Recommender Systems for Technology Enhanced Learning

Nikos Manouselis • Hendrik Drachsler
Katrien Verbert • Olga C. Santos
Editors

Recommender Systems for Technology Enhanced Learning

Research Trends and Applications

Foreword by Joseph A. Konstan

 Springer

Editors
Nikos Manouselis
Agro-Know
Athens, Greece

Katrien Verbert
Department of Computer Science
VUB & KU Leuven
Leuven, Belgium

Hendrik Drachsler
Welten Institute – Research Centre for
  Learning, Teaching and Technology
Faculty of Psychology and Educational
  Sciences
Open University of the Netherlands
Heerlen, The Netherlands

Olga C. Santos
aDeNu Research Group, Artificial
  Intelligence Department
Computer Science School, UNED
Madrid, Spain

ISBN 978-1-4939-4656-3   ISBN 978-1-4939-0530-0 (eBook)
DOI 10.1007/978-1-4939-0530-0
Springer New York Heidelberg Dordrecht London

Foreword

It was an inauspicious beginning in Barcelona in 2010. I had agreed to give talk to a workshop I hadn't heard of before on Recommender Systems for Technology Enhanced Learning. That morning was sunny and hot, and the city's usually efficient transit was on strike. I was advised that the easiest way to get to the workshop would be a long walk, so I set off for the workshop reflecting on the theme of my talk—that recommender systems had great potential in education, but that we weren't there yet. Arriving hot and tired, I re-told the story I'd been telling for almost 15 years—about how recommending products was relatively easy, and that it was a quick win for the technology. Product recommenders certainly have improved quality of life—making shopping and television watching easier. But for people seeking a deeper impact, they may fall short.

By contrast, education raised all sorts of challenges for recommender systems. But it also presented the potential for a deep win—for making a difference that would affect the quality of life for billions of people. The technical challenges are formidable. Education is fundamentally interdependent and sequential. A learning module or lesson that may be ideal for a student at one time may be completely useless too early or too late. So in a very real way, technology-enhanced learning should be a "grand challenge" for recommender systems researchers—but at that time, it mostly wasn't happening.

There were many reasons why. Making progress on educational recommenders presented at least three formidable obstacles to the typical recommender systems researcher. First, the researcher needed to gain understanding of education and learning research—any successful effort in education would require such an understanding. Second, the researcher would need real datasets—part of the challenge at the time was the lack of large datasets in general and of cases where there are more than one or two alternatives for given content modules specifically. And third, the researcher would need to learn how to conduct meaningful evaluation—this is no longer simply a question of which learning modules a student "prefers" but of what leads to actual learning, competence, and performance, not just on an immediate post-test basis, but later as the knowledge gets integrated. So while I was happy to lead the cheers for the whole area of RecSysTEL, and enjoyed seeing the work being done at the time, I left that day somewhat discouraged that this field would remain in the margins.

Three years later, how things have changed! Who knew that we'd have online courses with tens and hundreds of thousands of students? And who would have expected entire campuses (physical and virtual) committed to the idea of scientific exploration of personalised education? We are surely entering an era of new interest and new possibilities.

But what's most exciting is that we are entering that area through strength. As I look through the collection of articles in this book, I see a variety of advances that bring together the best ideas in recommender systems with important TEL applications. It is gratifying to see the expansion of available datasets that can allow researchers to explore ideas offline first, and even more gratifying to see the increased diversity of research approaches and questions—with issues ranging from trust to affect, and methods ranging from data analysis to field and experimental research.

So we are entering what may well become the golden age of RecSysTEL research, and this is a well-timed volume to help bring those new to the field up to speed.

Minneapolis, MN   Joseph A. Konstan

Preface

Technology-enhanced learning (TEL) aims to design, develop, and test socio-technical innovations that will support and enhance learning practices of both individuals and organisations. It is an application domain that generally addresses all types of technology research and development aiming to support teaching and learning activities, and considers meta-cognitive and reflective skills such as self-management, self-motivation, and effective informal and self-regulated learning. It was in 2007 when our first efforts to create opportunities for researchers working on topics related to recommender systems for TEL found their way in workshops like the Workshop on Social Information Retrieval for Technology Enhanced Learning (SIRTEL), the Workshop on Context-Aware Recommendation for Learning, and the Workshop Towards User Modelling and Adaptive Systems for All (TUMAS-A).

Still, it was only in 2010 when a really rare opportunity rose: during the same week of September and at the same location (Barcelona, Spain), two very prestigious and very relevant events (the fourth ACM Conference on Recommender Systems and the fifth European Conference on Technology Enhanced Learning) took place, giving us the chance to bring the two communities together. And so we did, by organising a joint event called the *1st Workshop on Recommender Systems for Technology Enhanced Learning (RecSysTEL)*.

Since then, lots of things have happened to mainstream educational applications in recommender systems' research. The most important achievement is an initial pool of datasets that have been collected and can be used to compare the outcomes of different TEL Recommender Systems to create a body of knowledge about the effects of different algorithms on learners. Furthermore, running research projects like Open Discovery Space[1] and LinkedUp[2] aim to create a publicly accessible Linked Data cloud[3] that can be used as a reference dataset for RecSysTEL research. Along these infrastructure improvements various scientific events and publications

---

[1] www.opendiscoveryspace.eu/

[2] www.linkedup-project.eu/

[3] http://data.linkededucation.org/linkedup/catalog/

have been realised. The most relevant are the organisation of subsequent editions of the RecSysTEL workshop with bi-annual periodicity; authoring a review article for the Recommender Systems Handbook; expanding it to an introductory handbook on Recommender Systems for Learning; and contributing (as co-editors or as authors) to several relevant Special Issues in scientific journals and specialised books.

We thought that this is a good time to build upon this previous experience and to collect some state-of-the-art contributions to a volume that will give a fresh view of the status of this area. Our interest was to collect a representative sample of high-quality manuscripts that will illustrate some important research trends, identify key challenges and demonstrate some innovative applications. This volume is the result of an open call that helped us collect, peer-review, select and propose for publication 14 articles (out of 49 proposed works; 29 % acceptance rate) that give a very good picture of the current status of research in recommender systems for TEL. The first four chapters (Karampiperis et al.; Cenichel et al.; Dietze et al.; Bienkowski and Klo) deal with user and item data that can be used to support recommendation systems and scenarios. The next four (Hulpus et al.; Santos et al.; Schwind and Buder; Tang et al.) focus on innovative methods and techniques for recommendation purposes. And the last six (Fazeli et al.; Bielikova et al.; Nowakowski et al.; Fernandez et al.; Sie et al.; Petertonkoker et al.) present examples of educational platforms and tools where recommendations are incorporated.

The bibliography covered by this book is available in an open group created at the Mendeley research platform[4] and will continue to be enriched with additional references. We would like to encourage the reader to sign up for this group and to connect to the community of people working on these topics, gaining access to the collected bibliography but also contributing pointers to new relevant publications within this very fast developing domain.

We hope that you will enjoy reading this volume as much as we enjoyed editing it.

Athens, Greece   Nikos Manouselis
Heerlen, The Netherlands   Hendrik Drachsler
Leuven, Belgium   Katrien Verbert
Madrid, Spain   Olga C. Santos

---

[4] http://www.mendeley.com/groups/1969281/recommender-systems-for-learning/

Acknowledgements

We would like to thank all the people that are continuously inspiring and contributing to this application domain of recommender systems. We would particularly like to thank the people that are listed below (in alphabetical order), since they have contributed to the quality of this volume by reviewing the submissions received, providing valuable arguments that helped us select the most appropriate contributions as well as giving valuable feedback to the authors so that they improve their final articles. This list includes the people that have served as part of the RecSysTEL workshops Steering Committees and/or Program Committees as well as in the Review Committee for this volume.

Alexander Felfernig, Graz University of Technology (Austria)
Brandon Muramatsu, Massachusetts Institute of Technology (USA)
Carlos Delgado Kloos, University of Carlos III de Madrid (Spain)
Charalampos Karagiannidis, University of Thessaly (Greece)
Christina Schwind, Knowledge Media Research Center (Germany)
Christoph Rensing, Technische Universität Darmstad (Germany)
Cristian Cechinel, Fundação Universidade Federal do Pampa (Brazil)
Cristóbal Romero, University of Cordoba (Spain)
David Massart, ZettaDataNet, LLC (USA)
Davinia Hernández-Leo, Universitat Pompeu Fabra (Spain)
Denis Gillet, Swiss Federal Institute of Lausanne (Switzerland)
Denis Parra, University of Pittsburgh (USA)
Eelco Herder, L3S (Germany)
Elina Megalou, Computer Technology Institute and Press – Diophantus (Greece)
Erik Duval, Katholieke Universiteit Leuven (Belgium)
Felix Mödritscher, Vienna University of Economics and Business (Austria)
Fridolin Wild, Open University (UK)
Geert-Jan Houben, Technical University Delft (The Netherlands)
George Kyrgiazos, National Technical University of Athens (Greece)
Giannis Stoitsis, Agro-Know (Greece)

Hannes Ebner, Royal Institute of Technology (Sweden)
Hans-Christian Schmitz, Fraunhofer FIT (Germany)
Ivana Bosnic, University of Zagreb (Croatia)
Jad Najjar, Eummena (Belgium)
Jan Pawlowski, University of Jyväskylä (Finland)
Jesus G. Boticario, UNED (Spain)
Joel Duffin, Tatemae (USA)
Jon Dron, Athabasca University (Canada)
Joris Klerkx, Katholieke Universiteit Leuven (Belgium)
Julien Broisin, Université Paul Sabatier (France)
Katrin Borcea-Pfitzmann, Dresden University of Technology (Germany)
Leonardo Lezcano, University of Alcala (Spain)
Liliana Ardissono, Universita di Torino (Italy)
Maiga Chang, Athabasca University (Canada)
Martin Memmel, German Research Center for Artificial Intelligence (Germany)
Martin Wolpers, Fraunhofer FIT (Germany)
Miguel-Angel Sicilia, University of Alcala (Spain)
Mimi Recker, Utah State University (USA)
Nikolas Athanasiadis, Intrasoft Int. (Luxembourg)
Paul Libbrecht, Karlsruhe University of Education and Martin Luther University of
    Halle (Germany)
Pedro J. Munoz Merino, University of Carlos III de Madrid (Spain)
Peter Brusilovsky, University of Pittsburgh (USA)
Peter Scott, Open University (UK)
Ralf Klamma, RWTH Aachen University (Germany)
Rick D. Hangartner, Strands (USA)
Riina Vuorikari, European Schoolnet (Belgium)
Rita Kuo, Knowledge Square, Inc. (Taiwan)
Rosta Farzan, Carnegie Mellon University (USA)
Salvador Sanchez-Alonso, University of Alcala de Henares (Spain)
Sandy El Helou, Swiss Federal Institute of Lausanne (Switzerland)
Sergey Sosnovsky, DFKI GmbH (Germany)
Sotiris Konstantinidis, University of Athens (Greece)
Stavros Demetriadis, Aristotle University of Thessaloniki (Greece)
Stefan Dietze, University Hanover, (Germany)
Stefanie Lindstaedt, Know-Center Graz (Austria)
Sten Govaerts, K.U.Leuven (Belgium)
Tiffany Tang, Kean University (USA)
Toby Dragon, Saarland University (Germany)
Tomislav Šmuc, Rudjer Bošković Institute (Croatia)
Tsukasa Hirashima, Hiroshima University (Japan)
Wolfgang Greller, Open University of the Netherlands (Netherlands)
Wolfgang Nejdl – L3S & Leibniz Universitat (Germany)
Wolfgang Reinhardt, University of Paderborn (Germany)
Xavier Ochoa, Escuela Superior Politecnica del Litoral (Ecuador)

The compilation of the work presented in this book has been carried out with European Commission and national funding support. More specifically, the involvement of Nikos Manouselis has been supported by the EU project Open Discovery Space (ODS)—297229 of the CIP PSP Programme (http://opendiscoveryspace.eu), the work of Hendrik Drachsler by the EU project LinkedUp—317620 of the FP7 Programme, and the work of Olga C. Santos by the EU project "European Unified Approach for Accessible Lifelong learning" (EU4ALL)—034778 of the IST FP6 (http://www.eu4all-project.eu/) and the national project "Multimodal approaches for Affective Modelling in Inclusive Personalized Educational scenarios in intelligent Contexts" (MAMIPEC) funded by the Spanish Ministry of Science and Innovation (TIN2011-29221-C03-01). Katrien Verbert is a post-doctoral fellow of the Research Foundation—Flanders (FWO). This publication reflects the views only of the authors, and the funding bodies cannot be held responsible for any use that may be made of the information contained therein.

Contents

Part I
User and Item Data

Collaborative Filtering Recommendation of Educational Content in Social Environments Utilizing Sentiment Analysis Techniques

Pythagoras Karampiperis, Antonis Koukourikos, and Giannis Stoitsis

Abstract Collaborative filtering techniques are commonly used in social networking environments for proposing user connections or interesting shared resources. While metrics based on access patterns and user behaviour produce interesting results, they do not take into account qualitative information, i.e. the actual opinion of a user that used the resource and whether or not he would propose it for use to other users. This is of particular importance on educational repositories, where the users present significant deviations in goals, needs, interests and expertise level. In this paper, we examine the benefits from introducing sentiment analysis techniques on user-generated comments in order to examine the correlation of an explicit rating with the polarity of an associated text, to retrieve additional explicit information from user comments when a standard rating is missing and expand tried recommendation calculation with qualitative information based on the community's opinion before proposing the resource to another user.

Keywords Recommender systems • Educational repositories • Sentiment Analysis • Qualitative analysis

P. Karampiperis (✉) • A. Koukourikos
Software and Knowledge Engineering Laboratory, Institute of Informatics
and Telecommunications, National Center for Scientific Research "Demokritos"Agia
Paraskevi Attikis, P.O.Box 60228, 15310 Athens, Greece
e-mail: pythk@iit.demokritos.gr; kukurik@iit.demokritos.gr

G. Stoitsis
Agro-Know Technologies, Grammou 17 Str., Vrilissia Attikis, 15235 Athens, Greece

Universidad de Alcalá, Pza. San Diego, s/n, 28801 Alcalá de Henares, Madrid, Spain
e-mail: stoitsis@ieee.org

N. Manouselis et al. (eds.), *Recommender Systems for Technology Enhanced Learning:*   3
Research Trends and Applications, DOI 10.1007/978-1-4939-0530-0_1,
© Springer Science+Business Media New York 2014

Introduction

Recommender Systems are of particular importance within social environments, where users share access to a common set of resources. The variability of crucial user characteristics, like their background, their special interests, their degree of expertise, pose interesting issues in terms of proposing a resource that is interesting, useful and comprehensible to a particular user.

Collaborative filtering approaches based on explicitly given user ratings do not always reflect the differentiation between the various criteria that apply to a resource and the weight that the users give to each criterion. On the other hand, techniques that examine access patterns may suffer from the appearance of stigmergy phenomena. That is, the resources that are more popular or favourably regarded by the community at a given time tend to be favoured as recommendations to new users. The visibility of a resource, or even more elaborate features like the time spent in a resource, the amount of downloads etc. are not directly connected to its quality or suitability. Hence, the examination of access and use patterns can lead to poor recommendation that will be further propagated due to the users continuing to follow previously defined paths within the repository of available content.

The evolvements of Web 2.0, however, led to the provision of more explicit information from the user side. User comments, discussions and reviews can constitute valuable information for determining the quality, appeal and popularity of a resource.

In this context, we propose the exploitation of user generated comments on the resources of a repository of educational content in order to deal with the lack of explicit ratings and discover qualitative information related to a specific resource and the impressions it left to the users that accessed it. To this end, we applied sentiment analysis to comments on educational content and examined the accuracy of the results and the degree to which these comments reflect the perceived user satisfaction from the content. At this stage, a Collaborative Filtering Recommendation system was built, that is, content characteristics and features were not taken into account in the analysis.

The rest of the paper is structured as follows. We provide an overview of Collaborative Filtering approaches in "Collaborative Filtering Recommender Systems". Our quality-centric approach on Collaborative Filtering Recommendation is analysed in "Quality-Centric Recommender System Methodology". "Sentiment Analysis Techniques for Collaborative Filtering Recommender Systems" describes the Sentiment Analysis techniques that were implemented and examined for incorporation in a Recommender System. The experimental setup for determining the appropriateness of these Sentiment Analysis techniques and evaluating our Recommender System is described in "Experimental Setup", while the experimental results are presented in "Experimental Results." We conclude and define our next steps in "Conclusions and Future Work".

Collaborative Filtering Recommender Systems

Recommender systems aim to predict the preferences of an individual (user/customer) and provide suggestions of further resources or entities (other users of the same system, resources, products) that are likely to be of interest.

In broad terms, a recommender system can be defined formally as follows; Let U be the set of all users of a system and R the set of all items (resources) that are available within the system and accessible by the users. A utility function $f: U \times R \rightarrow S$, associates a score to user-resource pairs, which indicates the suitability of the specific resource to the specific user. As it is obvious, the common case for environments with that structure is that there do not exist scores for every pair in $U \times R$. To this end, the role of a recommender system is to "predict" the scores for the user-resource pairs that do not have a score readily available.

The main approaches for building a recommender system, i.e. defining the characteristics that are taken into account by the utility function employed, are the following:

- Content-based approaches; the utility function examines the similarity of new/unknown items with the ones already declared as likeable by the user and proposes the most similar to him/her.
- Collaborative filtering approaches; the recommendations provided to the user are based on the explicit usefulness declared by other users with similar tastes and activity with him/her.
- Hybrid approaches that combine the characteristics of the previous methods.

Collaborative recommender systems can generally be grouped into heuristic-based and model-based systems [1, 2]. In the first case, the score for a user-resource pair is calculated using the scores of other users for the examined resource. The main goals in heuristic-based approaches are to determine user similarity and the way that the degree of similarity is used to weigh the effect of a user's activity to another user's preferences. Various metrics have been examined for computing user similarity, like calculating the angle between the rating vectors of the users [3], computing the mean squared difference of users' ratings [4] and calculating the correlation coefficient between a given pair of users [5]. In the latter case, existing scores are used to construct a rating model, to which the predicted scores are expected to conform. Similarly, the aggregation of peer ratings to produce a predicted rating can be achieved in various ways, such as calculating the average of the ratings of similar users, using a weighted average where the weights are based on the degree of similarity etc. In the case of model-based approaches,

The usage of recommender systems is widely spread in e-commerce environments [6] but the general principle is applicable to multiple and diverse environments. In the case of TEL, multiple solutions have been proposed and examined [7, 8]. The proposed systems use a variety of methods and elements for producing recommendations. For example, RACOFI [9] takes into account user ratings and content associations, CoFind [10] applies folksonomies to better define context and purpose before producing a recommendation, while [11] exploits a multi-attribute rating of educational resources. Further techniques from different fields have been used in TEL Recommenders, like creating clusters of users based on their interests [12], ontology-based strategies [13] and methods that combine social and contextual information [14].

Due to the particularities of the domain, some of the most common algorithms for collaborative filtering have been shown to struggle in the setting of a learning object repository [15, 16]. Furthermore, the explosion of Social Networking environments in the context of Web2.0 has established new interesting issues and proposed solutions for the field [17–19] and urged the pre-dominance of collaborative filtering methods in many environments with such functionality. The incorporation of social networking functionality in educational repositories is continuously increasing. Platforms like MERLOT [20] and Organic. Edunet [21] offer to their users the ability to comment on the presented material, stating their opinions or remarks regarding various aspects of the available content.

Taking into account the previous two statements, the presented service tries to exploit the newly-introduced information from user comments and reviews and examine an alternative approach for producing recommendations of educational resources. As mentioned, the presented techniques are to be incorporated in a recommender system over a social platform that provides access to educational content. Linguistic techniques, such as sentiment analysis, can be of use for alleviating some of the drawbacks of traditional algorithms in terms of differentiating users belonging in different audiences (e.g. teachers from students) and bypassing the need for explicit ratings (via a star system).

Quality-Centric Recommender System Methodology

The proposed Collaborative Filtering methodology is based on the users' social connectivity and their rating activities within the relevant Social environment in order to compute the expected ratings for resources unknown to the user. It should be noted that the approach is domain-agnostic; hence additional information for the resources (metadata, categorization, keywords etc.) is not examined by the method. In this paper, the equations and scores rely on the widely used 5-scale rating system.

For the purposes of our research we consider a social service that incorporates the following functionalities:

- Membership: The service enables user registration and associates each user with a unique account.
- Organisation in Communities: Users can create communities (groups) within the social environment. The communities can be considered as subsets of the overall social network.
- Rating attribution: The users of the service can apply a rating to the resources available through the system, by assigning 1–5 stars to the resource.

- Comment submission: The users can comment on resources, essentially providing a review in natural language. The length of a comment can be arbitrary. For the purposes of the experiment, we consider comments written in English.

In this context, the activities of interest from a registered user are the ones of (a) assigning a rating to a resource and (b) commenting on a resource. The purpose of the recommendation service, therefore, is twofold; to generate a rating of the user from his/her actual activities (ratings and comments); and to generate a rating for resources for which there is no activity from the particular user. We consider the first case as an *explicit* rating for the user-resource pair, while in the second case, we consider the rating *implicit*. In the next paragraphs, we proceed to elaborate on the two types of ratings and their formal definition for the proposed recommender system.

Explicit Rating: The proposed system relies on the attribution of a rating to a resource by a user. This rating could be direct, via the aforementioned star system, or indirect, via the analysis of comments/discussion related to the specific resource. These ratings—if existent—are used to provide a *score* for a user-resource pair. The score is defined as:

$$
Score(u,r) = \begin{cases} Rating(u,r), \left[\exists Rating(u,r)\right] AND \left[\nexists Comment(u,r)\right] \\[2ex] Sentiment(u,r), \left[\nexists Rating(u,r)\right] AND \left[\exists Comment(u,r)\right] \\[2ex] \dfrac{Rating(u,r)+Sentiment(u,r)}{2}, otherwise \end{cases} \quad (1)
$$

Where *Rating(u,r)* is the explicit rating of the resource *r* by user *u* and *Sentiment(u,r)* is the sentiment score assigned by the sentiment analysis that will be applied to user comments and is described in detail in "Sentiment Analysis Techniques for Collaborative Filtering Recommender Systems".

Implicit Rating using User Similarity: In the case that a user has not explicitly provided a rating for a specific resource, the recommender system provides a predicted rating, taking into account the user's similarity with other users who have actually provided a rating for this resource.

This similarity represents the trust of a certain user to the expressed opinion of other users of the social service. In the relevant literature, it is evident that this type of information can provide meaningful recommendations in the case where no explicit qualitative information has been provided by the user himself/herself [17, 18, 22].

The calculation of the predicted rating relies on the similarity and distribution of scores provided by the system's users. Specifically, the predicted score given to a resource r by user *u* is defined as:

$$
Score(u,r) = \frac{1}{2|S|} \cdot \left(\sum_{i=1}^{|S|} \left(L(u,S_i) + P(u,S_i) \right) Score(S_i,r) \right) \quad (2)
$$

In this function, S is the set of system users that have provided an explicit score for the resource r. The L metric is a modification of the trust-centred algorithm proposed by [23] and is defined as:

$$L(a,b) = \left(1 - \frac{1}{5 \cdot |C|} \sum_{i=1}^{|C|} \left| Score(a,i) - Score(b,i) \right| \right)$$

The set $C = R_a \cap R_B$ is the conjunction of the sets R_a and R_b of resources that bear explicit scores provided by users a and b respectively. So, in broad terms, L is a measure for the similarity in the ratings of users a and b. The score difference is normalized to the [0, 1] space, since the ratings on the examined dataset belong in the (0, 5] range.

P is the normalized Pearson correlation metric as applied to our system. Specifically,

$$P(a,b) = \begin{cases} \frac{1}{5} \overline{Score(a,Ra)}, & \left[Score(a,i) = \overline{Score(a,R_a)} \forall i \in C \right] \\\\ \frac{1}{5} \overline{Score(b,R_b)}, & \left[Score(b,i) = \overline{Score(b,R_b)} \forall i \in C \right] AND \\\\ & \left[\neg \left(Score(a,i) = \overline{Score(a,R_a)} \forall i \in C \right) \right] \\\\ \left(\dfrac{\sum_{i=1}^{|C|} \left(Score(a,i) - \overline{Score(a,R_a)} \right) \cdot \left(Score(b,i) - \overline{Score(b,R_b)} \right)}{\sqrt{\sum_{i=1}^{|C|} \left(Score(a,i) - \overline{Score(a,R_a)} \right)^2} \cdot \sum_{i=1}^{|C|} \left(Score(b,i) - \overline{Score(b,R_b)} \right)^2} \right) \end{cases}$$

The $Score(u,R_u)$ construct denotes the complete set of scores provided by a user u. Hence, the average of these scores is $\overline{Score(u,R_u)}$.

Both quantities participate in the definition of the proposed score, as L reflects the "trust" that the examined user can have in the opinions of others, while P computes the differentiations on their rating habits and adjusts the score accordingly.

Community-driven Implicit Rating: In the case that a user has not explicitly provided a rating for a specific resource and, additionally, does not have any common activities with the other users of the system, i.e. $R_u \cap R_k = \emptyset \forall k \in U, k \neq u$, where U is the set of users known to the system, the recommendation module provides a rougher estimate for the scores to be proposed to the user by calculating the average of the scores provided by users belonging to the same communities with user u.

Formally, let $M(u,c)$ denote that user u is a member of community c. If $R_u \cap R_k = \varnothing\, \forall k \in U, k \neq u$ the estimated score of user u or a resource r is calculated by the following formula:

$$Score(u,r) = \begin{cases} \dfrac{5}{2}, T = \varnothing \\[2ex] \dfrac{\sum\limits_{i=1}^{|T|} Score(T_i, r)}{|T|} \end{cases} \tag{3}$$

$$T = \{p \in U : \exists c\, M(p,c), M(a,c)\}$$

Sentiment Analysis Techniques for Collaborative Filtering Recommender Systems

Sentiment analysis regards extracting opinion from texts and classifying it into positive, negative or neutral valence [24]. Work on the field focuses on two general directions; lexical approaches and solutions using supervised machine learning techniques.

Lexical approaches rely on the creation of appropriate dictionaries. The terms present in the dictionary are tagged with respect to their polarity. Given an input text, the presence of dictionary terms is examined and the overall sentiment of the text is computed based on the existence of "positive" and "negative" terms within it. Despite its simplicity, the lexical approach has produced results significant better than "coin-toss" [25–27]. The way of constructing the lexica that are used for sentiment analysis is the subject of several works. In [27] and [28] the lexicons comprised solely adjective terms.

The usage of pivot words (like "good" and "bad") and their association with the target words is also a frequently met approach. In [29] and [30], the minimum path between each target word and the pivot terms in the WordNet hierarchy was calculated in order to determine the polarity of the term and its inclusion in the dictionary. In [26], the authors executed search queries with the conjunction of the pivot words and the target word given as input. The query that returned the most hits determined the polarity of the given word.

Machine learning techniques focus on the selection of feature vectors and the provision of tagged corpora to a classifier, which will be used for analysing untagged corpora. The most frequent routes for choosing the feature vectors are the inclusion of unigrams or n-grams, counting the number of positive/ negative words, the length of the document etc. The classifiers are usually implemented as a Naive Bayes classifiers or as Support Vector Machines [27, 31]. Their accuracy is dependent on the selection of the aforementioned feature vectors, ranging in the same space as the lexical approaches (63–82 %).

This section presents the sentiment analysis techniques that were examined and tested in order to identify the most suitable method for the case of the proposed Social Recommendation Service in terms of precision, recall and execution time. Sentiment analysis in the context of the Social Recommendation Service refers to the task of extracting the polarity of an opinionated text segment with respect to the quality of a certain resource. In this case, a number of different techniques could be applied (presented in the following subsections), with different performance and characteristics. The fact that we are dealing with user generated content drives us to take into account its unstructured nature and the potential unbalanced distribution it may present. This gives rise to the fact that our training set may be unbalanced and therefore learning may not be able to cope with such diversity in the number of instances per class. In this paper, we focus on lexical approaches for sentiment analysis, in order to avoid the consequences of erroneous training due to the distribution of the ratings in MERLOT (i.e. the positive ratings are much more than the negative ones). The following subsections discuss the techniques that we have implemented and tested for inclusion in the proposed recommender system.

Affective Term Frequency

This technique relies on the existence of sets of terms that bear a predetermined polarity. In most cases, there are two sets of terms; a set containing terms with positive polarity and a set containing terms with negative polarity. Let P be the set of terms bearing positive polarity and N the set of terms bearing negative polarity. Also, let $T = \{t_1, t_2, \cdots, t_n\}$, the set of distinct tokens in the text segment to be examined. We define a positive score for a token t as:

$$PosScore(t, P) = \begin{cases} 1, & t \in P \\ 0, & t \notin P \end{cases}$$

Similarly, the negative score for a token is defined as:

$$NegScore(t, N) = \begin{cases} 1, & t \in N \\ 0, & t \notin N \end{cases}$$

For the entire text, i.e. the complete set of tokens T, we define the positive score as:

$$PosScore(T, P) = \sum_{i=1}^{|T|} PosScore(t_i, P)$$

Similarly, the negative score for the entire text is defined as:

$$NegScore(T,N) = \sum_{i=1}^{|T|} NegScore(t_i,N)$$

We describe two distinct variations of this approach below.

Domain-agnostic Term Frequency

In this case, the sets of positive and negative terms are constant and known before-hand [27]. The algorithm discovers all the terms of a text segment that can be found in the positive set and all the terms that can be found in the negative set. For example, in the sentence "Don't you just love this camera? It's great!", the presence of sentiment-bearing terms determines the polarity of the overall statement.

Keeping in mind the previous definitions, the overall polarity of the text segment (normalized to the [−1, 1] space) is defined as:

$$Sentiment(T,P,N) = \frac{PosScore(T,P) - NegScore(T,N)}{\max\{PosScore(T,P), NegScore(T,N)\}} \quad (4)$$

Domain-Aware Term Frequency

In this variation of the term frequency approach, the sets of polarized terms are constructed from a corpus of already classified, in-domain text segments [31]. Every term found in segments characterized as positive is added to the positive set P. Similarly, every term found in segments characterized as negative is added to the negative set N. An example for showcasing the differentiation of term polarity with respect to the domain at hand is a text segment such as "This phone is amazing! It's so small and light", where the term "small" carries a positive valence, in contrast with the general notion that small is a negative attribute. In this method, we introduce the notion of neutral polarity, where the text segment was characterized as neither positive nor negative. Hence, the algorithm uses another set of terms Neu, in which the terms found in segments characterized as neutral are added. Similar to the cases of positive and negative sets, the neutral score of a token is equal to:

$$NeuScore(t, Neu) = \begin{cases} 1, & t \in Neu \\ 0, & t \notin Neu \end{cases}$$

And the neutral score for the entire text equals to:

$$NeuScore(T, Neu) = \sum_{i=1}^{|T|} NeuScore(t_i, Neu)$$

In this case, the function for determining the polarity of a text segment T is formulated as follows.

$$Sentiment(T,P,N,Neu) = \begin{cases} 0, & \begin{bmatrix} NeuScore(T,Neu) > PosScore(T,P) \end{bmatrix} AND \\ & \begin{bmatrix} NeuScore(T,Neu) > NegScore(T,N) \end{bmatrix} \\ \dfrac{PosScore(T,P) - NegScore(T,N)}{\max\{PosScore(T,P), NegScore(T,N)\}}, & otherwise \end{cases}$$

Affective and Domain Terms Correlation

The main drawback of the previous approach is that it does take into account the fact that a certain text segment may express opinions not directly related to the entity we are actually interested in. For example, a comment on an educational object may contain praises for a similar work that is recommended as a possible reference. The following techniques try to address this problem by examining ways to associate the affective terms with specific tokens that refer to the entity for which we want to mine the writer's opinion.

Distance-Based Correlation

This method relies on the proximity of the domain and affective terms in order to determine which of the latter are more likely to determine the polarity of the text towards the entity of interest. Let $D = \{D_1, D_2, \cdots, D_n\}$ the set of terms/phrases that are used to define the entity of interest (e.g. "the paper", "the article", the title of the article etc.). For each element of D, we calculate the distance between the term and all the affective terms in the positive and negative sets, i.e. the number of words between the descriptive and the affective term. If there is not an affective term within the text segment, the distance is set to zero.

Dependency-Based Correlation

A more sophisticated approach for estimating the polarity of a text towards a specific entity is to examine if the terms associated with the latter are syntactically linked with one or more affective terms.

In this method, we split the input text into sentences and obtain the parse tree for each sentence by employing a shallow parser. For sentences containing a term or phrase that describes the entity of interest, we examine the dependencies of these terms from the parse tree. If the connected terms are also found in the positive or the negative sets, the PosScore and NegScore are respectively incremented by 1. Finally, we employ (4) to calculate the overall polarity of the text.

Experimental Setup

Experimental Corpus

The conducted experiments used the material available in the MERLOT platform. MERLOT is an online repository, providing open access to resources for learning and online teaching. It provides learning material of higher education aiming at promoting access to scientific data and as a result to their manipulation and exploitation by research communities.

MERLOT users can evaluate the available resources in two distinct ways. They can write comments on the resource, along with providing a rating in the 0–5 scale. We consider ratings of 0–2 as negative, ratings of 3 as neutral and ratings of 4–5 as positive. Additionally, MERLOT users can provide comments in a more formal manner, by submitting an "expert review". Expert reviews follow a structured template. Reviewers can provide an overview of the examined content and evaluate it with respect to its (a) Content Quality; (b) Effectiveness as a teaching tool; and (c) Ease of Use for students and faculty. Figures 1, 2 and 3 depict a resource description, a user comment and an expert review respectively, as they are presented within MERLOT.

Fig. 1 A MERLOT resource as represented in the constructed XML file

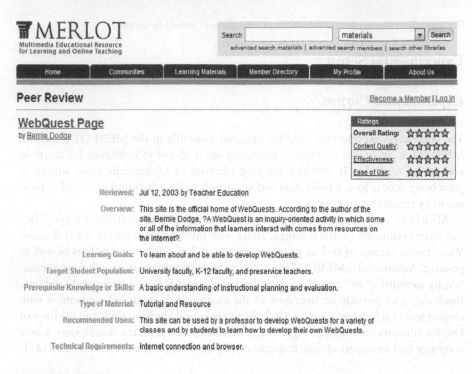

Fig. 2 Structure of the reviews element in a MERLOT resource description

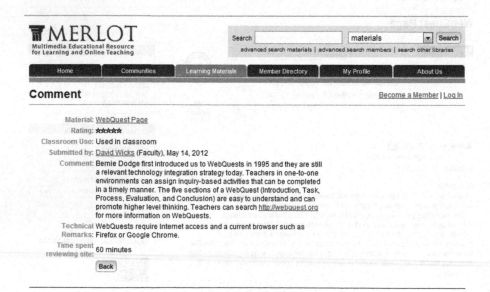

Fig. 3 Structure of the comments element in a MERLOT resource description

In order to build our test corpus, the MERLOT user-generated content was retrieved via the following process: starting from a list of resources presented via the MERLOT web environment, we crawled the pages of each individual included object by following the appropriate hyperlinks in the object's page. For each resource, we retrieved the following elements:

- The title of the resource
- The description provided within MERLOT
- The keywords associated with the resource
- User comments provided for the resource
- Expert reviews submitted to MERLOT

For the user comments, we store the URL of the comment and the actual comment text. For the expert reviews associated with a resource, we store the following information:

- The URL of the review
- The ID code of the user that provided the review
- Information pertaining to the quality of the content, as expressed by the reviewer. This includes descriptions in natural language, of the strengths and concerns regarding the content quality.
- Information pertaining to the effectiveness of the examined resource, as a learning object. This includes descriptions, in free-form text, of the strengths and concerns regarding the effectiveness of the resource.
- Information pertaining to the ease of use of the resource, again indicating the strengths and weaknesses in free text.

All of the above information is organized and stored in an XML file, in order to facilitate the extraction of information with respect to the resources and the contributing users (via XPath querying). Each tag associated with a MERLOT resource encloses all the elements associated with it.

The dataset used for our experiments incorporates information for 6,720 MERLOT resources. There are 9,623 comments and 3,459 expert reviews in total. Hence, the average comment count is 1.43 comments per resource and 0.514 expert reviews per resource. The majority of the resources had 1 or 2 comments and no reviews. However, the maximum number of comments in the examined datasets was 23, while the maximum number of expert reviews was 4.

Sentiment Analysis Techniques

The described methods were tested in terms of precision, recall and execution time in order to reach to a decision for their suitability in the context of a recommendation service. As the recommendation methodologies have an execution overhead, we incorporate the execution time metric into the quality analysis of each implementation. This section provides a description of the dataset used for the experiments, the definition of the quality score for a sentiment analysis method and the results of the experiments on the given dataset.

Corpus Preparation

In order to build our test corpus, the MERLOT user-generated content was retrieved and underwent trivial linguistic processing (HTML cleaning, Stop-word removal, Lemmatization) before being fed to implementations of the aforementioned sentiment analysis methods.

Sentiment Analysis Quality Score

As mentioned, besides the precision and recall performance of a sentiment analysis method, we are especially concerned with the execution time of the respective module, as it will be incorporated into an already time-demanding recommendation process.

In this regard, we introduce a Quality Score (QS) metric for the implementation of each method. Let P denote the achieved precision from the application of the method on the MERLOT corpus, and R the achieved recall. Let also T denote the execution time (in milliseconds) for 1,000 iterations of the method (that is, the analysis of 1,000 specific textual segments) and $maxT$, $minT$ the worst and best observed execution times, that is, the execution time of the slowest and fastest method respectively. The Quality Score for the method is defined as:

$$QS = \frac{2}{3} \cdot \left(\frac{P+R}{2} \right) + \frac{1}{3} \cdot \left(\frac{maxT-T}{maxT - minT} \right)$$

Since $0 \leq P \leq 1$, $0 \leq R \leq 1$ and $T \leq maxT$, it is obvious that $0 \leq QS \leq 1$ and that a higher Quality Score indicates a more suitable method. The QS metric assigns a higher weight to the effectiveness of the method in comparison to its execution speed.

Quality-Centric Collaborative Filtering Recommender

Building the Training and Evaluation Sets

In this phase of the experiment, the retrieved corpus was divided in two subsets; the first subset was considered the initial input of the recommender system, that is, the records were considered as the information known to the service; the second subset was held as the evaluation corpus, that is, the information present was considered unknown and the results of the recommendation service are to be compared with these data. For this first run, 60 % of the corpus was used as the input set, while the remaining 40 % was held for the comparison of the results.

Evaluation Metrics

The creation of a test corpus allows us to obtain a set of ratings that are comparable to the one generated by the recommender system. As mentioned, the ratings provided by the recommender system are normalized to the [0, 5] space, while the ratings available from MERLOT hold values in the $\{1,2,3,4,5\}$ set. Therefore, the produced ratings were rounded to the closest integer and compared to the actual rating provided by the user. The mean distance of the two ratings provide a measure for the accuracy of the acquired results. We examined the accuracy of the service's results with two different thresholds. The first one was set to zero, that is, the result was considered correct when the (rounded) rating for the resource predicted by the service was exactly the one provided by the user in the test set. The second threshold was set to 0.5, that is, the (exact) rating predicted by the service was within 0.5 stars from the actual rating. Furthermore, we applied the standard Mean Average Error (MAE) metric to our results.

It should be noted that a differentiation between the MERLOT structure and our definition for a social environment is the lack of organisation in user communities within the former. To overcome this obstacle, we defined an ad-hoc classification of the users, based on their profile. To this end, users that share at least two common interests, as declared in the "skills and interests" section of their MERLOT profile, were considered to belong in the same community.

Experimental Results

Sentiment Analysis Techniques

This section presents the produced results of the experiments over the constructed MERLOT corpus for each class of polarity (positive, negative and neutral). We distinguish the two cases of MERLOT input (comments and expert reviews) in terms of the formality of their structure. The expert reviews—clearly divided in subjects of evaluation and strengths and concerns—are considered as "structured" content, while user comments are considered unstructured, as there is not a clear distinction of the positive and negative points made by the commenter.

Table 1 summarizes the Precision, Recall and overall Quality Score over structured content (Expert Reviews) for positive reviews and for each sentiment analysis method.

Accordingly, Table 2 presents the results over structured content for negative reviews and for each sentiment analysis method.

Table 1 Quality scores over structured input with positive polarity

Method	Precision	Recall	Execution time	QS
Domain-agnostic term frequency	0.577	0.786	1,500	**0.788**
Domain-aware term frequency	0.622	0.802	1,700	0.764
Distance-based correlation	0.645	0.821	1,800	0.756
Dependency-based correlation	0.691	0.826	3,000	0.506

Table 2 Quality Scores over structured input with negative polarity

Method	Precision	Recall	Execution time	QS
Domain-agnostic term frequency	0.569	0.810	1,500	**0.793**
Domain-aware term frequency	0.596	0.829	1,700	0.764
Distance-based correlation	0.671	0.838	1,800	0.770
Dependency-based correlation	0.710	0.850	3,000	0.520

Table 3 Quality scores over unstructured input with positive polarity

Method	Precision	Recall	Execution time	QS
Domain-agnostic term frequency	0.563	0.740	1,500	**0.768**
Domain-aware term frequency	0.573	0.760	1,700	0.733
Distance-based correlation	0.610	0.779	1,800	0.730
Dependency-based correlation	0.634	0.788	3,000	0.474

Table 4 Quality Scores over structured input with negative polarity

Method	Precision	Recall	Execution time	QS
Domain-agnostic term frequency	0.517	0.762	1500	**0.760**
Domain-aware term frequency	0.525	0.781	1700	0.724
Distance-based correlation	0.623	0.800	1800	0.741
Dependency-based correlation	0.640	0.804	3000	0.481

In similar fashion, Tables 3 and 4 presented the results for each polarity class and for each sentiment analysis method over unstructured data (User Comments).

The experimental results indicated that the benefits of applying more sophisticated methods of sentiment analysis do not overcome the decrease in performance. Furthermore, the methods examining the correlation between descriptive and affective terms have the additional drawback that they do not offer an intuitive way to obtain sentiment values in a continuous space. That is, they have good performance on indicating the general polarity of the examined text but they operate on the quantized space of $\{-1, 0, 1\}$.

Therefore, the sentiment analysis module that was incorporated in the proposed Recommendation Service uses the Domain-agnostic variation of the Term Frequency

Table 5 Accuracy of the proposed recommendation service

Audience	Threshold 1 (=0)	Threshold 2 (=0.5)
Users (commenters)	0.71	0.84
Reviewers	0.74	0.87

Table 6 Mean average error scores of the proposed recommendation service

Audience	MAE
Users (commenters)	0.76
Reviewers	0.72

Calculation algorithm. In order to transfer the results of sentiment analysis to the [0, 5] space, we formulate the sentiment analysis equation (4) that will be used within the service as follows.

$$Sentiment(T,P,N) = \frac{5}{2}\left(1 + \frac{PosScore(T,P) - NegScore(T,N)}{\max\{PosScore(T,P), NegScore(T,N)\}}\right) \quad (5)$$

Quality-Centric Collaborative Filtering Recommender

Table 5 presents the accuracy of the service's prediction for the two thresholds we set. As explained in the experimental setup, we employ two different thresholds for comparing the obtained results with the explicit ratings provided by the MERLOT users. In the first case, we required that the produced rating for a resource in the 5-star scale was exactly equal to the rating provided by the users or the reviewers of the resource. In the second case, we required that the produced rating had a distance of 0.5 from the explicit rating provided by the users or reviewers.

Similarly, Table 6 depicts the MAE results for the proposed service.

As can be seen in Table 5, in 71 % of the examined cases the recommender system produced the exact same star rating that was actually assigned by the user commenting on a resource. In the case of expert reviews, the percentage rises slightly to 74 %. When relaxing the threshold for deeming a produced rating correct, the accuracy of the system naturally increases. Essentially, the produced ratings were within 0.5 stars from the actual rating provided by the user in 84 % of the cases for comments and in 87 % of the cases for expert reviews.

Taking into account the results on the accuracy of the proposed recommender system, the achieved MEA is relatively high. This is a direct consequence of using the Term Frequency Sentiment Analysis method, which, while having the best QS and an acceptable precision, tends to produce inaccurate results when the examined text bears certain characteristics. For example, the method does not handle comparisons or negations particularly well, causing significant diversions between the perceived and the real sentiment expressed by a text segment. In other words, in cases that the text bears such syntactic characteristics, the method computes a sentiment that is substantially different, therefore it produces a small set of results that have a big error margin (e.g. a distance over two from the real rating) and affect the MAE for the entire dataset.

The results are indicative of a system that performs generally well. However, a bias factor is inserted by the fact that the ratings within MERLOT are not evenly distributed. There is a relatively strong tendency towards high ratings, while the comments do not use strong language for the negative aspects of a resource and—on the other hand—show clearly the appraisal of the positive aspects.

Conclusions and Future Work

This article presents our first steps towards introducing qualitative information into collaborative filtering recommender systems over social platforms. The preliminary results of the sentiment analysis on user comments in the context of a repository of educational resources indicated that there can be valuable qualitative information that can be added to a recommendation service and be used to adjust the perceived "rating" of a given resource by a specific user. The accuracy of the examined algorithms, while satisfactory, leaves room for improvement. We expect that more elaborate techniques that introduce association of entities and contextual information will produce better results, always taking into account performance issues, as quantified by the introduced QS metric. However, it is important to note that sentiment analysis does not suffer much from domain differentiation or variability on user roles (that is, the results for expert reviews and general user comments presented similar success). An interesting remark regarding the linguistic characteristics of the examined content is that the criticism is usually employed using mild terminology, which is in contrast of user-generated reviews for products/movies etc. In the future, we will examine refinements of the way QS is calculated, and examine the accuracy of other sentiment analysis methods. User evaluations will be an important part of this process, as we should examine if the unavoidable increased delay that will be introduced from more complex sentiment analysis methods will have a negative impact on user acceptance despite offering better recommendations.

Regarding the evaluation of the quality-centric recommender system itself, it was revealed that the introduction of more elaborate analysis on user-provided information can produce a more accurate picture for the individual opinions expressed. Furthermore, the extraction of ratings from textual information helps in obtaining additional explicit scores for a user-resource pair. However, there are several steps needed to be completed for obtaining a clearer picture of the system's potential and the overall effect of the sentiment analysis in the improvement of the system. The presented service will be used for producing recommendations for the users of the VOA3R platform [31], an environment that bears all the characteristics that are exploited by our approach (explicit ratings, user discussions, user comments and reviews, organizations of the users into communities). The examination of the system's efficiency in real-life settings is expected to provide valuable feedback for the refinement of our methodology.

The next step for expanding the scope of the recommendation service is to move to a hybrid approach, where content characteristics are taken into account. Furthermore, further details for the user profiles can be incorporated in the service, in order to modify the weights of ratings provided by other users, based on their profile and not only their behavioural similarity with the examined user. Finally, it is worth examining the possibilities of incorporating semantic information in the recommendation algorithm, by analysing the actual content of the resource, associating distinct scores for different perspectives of a resource and relating them to more detailed user interests, as the latter are deduced by their profiles and the analysis of their comments.

Acknowledgments The research leading to these results has received funding from the European Union Seventh Framework Programme, in the context of the SYNC3 (ICT-231854) project.

This paper also includes research results from work that has been funded with support of the European Commission, and more specifically the project CIP-ICT-PSP-270999 "Organic.Lingua: Demonstrating the potential of a multilingual Web portal for Sustainable Agricultural & Environmental Education" of the ICT Policy Support Programme (ICT PSP).

References

1. Adomavicius G, Tuzhilin A (2005) Toward the next generation of recommender systems: a survey of the state-of-the-art and possible extensions. IEEE Trans Knowl Data Eng 17(6): 734–749
2. Breese JS, Heckerman D, Kadie C (1998) Empirical analysis of predictive algorithms for collaborative filtering. In: Proceedings of the fourteenth conference on uncertainty in artificial intelligence, Madison, WI, July 1998
3. Sarwar B, Karypis G, Konstan J, Riedl J (2001) Item-based collaborative filtering recommendation algorithms. In Proceedings of the 10th international conference on World Wide Web (WWW '01), New York, NY, USA, pp 285–295
4. Shardanand U, Maes P (1995) Social information filtering: algorithms for automating 'word of mouth'. In: Proceedings of the conference on human factors in computing systems, Denver, Co, 1995, pp 210–217
5. Resnick P, Iakovou N, Sushak M, Bergstrom P, Riedl J (1994) Group Lens: an open architecture for collaborative filtering on netnews. In: Proceedings of the 1994 ACM conference on Computer Supported cooperative work, New York, NY, USA, 1994, pp 175–186
6. Sarwar B, Karypis G, Konstan J, Riedl J (2000) Analysis of recommendation algorithms for e-commerce. In: Proceedings of the 2nd ACM conference on electronic commerce, Minneapolis, MN, October 2000, pp 158–176
7. Manouselis N, Vuorikari R, Van Assche F (2010) Collaborative recommendation of e-Learning resources: an experimental investigation. J Comput Assist Learn 26(4):227–242
8. Manouselis N, Drachsler H, Vuorikari R, Hummel H, Koper R (2011) Recommender systems in technology enhanced learning. In: Kantor P, Ricci F, Rokach L, Shapira B (eds) Recommender systems handbook. Springer, NY, pp 387–415
9. Anderson M, Ball M, Boley H, Greene S, Howse N, Lemire D McGrath S (2003) RACOFI: a rule-applying collaborative filtering system. In: Proceedings of IEEE/WIC COLA'03, Halifax, Canada, October 2003
10. Dron J, Mitchell R, Boyne C, Siviter P (2000) CoFIND: steps towards a self-organising learning environment. In: Proceedings of WebNet Proceedings of WebNet World Conference on the WWW and Internet 2000, San Antonio, TX, 2000, pp 146–151

11. Manouselis N, Vuorikari R, Van Assche F (2007) Simulated analysis of MAUT collaborative filtering for learning object recommendation. In: Proceedings of the workshop on social information retrieval in technology enhanced learning (SIRTEL 2007), Crete, Greece, 2007, pp 17–20
12. Tang T, McCalla G (2003) Smart recommendation for an evolving e-learning system. In: Proceedings of the workshop on technologies for electronic documents for supporting learning, international conference on artificial intelligence in education (AIED 2003), Sydney, Australia, July 20–24 2003
13. Nadolski R, Van den Berg B, Berlanga A, Drachsler H, Hummel H, Koper R, Sloep P (2009) Simulating light-weight personalised recommender systems in learning networks: a case for pedagogy-oriented and rating based hybrid recommendation strategies. J Artif Soc Soc Simulat 12(14)
14. Hummel H, Van den Berg B, Berlanga AJ, Drachsler H, Janssen J, Nadolski RJ, Koper EJR (2007) Combining social- and information-based approaches for personalised recommendation on sequencing learning activities. Int J Learn Tech 3(2):152–168
15. Herlocker JL, Konstan J, Terveen LG, Riedl J (2004) Evaluating collaborative filtering recommender systems. ACM Trans Inf Syst 22(1):5–53
16. Sicilia MA, Garca-Barriocanal E, Sanchez-Alonso S, Cechinel C (2010) Exploring user-based recommender results in large learning object repositories: the case of MERLOT. In: Manouselis N, Drachsler H, Verbert K, Santos OC (eds) Proceedings of the 1st workshop on recommender systems for technology enhanced learning (RecSysTEL 2010). Procedia Computer Science, 1(2):2859–2864
17. Massa P, Avesani P (2007) Trust-aware recommender systems. In: Proceedings of the 2007 ACM conference on recommender systems (RecSys 07), New York, NY, USA, 2007, pp 17–24
18. Bedi P, Kaur H, Marwaha S (2007) Trust based recommender system for the semantic web. In Proceedings of the 20th international joint conference on artificial intelligence (IJCAI 07), San Francisco, 2007, pp 2677–2682
19. Andersen R, Borgs C, Chayes J, Feige U, Flaxman A, Kalai A, Mirrokni V, Tennenholtz M (2008) Trust-based recommendation systems: an axiomatic approach. In: Proceedings of the 17th ACM international conference on World Wide Web (WWW 08), New York, 2008, pp 199–208
20. MERLOT (2013) Multimedia educational resource for learning and online teaching. http://www.merlot.org. Accessed Feb 2013
21. (2013) Organic.Edunet. http://portal.organic-edunet.eu/. Accessed Feb 2013
22. Weng J, Miao C, Goh A (2006) Improving collaborative filtering with trust-based metrics. In: Proceedings of the ACM symposium on applied computing, 2006, pp 1860–1864
23. Lathia N, Hailes S, Capra L (2008) Trust-based collaborative filtering. In: Proceedings of the Joint iTrust and PST conferences on privacy, trust management and security (IFIPTM), 2008, pp 14–29
24. Pang B, Lee L (2008) Opinion mining and sentiment analysis. Now Publishers Inc., Hanover, MA
25. Durant K, Smith M (2006) Mining sentiment classification from political web logs. In: Proceedings of workshop on web mining and web usage analysis of the 12th ACM SIGKDD international conference on Knowledge Discovery and Data Mining (WebKDD-2006), Philadelphia, PA, USA, August 2006
26. Turney P (2002) Thumbs up or thumbs down? Semantic orientation applied to unsupervised classification of reviews. In: Proceedings of the 40th Annual Meeting on Association for Computational Linguistics (ACL '02), Philadelphia, PA, July 2002, pp 417–424
27. Kamps J, Marx M, Mokken RJ (2004) Using WordNet to measure semantic orientation of adjectives. In: LREC 2004, vol IV. pp 1115–1118
28. Hatzivassiloglou V, Wiebe J (2000) Effects of adjective orientation and gradability on sentence subjectivity. In: Proceedings of the 18th international conference on computational linguistics, Stroudsburg, PA, USA, 299–305

29. Kennedy A, Inkpen D (2006) Sentiment classification of movie reviews using contextual valence shifters. Computational Intelligence (special issue), Vol. 22, No. 2, 2006, pp 110–125
30. Andreevskaia A, Bergler S, Urseanu M (2007) All blogs are not made equal: exploring genre differences in sentiment tagging of blogs. In: Proceedings of the International Conference on Weblogs and Social Media (ICWSM-2007), Boulder, CO, March 2007
31. Akshay J (2007) A framework for modeling influence, opinions and structure in social media. In: Proceedings of the twenty-second AAAI conference on artificial intelligence, Vancouver, BC, July 2007, pp 1933–1934

Towards Automated Evaluation of Learning Resources Inside Repositories

Cristian Cechinel, Sandro da Silva Camargo, Salvador Sánchez-Alonso, and Miguel-Ángel Sicilia

Abstract It is known that current Learning Object Repositories adopt strategies for quality assessment of their resources that rely on the impressions of quality given by the members of the repository community. Although this strategy can be considered effective at some extent, the number of resources inside repositories tends to increase more rapidly than the number of evaluations given by this community, thus leaving several resources of the repository without any quality assessment. The present work describes the results of two experiments to automatically generate quality information about learning resources based on their intrinsic features as well as on evaluative metadata (ratings) available about them in MERLOT repository. Preliminary results point out the feasibility of achieving such goal which suggests that this method can be used as a starting point for the pursuit of automatically generation of internal quality information about resources inside repositories.

Keywords Learning repositories • Quality metrics • Automatic assessment

C. Cechinel (✉)
Distance Learning Center, Federal University of Pelotas,
Felix da Cunha, 630 Centro, Pelotas, RS, Brazil
e-mail: contato@cristiancechinel.pro.br

S.da Silva Camargo
Computer Engineering Course, Federal University of Pampa,
Caixa Postal 07, 96400-970 Bagé, RS, Brazil
e-mail: camargo.sandro@gmail.com

S. Sánchez-Alonso • M.-Á. Sicilia
Information Engineering Research Unit, Computer Science Department, University
of Alcalá, Ctra. Barcelona km. 33.6, 28871 Alcalá de Henares, Madrid, Spain
e-mail: salvador.sanchez@uah.es; msicilia@uah.es

N. Manouselis et al. (eds.), *Recommender Systems for Technology Enhanced Learning:*   25
Research Trends and Applications, DOI 10.1007/978-1-4939-0530-0_2,
© Springer Science+Business Media New York 2014

Introduction

Current Learning Object Repositories (LORs) normally adopt strategies for the establishment of quality of their resources that rely on the impressions of usage and evaluations given by the members of the repository community (ratings, tags, comments, likes, lenses). All this information together constitute a collective body of knowledge that further serves as an external memory that can help other individuals to find resources according to their needs. Inside LORs, this kind of evaluative metadata [1] is also used by search and retrieval mechanisms for properly ranking and recommending resources to the community of users of the repository.

Although such strategies can be considered effective at some extent, the amount of resources inside repositories is rapidly growing every day [2] and it becomes impractical to rely only on human effort for such a task. For instance, on a quick look at the summary of MERLOT's recent activities, it is possible to observe that in a short period of 1 month (from May 21 to June 21, 2011), the amount of new resources catalogued in the repository was nine times more than the amount of new ratings given by experts (peer-reviewers), six times more than the amount of new comments (and users ratings) and three times more than the amount of new bookmarks (personal collections). This situation of leaving many resources of the current repositories without any measure of quality at all (and consequently unable or at least on a very disadvantaged position to compete for a good position during the process of search and retrieval) has raised the concern for the development of new automated techniques and tools that could be used to complement existing manual approaches. On that direction, Ochoa and Duval [3] developed a set of metrics for ranking repository search results according to three dimensions of relevance (topical, personal and situational) and by using information obtained from the learning objects metadata, from the user queries, and from other external sources such as the records of historical usage of the resources. This authors contrasted the performance of their approach against the text-based ranking traditional methods and have found significant improvements in the final ranking results. Moreover, Sanz-Rodriguez et al. [4] proposed to integrate several distinct quality indicators of learning objects of MERLOT along with their usage information into one overall quality indicator that can be used to facilitate the ranking of learning objects.

These mentioned approaches for automatically measuring quality (or calculating relevance) according to specific dimensions depend either on the existence and availability of metadata attached to the resources (or inside the repositories), or on measures of popularity about the resources that are obtained only when the resource is publicly available after a certain period of time. As metadata may be incomplete/inaccurate [5] and these measures of popularity will be available just for "old" resources, we propose to apply an alternative approach for this problem. The main idea is to identify intrinsic measures of the resources (i.e., features that can be calculated directly from the resources) that are associated to quality and that can be used in the process of creating models for automated quality assessment.

In fact, this approach was recently tested by Cechinel et al. [6] who developed highly-rated profiles of learning objects available in MERLOT, and have generated Linear Discriminant Analysis (LDA) models based on 13 learning objects intrinsic features. The generated models were able to classify resources between good and not-good with 72.16 % of precision, and between good and poor with 91.49 % of precision. Among other things, these authors concluded that highly-rated learning objects profiles should be developed taking into consideration the many possible intersections among the different disciplines and types of materials available in MERLOT, as well as the group of evaluators who rated the resources (whether they are formed by experts or by the community of users). For instance, the mentioned models were created for materials of *Simulation* type belonging to the discipline of *Science & Technology*, and considering the perspective of the peer-reviewers ratings.

The present chapter reviews two experiments conducted towards the creation of models for automated quality assessment of learning resources inside MERLOT and that expand the previous work developed by Cechinel et al. [6]. The first experiment explores the creation of statistical profiles of highly-rated learning objects by contrasting information from *good* and *not-good* resources of three subsets of MERLOT repository and by using these profiles to generate models for quality assessment. The second experiment tests a slightly different and more algorithmic approach, i.e., the models are generated exclusively through the use of data mining algorithms. In this second experiment we also worked with a larger collection of resources and a considerably higher number of MERLOT subsets.

The rest of this chapter is structured as follows. "Background" presents existing research focused on identifying intrinsic quality features of resources. "Data Collection" describes the data collected for the experiments. "First Experiment: Statistical profiles of highly-rated resources" and "Second experiment: Algorithmic Approach" present the experiments and some discussion about the results on the generation and evaluation of automated models for quality assessment. Finally, conclusions and outlook are provided in "Conclusions and Outlook".

Background

Apart from the recent works by Cechinel et al. [6, 7], there is still no empirical evidence of intrinsic metrics that could serve as indicators of quality for LOs. However, there are some works in adjacent fields which can serve us as a source of inspiration. For instance, empirical evidence of relations from intrinsic information and other characteristics of LOs have been found in [8], where the authors developed a model for classifying the didactic functions of a learning object based on measures about the length of the text, the presence of interactivity and information contained in the HTML code (lists, forms, input elements). Mendes et al. [9] have identified evidence in some measures to evaluate sustainability and reusability of educational hypermedia applications, such as, the type of link and the structure and size of the application. Blumenstock [10] has found the length of an article (measured in words) as a predictor of quality in Wikipedia. Moreover, Stvilia et al. [11] have been able to automatically discriminate high quality articles voted by the community of users from the rest of the articles of the collection. In order to do that, the authors developed profiles by contrasting metrics of articles featured as best articles by Wikipedia editors against a random set. The metrics were based on measures of the article edit history (total number of edits, number of anonymous user edits, for instance) and on the article attributes and surface features (number of internal broken links, number of internal links, number of images, for instance). At last, in the field of usability, Ivory and Hearst [12] have found that good websites contain (for instance) more words and links than the regular and bad ones.

Our approach is initially related exclusively to those aspects of learning objects that are displayed to the users and that are normally associated to the dimensions of presentation design and interaction usability included in LORI [13] and the dimension of information quality (normally mentioned in the context of educational digital libraries). Precisely, the references for quality assurance used in here are the ratings given by the peer-reviewers (experts) of the repository.

Data Collection

Two databases were collected from MERLOT (2009 and 2010) through the use of a crawler that systematically traversed the pages and collected information related to 34 metrics of the resources. The decision of choosing MERLOT lays mainly on the fact that MERLOT has one of the largest amount of registered resources and users, and it implements a system for quality assurance that works with evaluations given by experts and users of the repository. Such system can serve as baseline for the creation of the learning object classes of quality. As MERLOT repository is mainly formed by learning resources in the form of websites, we evaluated intrinsic metrics that are supposed to appear in such technical type of material (i.e., link measures, text measures, graphic measures and site architecture measures). The metrics collected for this study (see Table 1) are the same as used by Cechinel et al. [6] and some of them have also been mentioned in other works which tackled the problem of assessing quality of resources (previously presented in "Background").

Given that the resources in MERLOT vary considerably in size, a limit of two levels of depth was established for the crawler, i.e., metrics were computed for the root node (level 0—the home-page of the resource), as well as for the pages linked by the root node (level 1), and for the pages linked by the pages of the level 1 (level 2[1]). As it is shown in Table 1, some of the metrics refer to the total sum of the occurrences of a given attribute considering the whole resource, and other metrics refer to the average of this sum considering the number of the pages computed.

---

[1]Although this limitation may affect the results, the process of collecting the information is extremely slow and such limitation was needed. In order to acquire the samples used in this study, the crawler kept running uninterruptedly for 2 (in 2009) and 4 (in 2010) full months.

Table 1 Metrics collected for the study

Class of measure	Metric
Link measures	Number of links, number of unique[a] links, number of internal links[b], number of unique internal links, number of external links, number of unique external links
Text measures	Number of words, number of words that are links[c]
Graphic, interactive and multimedia measures	Number of images, total size of the images (in bytes), number of scripts, number of applets, number of audio files, number of video files, number of multimedia files
Site architecture measures	Size of the page (in bytes), number of files for downloading, total number of pages

[a]The term unique stands for "non-repeated"
[b]The term internal refers to those links which are located at some directory below the root site
[c]For these metrics the average was not computed or does not exist

For instance, an object composed by 3 pages and containing a total of 30 images will have a total number of images equals to 30, and an average number of images equals to 10 (= 30/3).

Classes of Quality

As the peer-reviewers ratings tend to concentrate above the intermediary rating 3, classes of quality were created using the terciles of the ratings for each subset (ratings in MERLOT vary from 1 to 5). Resources with ratings below the first tercile are classified as *poor*, resources with ratings equal or higher the first tercile and lower than the second tercile are classified as *average*, and resources with ratings equal or higher the second tercile are classified as *good*. The classes of quality *average* and *poor* were then joined in another class called *not-good* and were used as the output reference for generating and testing models for automated quality assessment of the resources

First Experiment: Statistical Profiles of Highly-Rated Resources

The collected sample contained 6,470 learning resources classified into 7 different disciplines and 9 distinct types of material, thus totalizing 63 different classes of possible learning object profiles. From the total, 1,257 (19.43 %) had at least one peer review rating and formed the final data sample. We have selected resources from the three subsets with the highest number of occurrences to generate and evaluate models for automated quality assessment in the context of peer-reviews thresholds. The selected subsets are (amounts in parenthesis): *Simulation* ∩ *Science and Technology* (97), *Simulation* ∩ *Mathematics and Statistics* (83), and *Tutorial* ∩ *Science and Technology* (83).

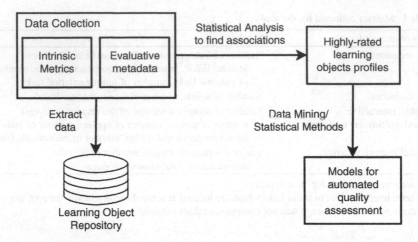

Fig. 1 Methodology for generating models for automated quality assessment

The methodology used for the present study was the development of highly-rated learning object profiles of MERLOT. The study described in this chapter is based on the methodology applied by Ivory and Hearst [12], as well as on the methodology described on García-Barriocanal and Sicilia [14] and Cechinel et al. [6]. The created profiles were then further used to generate models for automated quality assessment of learning objects. Figure 1 gives a general idea of the methodology applied here.

The analysis was conducted by contrasting intrinsic metrics from the groups between *good* and *not-good*[2] resources, and by observing if they presented significant differences between them. As the samples did not follow a normal distribution, a Mann-Whitney (Wilcoxon) test was performed to evaluate whether the classes presented differences between their medians, and a Kolmogorov-Smirnov test was applied to evaluate if the classes presented distinct distributions. When both distributions and medians presented significant differences, the metric was considered as a potential indicator of quality. The tendency of each metric (whether they influence negatively or positively the quality of the resource) was observed by comparing the median values of the samples. Table 2 presents the metrics that are associated to highly rated learning objects and their tendencies for each analyzed subset.

As it can be seen in Table 2, the metrics present different associations and tendencies depending on the given subsets. For instance, for the subset *Simulation ∩ Science and Technology*, seven metrics are positively associated to quality and six metrics negatively associated. On the other hand, for the subset of *Simulation ∩ Mathematics and Statistics* all metrics associated to quality present positive tendencies and for the subset of *Tutorial ∩ Science and Technology* all metrics associated to quality present negative tendencies.

---

[2] The so-called not-good group was formed by the union of the *average* group and the *poor* group.

Table 2 Significant discriminators and tendencies of the metrics for the good category of the selected subsets

Metric	Simulation ∩ science and technology	Simulation ∩ mathematics and statistics	Tutorial ∩ science and technology
Number of links	–	Y↑	Y↓
Number of unique links	–	Y↑	(Y)↓
Number of internal links	–	(Y)↑	Y↓
Number of unique internal links	–	(Y)↑	(Y)↓
Number of external links	Y↓	–	(Y)↓
Number of unique external links	Y↓	–	–
Size of the page (in bytes)		Y↑	(Y)↓
Number of images	(Y)↑	Y↑	–
Total size of the images (in bytes)	Y↑	Y↑	–
Number of scripts	Y↑	Y↑	–
Number of words	–	–	(Y)↓
Number of words that are links	–	–	Y↓
Number of applets	Y↓	–	–
Average number of unique internal links	–	–	(Y)↓
Average number of internal links	–	–	Y↓
Average number of unique external links	Y↓	–	–
Average number of external links	Y↓	–	(Y)↓
Average number of unique links	–	(Y)↑	Y↓
Average number of links	–	–	Y↓
Average number of applets	Y↓	–	–
Average number of images	Y↑	–	–
Average size of the pages	Y↑	–	–
Average size of the images	Y↑	Y↑	–
Average number of scripts	Y↑	(Y)↑	–
Total	13	11	13

Note: Y stands for both differences (medians and distributions) at the same time. The overall analysis was conducted for a 95 % confidence level; information in parenthesis means the results are significant at the 90 % level. Moreover (↑) stands for a positive contribution and (↓) stands for negative contribution

The Models

We created models for automated quality assessment of the resources through Data Mining Classification Algorithms (DMCA). Classification algorithms aim to construct models capable of associating each record of a given dataset to a labeled category. We have used WEKA [15] to generate and test models for the classification of resources between *good* and *not-good*, and among *good*, *average* and *poor* resources through the following classification algorithms: J48, SimpleCart, PART, Multilayer Perceptron Neural Network and Bayesian Network. Tables 3, 4 and 5 present the results of these tests. For all tests we have used the same metrics previously identified as potential indicators of quality for each subset (Table 2).

Table 3 Results of DMCA for *Simulation ∩ Science and Technology* in the context of peer-reviews ratings thresholds

Classification algorithm	N	Classes in the model	Metrics used by the model[a]	Number of leaves / Number of rules	Size of the tree	MAE	K	Classification precision				Overall (%)
								Good (%)	Average (%)	Poor (%)	Not-good (%)	
J48	1	Good and not-good	2	3	5	0.31	0.38	33.33	–	–	98.43	76.29
	2	Good, average and poor	11	19	37	0.1	0.83	96.96	84.00	92.85	–	89.69
Simple cart	3	Good and not-good	2	3	5	0.30	0.53	57.57	–	–	92.18	80.41
	4	Good, average and poor	8	14	27	0.15	0.76	90.90	86.00	71.40	–	85.57
PART	5	Good and not-good	5	4	–	0.28	0.38	33.33	–	–	98.43	76.29
	6	Good, average and poor	8	11	–	0.16	0.74	97.00	72.00	92.9	–	83.51
Multilayer perceptron	7	Good and not-good	13	–	–	0.29	0.58	60.60	–	–	93.75	82.47
	8	Good, average and poor	13	–	–	0.26	0.53	60.60	92.00	42.90	–	74.23
Bayesian network	9	Good and not-good	3	–	–	0.30	0.37	84.84	–	–	57.81	67.01
	10	Good, average and poor	5	–	–	0.30	0.41	60.60	48.00	100	–	59.79

[a]All models were tested with 13 metrics.

Table 4 Results of DMCA for *Simulation ∩ Mathematics and Statistics* in the context of peer-reviews ratings thresholds

Classification algorithm	N	Classes in the model	Metrics used by the model[a]	Number of leaves / Number of rules	Size of the tree	MAE	K	Classification precision				
								Good	Average (%)	Poor	Not-good (%)	Overall (%)
J48	1	Good and not-good	2	4	7	0.36	0.44	58.1	–	–	84.60	74.70
	2	Good, average and poor	4	8	15	0.26	0.47	64.5	89.10	0	–	73.49
Simple cart	3	Good and not-good	1	2	3	0.4	0.37	48.4	–	–	86.50	72.29
	4	Good, average and poor	1	2	3	0.32	0.32	48.4	87.00	0	–	66.26
PART	5	Good and not-good	5	5	–	0.3	0.55	54.8	–	–	96.20	80.72
	6	Good, average and poor	5	–	–	0.23	0.55	77.4	87.00	0	–	77.11
Multilayer perceptron	7	Good and not-good	11	–	–	0.42	0.17	16.1	–	–	98.10	67.47
	8	Good, average and poor	11	–	–	0.34	0.13	16.1	97.80	0	–	60.24
Bayesian network	9	Good and not-good	0	–	–	0.47	0	0	–	–	100	62.65
	10	Good, average and poor	0	–	–	0.37	0	0	100	0	–	55.42

[a] All models were tested with 11 metrics.

Table 5 Results of DMCA for *Tutorial ∩ Science and Technology* in the context of peer-reviews ratings thresholds

Classification algorithm	N	Classes in the model	Metrics used by the model[a]	Number of leaves / Number of rules	Size of the tree	MAE	K	Classification precision				
								Good (%)	Average (%)	Poor (%)	Not-good (%)	Overall (%)
J48	1	Good and not-good	3	6	11	0.25	0.62	60.7	–	–	96.4	84.34
	2	Good, average and poor	2	4	7	0.37	0.21	0	97.2	47.4	–	53.01
Simple cart	3	Good and not-good	0	1	1	0.45	0	0	–	–	100	66.26
	4	Good, average and poor	5	10	19	0.24	0.64	82.1	83.3	57.9	–	77.11
PART	5	Good and not-good	4	6	–	0.24	0.66	67.9	–	–	94.5	85.54
	6	Good, average and poor	5	3	–	0.35	0.25	0	100	52.6	–	55.42
Multilayer perceptron	7	Good and not-good	13	–	–	0.40	0	0	–	–	100	66.26
	8	Good, average and poor	13	–	–	0.38	0.20	10.7	86.1	47.4	–	51.81
Bayesian network	9	Good and not-good	0	–	–	0.45	0	0	–	–	100	66.26
	10	Good, average and poor	0	–	–	0.43	0	0	100	0	–	43.37

[a] All models were tested with 13 metrics.

There are several possible criteria for evaluation the good prediction of classification models [16]. Here we selected a few of them to present the results of our analysis. In the tables, the column "metrics used by the model" presents the number of metrics that were included in the model generated by the given algorithm. The mean absolute error (MAE) measures the average deviation between the predicted classes and the true classes of the resources. The closer to 0 the MAE, the lower is the error of the prediction and the better the model. The K stands for "Kappa statistic" which is a coefficient that measures the overall agreement between the data observed and the data expected. This coefficient varies from −1 to 1, where 1 means total agreement, 0 means no agreement, and −1 means total disagreement. At last, the tables also present the overall precision of the model and the specific precisions for each one of the classes in the dataset. We adopted the MAE measure as the main reference of quality for the models, i.e., when we mention in this section that a given model is the best for a given subset, we mean that this model has presented the minimum MAE among all. In this first exploratory study the models were evaluated using the training dataset, i.e., the entire dataset was used for training and for evaluating.

As it can be seen in the tables, apparently there is no best classification algorithm that fits for all subsets for the generation of good models. The results vary signifi cantly depending on the algorithm used, the subset from which the models were generated and the classes of quality included in the datasets.

Simulation ∩ Science and Technology

Among the three subsets, the models presented (in general) the best results for the *Simulation ∩ Science and Technology* subset. For this subset, the best model was a decision tree generated by a J48 algorithm (model number 2 of Table 3) which was able to correctly classify resources among *good*, *average* and *poor* with an overall precision of 89.69 %, and presented a Kappa coefficient of 0.83, and a MAE of just 0.1. The percentages of precision of this model for classifying resources in the specific categories of quality are considerably similar. *Good* resources are classified with 96.96 % of precision, while *average* and *poor* resources are classified with precisions of 84 and 92.85 % respectively. The second and third best models for this subset were also focused on classify resources among *good*, *average* and *poor*. The second best model was a decision tree generated by a Simple Cart algorithm with an overall precision of 85.57 % (model number 4 of Table 3) and the third best model was a set of if-then-rules generated by the PART algorithm with an overall precision of 83.51 % (model number 6 of Table 3). The main difference between these two models (in terms of precisions) is that the former presented the worst precision percentages for classifying *poor* resources (71.40 %), where the latter presented the worst precision percentages for classifying *average* resources (72 %). At last, the best results for classifying resources between *good* and *not-good* were achieved by the PART algorithm and by a Multilayer Perceptron Neural Network. The PART model achieved an overall precision of 76.29 a MAE of 0.28 and Kappa Statistic of 0.38. Moreover, it classified *not-good* resources with a precision of 98.43 %, and *good* resources with a precision of only *33.33 %*. The Multilayer Perceptron presented an overall precision of 82.47 %, a MAE of 0.29 and a Kappa coefficient of 0.58. The drawback of these two models is the very low precision for classifying *good* resources.

Simulation ∩ Mathematics and Statistics

For the *Simulation ∩ Mathematics and Statistics* subset the best model was generated by the PART algorithm (model 5 of Table 4) for classifying resources between *good* and *not-good*. This model contains a set of 5 if-then-rules that uses 5 from the 11 metrics identified as possible indicators of quality. It achieved an overall precision of 80.72 %, a MAE of 0.30 and a Kappa coefficient equals to 0.55. Even though the overall results can be considered good, the model presents a serious limitation for the classification of *good* resources, with only 54.8 % of precision. The second best model for this subset is a decision tree generated by the J48 algorithm to classify resources between *good* and *not-good* (model 1 of the Table 4). Here the model achieved an overall precision of 74.70, a MAE of 0.36, and a Kappa coefficient of 0.44. The main problem with this model is the fact that it uses just 2 of the 11 possible indicators of quality. For this subset, all models for classifying resources among *good*, *average* and *poor* have completely failed on the classification of the *poor* category (presenting 0 % of precision). It is also possible to see that the precisions for classifying *good* and *average* resources in these models are very similar to the precisions for classifying *good* and *not-good* resources on the other models.

Tutorial ∩ Science and Technology

The best model for the subset *Tutorial ∩ Science and Technology* was generated by the PART algorithm to classify resources between *good* and *not-good* (model 5 of Table 5). The model presents an overall precision of 85.54 %, a MAE of 0.24 and a Kappa coefficient of 0.66. From the 13 metrics identified as quality indicators, the model has included only four in the six if-then-rules generated. Moreover, the model has a high precision for classifying *not-good* resources (94.5 %), but a low precision for classifying *good* resources (67.9 %). The second best model for this subset is a decision tree generated by a Simple Cart algorithm that classifies resources among *good*, *average* and *poor* (model 4 of Table 5). Here the model uses 5 from the 13 metrics identified as quality indicators; it has an overall precision of 77.11 %, a MAE of 0.24, and a Kappa coefficient of 0.64. The model is able to classify *good* resources with 82.1 % of precision, *average* resources with 83.3 % of precision, and *poor* resources with 57.9 % of precision. The third best model is a decision tree generated by a J48 algorithm (model 1 of Table 5). This model classifies resources between *good* and *not-good* with an overall precision of 84.34 %, a MAE of 0.25, and a Kappa coefficient of 0.62. The model uses only 3 from the 13 metrics identified as quality indicators. Moreover, similarly to the best model for this subset, this model also has a high precision for classifying *not-good* resources (96.4 %) and a low precision for classifying *good* resources (60.7 %).

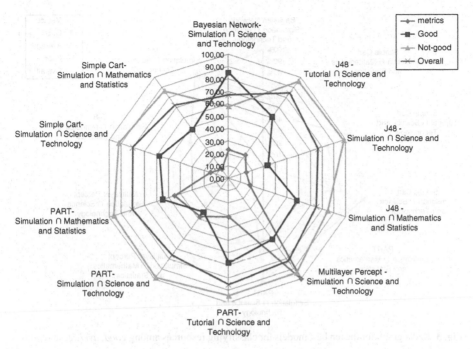

Fig. 2 Results of DMCA for *Tutorial ∩ Science and Technology* in the context of peer-reviews ratings thresholds

General Considerations at the light of the Results

The models normally exclude several of the metrics previously identified as indicators of quality. For instance, from the top ten best models for the classification of resources between Good and Not-Good, only one has used all metrics included in the dataset (a Multilayer Perceptron for the *Simulation ∩ Science and Technology* subset) (see Fig. 2). The rest of the models have used from just one to five metrics. It is also interesting to highlight that it was possible to generate models for all three subsets. Moreover, practically all models presented a higher precision for the classification of *not-good* resources than for *good* resources. Figure 2 presents this last observation more clearly. As it can be seen in the figure, from the ten best models, nine presented better precisions for classifying *not-good* resources and just one—a Bayesian Network for the *Simulation ∩ Science and Technology* subset—presented a higher precision for classifying *good* resources than *not-good* ones.

The best models generated for classifying resources among *good*, *average* and *poor* achieved lower MAEs and higher Kappa coefficients than the models for classifying resources between *good* and *not-good*. Moreover, as it can be seen in Fig. 3, the models here also tend to use more indicators of quality. The main problem found for this set of models is the fact that it was not possible to create good models for the subset of *Simulation ∩ Mathematics and Statistics* (all models presented 0.0 % of precision for

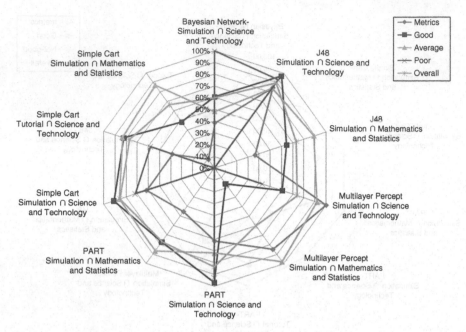

Fig. 3 Radar graph for the ten best models for classifying resources among *good*, *average* and *poor*

classifying *poor* resources). Another important thing to highlight is that the best three models presented more balanced precisions for the classification among the different classes. However, it is still possible to observe all kinds of models, i.e., those which classify more precisely *good* resources, those which classify more precisely *average* resources, and those which classify more precisely *poor* resources (see Fig. 3).

The results found here point out the possibility of generating models for automated quality assessment of learning resources inside repositories based on their intrinsic metrics. However, as the models are very heterogeneous (different MAEs, Kappa coefficients, number of metrics used, classification precisions), the decision of which one is the best will depend on the combination of several facts such as: the specific scenario to which the model is going to be applied, the specific subset (category of discipline versus material type) to which they are being generated for, and the classes of quality included in the dataset. Next section will describe another experiment towards automated evaluation and that was performed with a slightly different methodology and using a broader set of resources and subsets.

Second Experiment: Algorithmic Approach

For this second experiment we collected (in 2010) a total of 20,582 learning resources from MERLOT. From this amount, only 2,076 were peer-reviewed, and 5 of them did not have metadata regarding the category of discipline or the type of

Table 6 Frequency of materials for the subsets used in this study (intersection of category of discipline and material type)

Material type/discipline	Arts	Business	Education	Humanities
Collection		52	56	43
Reference material		83	40	51
Simulation	57	63	40	78
Tutorial		76	73	93

Material type/discipline	Mathematics and statistics	Science & technology	Social sciences
Collection	50	80	
Reference Material	68	102	
Simulation	40	150	
Tutorial	48	86	

material and were disregarded. Considering that many subsets are formed by very small amounts of resources, we restrained our experiment to just a few of them. Precisely, we worked with 21 subsets formed by the following types of material: *Collection, Reference Material, Simulation* and *Tutorial*, and that had 40 resources or more.[3] In total, we worked with information of 1,429 learning resources which represent 69 % of the total collected data. Table 6 presents the frequency of the materials for each subset used in this study.

As mentioned before, the methodology we followed for this experiment was slightly different from the one described in the previous section. Here we did not created statistical profiles of the learning resources, but used all collected metrics as input information for the generation and evaluation of models through the use of Artificial Neural Networks (ANNs).

This experiment was conducted with the Neural Network toolbox of Matlab. For each subset we randomly selected 70 % of the data for training, 15 % for testing and 15 % for validation, as suggested by Xu et al. [17]. We tested the Marquardt–Levenberg algorithm [18] using from 1 to 30 neurons in all tests. In order to obtain more statistically significant results (due to the small size of the data samples), each test was repeated 10 times and the average results were computed. Differently from the previous experiment, the models here were generated to classify resources between *good* and *not-good* (we did not tested models to classify resources among *good, average* and *poor*).

The choice of using ANNs rests on the fact that they are adaptive, distributed, and highly parallel systems which have been used in many knowledge areas and have proven to solve problems that require pattern recognition [19]. Moreover, ANNs are among the types of models that have also shown good precisions for some subsets in the previous experiment. At last, this experiment was initially

---

[3] The difficulties for training, validating and testing predictive models for subsets with less than 40 resources would be more severe.

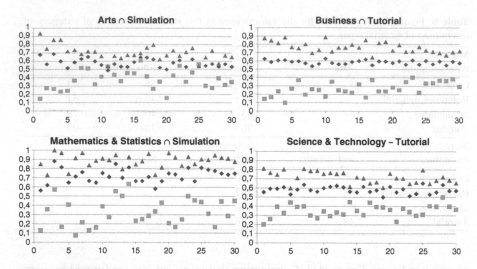

Fig. 4 Precisions of the some models versus number of neurons. Overall precision (*lozenges*), precision for the classification of *good* resources (*squares*) and *not-good* resources (*triangles*)

focused on populating the repository with hidden internal quality information that can be further used by ranking mechanisms [20], and for such a purpose we could use black-box models such as ANNs.

Results and Discussion

The models presented different results depending on the subset used for training. Most of the models tend to classify *not-good* resources better than *good* ones which can probably be a result of the uneven amount of resources of each class inside the datasets (normally formed by 2/3 of *not-good* and 1/3 of *good*). These tendencies can be observed in Fig. 4.[4]

The number of neurons used in the construction of the models has different influences depending on the subsets. A Spearman's rank correlation (r_s) analysis was carried out to evaluate whether there are associations between the number of neurons and the precisions achieved by the models. This test serves to the purpose of observing the pattern expressed by the models on predicting quality for the given subsets. For instance, assuming x as a predictive model for a given subset A, and y as a predictive model for a given subset B; if x has less neurons than y and both have the same precisions, the patterns expressed in A arc simpler than the ones expressed in B. This means to say that it is easier to understand what is *good* (or *not-good*) in the subset A. Table 7 shows the results of such analysis.

---

[4] Just some models were presented in the figure.

Table 7 Tendencies of the precisions according to the number of neurons used for training (*good | not-good*)

Subset	Arts	Business	Education	Humanities	Math & statistics	Science & tech
Collection	−|−	−|−	↑|↓	−|−	−|−	−|−
Reference material	−|−	−|−	−|−	−|↓	−|−	−|−
Simulation	−|↓	↑|−	−|↓	−|−	−|−	↑|↓
Tutorial	−|−	↑|↓	↑|↓	↑|−	−|−	−|↓

In Table 7 (−) stands for no association between the number of neurons and the precision of the model for classifying a given class, (↑) stands for a positive association, and (↓) stands for a negative association. The analyses considered a 95 % level of significance. As it can be seen in the table, the number of neurons influences on the precisions for some classes of quality of some subsets. For instance, the number of neurons presents a positive association with the precisions for classifying *good* resources in the 6 (six) following subsets: *Business ∩ Simulation, Business ∩ Tutorial, Education ∩ Collection, Education ∩ Tutorial, Humanities ∩ Tutorial*, and *Science & Technology ∩ Simulation*. Moreover, the number of neurons presents a negative association with the precisions for classifying *not-good* resources in the 8 (eight) following subsets: *Arts ∩ Simulation, Business ∩ Tutorial, Education ∩ Collection, Education ∩ Simulation, Education ∩ Tutorial, Education ∩ Humanities, Science & Technology ∩ Simulation*, and *Science & Technology ∩ Tutorial*. Finally, there are no positive associations between the number of neurons and the precisions for classifying *not-good* resources; neither there are negative associations between the number of neurons and the precisions for classifying *good* resources.

In order to evaluate how to select the best models for quality assessment, it is necessary to understand the behavior of the models for classifying both classes of quality included in the datasets. Considering that, a Spearman's rank correlation (r_s) analysis was also carried out to evaluate whether there are associations between the precisions of the models for classifying *good* and *not-good* resources. Such analysis serves to evaluate the trade-offs of selecting or not a given model for the present purpose. Most of the models have presented strong negative correlations between the precisions for classifying *good* and *not-good* resources. The results of both analyses suggest that the decision of selecting a model for predicting quality must take into account that, as the precision for classifying resources from one class increases, the precision for classifying resources of the other class decreases. Considering that, the question lies on establishing which would be the cutting point for acceptable precisions so that the models could be used for our purpose. In other words, it is necessary to establish the minimum precisions (cutting point) that the models must present for classifying both classes (*good* and *not-good*) so that they can be used for generating hidden quality information for the repository.

For the present study, we are considering that the models must present precisions higher than 50 % for the correct classification of *good* and *not-good* resources (simultaneously) in order to be considered as useful. It is known that the decision of selecting the minimum precisions for considering a model as efficient or not will depend on

Table 8 Two best models for each subset (ordered by the precisions for classifying *good* resources)

Subset	N	OP	G	NG	Subset	N	OP	G	NG
Arts ∩ Simulation	16	0.65	0.61	0.70	*Business ∩*	11	0.56	0.61	0.60
	25	0.55	0.56	0.54	*Collection*	25	0.57	0.60	0.59
Business ∩ Reference	8	0.58	0.54	0.59	*Business ∩*	24	0.64	0.67	0.60
	5	0.59	0.53	0.68	*Simulation*	30	0.57	0.62	0.55
Business ∩ Tutorial	23	0.61	0.40	0.72	*Education ∩*	26	0.51	0.6	0.49
	29	0.59	0.38	0.71	*Collection*	29	0.51	0.6	0.44
Education ∩ Reference	16	0.60	0.63	0.70	*Education ∩*	20	0.52	0.62	0.5
	20	0.58	0.54	0.71	*Simulation*	12	0.53	0.59	0.56
Education ∩ Tutorial	27	0.47	0.49	0.47	*Humanities ∩*	14	0.6	0.75	0.51
	29	0.53	0.43	0.61	*Collection*	19	0.63	0.69	0.68
Humanities ∩	29	0.47	0.59	0.49	*Humanities ∩*	4	0.69	0.76	0.69
Reference Mat.	10	0.58	0.5	0.65	*Simulation*	9	0.79	0.75	0.79
Humanities ∩ Tutorial	25	0.56	0.60	0.58	*Math.& Statistics ∩*	28	0.5	0.61	0.54
	21	0.51	0.59	0.54	*Collection*	27	0.49	0.57	0.46
Math. ∩ Reference Mat.	22	0.63	0.54	0.72	*Math.& Statistics ∩*	14	0.81	0.63	0.93
	18	0.53	0.48	0.60	*Simulation*	3	0.88	0.57	1
Mathematics ∩ Tutorial	26	0.69	0.79	0.64	*Science & Tech. ∩*	17	0.58	0.60	0.54
	25	0.70	0.77	0.61	*Collection*	3	0.56	0.54	0.60
Science & Tech. ∩	19	0.59	0.63	0.56	*Science & Tech. ∩*	29	0.57	0.58	0.61
Reference Mat.	16	0.55	0.58	0.58	*Simulation*	19	0.58	0.52	0.62
Science & Tech. ∩	28	0.64	0.50	0.72					
Tutorial	14	0.56	0.45	0.61					

the specific scenario/problem for which the models are being developed for. Here we are considering that precisions higher than 50 % are better than the merely random.

Table 8 presents the top-2 models for each subset considering their overall precisions, and their precisions for classifying *good* and *not-good* resources (ordered by the precision for classifying *good* resources).

In Table 8, N stands for the number of neurons in the model, OP stands for the overall precision, G for the precision for classifying good resources and NG for the precision for classifying not-good resources. As it can be seen in the table, and considering the established minimum cutting-point, it was possible to generate models for almost all subsets. From the 42 models presented in the table, only 10 did not reach the minimum precisions (white in the table). Moreover, 22 of them presented precisions between 50 and 59.90 % (gray hashed in the table), and nine presented both precisions higher than 60 % (black hashed in the table). We have also found 1 (one) model with precisions higher than 70 % (for *Humanities ∩ Simulation*). The only three subsets where the models did not reach the minimum precisions were: *Business ∩ Tutorial, Education ∩ Collection* and *Education ∩ Tutorial*. On the other hand, the best results were found for: *Humanities ∩ Simulation, Mathematics ∩ Tutorial, Humanities ∩ Collection, Business ∩ Simulation, Arts ∩ Simulation* and *Business ∩ Collection*. One of the possible reasons why it was not feasible to generate good models for all subsets may rest on the fact that the real features associated to quality on those given subsets might not have been collected by the crawler.

In order to select the most suitable model one should take into consideration that the model's output is going to be used as information during the ranking process, and to evaluate the advantages and drawbacks of a lower precision for classifying *good* resources in contraposition to a lower precision for classifying *not-good* resources. The less damaging situation seems to occur when the model classifies as *not-good* a *good* material. In this case, *good* materials would just remain hidden in the repository, i.e., in bad ranked positions (a similar situation to the one of not using the models). On the other hand, if the model classifies as *good* a resource that is *not-good*, it is most likely that this resource will be put at a higher rank position, thus increasing its chances of being accessed by the users. This would mislead the user towards the selection of a "not-so-good" quality resource, and it could put in discredit the ranking mechanism.

Conclusions and Outlook

It is known that LORs normally use evaluative information to rank resources during the process of search and retrieval. However, the amount of resources inside LORs increases more rapidly than the number of contributions given by the community of users and experts. Because of that, many LOs that do not have any quality evaluation receive bad rank positions even if they are of high-quality, thus remaining unused (or unseen) inside the repository until someone decides to evaluate it.

The present chapter presented two experiments that used intrinsic features of the resources in order to generate models for their automated quality assessment. For that, we collected information from MERLOT and used the ratings associated to the resources as baseline for the creation of classes of quality.

In the first experiment we tested the generation of automated models through the creation of statistical profiles and the further use of data mining classification algorithms for three distinct subsets of MERLOT materials. On these studies we were able to generate models with good overall precision rates (up to 89 %) but we highlighted that the feasibility of the models will depend on the specific method used to generate them, the specifics subsets to which they are being generated for, and the classes of quality included in the dataset. Moreover, the models were generated by using considerably small datasets (around 90 resources each), and were evaluated using the training dataset, i.e., the entire dataset was used for training and for evaluating. Such kind of evaluation is always too optimistic and is susceptible to over fitting (i.e. the model just memorizes the data and can fail to predict well in the future).

In the second experiment we used all collected intrinsic features as input information for the generation of models represented by Artificial Neural Networks. We also changed the method for the evaluation of the models in order to better deal with the small amount of resources in the samples and to avoid over fitting. Among other good results, one can mention the model for *Humanities* ∩ *Simulation* that is able to classify *good* resources with 75 % of precision and *not-good* resources with 79 %; and the model developed for *Mathematics* ∩ *Tutorial* with 79 % of precision for classifying *good* resources and 64 % for classifying *not-good* ones. As the models would be used inside repository and the classifications would serve just as input information for searching mechanisms, it is not necessarily required that the models provide explanations about their reasoning. Models constituted of neural networks (as the one tested in the present study) can perfectly be used in such a scenario.

The models developed here could be used to provide internal quality information for those LOs still not evaluated, thus helping the repository in the stage of offering resources. Resources recently added to the repository would be highly benefited by such models since that they hardly receive any assessment just after their inclusion. Once the resource finally receives a formal evaluation from the community of the repository, the initial implicit quality information provided by the model could be disregarded. Moreover, this "real" rating could be used as feedback information so that the efficiency of the models could be analyzed, i.e. to evaluate whether or not the users agree with the models decisions.

Future work will try to include more metrics still not implemented, such as, for instance, the number of colors and different font styles, the existence of adds, the number of redundant and broken links, and some readability measures (e.g. Gunning Fog index and Flesch-Kincaid grade level). We would also like to repeat the experiments, but now using the same method to train and evaluate the models so that we can compare the results of these two approaches. Besides, as pointed out by Cechinel and Sánchez-Alonso [21], both communities of evaluators in MERLOT (users and peer-reviewers) are communicating different views regarding the quality of the learning objects refereed in the repository. The models tested here are related to the perspective of quality given by peer-reviewers. Future work will test models created with the ratings given by the community of users and will compare their performances with the present study. Moreover, as the present work is context sensitive, it is important to evaluate whether this approach can be extended to other repositories. As not all repositories adopt the same kind of quality assurance that MERLOT does, alternative quality measures for contrasting classes between *good* and *not-good* resources must be found. Another interesting possible direction is to classify learning resources according to their granularity, and use this information as input for the generation of the models. At last, we could use the values calculated by the models for all the resources and compare the ranking of MERLOT with the ranking performed through the use of these "artificial" quality information.

It is important to mention that the present approaches do not intend to replace traditional evaluation methods, but complement them providing a useful and inexpensive quality assessment that can be used by the repositories before more time and effort consuming evaluation is performed.

Acknowledgments The work presented here has been partially funded by the European Commission through the project IGUAL (www.igualproject.org)—Innovation for Equality in Latin American University (code DCIALA/19.09.01/10/21526/245-315/ALFAIII (2010)123) of the ALFA III Programme, by Spanish Ministry of Science and Innovation through project MAVSEL: Mining, data analysis and visualization based in social aspects of e-learning (code TIN2010-21715-C02-01) and by CYTED (Ibero-American Programme for Science, Technology and Development) as part of project "RIURE - Ibero-American Network for the Usability of Learning Repositories " (code 513RT0471).

References

1. Vuorikari R, Manouselis N, Duval E (2008) Using metadata for storing, sharing and reusing evaluations for social recommendations: the case of learning resources. Social information retrieval systems: emerging technologies and applications for searching the web effectively. Idea Group, Hershey, PA, pp 87–107
2. Ochoa X, Duval E (2009) Quantitative analysis of learning object repositories. IEEE Trans Learn Technol 2(3):226–238
3. Ochoa X, Duval E (2008) Relevance ranking metrics for learning objects. IEEE Trans Learn Technol 1(1):34–48. doi:10.1109/TLT.2008.1, http://dx.doi.org/
4. Sanz-Rodriguez J, Dodero J, Sánchez-Alonso S (2010) Ranking learning objects through integration of different quality indicators. IEEE Trans Learn Technol 3(4):358–363. doi:10.1109/TLT.2010.23
5. Cechinel C, Sánchez-Alonso S, Sicilia M-Á (2009) Empirical analysis of errors on human-generated learning objects metadata. In: Sartori F, Sicilia MÁ, Manouselis N (eds) Metadata and semantic research, vol 46, Communications in computer and information science. Springer, Berlin, pp 60–70. doi:10.1007/978-3-642-04590-5_6
6. Cechinel C, Sánchez-Alonso S, García-Barriocanal E (2011) Statistical profiles of highly-rated learning objects. Comput Educ 57(1):1255–1269. doi:10.1016/j.compedu.2011.01.012
7. Cechinel C, Silva Camargo S, Sánchez-Alonso S, Sicilia M-Á (2012) On the search for intrinsic quality metrics of learning objects. In: Dodero J, Palomo-Duarte M, Karampiperis P (eds) Metadata and semantics research, Communications in computer and information science. Springer, Berlin, pp 49–60. doi:10.1007/978-3-642-35233-1_5
8. Meyer M, Hannappel A, Rensing C, Steinmetz R (2007) Automatic classification of didactic functions of e-learning resources. Paper presented at the Proceedings of the 15th international conference on multimedia, Augsburg, Germany
9. Mendes E, Hall W, Harrison R (1998) Applying metrics to the evaluation of educational hypermedia applications. J Univers Comput Sci 4(4):382–403. doi:10.3217/jucs-004-04-0382
10. Blumenstock JE (2008) Size matters: word count as a measure of quality on Wikipedia. Paper presented at the Proceedings of the 17th international conference on World Wide Web, Beijing, China
11. Stvilia B, Twidale MB, Smith LC, Gasser L (2005) Assessing information quality of a community-based encyclopedia. In: Proceedings of the international conference on information quality – ICIQ 2005, pp 442-454. Doi:citeulike-article-id:1833325
12. Ivory MY, Hearst MA (2002) Statistical profiles of highly-rated web sites. Changing our world, changing ourselves. Paper presented at the proceedings of the SIGCHI conference on Human factors in computing systems, Minneapolis, MA, 2002
13. Nesbit JC, Belfer K, Leacock T (2003) Learning object review instrument (LORI). E-learning research and assessment network. http://www.elera.net/eLera/Home/Articles/LORI%20manual
14. García-Barriocanal E, Sicilia M-Á (2009) Preliminary explorations on the statistical profiles of highly-rated learning objects. In: Sartori F, Sicilia MÁ, Manouselis N (eds) Metadata and semantic research, vol 46, Communications in computer and information science. Springer, Berlin, pp 108–117. doi:10.1007/978-3-642-04590-5_10
15. Hall M, Frank E, Holmes G, Pfahringer B, Reutemann P, Witten IH (2009) The WEKA data mining software: an update. SIGKDD Explor Newsl 11(1):10–18.doi:10.1145/1656274.1656278
16. Cichosz P (2011) Assessing the quality of classification models: performance measures and evaluation procedures. Cent Eur J Eng 1(2):132–158. doi:10.2478/s13531-011-0022-9
17. Xu L, Hoos HH, Leyton-Brown K (2007) Hierarchical hardness models for SAT. Paper presented at the Proceedings of the 13th international conference on principles and practice of constraint programming, Providence, RI
18. Hagan MT, Menhaj MB (1994) Training feedforward networks with the Marquardt algorithm. IEEE Trans Neural Netw 5(6):989–993. doi:10.1109/72.329697
19. Bishop CM (2006) Pattern recognition and machine learning, Information Science and Statistics. Springer, New York

20. Cechinel C, Camargo SdS, Ochoa X, Sánchez-Alonso S, Sicilia M-Á (2012a) Populating learning object repositories with hidden internal quality information. In: Manouselis N, Drachsler H, Verbert K, Santos OC (eds) Recommender systems in technology enhanced learning, CEUR workshop proceedings, Saarbrücken, pp 11–22

21. Cechinel C, Sánchez-Alonso S (2011) Analyzing associations between the different ratings dimensions of the MERLOT repository. Interdisciplinary Journal of E-Learning and Learning Objects 7:1–9

A Survey on Linked Data and the Social Web as Facilitators for TEL Recommender Systems

Stefan Dietze, Hendrik Drachsler, and Daniela Giordano

Abstract Personalisation, adaptation and recommendation are central features of TEL environments. In this context, information retrieval techniques are applied as part of TEL recommender systems to filter and recommend learning resources or peer learners according to user preferences and requirements. However, the suitability and scope of possible recommendations is fundamentally dependent on the quality and quantity of available data, for instance, metadata about TEL resources as well as users. On the other hand, throughout the last years, the Linked Data (LD) movement has succeeded to provide a vast body of well-interlinked and publicly accessible Web data. This in particular includes Linked Data of explicit or implicit educational nature. The potential of LD to facilitate TEL recommender systems research and practice is discussed in this paper. In particular, an overview of most relevant LD sources and techniques is provided, together with a discussion of their potential for the TEL domain in general and TEL recommender systems in particular. Results from highly related European projects are presented and discussed together with an analysis of prevailing challenges and preliminary solutions.

Keywords Linked data • Education • Semantic web • Technology-enhanced learning • Data consolidation • Data integration

S. Dietze (✉)
L3S Research Center, Leibniz University, Hannover, Germany
e-mail: dietze@l3s.de

H. Drachsler
Faculty of Psychology and Educational Sciences, Welten Institute – Research Centre
for Learning, Teaching and Technology, Open University of the Netherlands, CELSTEC,
Heerlen, The Netherlands
e-mail: hendrik.drachsler@ou.nl

D. Giordano
DIEEI, University of Catania, Catania, Italy
e-mail: dgiordan@diit.unict.it

N. Manouselis et al. (eds.), *Recommender Systems for Technology Enhanced Learning: Research Trends and Applications*, DOI 10.1007/978-1-4939-0530-0_3,
© Springer Science+Business Media New York 2014

Introduction

As personalisation, adaptation and recommendation are central features of TEL environments, TEL recommender systems apply information retrieval techniques to filter and deliver learning resources according to user preferences and requirements. While the suitability and scope of possible recommendations is fundamentally dependent on the quality and quantity of available data, e.g., data about learners, and in particular metadata about TEL resources, the landscape of standards and approaches currently exploited to share and reuse educational data is highly fragmented.

This landscape includes, for instance, competing metadata schemas, i.e., general-purpose ones such as Dublin Core[1] or schemas specific to the educational field, like IEEE Learning Object Metadata (LOM) [5] or ADL SCORM[2] but also interface mechanisms such as OAI-PMH[3] or SQI.[4] These technologies are exploited by educational resources repository providers to support interoperability. To this end, although a vast amount of educational content and data is shared on the Web in an open way, the integration process is still costly as different learning repositories are isolated from each other and based on different implementation standards [4].

In the past years, TEL research has already widely attempted to exploit Semantic Web technologies in order to solve interoperability issues. However, while the Linked Data (LD) [2] approach has established itself as the de-facto standard for sharing data on the Semantic Web, it is still not widely adopted by the TEL community. Linked Data is based on a set of well-established principles and (W3C) standards, e.g., RDF, SPARQL [6] and use of URIs, and aims at facilitating Web-scale data interoperability. Despite the fact that the LD approach has produced an ever growing amount of data sets, schemas and tools available on the Web, its take-up in the area of TEL is still very limited. Thus, LD opens up opportunities to substantially alleviate interoperability issues and to substantially improve quality, quantity and accessibility of TEL data.

In particular, we expect LD to facilitate TEL community with relevant datasets in order to gain more knowledge about personalisation of learning and build better recommender systems. So far the outcomes of different recommender systems and personalisation approaches in the educational domain are hardly comparable due to the diversity of algorithms, learner's models, datasets and evaluation criteria [40]. A kind of reference dataset is needed for the TEL recommender systems field, as is the MovieLens dataset[5] in the e-commerce field. Initial characteristics of such a reference dataset for TEL have been described in [40]. Recently, some initiatives

---

[1] http://dublincore.org/documents/dces/.

[2] Advanced Distributed Learning (ADL) SCORM: http://www.adlnet.org.

[3] Open Archives Protocol for Metadata Harvesting http://www.openarchives.org/OAI/openarchives protocol.html.

[4] Simple Query Interface: http://www.cen-ltso.net/main.aspx?put=859.

[5] http://www.grouplens.org/node/73.

like LinkedEducation.org and the Special Interest Group dataTEL of the European Association of TEL started to collect representative datasets that can be used as a main set of references for different personalisation approaches within TEL [43]. Data driven companies like the Mendeley reference systems[6] are pioneers with this respect as they provided a reference dataset for Science2.0 research [54]. Similar, initiatives for TEL are highly needed to stimulate data driven research for education. Recently, the SOLAR foundation for Learning Analytics presented a concept paper that also contributes to this idea, and outlines an Open Learning Analytics platform for online data-driven studies [41]. At the Learning Analytics and Knowledge Conference 2012, the first workshop on Learning Analytics and Linked Data (LALD12) has raised the idea to use LD sources as reference dataset for these kinds of research [42]. The workshop was inspired by the FP7 *LinkedUp* project[7] that aims to provide a data pool of linked educational datasets that can be used for developing and testing advanced TEL recommender systems and other data driven educational tools. Using LD as the foundation for the TEL references datasets provides various advantages due to two main reasons: (a) LD and the Social Web offer vast amounts of often publicly available data and resources of high relevance to educational contexts; and (b) LD techniques offer solutions for fundamentally improving quality and interoperability of existing data by, for instance, allowing to match schemas and interlink previously unrelated datasets. To this end, LD and the Social Web show high potential to alleviate data sparseness and interoperability problems towards Web-scale application of recommender systems.

In this article, we first provide a state of the art review of approaches to TEL resource data sharing on the Web, and of educational datasets relevant for TEL recommender research, including those that are available in the Linked Data landscape (section "TEL resource data sharing on the Web: State of the Art"). Afterwards, in section "Challenges for using LD as references datasets for TEL research," we describe the challenges that currently hinder the use of LD as data repository. In section "Towards integration and exploitation of heterogeneous educational resource data," we outline a set of principles that need to be considered to overcome these challenges and create a suitable LD repository. To this aim we show how some of these challenges are being addressed by some key past and on-going European projects. Section "Integration of social data" describes suitable data formats for dealing with data generated in the social web and from the tracking of user's activities. Section "Bridging the gap between Linked Data and the Social Web" describes how these data sources can be exposed to the general LD cloud, providing some examples of social and linked data sources integrated for recommendations. Finally, we summarise the article and outline the main aspects to develop a LD repository for TEL recommender systems.

---

[6] http://www.mendeley.com/.
[7] LinkedUp: Linking Web Data for Education Project—Open Challenge in Web-scale Data Integration (http://www.linkedup-project.eu).

TEL Resource Data Sharing on the Web: State of the Art

Open Educational Resources (*OER*) are educational material freely available online. The wide availability of educational resources is a common objective for universities, libraries, archives and other knowledge-intensive institutions raising a number of issues, particularly with respect to Web-scale *metadata interoperability* or legal as well as *licensing aspects*. Several competing standards and educational metadata schemata have been proposed over time, including IEEE LTSC LOM[8] (*Learning Object Metadata*), one of the widest adopted, IMS,[9] Ariadne, ISO/IEC MLR—ISO 19788[10] Metadata for Learning Resources (MLR) and Dublin Core (see also [21]). The adoption of a sole metadata schema is usually not sufficient to efficiently characterize learning resources. As a solution to this problem, a number of taxonomies, vocabularies, policies, and guidelines (called *application profiles*) are defined [20]. Some popular examples are: UK LOM Core,[11] DC-Ed[12] and ADL SCORM.

Due to the diversity of exploited standards, existing *OER repositories offer very heterogeneous datasets*, differing with respect to schema, exploited vocabularies, and interface mechanisms. Examples are the MIT Open Courseware[13] (OCW), and OpenLearn,[14] the UK Open University's contribution to the OER movement (OpenLearn is also member of the MIT OCW Consortium). Video material from OpenLearn, distributed through iTunes U has reached more than 40 million downloads in less than 4 years.[15] One of the largest and diverse collections of OER can be found in the GLOBE[16] (Global Learning Objects Brokered Exchange) where jointly, nearly 1.2 million learning objects are shared. KOCW,[17] LACLO[18] and OUJ[19] expose a single collection of metadata instances with a common provenance. Other repositories, such as ARIADNE, LRE,[20] OER and LORNET[21] expose the result of the aggregation of several metadata collections that have different provenance.

Regarding the presence of *educational information in the linked data landscape*, two types of linked datasets need to be considered: (1) datasets directly related to educational material and institutions, including information from open educational

---

[8] http://ltsc.ieee.org/wg12/par1484-12-1.html.

[9] http://www.imsglobal.org/metadata/.

[10] http://www.iso.org/iso/.

[11] http://zope.cetis.ac.uk/profiles/uklomcore/.

[12] http://www.dublincore.org/documents/education-namespace/.

[13] http://ocw.mit.edu/index.htm.

[14] http://openlearn.open.ac.uk/.

[15] http://www.bbc.co.uk/news/education-15150319.

[16] http://globe-info.org/.

[17] http://www.koreabrand.net/.

[18] http://www.laclo.org/.

[19] http://www.ouj.ac.jp/eng/.

[20] http://lreforschools.eun.org/.

[21] http://www.lornet.org/.

repositories and data produced by universities; (2) datasets that can be used in teaching and learning scenarios, while not being directly published for this purpose. This second category includes, for example, datasets in the cultural heritage domain, such as the ones made available by the Europeana project,[22] as well as by individual museums and libraries (such as the British Museum,[23] who have made their collection available as linked data, representing more than 100 Million triples, or the Bibliothèque Nationale de France,[24] who made available information about 30,000 books and 10,000 authors in RDF, representing around 2 Million triples). It also includes information related to research in particular domains, and the related publications (see PubMed[25] which covers more than 21 Million citations, in 800 Million triples), as well as general purpose information for example from Wikipedia (see DBPedia.org).

Regarding category (1), initiatives have emerged recently using linked data to expose, give access to and exploit public information for education. The Open University in the UK was the first education organization to create a linked data platform to expose information from across its departments, and that would usually sit in many different systems, behind many different interfaces (see http://data.open.ac.uk which includes around 5 Million triples about 3,000 audio-video resources, 700 courses, 300 qualifications, 100 Buildings, 13,000 people [24, 25]). Many other institutions have since then announced similar platforms, including in the UK the University of Southampton (http://data.southampton.ac.uk) and the University of Oxford (http://data.ox.ac.uk). Outside the UK, several other universities and education institutions are joining the Web of Data, by publishing information of value to students, teachers and researchers with linked data. Noticeable initiatives include the Linked Open Data at University of Muenster[26] and the LODUM[27] project in Germany or the Norwegian University of Science and Technology exposing its library data as linked open data.[28] In addition, educational resources metadata has been exposed by the mEducator project [3, 22]. A more thorough overview of educational Linked Data is offered by the Linked Education[29] platform and in [4].

In the TEL field many research projects are working with rather small internal datasets which cannot be shared with other research institutes [45, 46]. Therefore, the EATEL Special Interest Group *dataTEL* was founded [40] with a focus on the analysis of issues around the development, sharing and using of TEL datasets for research. Recently, the dataTEL project published an initial list of 20 available TEL datasets for research and compared the different datasets according to certain criteria (see Table 1) [43]. With this initiative the amount of available TEL datasets has

---

[22] http://www.europeana.eu/.

[23] http://collection.britishmuseum.org/.

[24] http://data.bnf.fr/.

[25] http://www.ncbi.nlm.nih.gov/pubmed/ and http://thedatahub.org/dataset/bio2rdf-pubmed.

[26] http://data.uni-muenster.de.

[27] http://lodum.de.

[28] http://openbiblio.net/2011/09/08/ntnu/.

[29] http://linkededucation.org.

Table 1 Overview of datasets from dataTEL project [43]

dataTEL	Environment/application	Collection period	Statistics	Access rights	Educational context
Mendeley	Web portal	1 year	200,000 users 1,857,912 items 4,848,725 actions	Open access	Science
APOSDLE	PLE	3 months	6 users 163 items 1500 actions	Open access	Workplace learning
ReMashed	PLE/Mash-up environment	2 years	140 users 960,000 items 23,264 actions	Legal protection	Computer science
Organic. Edunet		9 months	1,000 users 11,000 items 920 actions	Legal protection	Agriculture
MACE	Web portal	3 years	1,148 users 12,000 items 461,982 actions	Legal protection	Architecture
Travel well	Web portal	6 months	98 users 1,923 items 16,353 actions	Open access	Various
ROLE	PLE	6 months	392 users 11,239 items 28,554 actions	Legal protection	Computer science
SidWeb	LMS	4 years	4,013,208 users 35,041 items 4,009,292 actions	Legal protection	Various
UC3M	Virtual machine LMS	3 months	284 users 8,669 items 49,000 actions	Legal protection	Computer science
CGIAR	LMS	6 years	841 users 14,693 items 326,339 actions	Legal protection	Agroforestry

PSLC DataShop	Algebra 2008–2009	ITS	3,310 users 3,918,055 actions 206,597 items	1 year	Math/algebra	Legal protection
	Bridge to algebra	ITS	6,044 users 20,012,499 actions 187 items	1 year	Math/algebra	Legal protection
	Geometry area	ITS	59 learners 139 items 6,778 actions	1 year	Math/geometry	Open access
	Electric fields—pitt	ITS	25 learners 139 items 5,347 actions	1 month	Math	Open access
	Chinese vocabulary fall 2006	ITS	101 learners 9,884 items 107,910 actions	4 years	Language learning	Open access
	Handwriting 2/examples spring 2007	ITS	54 users 11,162 items 20,016 actions	2 months	Math	Open access
Mulce	Virtual math team (VMT)	Chat	13 users 2,488 actions/items	10 days	Math	Open access
	mce-simu	Forum Email Chat	44 users 12,428 actions/items	10 weeks	Language learning	Open access
	mce-copeas	Video conferencing	14 users 37 videos	10 weeks	Language learning	Open access

increased and initial comparison study's are emerging that use the same dataset for different personalisation techniques [44–47]. The overall aim of the dataTEL initiative is to make different personalisation approaches more comparable to gain a body of knowledge about the effects of personalisation on learning. Still, there are several issues as described in [50] that need to be resolved before the uptake and usage of such datasets can become standard practice as in other domains [48].

The emergence of several Linked Open Data initiatives is promising to overcome these issues by providing: (1) A vast and increasing amount of data, (2) An established set of exchange principles and standards, and (3) Standardised publication and licensing approaches for TEL datasets.

Challenges for Using LD as References Datasets for TEL Research

While there is already a large amount of educational data available on the Web via proprietary and/or competing schemas and interface mechanisms, the main roadmap for improving impact of TEL recommender systems includes (a) start adopting LD principles and vocabularies while (b) leveraging on existing educational data available on the Web by non-LD compliant means. Following such an approach, major research challenges need to be taken into consideration towards Web-scale interoperability [4]:

(C1) *Integrating distributed data from heterogeneous educational repositories*: educational data and content is usually exposed by heterogeneous services/ APIs such as OAI-PMH or SQI. Therefore, interoperability is limited and Web-scale sharing of resources is not widely supported yet.

(C2) *Metadata mediation and transformation*: educational resources and the services exposing those resources are usually described by using distinct, often XML-based schemas and by making use of largely unstructured text and heterogeneous taxonomies. Therefore, schema and data transformation (into RDF) and mapping are important requirements in order to leverage on already existing TEL data.

(C3) *Enrichment and interlinking of unstructured metadata*: existing educational resource metadata is usually provided based on informal and poorly structured data. That is, free text is still widely used for describing educational resources while use of controlled vocabularies is limited and fragmented. Therefore, to allow machine-processing and Web-scale interoperability, educational metadata needs to be enriched, that is transformed into structured and formal descriptions by linking it to widely established LD vocabularies and datasets on the Web.

(C4) *Integration of personal and social data*: While the above mentioned challenges focus on educational resource data and metadata, the user perspective has to be considered by integrating personal as well as social data into the data environment. In particular, the LD cloud is populated mainly with content driven information and less data available via the social web. Hence, knowledge obtained via the LD approach has to be complemented with data obtained from the social Web. This results in additional challenges with regards to integration of such diverse data sources in order to make them available as resources for recommender systems and other social web applications.

Our work builds on the hypotheses that Linked Data offers high potential to improve take-up and impact of TEL recommender systems and introduces key past and on-going projects which serve as building blocks towards *Linked Education,*[30] i.e., educational data sharing enabled by adoption of Linked Data principles.

In particular, we focus on three projects which address the aforementioned challenges by providing innovative approaches towards (a) integration of heterogeneous TEL data (as part of the *mEducator*[31] project), (b) exploitation of large scale educational open data addressed by the *LinkedUp*[32] project, and (c) exploitation of social data as linked data (as part of the Open Discovery Space[33] project). In the next section we focus on approaches to address challenges C1, C2, and C3, whereas in section "Integration of social data" we focus on challenge C4 and point (c), exploitation of social data.

Towards Integration and Exploitation of Heterogeneous Educational Resource Data

With respect to the key issue —integration of heterogeneous TEL data—we first identify a set of principles (see [3, 7]) to address the above mentioned challenges:

(P1) *Linked Data-principles*: are applied to model and expose metadata of both educational resources and educational services and APIs. In this way, resources are interlinked but also services' description and resources are exposed in a standardized and accessible way.

(P2) *Services integration*: Existing heterogeneous and distributed learning repositories, i.e., their Web interfaces (services) are integrated on the fly by reasoning and processing of LD-based service semantics (see P1).

(P3) *Schema matching*: metadata retrieved from heterogeneous Web repositories, is automatically lifted into RDF, aligned with competing metadata schemas and exposed as LD accessible via de-referenceable URIs.

(P4) *Data interlinking, clustering and enrichment*: Automated enrichment and clustering mechanisms are exploited in order to interlink data produced by (P3) with existing datasets as part of the LD cloud.

---

[30] http://linkededucation.org: an open platform to share results focused on educational LD. Long-term goal is to establish links and unified APIs and endpoints to educational datasets.

[31] http://www.meducator.net.

[32] LinkedUp: Linking Web Data for Education Project—Open Challenge in Web-scale Data Integration (http://www.linkedup-project.eu).

[33] http://www.opendiscoveryspace.eu/.

In the following we provide examples of how the above principles can be applied, starting from the conversion of data into RDF and touching on various approaches to harmonize educational metadata and on the available tools and techniques to achieve metadata enrichment and dataset interlinking.

Integration of Educational Resources Data

The problems connected to the heterogeneity of metadata can be addressed by converting the data into a format that allows for implementing the Linked Data principles [2]. Most often this means that the data which is provided as part of RDBMS or in XML format—or, on occasion, in other formats—are converted into RDF. The data model of RDF is a natural choice as it allows for unique identification, interlinking to related data, as well as enrichment and contextualization. Therefore, general-purpose tools such as D2R,[34] Virtuoso[35] and Triplify[36] are often used to convert proprietary datasets into RDF.

It is common to use DBpedia or other big datasets as "linking hubs" [1]. One of the advantages of such an approach is that such datasets are commonly used by other datasets, which automatically leads to a plurality of indirect links. In the case of more specialized applications it is beneficial if domain specific datasets or ontologies can be found and linked to. This has been successfully demonstrated by specialized projects such as Linked Life Data[37] in the biomedical domain, Organic. Edunet[38] in organic agriculture and agroecology [27], and mEducator[39] in medical education [3, 23].

The approaches applied for creating links between datasets can be fully automatic, semi-automatic and fully manual. A lot of tasks required for interlinking and enhancing (enriching) metadata can be automated by analyzing textual content using Information Extraction (IE) and Natural Language Processing (NLP) techniques. Most commonly this includes the detection of sentences, named entities, and relationships, as well as disambiguation of named entities. However, quality control implies that the process has to be supervised at some point. The links can be created manually; alternatively the automatically detected links can be approved manually. NLP has its roots in machine learning which implies the use of learning algorithms which are trained on large textual corpora which eventually are

---

[34] http://www4.wiwiss.fu-berlin.de/bizcr/d2r-server/.

[35] http://virtuoso.openlinksw.com/.

[36] http://triplify.org/.

[37] http://www.linkedlifedata.com.

[38] http://www.organic-edunet.eu.

[39] http://www.meducator.net.

domain-specific. Public services such as DBpedia Spotlight[40] and OpenCalais[41] offer NLP services relevant for linking data and also provide their output in RDF. In addition to these services which are ready to use, frameworks such as Apache Stanbol[42] can be easily integrated and provide solutions for the most common tasks involved in the creation of Linked Data, such as textual analysis and metadata extraction. A RESTful API allows for easy integration which should help projects dealing with metadata management using semantic technologies to hit the ground running.

Traditional ways of managing metadata often take a document-centric approach and use XML as it is an established standard for expressing information. Transformation of metadata into other formats requires a thorough mapping to be crafted, which often involves an analysis of the exact semantics of the involved standards. If such heterogeneous formats are to be transformed into Linked Data, good knowledge of existing standards is required, as it is good practice to reuse established terms from other RDF-based standards [14] whenever possible. There are situations where the conceptual model of the origin data cannot be cleanly mapped to the RDF model and information may be lost. To avoid such situations, RDF should be considered as a basis for metadata interoperability [14]—a common carrier—when adapting existing or creating new metadata standards.

The joint working group from IEEE LTSC and Dublin Core made an attempt to address heterogeneity of educational metadata by developing a mapping of IEEE LOM into the Dublin Core Abstract Model. This work resulted in a draft report in 2008, but the uptake has not been overwhelming. To date, the only known project to implement this draft[43] is the Organic.Edunet project, whose achieved goal was to build a federation of learning repositories with material on organic agriculture and agroecology. The EntryStore backend[44] (the basic concepts behind it are described in [26] and [27]) is used across all Organic.Edunet repositories and stores all information in RDF. This requires that all metadata that are harvested for enriching in the Organic.Edunet repositories are converted from LOM/XML (which is the primary format in most of the source repositories) to an RDF representation. This makes it also possible to freely combine different standards and vocabularies, resulting in enriching LOM metadata with more specific terms from vocabularies such as EUN's LRE and blending in some FOAF and relational predicates from OWL and DC to create interlinkage between resources.

A similar yet even more exhaustive approach was followed by the mEducator project addressing two central challenges for educational data integration: integration at the repository-level facilitated by repository-specific APIs and integration at

---

[40] http://dbpedia.org/spotlight.

[41] http://www.opencalais.com.

[42] http://incubator.apache.org/stanbol/.

[43] The reference implementation is part of EntryStore which is Free Software.

[44] http://code.google.com/p/entrystore/.

the (meta)data-level [3]. The former aims at integrating educational services and APIs in order to facilitate repository-level integration. To this end, it is concerned with resolving heterogeneities between individual API standards (e.g., SOAP-based services vs. REST-ful approaches) and distinct response message formats and structures (such as JSON, XML or RDF-based ones) where details are described in [28]. In order to enable integration of such heterogeneous APIs, Linked Data principles were used to annotate individual APIs in terms of their interfaces, capabilities and non-functional properties. This enables the automatic discovery and execution of APIs for a given educational purpose (for instance, to retrieve educational metadata for a given subject and language) while it resolves heterogeneities between individual API responses. All metadata of educational content retrieved from these services are transformed from their native (standardized or proprietary) formats into RDF. The second step deals with the actual integration of the retrieved heterogeneous educational (meta)data by exposing all retrieved educational (RDF) metadata as well-interlinked Linked Data. As starting point, all generated RDF is stored in a dedicated, public RDF store[45] which supports two main purposes: to expose existing educational (non-RDF) data in a LD-compliant way and allow content/data providers to publish new educational resource metadata. Automated interlinking of dataset as well as clustering and classification is employed to enrich and interlink the educational data. Transformation of heterogeneous metadata into RDF is indeed a substantial step towards integration, however, mere transformation does not improve metadata quality. Thus, it is even more challenging to enrich descriptions by automated data enrichment techniques to establish links with established vocabularies available on the LD cloud. Enrichment takes advantage of available APIs such as the ones provided by DBpedia Spotlight or Bioportal,[46] which allow access to a vast number of established taxonomies and vocabularies. This way, unstructured free text is enriched with unique URIs of structured LD entities to allow further reasoning on related concepts and to enable the formulation of queries by using well-defined concepts and terms. In addition, automated clustering and classification mechanisms are exploited in order to enable data and resource classification across previously disconnected repositories.

Another attempt to harmonize educational metadata is currently carried out by the Learning Resource Metadata Initiative[47] (LRMI) whose goal is to build a common metadata vocabulary for the description of educational resources. LRMI is led by both the Association of Educational Publishers and the Creative Commons.[48] The applied approach is based on schema.org and has the declared goal of providing mappings to the most common standards for describing education resources, such as LOM and DC.

---

[45] http://ckan.net/packages/meducator.

[46] http://www.bioontology.org/wiki/index.php/BioPortal_REST_services.

[47] http://wiki.creativecommons.org/LRMI.

[48] http://creativecommons.org/.

Large Scale Exploitation of Educational Open Data

An issue complementary to the integration of heterogenous educational data is the large scale exploitation of open educational data, is addressed by the *LinkedUp* project, setting up to push forward the exploitation of the vast amounts of public, open data available on the Web, in particular by educational institutions and organizations. This will be achieved by identifying and supporting highly innovative large-scale Web information management applications through an open competition (the *LinkedUp Challenge*) and a dedicated evaluation framework. The vision of the LinkedUp Challenge is to realise personalised university degree-level education of global impact based on open Web data and information. Drawing on the diversity of Web information relevant to education, ranging from OER metadata to the vast body of knowledge offered by the LD approach, this aim requires overcoming substantial issues related to Web-scale data and information management involving Big Data, such as performance and scalability, interoperability, multilinguality and heterogeneity problems, to offer personalised and accessible education services. Therefore, the LinkedUp Challenge provides a focused scenario to derive challenging requirements, evaluation criteria, benchmarks and thresholds which are reflected in the LinkedUp evaluation framework. Information management solutions have to apply data and learning analytics methods to provide highly personalised and context-aware views on heterogeneous Web data. Building on the strong alliance of institutions with expertise in areas such as open Web data management, data integration and Web-based education, key outcomes of LinkedUp include a general-purpose evaluation framework for Web-data driven applications, a set of quality-assured educational datasets, innovative applications of large-scale Web information management, community-building and clustering crossing public and private sectors and substantial technology transfer of highly innovative Web information management technologies.

Integration of Social Data

Social data can be defined in many ways when seen from different disciplines or perspectives. From the LD perspective we see social data as an end user added information that is publicly available on the Web and provides an indication of the quality of an artefact on the Web. We further distinguish between '*social data*' and '*para-data*'. The main difference between '*social data*' and '*paradata*' whether they have been contributed by the user intentionally or were tracked by the system in the background. The CIP ICT-PSP eContentPlus project *Open Discovery Space* (ODS) has a work package dedicated to develop a social metadata cloud that can contribute social activity data like ratings, tags, bookmarks and comments to the LD cloud. ODS represents large amount of data in the field of education with a critical mass of approximately 1,550,000 eLearning resources from 75 content repositories, as well as 15 educational portals of regional, national or thematic coverage connected to it that will be exposed as LD. This vast amount of data and the emerging social activities around it will be captured and exposed in an anonymised way to the LD cloud. A first design of this social data cloud has been already specified in one deliverable [49]. In this section we discuss suitable data formats that could be applied to store the social activities of the users and expose it as LD.

According to the ODS project social data and paradata are defined as follows [49]:

1. *Social Metadata* which refers to the direct interaction users have with an artefact or with other actors around the artefact. Interactions with artefacts can include the adding of keyword, ratings, tags, bookmarks, or comments.
2. *Paradata*, is another type of social data as it requires further processing of the data before it can be meaningful. Paradata consists of *automatic traces* of the interaction the user has with various artefacts together with appropriate contextual information.

The following four metadata schemas [(1) CAM, (2) Organic.Edunet, (3) Learning Registry Paradata, (4) NSDL Paradata] have been investigated by the ODS project and are suitable to store social data in a database. So far there is no LD RDF schema available for these data formats but it is the intention of the ODS project to first select the most appropriate data format, and second design a suitable RDF schema to expose the social data as LD. In the following subsections we shortly introduce the different data formats and conclude by presenting an initial comparison of the candidate data formats. This analysis is mainly based on the findings of [49] (*Review of Social Data Requirements*). A more in depth analysis of the different formats and how they can be interconnected can be found in [13, 52, 53].

Contextualized Attention Metadata (CAM)

Contextualized Attention Metadata[49] (CAM) [16–18] is a format to describe *events* conducted by a human user, e.g., accessing a document or sending an e-mail. As little information as possible is stored in the CAM instance itself, e.g., the event type and the time stamp. All other information, e.g., metadata describing users or documents involved in the event, are linked. This way, every entity/session can be described in a different and suitable format and no information is duplicated.

The main element of each CAM instance is the *event* entry which comprises its *id*, the *event type*, the *timestamp*, and a *sharing level reference*. Examples for *event types* are "send," "update" or "select." CAM is used in a couple of European projects such as ROLE[50] and OpenScout[51] that already started to define a collection of

---

[49] https://sites.google.com/site/camschema/.
[50] http://www.role-project.eu/.
[51] http://www.openscout.net/.

various *event types*. Depending on the *event*, various *entities* with different *roles* can be involved. For example: When bookmarking a file at a social bookmarking service, there's a person with the role *sender*, and at least one person or a community with the role *receiver* and a *document* with the role *website*. Each event can be conducted in a *N:M relation*.

Organic.Edunet Format

The Organic.Edunet portal[52] [9] is a learning portal that provides access to more than 10,000 digital learning resources on organic agriculture and agro-ecology hosted in a federation of external repositories. Regarding social data, Organic. Edunet relies on a representation model detailed in [10] which to some degree is based on CAM, since it stores data about which tags, reviews, ratings and recommendations were assigned to learning resources by which user. This conceptual model, not specific of any portal, context or particular application, was intended as a structured, reusable and interoperable way of representing the different types of user feedback and was used as a basis for the social module in the Organic. Edunet portal. The model by Manouselis and Vuorikari [10] is based on the concept of an *annotation schema*, a formal declaration of the type(s) of feedback (i.e., rating, review, tags, etc.) including the exact structure and value spaces of the collected feedback. For instance, ratings may be collected upon one or more attributes (criteria), and may use different rating scales, particularly in different application areas.

The Learning Registry Format

The Learning Registry model [8] collects social data such as tags, comments, ratings, clicked and viewed data, shared data, data aligned to a standard, and any other data about the usage of learning resources and shares this data in a common pool for aggregation, amplification and analysis.

By design, a loose format for the submission of metadata is defined without specifying what metadata schema should be used. The Learning Registry uses a Resource Data Description (RDD) document for submitting social metadata as a thin wrapper around the submitted metadata. The services built on top of the Learning Registry can provide extraction or crosswalk services across RDDs that use disparate standards, or can assemble metadata fields from different schemas into custom views.

---

[52] http://portal.organic-edunet.eu.

National Science Digital Library Format

National Science Digital Library (NSDL) is an online portal for education and research on learning in Science, Technology, Engineering, and Mathematics. NSDL's mission is to provide quality digital resources to the science, technology, engineering, and mathematics (STEM) education community, both formal and informal, institutional and individual. The STEM Exchange is a collaboration with a range of education partners that has been initiated for the implementation of an NSDL web service to capture and share social media-generated information and other networked associations about educational resources.

Collections and records stored in the NSDL repository are made available through the Search API and the NSDL OAI data provider. In addition, the Strand Map Service APIs provide access to Benchmarks, Maps and visualizations. Developers can use the Search API, SMS APIs and OAI data provider to build customized search and browse interfaces and other applications.

In creating the concept of the STEM Exchange, two different kinds of Item-Level Metadata evolved, i.e., the NSDL Annotation and NSDL Paradata. The main purpose of NSDL Annotation is to capture user comments, reviews, and teaching tips. It also allows annotations to include additional information, e.g., the metadata record contributor, annotator, or the subject. NSDL Paradata was defined to capture usage data about a resource, such as downloaded or rated [15].

Definition of the Standards and a Comparison

In order to evaluate the four described candidate schemes and for selecting the best suited format for social metadata and paradata recording we applied a social media use case called 'Irma.' A detailed description of the use case can be found in [49]. Table 2 illustrates a feature comparison of the four mentioned data formats: CAM, Organic.Edunet, Learning Registry, and NSDL Paradata. Each of the formats are either rated with a (+) to indicate it supports a requirement derived from Irma, or with a (−) meaning it does not support this requirement. The first nine requirements relate to social metadata, the second nine requirements show support of paradata.

The comparison expressed in Table 2 emphasises that any of the described formats can store common social activities like rating, tagging and commenting in the social web.

Differences in applicability of the various schemata appear between the formats when we consider paradata aspects. The most promising data format therefore is CAM, as it covers all 18 requirements from the Irma use case, while NSDL supports only 9 of them. Learning Registry and Organic.Edunet have also 14 and 13 points in Table 2, respectively. All the mentioned formats use application specific models and services for implementing social services for their users.

Table 2 Overview comparison of suitable data formats to store social data [49]

No.	Social metadata requirements from Irma	CAM	Organic Edunet format	Learning registry paradata	NSDL paradata
1	Rate	+	+	+	+
2	Tag	+	+	+	+
3	Bookmark	+	+	+	+
4	Share (FB, twitter, e-mail)	+	−	+	+
5	Share count	+	+	−	+
6	Comment	+	+	+	+
7	Join groups	+	−	+	−
8	Posts (discussion, blog, etc.)	+	−	+ (Google discussion)	−
9	Following/followers	+	−	+	−
	Social data sum (+)	9	5	8	6
10	Login/logout	+	+	+ (Google)	−
11	Access learning object metadata	+	+	+	+
12	Navigation history of users	+	+	+	−
13	Search history of users	+	−	−	−
14	History of LO (new upload or edit)	+	+	−	−
15	IP location of user	+	+	+	−
16	Language of LO (and of browser of the user)	+	+	+	+
17	Language of user browser	+	+	+	+
18	Group metadata to extend user profile (new interests)	+	+	−	−
	Total sum (+)	18	13	14	9

From the analysis, it appears that Organic. Edunet might be a suitable candidate for collecting social metadata in a database and become exposed as Linked Data. This would also be aligned with privacy aspects, as Organic.Edunet mainly focuses on social metadata that is publicly available on the web whereas CAM, for instance, first needs to be filtered to not expose all private data of a user. CAM, on the other hand, clearly turns out to be the most suitable data format for tracking and storing paradata. Both formats have a strong European community behind them and some ready-to-use services that are already applied in different EU projects.

Bridging the Gap Between Linked Data and the Social Web

In this section we focus on some current efforts that are relevant to the integration of linked data and the social web, with the goal of providing more sophisticated recommender systems. In the previous section some schemas meant to capture social data and paradata have been discussed. Here we turn to ontologies and vocabularies written in RDF/OWL that can be instrumental to exposing social data and paradata to the Linked Data Cloud and survey some first applications that demonstrate their potential.

SIOC and Its Applications

A fundamental component towards the goal of exposing social data and paradata as LD is provided by the SIOC (Semantically-Interlinked Online Communities) initiative.[53] SIOC [29] is an ontology to describe user-generated content on forums, weblogs, and web2.0 sites, and link online communities. The goal of SIOC is to harness, across online communities, discussions on interrelated topics relevant to a post, either from similar members profiles of from common-topic discussion forums. By narrowing the scope of a search to a set of interlinked community sites a first advantage is that the problem of low precision of a query issued in the web can be addressed. Also, concepts such as Site, Forum, Post, Event, Group and UserAccount are described in the SIOC ontology with a focus on the relationships, sub-classes and properties of these concepts relevant to the arena of online discussion methods, in such a way to enable use cases not previously possible with other ontologies describing similar concepts. The SIOC community provides mappings and interfaces to commonly-used ontologies such as Dublin Core, FOAF and RSS 1.0. and several tools to import and export data from SIOC.

In particular, SIOC is often used in conjunction with FOAF[54] (Friend of a Friend) vocabulary for describing users and their connections to interests and other users profiles. In such a way, the contribution of Social Web sites to the linked data cloud is explicated from two synergistic points of view: via the direct links from person to person and by the links arising from the notion of "object centred sociality" [30], i.e., people in a community are indirectly connected because they share objects of a social focus (e.g., a topic in a post or a link to the song of a band).

Currently, SIOC is generating much interest and is widely adopted, resulting in an active support for the development of tools, API and applications. For example, in [31] user-generated contents are lifted to SIOC by a method that extracts users comments directly from HTML pages, without requiring any a priori knowledge about the webpage. This approach circumvents the problem of SIOC data scarcity, which is a consequence of the fact that SIOC exporter plugins often are not enabled be the site administrators. One remarkable aspect of SIOC is that its high-level description of communities can be easily integrated with more specific ontologies to bridge the Social Semantic Web and more application domains. An example is the SWAN/SIOC project[55] that defines a coherent ontology capable of representing both

---

[53] http://sioc-project.org/.

[54] http://www.foaf-project.org/.

[55] http://www.w3.org/TR/hcls-swansioc/.

high-level descriptions of communities (thanks to SIOC) and the argumentative discussions (using the SWAN ontology) taking place in that communities [32]. The goal of this alignment is to make the discourse structure and component relationships accessible to computation, so that information can be better navigated, compared and understood, across and within domains.

Another example of leveraging on SIOC extensibility is provided in [33], where MediaWiki integration is accomplished by resorting to SKOS ontology to model topic and categories and to other vocabularies that model user tagging and are helpful in alleviating issues such as ambiguity between tags. From a methodological point of view, the two examples above are representative of the type of efforts that can be pursued to create datasets that integrate social, user-centric, and linked data to generate novel types of recommendations that can certainly find a space in the TEL scenario.

A first example of the joint usage of SIOC and linked data in recommender systems is in the music domain [34], where social data encompasses the publishing and sharing of music-related data on the Web, whatever their format is (blog posts, wiki pages, community databases, mp3s or playlists). This work demonstrates how FOAF, SIOC and linked data can be used to provide a completely open and distributed social graph, where SPARQL queries can implement a simple collaborative filtering algorithm, and the wide range of interlinked data in multiple domains allow the user to get more data rich, justified recommendations. This latter aspect (justified recommendations) seems to play an important role in the acceptance and trust of end-users towards recommender systems, e.g., [35].

The CAM-RDF Binding and the Atom Activity Stream RDF Mapping

An RDF binding of the Contextualised Attention Metadata (CAM) model discussed in the previous section has been recently proposed [36]. Among the advantages pointed out in [36] for the CAM-RDF binding with respect to the CAM-XML one, are the following ones: first, it facilitates the integration of CAM into RDF-based learning systems; second, the underlying graph-based representation may support more convenient ways of analyzing the observations, i.e., by resorting to graph algorithms. The binding has been tested for equivalence to the CAM-XML binding with respect to tasks such as creating statistics over the MACE dataset (consisting of learning resources in the architectural domain), and by developing, over the same learning data set and collected CAM data, a "find similar users" application. Another application of this binding in the learning domain has been done in the context of an exercise system that provides personalized help to learners in the form of hints [37]. Personalization is achieved in terms of the content of hints and of the appropriate hint-giving approach. The CAM-RDF binding is available at: http://www.fit.fraunhofer.de/~wolpers/ontologies/cam/cam.owl.

A representation of activity alternative to RDF-CAM, is provided by the Atom Activity Streams RDF mapping.[56] Atom Activity Streams[57] extends the Atom specification, which is a widely used syndication format to transmit various types of web content such as weblog posts, news headlines, as well as user activities within social sites. This extension provides the ability to express within existing Atom entries and feeds much of the activity-specific metadata in a machine-parseable format. Within the NoTube project[58] an RDF mapping of the Atom Activity Streams (AAIR) has been developed, in conjuction with the W3C Semantic Web Interest group. The specification is available at http://xmlns.notu.be/aair/. A typical expression in AAIR would have the form (Actor, Verb, Object, Context), where typical verbs include "Play" (open resource), "MarkAsFavorite," "Save" (download), "Rate," "Share" and so on.

AAIR was chosen, mostly due to its intuitiveness and fair coverage of both social data and paradata, as the starting reference point of a line of action pursued within the mEducator project, concerned with modeling data about activities on social learning resources and make them portable across learning platforms and provide resources useful for recommendations. To achieve this goal some extensions to AAIR were done to track the user activities. In particular, the proposed extensions were devised to deal with the need to model Search activities within the mEducator platforms, keeping track of the queries executed by the user, the results of the queries, and of the activites executed by the users on the results of a given query. This was accomplished by extending the lists of verbs by *ActivityVerb:Search*, by creating a recursive reference to Activity and by introducing the notion of session. These extensions are sketched in Fig. 1. In particular, *hasQueryString:* is the property that represents the user's keyword sequence to describe the query search; *isRelatedTo:* is a property to bind an activity to another one, so that it is possible to model an action performed on an object returned by a query, and *activitySession:* is a property that binds an activity to a specific user session.

A proof of concept recommender systems architecture based on this extension has been developed and deployed in one of the mEductor platforms,[59] where an Activity Monitor collects AAIR data and sends the activity to an external web service providing the recommendations.

In Fig. 2 is an example of how data generated by the Activity Monitor can be expressed as Linked Data. The example refers to a user "John Smith" who has an account in a mEducator platform, where he performs a search about "Magnetic Resonance Imaging" and saves one of the results of this search. In a subsequent session he comments on the saved resource. The example uses the AAIR extension, SIOC and FOAF vocabularies and the mEducator vocabulary to describe a learning resource.

---

[56] http://xmlns.notu.be/aair/.

[57] http://activitystrea.ms/specs/atom/1.0/.

[58] http://notube.tv/.

[59] http://www.meducator2.net/.

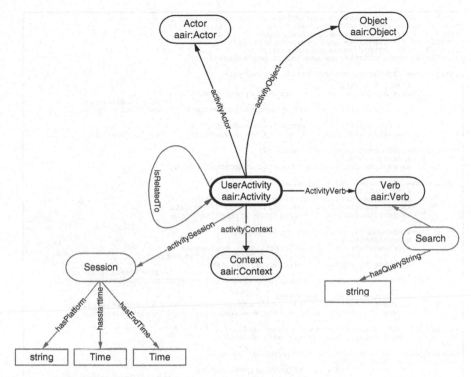

Fig. 1 AAIR extension adopted in mEducator to support recommendations

Summary

The above approaches and applications point to a scenario where the first efforts and concrete demonstrations of the possibilites of bridging the Linked Data and the Social Web world are beginning to emerge. Beyond the sketching of the potentialities, there is also some early evidence of the tangible benefits. In particular, the early evaluations that have been perfomed, although not necessarily in the TEL domain, show some advantages of the novel resulting data infrastructure. Evaluation research has shown that by using linked data to build open, collaborative recommender systems, the the "cold start" problem (related to to initial lack of data about new users and new items) is ameliorated, and it is possible to improve precision and recall with respect to simple collaborative filtering (CF) approaches [38]. In particular, the evaluation in [38] reports an improvement from an average precision of 2 % and average recall of 7 % of a simple collaborative filtering recommendation applied to a music streaming database to an average precision of 14 % and average recall of 33 % achieved by augmenting the initial data set with linked data from another music social platform (DbTune MySpace) and DBpedia. The use of social trust to improve the data sparsity problem of recommender systems has been investigated in

```
@prefix rdf: <http://www.w3.org/1999/02/22-rdf-syntax-ns#> .
@prefix sioc: <http://rdfs.org/sioc/ns#> .
@prefix foaf: <http://xmlns.com/foaf/0.1/> .
@prefix mdc: <http://www.purl.org/meducator/ns/> .
@prefix aair: <http://xmlns.notu.be/aair/> .
@prefix aairext: <http://www.mEducator2.net/aairext/> .

<http://www.mEducator2.net/Activities/Activity15>
        a aair:Activity ;
        aair:ActivityActor   [a aair:Actor; owl:sameAs
                                               [a sioc:UserAccount;
                       owl:sameAs <http://www.mEducator2.net/Account/JohnSmith>]
                                      ] ;
        aairext:ActivityVerb   <http://www.mEducator2.net/Verb/Search_50> ;
        aairext:ActivitySession <http://www.mEducator2.net/Session/Session1> .

<http://www.mEducator2.net/Verb/Search_50>
        a aairext:Search ;
        aairext:hasQueryString "Magnetic resonance imaging" .

<http://www.mEducator2.net/Session/Session1>
        a aairext:Session ;
        aairext:hasPlatform  <http://www.mEducator2.net> ;
        aairext:hasStartTime  "21/08/2010 12:27"^^xsd:date ;
        aairext:hasEndTime    "21/08/2010 12:32"^^xsd:date .

<http://www.mEducator2.net/Activities/Activity16>
        a aair:Activity ;
        aair:isRelatedTo    [a aair:Activity; owl:sameAs
                       <http://www.mEducator2.net/Activities/Activity15>] ;
        aair:ActivityActor  [a aair:Actor; owl:sameAs
                                               [a sioc:UserAccount;
                       owl:sameAs <http://www.mEducator2.net/Account/JohnSmith>]
                                      ] ;
        aair:ActivityVerb    aair:Save ;
        aair:ActivityObject  <http://www.mEducator2.net/Resources/resource123> ;
        aairext:ActivitySession <http://www.mEducator2.net/Session/Session1> .

<http://www.mEducator2.net/Resources/resource123>
        a mdc:Resource owl:sameAs  aair:Object .

<http://www.mEducator2.net/Activities/Activity17>
        a aair:Activity ;
        aair:ActivityActor  [a aair:Actor; owl:sameAs
                                               [a sioc:UserAccount;
                       owl:sameAs <http://www.mEducator2.net/Account/JohnSmith>]
                                      ] ;
        aair:ActivityVerb    aair:Post ;
        aair:ActivityObject  <http://www.mEducator2.net/Post/Comment1>  ;
        aairext:ActivitySession <http://www.mEducator2.net/Session/Session2> .

<http://www.mEducator2.net/Post/Comment1>
        a aair:Comment owl:sameAs sioc:Comment ;
        aair:Commenter <http://www.mEducator2.net/Account/JohnSmith> ;
        aair:Content "Provides one of the best explanation of MRI functioning" ;
        sioc:reply_of <http://www.mEducator2.net/Resources/resource123> .

<http://www.mEducator2.net/Session/Session2>
        a aairext:Session ;
        aairext:hasPlatform  <http://www.mEducator2.net> ;
        aairext:hasStartTime  "21/08/2010 18:15"^^xsd:date ;
        aairext:hasEndTime   "21/08/2010 18:42"^^xsd:date .

<http://www.mEducator2.net/Account/JohnSmith>
        a sioc:UserAccount ;
        sioc:email_sha1 "f4d5b3eaaff75fa981e626a3492d9030cb15191d" .

<http://www.mEducator2.net/Person/JohnSmith>
        a foaf:Person ;
        foaf:name "John Smith" ;
        foaf:knows <http://www.mEducator2.net/Person/Ernest> .
```

Fig. 2 Example of the Activity Monitor data, including social data and paradata generated during two sessions, and expressed as Linked Data (Turtle format)

[35], on the Movielens dataset. The results are reported in terms of F-score (harmonic mean of precision and recall), at various sparsity percentages, and show an improvement of of the F-score in the range 7–18 % with respect to the baseline obtained with a standard collaborative filtering approach. Interestingly, the peak if the advantage is achieved when it is most needed, i.e., at high data sparsity

percentages (98.57 %). Still, it is also clear that targeted, task-dependent strategies are needed to leverage on this wealth of data since, as it is demonstrated in the case of harnessing LOD evidence for profiling expertise and, accordingly, recommend experts [39]. This work, in particular, points out how, with respect to the expertise recommendation task, the LOD offers data that are decoupled from any specific hypothesis about what constitutes expertise, and, as such, are flexible and can serve multiple approaches in defining expertise, besides offering the clear advantage of harnessing richer, cross-platform evidence. On the other hand, it must be ensured that the type of data that are needed is available in the LOD with the necessary level of detail and that relevant datasets are accessible through effective interlinking, which are two current shortcomings that can be addressed by more informed data publishing strategies and better interlinking services. Whereas TEL related, task specific recommendation algorithms and relevant strategies to harness the LOD will be the object of future research, in the meantime some prior challenges related to fulfilling the vision of integrated social and linked data infrastructure are to be addressed, as pointed out in the next section.

Conclusions: Open Challenges and Scenarios

In the previous sections, we provided an overview of different efforts aiming at utilising Linked Data as well as social and user-centric data for recommender systems in TEL. While the accessibility of large-scale amounts of data is a foundation for TEL recommender systems, these efforts contribute to improvements in scope, quantity and quality of recommendations in TEL environments. This includes both TEL recommender systems in research, where data is required for evaluation and benchmarking, as well as in practice, where data is a core requirement for offering suitable recommendations to users.

There is still a range of shortcomings that need to be addressed. Social data is usually stored locally in the content management system of a single portal. Harvesting and aggregating such data from various learning object repositories will allow the generation of a social data cloud and will enable the provision of new services across multiple portals. For instance, more accurate recommendations can be generated by taking into account social data from more than one learning object repository or social environment, even non-TEL platforms. Collecting heterogeneous social data from different sources is not a trivial task and requires the adoption of efficient technologies and protocols. The main aspects that should be taken into account are therefore:

Data Quality and Trust

One fundamental issue in distributed data environment is related to diversity of quality, provenance and trustworthiness of data. While, for instance, the LD cloud has received a lot of attention due to its large quantities of data covering a wide variety of topics, take-up by data consumers is slow and usually focused on a small set of well-established datasets [4]. This can be attributed to the varied quality of the datasets and hence, the lack of trust on the data consumer side. Therefore, assessment of data, better and more structured approaches towards labeling and cataloging data and the exhaustive provisioning of provenance information are crucial for enabling a widespread take-up of distributed data.

Licensing and Privacy Issues

Licensing as well as privacy issues are related challenges which apply to educational resources metadata (licensing) and social data (privacy). Reuse of distributed datasets and exploitation by applications and data mashups have to consider and address the diversity of license models used by distributed datasets and the potential impact on any derived datasets. In addition, sharing of social and learner-centric data requires the consideration of privacy problems and how these can be addressed, in particular within distributed data environments such as the Web. Within the Open Discovery Space project a specific paragraph was written for the Terms-Of-Use of the platform to cover this aspect. This paragraph informs the users about the usage of their personal data within the ODS portal. If they sign-up for ODS platform they also agree to support certain personalization services with their personal data. The following services will be activate for all registered users to provide personalized access to the information of the platform:

- Personalized recommendations for learning material
- Bookmark items
- Utilize personal history (i.e., on searches undertaken, objects viewed, etc.)
- Upload and share learning material (publish)
- Utilize upload library
- View user stats
- Rate and comment items, follow discussions, comments and groups, etc.

If users do not agree with theses Term-Of-Use they are free to use the ODS platform without having a registered user account and by anonymised browsing of the educational resources. We believe that such legal solutions will be more frequently used in the close future.

Common Schemas and Vocabularies for Social
and Attention Data

Platforms usually deploy proprietary schemas and vocabularies for representing learner activities and social information. Common schemas are important to manage and process social and attention data. Potential options for such a schema are CAM for paradata in combination with Organic.Edunet for social metadata. Although these seem to be promising and most feasible, it needs to be analysed how Organic.Edunet can be aligned to events stored in CAM. The Organic.Edunet partners are preparing a new release of their social data schema by the end of the year 2012 that will address this issue and provide required adjustments to link CAM to Organic.Edunet.

Interoperability Between Different Social and Resource Data Formats

Complementary to unified schemas and vocabularies, LD approaches to representation of social and attention data (Section "Bridging the gap between Linked Data and the Social Web") can further alleviate interoperability issues. LD principles in particular provide standard query and interfacing mechanisms together with dereferencable URIs, which allows data consumers to easily interact with remote data repositories containing resource or social or activity data.

Scalability of Web Data Processing

Dealing with distributed Web data sources, in particularly graph- and reasoning-based environments such as the Semantic Web, poses challenges with respect to scalability and performance [3]. Performance issues arise from distributed processing, often requiring large quantities of HTTP-based message exchanges, lack of parallelisation techniques and the still often comparably poor performance of graph-based data storage. Previous work has shown [51] that still, with a limited amount of data sources acceptable performance can be achieved, also in distributed data settings. Additionally, techniques such as map/reduce, local replication of datasets or indexing are required to further alleviate this issue in actual large-scale data scenarios.

Towards Federated Recommendation

Very large, cloud-based data infrastructures like the one that Learning Registry is setting up for the US, are expected to provide a new perspective into the way that intelligent systems (in general) and socially-generated data-based services (in particular) will be developed [11, 12, 19]. Such global learning data infrastructures can help in scaling up the existing data-driven services, by allowing them to consume, process and use a rich variety of usage data streams, and thus enable novel forms of real time intelligence and cross-platform recommendations that can only become possible on extremely large data volumes.

Future work, in particular in highly related projects such as LinkedUp and ODS will address these issues in order to enabling the widespread adoption of data—resource metadata as well as learner-centric and social data—by TEL environments.

Acknowledgments This work is partly funded by the European Union under FP7 Grant Agreement No 317620 (LinkedUp) and the CIP ICT PSP eContentPlus project Open Discovery Space.

References

1. Auer S, Bizer C, Kobilarov G, Lehmann J, Cyganiak C, Ives Z (2007) DBpedia: a nucleus for a Web of open data. Proceedings of the 6th international semantic conference (ISWC2007)
2. Bizer C, Heath T, Berners-Lee T (2009) Linked Data—The Story So Far. International Journal on Semantic Web and Information Systems 5(3):1–22. doi:10.4018/jswis.2009081901. ISSN 1552-6283
3. Dietze S, Yu HQ, Giordano D, Kaldoudi E, Dovrolis N, Taibi D (2012) Linked education: interlinking educational resources and the Web of data, Proceedings of the 27th ACM symposium on applied computing (SAC-2012), Special track on semantic Web and applications, Riva del Garda (Trento), Italy
4. Dietze S, Sanchez-Alonso S, Ebner H, Yu H, Giordano D, Marenzi I, Pereira Nunes B (2013) Interlinking educational resources and the Web of data – a survey of challenges and approaches, accepted for publication in Emerald program: electronic library and information systems. 47(1)
5. IEEE (2002) IEEE standard for learning object metadata. IEEE Std 1484.12.1-2002, pp i–32. Doi: 10.1109/IEEESTD.2002.94128
6. World Wide Web Consortium (2008) W3C Recommendation, SPARQL query language for RDF. www.w3.org/TR/rdf-sparql-query/
7. Yu HQ, Dietze S, Li N, Pedrinaci C, Taibi D, Dovrolls N, Stefanut T, Kaldoudi E, Domingue J (2011) A linked data-driven & service-oriented architecture for sharing educational resources. In: Linked learning 2011. Proceedings of the 1st international workshop on eLearning approaches for linked data age, 29 May 2011, Heraklion, Greece
8. Bienkowski M, Brecht J, Kio J (2012) The learning registry: building a foundation for learning resource analytics. Proceedings of the 2nd international conference on learning analytics and knowledge, Vancouver, BC, Canada, Accessed 29 April–02 May 2012
9. Kosmopoulos T, Kastrantas K, Manouselis N (2009) Social navigation module specification Web services API for Organic.Edunet, eContentplus Deliverable Document D5.3 Mar 2009
10. Manouselis N, Vuorikari R (2009) What if annotations were reusable: a preliminary discussion. In: Spaniol M (Ed) Proceedings of the 8th international conference on advances in Web-based learning – ICWL 2009, Lecture notes in computer science, vol 5686, Springer, Berlin/Heidelberg, pp 255–264
11. Manouselis N, Drachsler H, Verbert K, Duval E (2012) Recommender systems for learning, Springer briefs, ISBN 978-1-4614-4360-5, 2012. http://www.springer.com/computer/information+systems+and+applications/book/978-1-4614-4360-5
12. Manouselis N, Kosmopoulos T, Kastrantas K (2009) Developing a recommendation web service for a federation of learning repositories. In Proceedings of international conference on intelligent networking and collaborative systems (INCoS 2009), IEEE Computer Press, Barcelona, Spain
13. Niemann K, Scheffel M, Wolpers M (2009) A comparison of usage data formats for recommendations in TEL. In: Manouselis N, Drachsler H, Verbert K, Santos OC (eds) Proceedings of the 2nd workshop on recommender systems in technology enhanced learning 2012, 7th

European conference on technology enhanced learning (EC-TEL 2012), CEUR Workshop Proceedings, ISSN 1613-0073, vol 896, 95-100, 2012. http://ceur-ws.org/Vol-896/

14. Nilsson M (2010) From interoperability to harmonization in metadata standardization: designing an evolvable framework for metadata harmonization. PhD thesis, KTH Royal Institute of Technology, Sweden

15. NSDL Annotation (2012) https://wiki.ucar.edu/display/nsdldocs/comm_para+%28paradata+-+usage+data%29

16. Paradata Specification v1.0. https://docs.google.com/document/d/1IrOYXd3S0FUwNozaEG5t M7Ki4_AZPrBn-pbyVUz-Bh0/edit

17. Schmitz HC, Wolpers M, Kirschenmann U, Niemann K (2012) Contextualized attention metadata. In: Roda C (ed) Human attention in digital environments. Cambridge University Press, Cambridge, USA

18. Wolpers M, Najjar J, Verbert K, Duval E (2007) Tracking actual usage: the attention metadata approach. J Educ Technol Soc 10(3):106–121

19. Zhou L, El Helou S, Moccozet L, Opprecht L, Benkacem O, Salzmann C, Gillet D (2012) A federated recommender system for online learning environments. Advances in Web-based learning – ICWL 2012. Lect Notes Comput Sci vol 7558/2012, 89–98, 2012 Doi: 10.1007/978-3-642-33642-3_10

20. Duval E, Hodgins W, Sutton S, Weibel S (2002) Metadata principles and practicalities. D-Lib Mag 8(4), Doi:10.1045/april2002-weibel

21. Koutsomitropoulos DA, Alexopoulos AD, Solomou GD, Papatheodorou TS (2010) The use of metadata for educational resources in digital repositories: practices and perspectives. D-Lib Mag 16(1/2). http://www.dlib.org/dlib/january10/kout/01kout.print.html#14

22. Mitsopoulou E, Taibi D, Giordano D, Dietze S, Yu HQ, Bamidis P, Bratsas C, Woodham L (2011) Connecting medical educational resources to the linked data cloud: the mEducator RDF schema, store and API. In: Linked learning 2011, Proceedings of the 1st international workshop on eLearning approaches for the linked data age, CEUR-WS, vol 717

23. Yu HQ, Dietze S, Li N, Pedrinaci C, Taibi D, Dovrolls N, Stefanut T, Kaldoudi E, Domingue J (2011) A linked data-driven & service-oriented architecture for sharing educational resources. In: Linked learning 2011, Proceedings of the 1st international workshop on eLearning approaches for linked data age, Heraklion, Greece, 29 May 2011

24. Zablith F, d'Aquin M, Brown S, Green-Hughes L (2011b) Consuming linked data within a large educational organization. Proceedings of the 2nd international workshop on consuming linked data (COLD) at International Semantic Web Conference (ISWC), Bonn, Germany, 23–27 Oct 2011

25. Zablith F, Fernandez M, Rowe M (2011a) The OU linked open data: production and consumption. In: Linked learning 2011. Proceedings of the 1st international workshop on elearning approaches for the linked data age, at the 8th extended semantic Web conference (ESWC), Heraklion, Crete, 29 May 2011

26. Ebner H, Palmér M (2008) A Mashup-friendly resource and metadata management framework. In: Wild F, Kalz M, Palmér M (eds) Mash-up personal learning environments, proceedings of the 1st workshop MUPPLE, European conference on technology enhanced learning (EC-TEL), Maastricht, The Netherlands, CEUR vol 388, http://ceur-ws.org/Vol-388/

27. Ebner H, Manouselis M, Palmér M, Enoksson F, Palavitsinis N, Kastrantas K, Naeve A (2009) Learning object annotation for agricultural learning repositories. Proceedings of the IEEE international conference on advanced learning technologies, Riga, Latvia

28. Dietze S, Yu HQ, Pedrinaci C, Liu D, Domingue J (2011) SmartLink: a Web-based editor and search environment for linked services. In: Proceedings of 8th extended semantic Web conference. Heraklion, Greece

29. Breslin GC, Harth A, Bojars U, Decker S (2005) Towards semantically-interlinked online communities. In: Proceedings of the 2nd European semantic Web conference (ESWC '05), Heraklion, Greece, LNCS 3532, pp 500–514

30. Bojars U, Passant A, Cyganiak R, Breslin J (2008) Weaving sioc into the web of linked data. In: Linked data on the Web workshop

31. Subercaze J, Gravier C (2012) Lifting user generated comments to SIOC. Proceedings of the 1st international workshop on knowledge extraction & consolidation from social media (KECSM 2012), vol 895, CEUR-WS.org

32. Passant A, Ciccarese P, Breslin JG, Clark T (2009) SWAN/SIOC: aligning scientific discourse representation and social semantics. Workshop on semantic web applications in scientific discourse (SWASD 2009), vol 523, Washington, DC, USA, CEUR-WS.org

33. Orlandi F, Passant A (2009) Enabling cross-wikis integration by extending the SIOC ontology. In: Proceedings of the fourth workshop on semantic wikis (SemWiki2009) workshop at 6th European semantic Web conference (ESWC2009)

34. Passant A, Raimond Y (2008) Combining social music and semantic Web for music-related recommender systems. In: Proceedings of the first workshop on social data on the Web (SDoW2008), vol 405, CEUR-WS.org. Workshop at International Semantic Web Conference

35. Pitsilis G, Knapskog SJ (2009) Social trust as a solution to address sparsity-inherent problems of recommender systems. ACM RecSys 2009, Workshop on Recommender Systems & The Social Web, Oct 2009, New York, USA

36. Muñoz-Merino PJ, Pardo A, Kloos CD, Muñoz-Organero M, Wolpers M, Katja Niemann K, Friedrich M (2010) CAM in the semantic Web world. Proceedings of iSemantics 2010 1–3 Sept 2010, ACM, Graz, Austria

37. Muñoz-Merino PJ, Kloos CD, Wolpers M, Friedrich M, Muñoz-Organero M (2010) An approach for the personalization of exercises based on contextualized attention metadata and semantic Web technologies. Proceedings 10th IEEE international conference on advanced learning technologies, pp 89–91

38. Heitmann B, Hayes C (2010) Using linked data to build open, collaborative recommender systems. In: AAAI spring symposium: linked data meets artificial intelligence, 2010. Association for the Advancement of Artificial Intelligence (www.aaai.org)

39. Stankovic M, Wagner C, Jovanovic J, Laublet P (2010) Looking for experts? What can linked data do for you? LDOW2010, Raleigh, USA, 27 Apr 2010

40. Drachsler H, Bogers T, Vuorikari R, Verbert K, Duval E, Manouselis N, Beham G et al (2010) Issues and considerations regarding sharable data sets for recommender systems in technology enhanced learning. In: Manouselis N, Drachsler H, Verbert K, Santos OC (eds) Procedia Comput Sci 1(2):2849–2858. http://www.sciencedirect.com/science/article/B9865-50YNHC8-B/2/6297391c895db31c1e10c1258443a201

41. Gasevic G, Dawson C, Ferguson SB, Duval E, Verbert K, Baker RSJD (2011) Open learning analytics: an integrated & modularized platform

42. Drachsler H, Dietze S, Greller W, D'Aquin M, Jovanovic J, Pardo A, Reinhardt W, Verbert K (2012) 1st international workshop on learning analytics and linked data. Proceedings of the 2nd international conference on learning analytics and knowledge – LAK '12. ACM Press, New York, NY, USA, p 9. http://dl.acm.org/citation.cfm?id=2330601.2330607

43. Verbert K, Manouselis N, Drachsler H, Duval E (2012) Dataset-driven research to support learning and knowledge analytics. Educ Technol Soc 15(3):133–148. http://www.ifets.info/journals/15_3/10.pdf

44. Verbert K, Drachsler H, Manouselis N, Wolpers M, Vuorikar R, Duval E (2011) Dataset-driven research for improving recommender systems for learning. First international conference on learning analytics and knowledge (LAK 2011). ACM Press, New York, http://dx.doi.org/10.1145/2090116.2090122

45. Manouselis N, Vuorikari R, van Assche F (2010) Collaborative recommendation of e-learning resources: an experimental investigation. J Comput Assist Learn 26(4):227–242, http://doi.wiley.com/10.1111/j.1365-2729.2010.00362.x

46. Sicilia M-Á, García-Barriocanal E, Sánchez-Alonso S, Cechinel C (2010) Exploring user-based recommender results in large learning object repositories: the case of MERLOT. Procedia Comput Sci 1(2):2859–2864, http://dx.doi.org/10.1016/j.procs.2010.08.011

47. Fazeli S, Drachsler H, Sloep P (submitted) Toward a trust-based recommender system for teachers. 13th international conference on knowledge management and knowledge technologies. 4–6 Sept 2013, Graz, Austria

48. Ekstrand MD, Ludwig M, Konstan JA, Riedl JT (2011) Rethinking the recommender research ecosystem. Proceedings of the fifth ACM conference on recommender systems – RecSys '11. ACM Press, New York, NY, USA, p 133. http://dl.acm.org/citation.cfm?id=2043932.2043958

49. Drachsler H, Greller W, Fazeli S, Niemann K, Sanchez-Alonso S, Rajabi E, Palmér M, Ebner H, Simon B, Nösterer D, Kastrantas K, Manouselis N, Hatzakis I, Clements K (2012) D8.1 Review of Social Data Requirements. Open Discovery Space project. http://hdl.handle.net/1820/4617

50. Drachsler H, Verbert K, Manouselis N, Vuorikari R, Wolpers M, Lindstaedt S (2012) Preface of the dataTEL special issue. Int J Technol Enhanced Learn 4(1/2) 1–10, http://www.inderscience.com/editorials/f841121129310576.pdf

51. Hendrix M, Protopsaltis A, Dunwell I, de Freitas S, Petridis P, Arnab S, Dovrolis N, Kaldoudi E, Taibi D, Dietze S, Mitsopoulou E, Spachos D, Bamidis P, Technical Evaluation of The mEducator 3.0 linked data-based environment for sharing medical educational resources, World Wide Web conference 2012, 2nd international workshop on learning and education with the Web of data, Lyon, France, April 2012

52. Niemann K, Wolpers M, Stoitsis G, Chinis G, Manouselis N (2013) Aggregating social and usage datasets for learning analytics: data-oriented challenges. In Proceedings of the Third International Conference on Learning Analytics and Knowledge (pp. 245–249). ACM

53. Rajabi E, Greller W, Kastrantas K, Niemann K, Sanchez-Alonso S (in press) Social data harvesting and interoperability in ER federations. In: Palavitsinis N, Klerkx J, Ochoa X (eds) Special issue on advances in metadata and semantics for learning infrastructures. IJMSO, Inderscience

54. Jack K, Hristakeva M, Garcia de Zuniga R, Granitzer M (2012) Mendeley's open data for science and learning: a reply to the DataTEL challenge. In: Drachsler H, Verbert K, Manouselis N, Vuorikari R, Wolpers M, Lindstaedt S (eds) Special Issue dataTEL – data supported research in technology-enhanced learning. Int J Technol Enhanced Learn 4(1/2):31–46. DOI: 10.1504/IJTEL.2012.048309

The Learning Registry: Applying Social Metadata for Learning Resource Recommendations

Marie Bienkowski and James Klo

Abstract The proliferation of online teaching, learning, and assessment resources is hampering efforts to make finding relevant resources easy. Metadata, while valuable for curating digital collections, is difficult to keep current or, in some cases, to obtain in the first place. Social metadata, paradata, usage data, and contextualized attention metadata all refer to data about *doing with* digital resources that can be harnessed for recommendations. To centralize this data for aggregation and amplification, the Learning Registry, a store and forward, distributed, de-centralized network of nodes was created. The Learning Registry makes it possible for disparate sources to publish learning resource social/attention metadata—data about users of and activity around resources. We describe our experimentation with social metadata, including that which describes alignment of learning resources to U.S. teaching standards, as a means to generate relationships among resources and people, and how it can be used for recommendations.

Keywords Metadata • Paradata • Digital resources

Introduction

Technology enhanced learning takes place in many contexts including, increasingly, over the Internet [1]. In online environments, educators and learners can take advantage of the web's broad reach to find online teaching, learning and assessment resources (resources, for short) with varying depth of content, level of interactivity, degree of accessibility, and the like. Teachers enliven their curriculum by inserting online resources into their classroom practice or using them to supplement class

M. Bienkowski (✉) • J. Klo
SRI International, Menlo Park, CA, USA
e-mail: marie.bienkowski@sri.com; jim.klo@sri.com

N. Manouselis et al. (eds.), *Recommender Systems for Technology Enhanced Learning: Research Trends and Applications*, DOI 10.1007/978-1-4939-0530-0_4,
© Springer Science+Business Media New York 2014

work or "flip" their teaching strategies [2, 26]; Students seeking resources to supplement their traditional course materials may look to these resources to help them see alternative presentations and representations of knowledge that deepen and reinforce their learning. Learners needing accommodations could find resources that adapt to visual, auditory, or cognitive differences. The Internet has paved the way for commercial, free, and openly licensed resources to be made widely available, supporting the democratization of education via increased access [24]. Resources can originate from government agencies, educational and research institutions, professional societies, and any other individual or organization with an interest in supporting improvements in learning, sharing their passion in a topic area, or fulfilling an outreach mission.

Although portals and online learning sites compete to be the "go to" location for finding, collecting, or playback of resources, a more user-centric vision is to allow online learning platforms to track experiences—including *learning* and *doing* interactions with online resources—and to have learner profiles be exportable, portable, and usable across platforms [10]. In the future, there may be capabilities for resources to be stitched together by individual learners or personalized learning assistants, or to be recommended by algorithms based on measured learner expertise and sophisticated analytics. (A good survey of recommender systems for technology-enhanced learning can be found in [13]). But at present, employing online resources for teaching, learning, and assessment still requires manual authoring, curating, and collecting into coherent lessons.

Various strategies are used to manage and deliver resources to educators and learners, including social networking and social recommendations at community-serving portals such as Better Lesson and ShareMyLesson. Resources are collected into repositories such as Merlot, OERCommons, European Schoolnet's Learning Resource Exchange, and the pan-European Open Discovery Space and popular resources may be available from many such places. Organizations that create *open* educational resources (e.g., the U.S. University of Colorado's PhET Interactive Simulations, the U.S. National Archives' DocsTeach, and Australia's National Film and Sound Archive) advertise their availability at teacher conferences and mailing lists as well as publishing them at government-sponsored, centralized digital libraries. As learning activities move to mobile platforms, "app stores" host educational content in the form of applications that can run on smartphones. With the availability of many thousands of widely dispersed online educational resources, there is the potential to create an online learning economy with a "long tail" demand curve for boutique resources [22].

But a long tail requires not just an easy means of production but also a means of locating resources [3]. And solutions to that problem still elude us; resources are distributed across many repositories and websites, using a variety of metadata standards and access mechanisms. Resources created for open use are, in principle, available for anyone to use—but in practice users must visit many websites, contend with their various interfaces, and then, clip or bookmark the sites. (Early efforts at resource location included social bookmarking sites such as Delicious.) Automatic harvesting of these resources for use elsewhere can involve complicated metadata crosswalks and web page analysis. A searcher should be able to search for all of the learning resources available on a particular topic or find ones that have been authored by a particular person or institution. Federated search or registries that collect metadata (e.g., the Ariadne system, see [27]) could provide a single access point to these repositories but require a centralized authority to maintain and prove difficult to upkeep; n-way connections among websites also suffer from the same difficulty. Updates to descriptive data could be obtained from information published on the web by scraping websites, use of microformats on learning resource pages [25], from search terms entered into repositories, or from analysis of online curriculum that uses embedded resources.

Nevertheless, there are still significant barriers to effective resource locating, sharing, and amplifying. The most damaging is the omission, decay, or irrelevance of metadata. Even if federated search and automated collection of metadata was achievable, searching for learning resources based on descriptive metadata (e.g., keywords, author, publication date) alone may still yield inadequate results. Newer methods of locating relevant items take into account characteristics of the *searcher* and their actions to provide recommendations (e.g., [28]). Online commerce and social networking sites using analytics have demonstrated the value and efficiency of recommendations. "Customers like you favorited product X." "People who bought this item also bought Y." "5000 people viewed this article in the past day." In technology-enhanced learning environments, recommenders have emerged as a topic of special interest to support personalized learning (see the 2010 and 2012 workshops on Recommender Systems for Technology Enhanced Learning, [14, 15]).

Recommendation requires that the search mechanism have access to both the properties of the object of search (metadata), the properties and actions of the learners who are searching, and the "learning networks" that learners form [12]. This richer set of data comes from user actions entered into interactive web sites, including counts of use (in the classroom), contexts of use (e.g., what sorts of classrooms, students, and teachers), and reflections by users (e.g., ratings, descriptions). Companies and the research community are taking advantage of the data exhaust or "big data" that comes from online interactions to characterize users, improve products, model user knowledge and judge engagement [5, 6]. It is worth asking the question, then, about where the "big data" for teaching, learning, and assessment resources comes from. Capturing the data exhaust is difficult to do with learning resource data because they are so broadly distributed, especially for open educational resources and live in their own environments.

Portals and repositories for educators and learners are effective in supporting specific needs of their user population (e.g., membership and community benefits that search engines lack) and should be enhanced, not replaced. Increasingly, these portals are capturing user activity with learning resources. However, these sites are collecting rich usage data in information silos. Rich social metadata—teachers downloading, favoriting, rating, commenting upon—are locked inside the portal and cannot be shared across a broad network of education stakeholders (including researchers). The Learning Registry provides a unique opportunity to

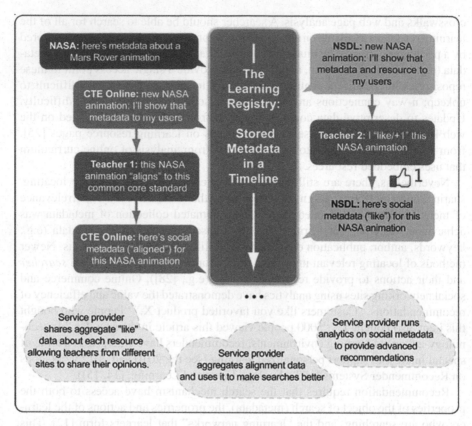

Fig. 1 A time series of learning resource data assertions via the Learning Registry

share data across siloes, and not just for data about government resources, but also education institutions, and for-profit and not-for-profit organizations. As shown in Fig. 1, the Learning Registry can collect time-stamped usage data that *any* service provider can leverage for learning-resource analytics and create services that are not now possible.

In the remainder of this chapter, we present the technical background for the Learning Registry and describe how it is implemented, what core functionality it provides, and what services can be built upon it that leverage the data it stores. Then, we expand on the perspective that the Learning Registry takes on social metadata or paradata, including motivating the need for collecting it (vs. relying only on metadata), and we present the data model for paradata used in the Learning Registry. Of particular interest for this application is the use of social metadata about the alignment of a learning resource to learning standards. We present our proof-of-concept implementation of a collaborative-filtering based recommender and then present our conclusions.

Technical Background

The Learning Registry was envisioned as a store-and-forward network of peer nodes based loosely on early content-distribution models (e.g., [7, 23]). The Learning Registry is a network to which providers of learning resources, metadata, and social metadata can distribute information for consumption and amplification by all communities [5, 6, 9]. To support these providers, the Learning Registry must accommodate a large volume of data expressed in a variety of metadata standards. The Learning Registry accepts, stores, and provides access to learning resource descriptions—metadata or social metadata—as documents expressed in JavaScript Object Notation (JSON). The storage and access mechanism used internally is a no-SQL, time-based data store: CouchDB (couchdb.apache.org). CouchDB is a lightweight, open-source document-based database. CouchDB provides data access in the form of views generated by MapReduce [8] functions written in JavaScript. CouchDB's replication mechanisms make it easy to stand up a network of nodes, which serves the goal of decentralizing the Learning Registry and eliminating single points of failure. Replication can also be leveraged by high-volume users to create their own local repository containing all or some Learning Registry data.

On top of CouchDB, the Learning Registry provides a layer of services (written in Python) as Application Programming Interfaces (APIs) to publish data to the Learning Registry, to query documents in the Learning Registry, and to retrieve documents from the Learning Registry (Fig. 2). These services are the principle public interface to the Learning Registry, though developers are welcome (and encouraged) to provide other services in addition to or on top of these services.

Documents (payload and wrapper) submitted are assigned a unique document identifier that is returned to the submitter; this identifier refers to the Learning Registry submission, not to the resource itself. One challenge in building the Learning Registry has been how to create a unique way to identify a teaching, learning, or assessment resource. This is important because the social metadata submitted about a resource do not refer to this document identifier (as that is specific to one submitter) but instead needs to reference the same resource identifier so metadata can be accumulated across many submitters. Indeed, in the Learning Registry, social metadata may be submitted for a learning resource before the resource itself has been registered with a metadata submission. At present, the Learning Registry is using URL as a unique resource locator but we have already found difficulties with this approach (e.g., the U.S. Public Broadcasting Service (PBS) Learning Media site, www.pbslearningmedia.org, desired to redirect its users to local PBS affiliates, turning the URL into something like ca.pbslearningmedia.org). While a solution such as OpenURL [20] could provide a standard URL to match resource metadata with social metadata, it requires a central service, which the Learning Registry has avoided. Over time, the Learning Registry community may develop more consistent URL conventions, adopt OpenURL, provide translation services, leverage "same as" social metadata assertions, or simply live with "islands" of data created by non-uniform naming.

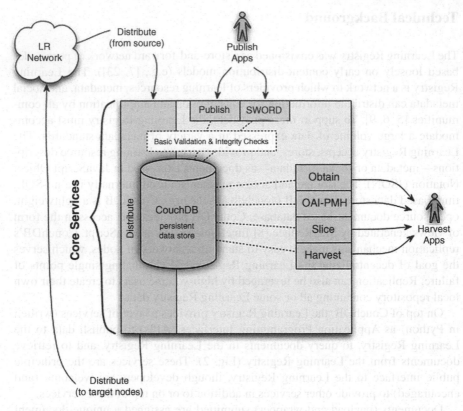

Fig. 2 High level structure and functions of the Learning Registry

The Learning Registry offers two core functions for data retrieval: obtain and harvest. Obtain is used to gather all documents at a node, or a subset based on the resource locator present in the document. Harvest is based on OAI-PMH Harvest [19] to gather documents or payload data for specific date ranges. Additionally, the Learning Registry Slice service allows users to retrieve documents based on pre-defined properties of the document wrapper such as identity of the resource owner, metadata author, or submitter; date of submission, and "tags" (including keywords, schema format, and the resource data type, i.e., paradata or metadata).

The Learning Registry is an infrastructure for application and service development, not a website, destination, or application itself. Developers build specialized services on Learning Registry APIs to extract data into other storage and tools in order to make use of it. For consumers of published data, basic obtain and harvest can yield volumes of resource data because the Learning Registry does not provide search or complex filtering functions, and data does not expire once published. The concept of Learning Registry *data services* was introduced as a design pattern for building MapReduce functions. Instantiating the design pattern allows developers to implement rules for identifying, filtering and formatting published content that conforms to a specific use case while maintaining a standardized, harvest-like interface. For the application described in this paper, we implemented a data service to create a harvest feed that filters and classifies standards alignment data in a format digestible for further analysis.

Social Metadata or Paradata

Metadata is largely about description and, by extension, classification. Classification metadata schemes refer to fixed characteristics of a resource: who created it, what organization hosts it, what grade level it is appropriate for and the like. Classification schemes can be as complex as variants of Dublin Core [17] or LRMI metadata (http://www.lrmi.net) or as simple as the taxonomies found in many applications such as genres of music and books, or types of software applications. Classification schemes support browsing and faceted search. For example, one can browse for apps under productivity, health and fitness, and the like. In the library, browsing the books on the shelves near the one you are seeking often yields other books of interest. Faceted search allows a user to select desired characteristics and see the set of resources that represents the intersection of the selected features, that is, those resources with all of the desired characteristics. Faceted search can be useful for finding similar items: an educator may want a resource at a different grade level for a student who is more or less advanced. These ways of finding resources can be useful and assume that the searcher is seeking specific material with given characteristics.

Metadata, as we have described, suffers from the burden of upkeep. Curators recognized the promise of capturing the social actions of users of resources, along with other characteristics [21]. Curators are also excited about the possibility of crowdsourcing of descriptive metadata, or collective tagging (e.g., http://www.steve.museum). Social metadata, then, supports the collection of assertions, in the Learning Registry, about the "social life" of a resource as acted upon by some person or organization. We use the term "social metadata" to show that this is a particular kind of metadata—data about usage, doing and action. The Learning Registry recommends a set of paradata "verbs" but does not impose any restrictions on what verbs are used (and it does no schema validation of paradata submissions). Table 1 shows an early categorization of social metadata derived from studies with educator-users of the U.S. National Science Digital Library (NSDL) learning resource library [18].

Independent of the work in the digital library community on social metadata, an Internet community was working on the concept of Activity Streams (http://activitystrea.ms). Their intent was to allow individuals to share that they did something specific, using a Real Simple Syndication (RSS) model. The Learning Registry paradata format was modeled on Activity Streams with the exception of organizations expressing social metadata on behalf of a user or users. While Activity Streams assumes that an individual will emit an RSS-like stream of activities, the Learning

Table 1 Categories of social metadata, or paradata, from U.S. National Science Digital Library

Annotational: refines descriptive metadata	Kinematic: illustrates diffusion through user actions	Pedagogical: refines educational context and utility
Tagged as	Clicked	User demographic aggregated by paradata contributor
Recommended	Viewed	Embedded in
Added to collection or playlist		
Commented/discussed	Downloaded	Correlated/aligned to
Rated	Favorited	Modified
	Added to personal collection	
Voted	Shared to social media	Implemented in a context
Related to other resources	Subscribed	Republished as
Cited	Linked to	Researched
Awarded	Featured	Saved/shared searches
Ranked		

Registry social metadata model assumes that a portal or website captures user actions about learning resource usage and asserts paradata for them. (This raises concerns, of course, about such entities releasing personal or personally identifiable information about their users.) Furthermore, the Activity Streams model does not support statements about aggregate activities (e.g., "watched 5 times"). The Learning Registry recommends (but, again, does not enforce) that social metadata for individuals be expressed using Activity Streams and, for organizational and aggregate activities, the extended model be used.

Social metadata is stored in the Learning Registry in JSON format and is saved in the CouchDB store unless explicitly deleted. Social metadata is connected to a learning resource by the URL of the resource. The general schema for social metadata or paradata is shown below.

actor (required, except for assertions): the person or group who does something; a string or a compound object (as shown below) that describes characteristics of the actor

> **object-type:** the actor value
> **description:** information about the actor

verb (required): the action that is taken; it can be a simple string. If it is a compound object, then **verb** contains:

> **action:** the verb value
> **measure:** the occurrences of the verb (whether counts, averages, ratings, or other things).
> **date** (optional): start time/stop time when the action occurs.
> **context** (optional): place where the action takes place

object (optional): the thing being acted upon. The important part of an object is the URL (or URI) where you can find out about the object (or get the object, or ideally both).

related (optional): describes a relationship between the object (above) and other objects listed within

content (optional): a human-readable string description of what the paradata item expresses

When paradata is being used to make assertions, as opposed to expressing the actions of an actor, the *actor* can be omitted. More information about paradata can be found at the Learning Registry GitHub site (https://github.com/LearningRegistry/), and a useful comparison among different usage data formats can be found in Niemann et al. [16].

An important piece of information about a learning resource is how it satisfies a curriculum standard. In the U.S., individual states are busy with adoption of the Common Core State Standards (also called the "Common Core," http://www.corestandards.org) for English Language Arts and Mathematics. Prior to the Common Core initiative, individual states had their own curriculum standards in these areas. Now, adopting states are conducting crosswalks between their existing state standards and these new standards, and anticipate a similar exercise once the Next Generation Science Standards (NGSS, http://www.nextgenscience.org) are finalized. Teaching, learning, and assessment resources formerly aligned to existing state standards now must be re-aligned to the Common Core and NGSS. Data in the Learning Registry is seen as a way to aid in this effort, for the simple reason that resources that are already aligned to a state standard will align to a Common Core or NGSS standard once crosswalks are done. This can rapidly increase the availability of resources aligned to common and state standards.

Alignment statements are not the only kind of social metadata that can help states: the following are examples that are of special interest to states adopting the registry:

- This resource has been aligned 214 times with Common Core Mathematics Standard 5.G.2.
- A fourth-grade science teacher bookmarked this National Geographic volcano diagram.
- An eighth-grade math teacher shared this Khan Academy video with her students.
- An anonymous user commented on this Common Core English Language Arts standard.
- A subject-matter expert matched this resource to three academic content standards.
- A resource was downloaded from the NSDL (National Science Digital Library) repository 1,354 times during May 2011.

The Learning Registry community is starting to explore what can be done with information derived from analysis assertions such as these. Applications include judging the popularity of resources, recommending sequences of resources organized by teachers for learning, and exploring trends in the use of resources. The Learning Registry could surface relationships between people based on their attention to resources: Which institutions, portals, or groups of users have shared/ curated the same resource? The Learning Registry enables solutions that rely on identity because it implements node-based signing (for submitting documents cryptographically signed, [4]) and by supporting OAuth and BrowserID (http://oauth. net; https://browserid.org/). Allowing users, as they deem fit, to expose more of their data will aid in relationship mining for learning resource analytics. In the next section we show an example of resource recommendation based on learning resource social metadata.

Leveraging Learning Registry Data for Resource Recommendations

Learning Registry data services provide more complex filtering and selection beyond the simple APIs that are part of the core infrastructure. Data services are good for extracting large amounts of filtered data, such as assertions about alignment to standards, to support the types of applications described in the previous section. To support discovery of new resources, and to provide an early proof-of-concept of the power of learning resource analytics with Learning Registry social metadata, we explored the capabilities provided by modeling standards alignment data as a graph of complex interconnections among resources, submitters, and standards. We employed Neo4j (http://www.neo4j.org/), a robust transactional property graph database that stores data as nodes and relationships, with properties for each. Traversal of the resulting graph reveals interesting relationships with direct application to resource recommendation.

Walt Grata of the U.S. Department of Defense's Advanced Digital Learning Initiative created the first version for leveraging crosswalks to discover new alignments (i.e., if Resource A aligns to Standard X, and Standard X is linked to Standard Y by a crosswalk, then Resource A aligns to Standard Y). This prototype used a technique that modeled resources and standards as nodes and relationships as edges. Specifics about the relationship or about the resource (e.g., submitter, curator, assertion type, ownership, rating, or collection) were represented as properties of the relationship. The result, shown in the example in Fig. 3, allows identification of possible relationships through graph traversal.

This representation can be extended to include simple activity data between an actor and the resource, shown in Fig. 4. With this addition of social activity metadata expression, we can begin to build a recommendation solution by intersecting features such as "resources related by shared standards that also have the most 'favorites' or the highest ratings".

As we investigated the applicability of this technique for collaborative filtering, we realized that it does not permit relationships to be weighted, for example, when multiple submitters make similar relationship statements, the strength of the relationship should increase. As illustrated (Fig. 3), while it is possible to create a

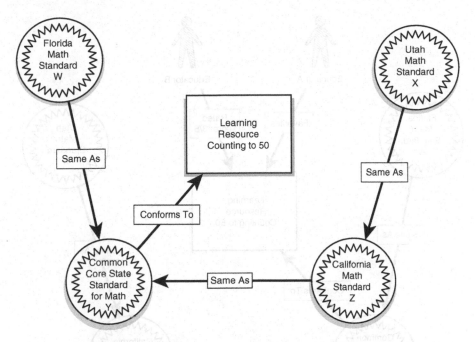

Fig. 3 Simple edges show relationships between standards and resources. In this example, once a relationship is defined between standards and resources, a resource can be cross-walked across standards

strength through numbers relationship for activities between two entities, such as in most favorited or highest ranked resource, this initial graph representation has no mechanism to create an edge between properties of an edge and another node. This would be used for building relationships between resources and standards where strength can be determined. However, as shown in Fig. 5, we are not able to extend the social popularity of the curricular standard using this simple technique. Neo4J does not permit the creation of more than one relationship type (Same As, Conforms To) between two nodes, as well as there is no mechanism of defining a relationship between a node and another relationship.

To be able to represent multiple submitters of alignment data, our next approach employed an alternative graph modeling technique that leverages hyperedges. Using this technique, each harvested document from the Learning Registry is represented as a node, and properties of the document that are relevant in determining the weight or impact of the relationship are also promoted to nodes (Fig. 6). Using this technique, multiple pathways describing the same relationship exist, but can be traversed through more than one author, allowing a more robust recommender system to be built. Hyperedge modeling permits the construction of links between more than two elements, and so richer relationships may be defined that may be used to influence the recommender system. For example, before we only could represent

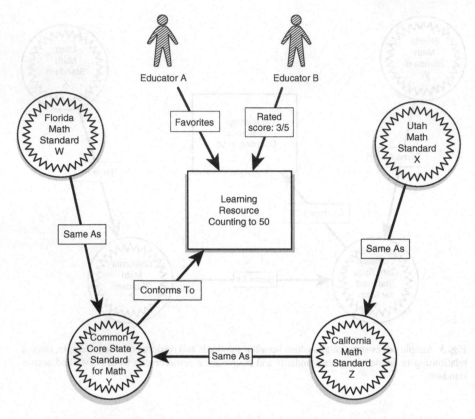

Fig. 4 Social activity data can be used to discover resources that are highly rated and "favorited"

that a rating relationship might have a score, we can now add context to identify that the rating uses a specific rubric. Transitioning to the use of hyper edges permits operations such as the following.

- Locating resources that are aligned to the same standards as a specified resource, ranking them by number of shared alignments.

  – Math activity for "learning to count to 50" shares ten of the same curricular alignments as a video "teaching to count to 50".

- Suggesting alternate resources that reference similar alignments but have more favorites and higher ratings by others.

  – There are 10 other resources that teach prepositional phrases that are similar to the specified resource, and 4 of these have received higher ratings than the one you are currently using.

- Identify actors who have submitted similar alignments as other actors, ranking by alignment type.

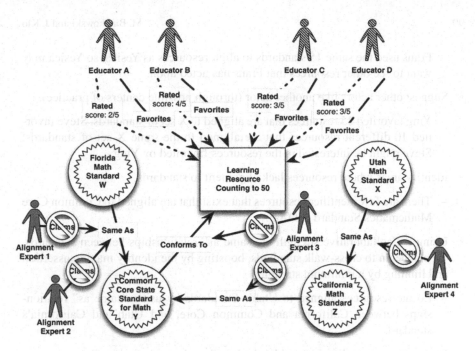

Fig. 5 Multiple actors can perform activities like ratings and "favoriting" but Neo4J does not support connecting relationships to relationships. Thus, in this graph representation, it is not possible to show that multiple experts have made the same alignment claims between two nodes

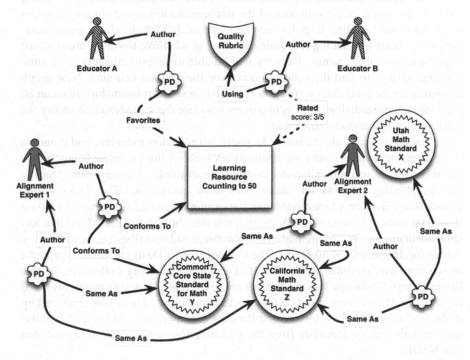

Fig. 6 A more complete representation of the relationships in Learning Registry data is enabled through the use of hyperedges

- Frans used the same 15 standards to align resources as Yesica, so Yesica may want to see other resources that Frans has acted upon.

• Suggest other actors like another actor (through possible centers of practice).

- Ying favorited 25 resources that are aligned to X set of standards. Steve favorited 10 different resources that are aligned to the same X set of standards. Steve might be interested in the resources favorited by Ying.

• Identify areas where resources lack alignment to standards.

- There are few identified resources that exist that are aligned to Common Core Mathematics Standard K.OA.5.

• Using the collaborative strength of "same as" relationships between standards, we can begin to cross-walk standards, boosting by the identity making assertion and limiting by a minimum strength.

- Locate resources aligned to Utah's Standards by using "same as" relationships between California and Common Core, and Utah and California's standard.

Each result set can be impacted by the length and count of paths from source to destination node.

In this section, we have shown a proof-of-concept implementation for employing Learning Registry standards alignment data for recommending resources. On-going work is examining the performance of the implementation as the amount of social metadata in the Learning Registry increases and using other kinds of social metadata as the basis for making recommendations. As we move toward a more robust implementation, the Learning Registry will be able to support educators in formal learning settings to find the right resources for their lesson planning. New graph databases can be built that capture other interesting social relationships that can be used for recommendation, such as two users who rate the same resource seeing the other resources that each other rated.

To understand how the Learning Registry helps gather metadata and paradata from disparate sources, and how applications built on the Learning Registry can use this data for recommendations, consider an example of several sites sharing and amplifying information about the same resources. The U.S. Public Broadcasting Service's LearningMedia, for example, created Anatomy of a Rover (based on content from the NOVA television series about the planet Mars) that lets students interactively explore features of the rover and describes how each feature solves specific technical problems. The Cooper Hewitt Design Museum created a lesson that was included in the NSDL Design Engineering collection. In this Rover Design Challenge lesson, students are given realistic design problems faced by previous Mars rovers based on unexpected conditions. These resources end up in the teacher portals CTE Online and Brokers of Expertise, respectively, because these portals harvest metadata from the Learning Registry and from repositories like NSDL.

In Brokers of Expertise, a curriculum expert aligns the Anatomy of a Rover resource to a Common Core standard, "Assess the extent to which the reasoning and evidence in a text support the author's claim or a recommendation for solving a scientific or technical problem" (RST.9-10-8). Independently, a CTE Online expert aligns the Rover Design Challenge resource to the same standard. Paradata assertions about each alignment go into the Learning Registry, referencing a machine-readable identifier for that standard.

A teacher using CTE Online is building a lesson that references the reasoning and evidence Common Core standard. This lesson is part of the model curriculum, The 10-Step Engineering Design Solution Process. When looking for resources to use in this lesson, the teacher is presented with suggestions from the Learning Registry, based on the standards alignment done on both the Brokers of Expertise platform and the CTE Online platform.

When the teacher incorporates the resource into the lesson, that action ("used in a lesson") is captured by CTE Online. CTE Online then publishes a notification of that action as paradata to the Learning Registry. Brokers of Expertise has a special Learning Registry data service set up to gather paradata information from users of CTE Online. Teachers and experts on any portal, repository, or lesson-sharing site can use this to locate new resources. As this example illustrates, this cross-site information flow enabled by the registry increases the shared pool of knowledge about the resources.

Conclusion and Future Work

The Internet is awash with data coming from the social and intellectual activities of individuals and organizations and the Learning Registry is creating the infrastructure and example applications that can improve access to online teaching, learning, and assessment resources through analytics. In this chapter, we have shown a work-in-progress recommendation application that exploits data relationships represented in graph form. Future work can build on this open-source example to create recommenders based on other relationships.

The Learning Registry has the potential to provide significant value to organizations adopting it for publishing and consuming, as described below.

1. Expanded access to trustworthy descriptive data on educational resources
   * The Learning Registry provides an easy-to-adopt and easy-to-operate mechanism for disseminating and consuming resource information.

Generalized search engines are not optimized to answer questions that are important to educators such as, what resources are available to teach a specific topic to a particular set of students? What kinds of students are those resources suitable for? Are any standards associated with those resources? The Learning Registry supports a model for organizations to share information for further amplification and discovery in an open, distributed network. No single entity owns or controls the Learning

Registry network. Anyone can freely publish data to the Learning Registry for any interested party to consume anytime, anywhere. The resources are thus made available to a broader network of educators. As a consumer of Learning Registry data, each organization can determine its set of trusted partners in the registry and consume data only from them. Such trust networks greatly reduce problems with quality and safety that are sometimes found with content on the Internet.

2. Pooling contextualized knowledge about learning resources
   • The Learning Registry enables sharing and aggregating resource usage data across disparate systems and platforms.

As educators interact online with portals and repositories, they generate useful information about resource usage and contexts of use, such as how often a resource is downloaded; what sort of users downloaded it; the classroom context the resource was used in; and for what kinds of students it was used. Commercial sites have proven the value of collecting this kind of social data across many users. For resources to be used and reused more effectively, social metadata must be shared widely and aggregated across many users, systems, and platforms. The Learning Registry enables this sharing.

3. Providing tools and services to make use of "big data" about resources
   • The Learning Registry provides a basis for building tools and applications to improve teaching and learning with digital resources.

The Learning Registry provides a core set of services on which applications and tools can be built to explore, analyze, and amplify big data in the registry, using such techniques as customized filtering, trend analysis, social network analysis, and more. Here are example learning-analytics applications for learning registry data

• User knowledge modeling: Learning Registry data could be used to compute what a student might be expected to know. In contrast to the coarse characterization of grade levels present in most metadata, Learning Registry assertions could be specific about the grade or level at which resources were successfully used.
• User experience modeling (Are users satisfied?): Learning Registry ratings paradata could be used to compute satisfaction.
• User profiling (What groups do users cluster into?): Learning Registry social metadata could be used to compute the types of actors who use resources. Submitters of paradata can also be clustered in categories based on how and when they submit.
• Domain modeling (How is content decomposed into components and sequenced?): Curriculum construction tools could gather data on sequencing of learning resources or alignment to standards.
• Trend analysis (What changes over time and how?): Trends in attention to different resources could be computed if a sufficiently fine-grain size of paradata is submitted, because the paradata specifies a date or date range.
• Recommendations (What next actions/resources can be suggested for the user?): As we have shown, the Learning Registry can support recommendations by

clustering users or by building a social network graph and then recommending resources among a cluster or social network.

- Feedback, Adaption, and Personalization (What actions should be suggested for the user? How should the user experience be changed for the next user?): Learning Registry data could provide feedback to developers about the utility of their resources, about who adapts them and how, and could eventually cause "widespread sharing" of learning resources to learners at the appropriate time.

As we have seen, the Learning Registry is designed to be flexible to accommodate different needs, user communities, and contexts. Learning Registry data are now ready to be consumed and put to use in a variety of ways. Excellent learning resources are being developed every day by public education agencies that are in need of finding the right audience. Publishing resource metadata descriptions to the Learning Registry gets that information out to the education community that needs it the most. Additionally, publishing activity and usage information completes the feedback loop that public and private learning resource publishers need in order to provide us with the most effective content.

At present, the Learning Registry community is exploring new and interesting ways to use shared data, such as recommending resources, visualizing trending resources, and analyzing connections among resources. California's Brokers of Expertise and CTE (Career and Technical Education) Online sites are active members of the Learning Registry network, sharing resources, ratings, and alignment data. The Public Broadcasting System, the National Science Digital Library and OER Commons have also connected to the Learning Registry network. The Shared Learning Collaborative, an initiative to create software to help teachers more efficiently enable effective, personalized instruction, is creating indexing and search applications for Learning Registry data. In the United Kingdom, JISC has been pioneering the use of the Learning Registry in higher education. Specific examples of CTE Online and JISC's work with the Learning Registry can be found in [11].

Acknowledgments Walt Grata of the Advanced Distributed Learning Initiative (ADL, U.S Department of Defense) designed and implemented an early version of the learning resource relationship graph described in this chapter. Steve Midgley, US Department of Education, first suggested creating a graph representation of Learning Registry data using Neo4j. SRI International's work on this project is supported by the US Department of Education (ED-04-CO-0040/0010).

References

1. Allen IE, Seaman J (2011) Going the distance: online education in the United States. Babson Survey Research Group http://www.babson.edu/Academics/centers/blank-center/global-research/Documents/going-the-distance.pdf
2. Allen IE, Seaman J (2012) Growing the curriculum: open education resources in U.S. higher education. Babson Survey Research Group http://www.onlinelearningsurvey.com/reports/growingthecurriculum.pdf
3. Anderson C (2006) The long tail: why the future of business is selling less of more. Hyperion, New York

4. Bienkowski M, Klo J (2011) Identity in the federal learning registry. Position Paper for W3C Workshop on Identity in the Browser (Mountain View, CA, USA, May 24–25, 2011). http://www.w3.org/2011/identity-ws/papers/idbrowser2011_submission_27.pdf
5. Bienkowski M, Brecht J, Klo J (2012) The learning registry: building a foundation for learning resource analytics. Learning Analytics and Knowledge 2012 (LAK'12): 29 April–2 May 2012, Vancouver, BC, Canada
6. Bienkowski M, Feng M, Means B (2012) Enhancing teaching and learning through educational data mining and learning analytics: an issue brief. U.S. Department of Education Report
7. Chang LK, Liu K-Y, Wu C-A, Chen H-Y (2005) Sharing web-based multimedia learning objects using NNTP news architecture. Proceedings of the Fifth IEEE International Conference on Advanced Learning Technologies (ICALT'05)
8. Dean J, Ghemawat S (2008) MapReduce: simplified data processing on large clusters. Commun ACM 51(1):107–113
9. Jesukiewicz P, Rehak D (2011) The learning registry: sharing federal learning resources. Presented at the Interservice/Industry Training, Simulation, and Education Conference (I/ITSEC)
10. Kyriacou D (2008) A scrutable user modelling infrastructure for enabling life-long user modelling. In: Adaptive hypermedia and adaptive Web-based systems, Springer, Heidelberg, pp 421–425
11. Lee A, Hobson J, Bienkowski M, Midgley S, Currier S, Campbell L, Novoseova T (2012) Towards networked knowledge: the learning registry, an infrastructure for sharing online learning resources. Educ Technol 52(6):14–19
12. Manouselis N, Drachsler H, Vuorikari R, Hummel H, Koper R (2011) Recommender systems in technology enhanced learning. In: Ricci F, Rokach L, Shapira B, Kantor PB (eds) Recommender systems handbook. Springer Science+Business Media, LLC, Boston, MA, pp 387–415. doi:10.1007/978-0-387-85820-3_12
13. Manouselis N, Drachsler H, Verbert K, Duval E (2013) Recommender systems for learning. Springer, New York, NY
14. Manouselis N, Drachsler H, Verbert K, Santos OC (eds) (2012) Proceedings of the 2nd workshop on recommender systems for technology enhanced learning (RecSysTEL-2012). Saarbrücken, Germany. http://ceur-ws.org/Vol-896/. Accessed 18–19 Sept 2012
15. Manouselis N, Drachsler H, Verbert K, Santos OC (eds) (2010) Proceedings of the 1st workshop on recommender systems for technology enhanced learning (RecSysTEL-2010). Procedia Computer Sci 1(2):2773–2998. Elsevier B.V., Amsterdam
16. Niemann K, Scheffel M, Wolpers M (2012) An overview of usage data formats for recommendations in TEL. In: Manouselis N, Drachsler H, Verbert K, Santos OC (eds) Proceedings of the 2nd workshop on recommender systems for technology enhanced learning (RecSysTEL-2012). http://ceur-ws.org/Vol-896/. p 95
17. NSDL (2007) NSDL_DC metadata guidelines, http://nsdl.org/contribute/metadata-guide
18. NSDL (2012) Paradata. http://nsdlnetwork.org/stemexchange/paradata
19. OAI-PMH (2008) The open archives initiative protocol for metadata harvesting, V2.0, www.openarchives.org/OAI/openarchivesprotocol.html
20. OCLC (2009) OpenURL. http://www.oclc.org/research/activities/openurl.html
21. OCLC (2012) Sharing and aggregating social metadata. http://www.oclc.org/research/activities/aggregating.html
22. Severance C, Teasley SD (2010) Preparing for the long tail of teaching and learning tools. Presented at the proceedings of the 9th international conference of the learning sciences-volume 1, International Society of the Learning Sciences, pp 758–764
23. Smith J, Klein M, Nelson M (2006) Repository replication using NNTP and SMTP. In: Gonzalo J et al (eds) Research and advanced technology for digital libraries. Springer, Berlin/Heidelberg, pp 51–62
24. Smith MS (2009) Opening education. Science 323(5910):89–93
25. Soylu A, Kuru S, Wild F, Mödrichter F (2008) e-Learning and microformats: a learning object harvesting model and a sample application. In: Proceedings Mupple'08 Workshop, pp 57–65

26. Staker H, Horn M (2012) Classifying K-12 Blended Learning. Innosight Institute. http://www.innosightinstitute.org/innosight/wp-content/uploads/2012/05/Classifying-K-12-blended-learning2.pdf
27. Ternier S, Verbert K, Parra G, Vandeputte B, Klerkx J, Duval E, Ordonez V, Ochoa X (2009) The Ariadne infrastructure for managing and storing metadata. IEEE Internet Comput 13: 18–25
28. Zhou L, Helou El S, Moccozet L, Opprecht L, Benkacem O, Salzmann C, Gillet D (2012) A federated recommender system for online learning environments. In: Popescu E, Li Q, Klamma R, Leung H, Specht M (Eds) Proceedings of the 11th international conference on advances in Web-based learning – ICWL 2012, Sinaia, Romania

Part II
Innovative Methods and Techniques

A Framework for Personalised Learning-Plan Recommendations in Game-Based Learning

Ioana Hulpuş, Conor Hayes, and Manuel Oliveira Fradinho

Abstract Personalised recommender systems receive growing attention from researchers of technology enhanced learning. The learning domain has a great need for personalisation as there is a general consensus that instructional material should be adapted to the knowledge, needs and abilities of learners. At the same time, the increase in the interest in game-based learning opens great opportunities for learning material personalisation, due to the complexity of life situations that can be simulated in serious games environments. In this paper, we present a model for competency development using serious games, which is supported by case-based learning-plan recommendation. While case-based reasoning has been used before for recommending learning objects, this work goes beyond current state-of-the-art, by recommending learning plans in a two-step hierarchical case-based planning strategy. First of all, several abstract plans are retrieved, personalised and recommended to the learner. In the second stage, the chosen plan is incrementally instantiated as the learner engages with the learning material. We also suggest how several learning strategies that resonate with a game-based learning environment, can drive the adaptation of learning material.

I. Hulpuş (✉)
INSIGHT Centre for Data Analytics, NUI Galway, Ireland
e-mail: ioana.hulpus@insight-centre.org

C. Hayes
College of Engineering and Informatics, NUI Galway, Ireland
e-mail: conor.hayes@nuigalway.ie

M.O. Fradinho
SINTEF, Trondheim, Norway
e-mail: manuel.oliveira@sintef.no

N. Manouselis et al. (eds.), *Recommender Systems for Technology Enhanced Learning: Research Trends and Applications*, DOI 10.1007/978-1-4939-0530-0_5,
© Springer Science+Business Media New York 2014

Introduction

Serious games for educational purposes have a number of potential advantages over more traditional learning methods and on-the-job training. Game-based learning is consistent with constructivist learning theories [42], which emphasize that learning is active and knowledge is built on top of own experiences. Serious games include tolerance and encouragement of risk within a safe environment [24], thus promoting and encouraging experimentation instead of passive learning [13, 27]. They can support learning that is active, experiential, situated, problem and inquiry-based, and they provide immediate feedback. They also involve communities of practice which provide collaborative support to learners [8].

Evidence for their efficacy as educational tools is growing with a growing number of research studies finding improved rates of learning and retention for serious games compared with more traditional learning methods [10, 11, 16]. A very recent literature review on empirical evidence of serious games [11] found that students enjoy the game-based approach and found it motivating. The same study shows that games can be used with success for both behavioural change and cognitive acquisition, but their benefits vary.

Like for all learning activities, the learning objects have to be designed and selected according to pedagogical foundations and the learning experience must be personalised in order to avoid the "one-size-fits-all" learning environment. In these paper, we are dealing with these two aspects of game-based-learning, namely: (i) the recommendation of learning paths that support the learner towards achievement of target competences, and (ii) personalisation through constant performance assessment and on-the-fly adaptation of the learning paths. The main contribution of this paper is twofold: (i) we research how case-based planning can be used for recommending personalised learning plans and (ii) we translate TEL recommendations from hypermedia to serious games, and exploit game adaptation strategies in accordance with the variation learning theory.

We propose a case-based approach to the generation of learning plans and game scenarios. While Case-Based Reasoning (CBR) has proven to yield good results for the adoption of on-line tutoring systems, the planning potential of CBR has yet to be exploited in relation to the creation of learning plans. We research how the game-based learning process can be continuously adapted towards the efficient development of required competencies for each individual learner. This entails the use of a planner that collects feedback from the learner interaction with the suggested plans and uses this feedback to learn which parts of the plan are failing and how to recover. As described by Hammond [21], case-based planning (CBP) systems have the capability of learning from the interaction with the human users. They can also anticipate problems and learn how to avoid them. These features make CBP attractive for use in learning environments.

We also research how alternative plans which target the same goals can be represented, and retrieved based on their outcomes for different learners. The retrieved plans are then incrementally instantiated during execution, taking into account the information derived from constant performance monitoring.

The objective of this article is to present a coherent framework for an on-the-fly adaptive planning system for game-based learning. We do not address narrative theory or specific game design. Rather, the focus is on providing a generic model of the atomic learning components for an adaptive personalised planner where competencies are taught through game-based learning strategies. At all times, we attempt to justify our models with reference to current learning theory and state-of-the-art techniques in case-based planning and personalisation.

This research was carried out within the context of the TARGET[1] European Project. TARGET's goal is to implement a new type of Technology Enhanced Learning (TEL) environment which shortens the time to competence for learners within enterprises. As such, the examples in this paper refer to learning topics such as innovation and project management.

The remaining of this paper is structured as follows. The next section summarises related work in personalised recommender systems for learning and related work that leverages the use of CBR for the purpose of supporting human learning. Section "Overview" presents an overview of our research direction in the field of CBP and learning with serious games, and in section "Learning Theory Principles", we show how some modern learning theories can drive the planning and story personalisation. In section "Hierarchical CBP for Personalised Learning Plans" we provide a detailed description of our model of hierarchical CBP for personalised learning plans. Section "Discussion and Future Work" presents a discussion of the implications of our system and some remarks on future work, and then we conclude in section "Conclusion".

Background

Personalised Recommendations in Technology Enhanced Learning

There has been a growing interest in applying recommendation techniques from the e-commerce domain to that of technology enhanced learning. However, for efficient learning, non-technical particularities of the e-learning domain must be considered. Previous work like [14, 32, 41] raises awareness of the differences between personalised recommendations in e-commerce and e-learning. The main guidelines for personalisation stress the importance of considering (i) the learning goal, (ii) prior knowledge of the learner, (iii) the learner's model, (iv) groups of similar learners, (v) rated learning activities, (vi) emerging learning paths and (vii) pedagogical strategies for learning. Our work considers all these aspects, and focuses on how the aspects captured by points (i)–(v) can be used to identify and reuse (vi)—emerging

---

[1] http://www.reachyourtarget.org.

learning paths—, by incorporating (vii)—pedagogical strategies—into the adaptive, personalised recommendation process.

TEL Recommender systems belong to three main categories, similar to their e-commerce ancestors: content-based, collaborative filtering, and hybrid [32]. While TEL recommenders extend classical recommenders by considering the pedagogical needs of the learners rather than only the preferences, they are still subject to drawbacks like: cold-start problem (new learner or new item) and data sparsity [2]. Hybrid recommenders usually overcome part of these problems. In our work, we consider a hybrid approach, combining collaborative filtering techniques with case-based reasoning (CBR) recommenders, a type of content-based approaches [47]. However, in this paper, the main focus lies on the case-based recommendation component. Next section analyses in more detail the related work on CBR and human learning.

Another aspect of interest regarding TEL recommender systems, is the type of recommended material. Most of the works focus on recommending individual learning objects, but in [15], the authors acknowledge the need of suggesting learning paths, where the sequence of the recommended material guides the learner towards achieving his goals. In [26], the authors suggest an adaptive learning plan generator for educational hypermedia. Several alternative paths are generated by analysing the domain concepts ontology and the relations between educational resources, for example, prerequisites. The personalised learning plan is created by computing the suitability of each path to the learner's profile. This work is similar to ours as it uses several abstraction layers in order to extract and personalise learning plans. However, it does not use any machine learning mechanism, therefore constant usage of the system will not improve its performance. More over, as opposed to our work, this model does not consider on-the-fly assessment and adaptation. Nevertheless, the work presented in [26] can be considered complimentary to ours and can be used in a hybrid system as a backup to the CBP approach, which (1) generates learning plans in case of cold-start problems like *data sparsity* and *new item*, (2) validates the ordering of learning resources, and (3) avoids the so-called "conceptual holes" [26] from the learning path.

Case-Based Reasoning and Human Learning

Case-Based Reasoning (CBR) is an artificial intelligence paradigm that involves reasoning from prior experiences: it retains a memory of previous problems and their solutions and solves new problems by reference to that knowledge. This is the main difference from rule-based reasoning systems, that normally rely on general knowledge of a problem domain, and tend to solve problems from scratch or from first principles. Usually, the case-based reasoner is presented with a problem (the current case). In order to solve it, the reasoner searches its memory of past cases (the case base) to find and retrieve cases that most closely match the current case, by using similarity metrics. When a retrieved case is not identical to the current case, an adaptation phase occurs. During this phase, the retrieved case is modified, taking the differences into account [37]. Finally, the cases are retained in the case base for future use. These four steps are defined by Aamodt and Plaza [1] as Retrieve, Reuse, Revise, and Retain.

Developed from CBR, case-based planning (CBP) systems address problems that are represented by goals and have solutions that are plans. Like traditional case-based reasoners, CBP systems build new cases out of old ones. Unlike CBR systems, CBP systems put emphasis on the prediction of problems: when encountering a new plan, CBP systems anticipate the problems that can arise and find alternative plans to avoid the problems. Plans are indexed by the goals satisfied and problems avoided [21].

CBR for human learning purposes has been a topic of study for a number of years, with significant developments in the fields of intelligent tutoring systems and adaptive hypermedia. The appeal of a CBR approach is partly due to its roots in cognitive science which focuses on modeling human problem-solving behaviour [39]. There are many examples in the literature of day-to-day human reasoning and planning that highlight the important role of previously experienced situations and of analogy in human problem solving [29, 43, 44]. In [44], Schank argues for a goal-based approach to education, in which case acquisition plays a central role. In [29], Kolodner suggests how CBR can enhance problem-based learning by recommending relevant problems to learners. In both goal-based and problem-based learning, learning occurs in the context of attempting to achieve a mission or find a result.

The research done by Jonassen and Hernandez-Serrano [25], also supports the use of CBR for instructional design based on problem solving. The authors argue for a story-based system supported by CBR that would enable learning from other people's experiences. These experiences form a case library of narratives from employees that describe real-life work-related problems and their solutions. Each experience must have a particular lesson to be learned that the user can reference in a similar situation. This idea resonates well with a game-based learning environment where learners' experiences are saved in common accessible repository. However, we are focused on how to create a suitable learning plan, rather than on how to retrieve a similar narrative.

The ILMDA (Intelligent Learning Material Delivery Agent), designed by Soh and Blank [51] focuses on the learning domain of computer science of undergraduates. It combines CBR with system meta-learning that demonstrating that a detailed analysis and adaptation of the learning process can be used to improve students' results. An approach that comes closer to serious games is presented by Gomez-Martin et al. [18, 19]. They present a metaphorical simulation of the Java Virtual Machine to help students learn Java language compilation and reinforce their understanding of object-oriented programming concepts. Unlike these two systems, where the problems have direct mapping to the correct solution and the targeted domains are well defined, we are creating a system for use in two very complex domains: Project Management and Innovation. In these domains, the problems are open-ended and the required competences are complex and difficult to model. Therefore, our approach is to create an open environment capable of reasoning with very complex, poorly structured domain knowledge. Furthermore, we focus on long term learning goals. For this, a single learning episode is not enough; the system must design consistent and coherent *learning plans*. As such, we use a CBP approach rather than classical CBR.

However, none of these approaches use CBR as a recommendation engine. CBR can be used for recommendations as shown in [47]. Technically, the main difference we consider between a case-based reasoning system and a case-based recommender system, is that while the former imposes the top solution, the latter returns top-n solutions and recommends them. The inner processing done to rank the results is similar in both types of systems. Previous research that considered CBR for recommending learning activities is presented in [17]. The work provides a simplified CBR model, without the revision/adaptation phase. Our model extends this work by exploiting adaptation methodologies inspired by learning theories. More over, our work also looks into recommending learning paths. In [14], the authors also consider case-based recommendations as a possible approach, and identify as a main disadvantage of the methodology the fact that "the user is limited to a pool of items that are similar to the items he already knows". We argue that this problem can be avoided by adapting the case retrieval methodology.

Overview

In this section, we introduce the fundamental aspects of case-based reasoning as it pertains to the support of an adaptive learning system. These ideas will be further elaborated by the model presented in section "Hierarchical CBP for Personalised Learning Plans".

In Fig. 1, we illustrate how CBR can be incorporated into the learning process within a game-based learning environment. The core unit of instruction is represented by *stories* which are interactive narratives the learner engages with as he

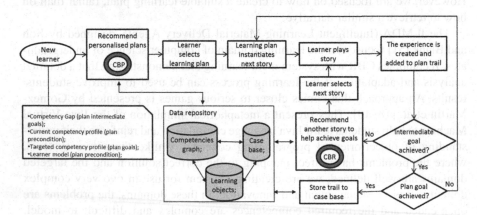

Fig. 1 Proposed CBR-supported learning process

assumes a specific role, with a specific mission. A learning plan is composed of a personalised sequence of stories. The learning plan is created in a two stage process. First, several *abstract plan* are created and recommended, as a sequence of story templates. Then, the actual learning plan is instantiated incrementally, each story being created starting from the corresponding story template, when the plan execution thread reaches it. This process is the central focus of our paper and is described in more detail in the section "Hierarchical CBP for Personalised Learning Plans".

Throughout a story execution, towards the achievement of his mission, the learner is put in various *situations* meant to develop and evaluate his competencies. Each story has at its core a *story template* which can accommodate several situations. In order to create a story starting from a story template, a sequence of these potential situations is selected, based on the learner needs and requirements.

The Data Repository

In this section, we describe the repositories that contain the competency knowledge, the raw learning objects and the cases.

The Competencies Graph

The term competency carries many definitions in the related literature [22]. The definition that matches the best the way we use and assess competencies is that they are a set of personal characteristics, knowledge, skills and abilities that help successfully perform certain tasks, actions or functions and are relatively stable across different situations [54]. Many companies use the IPMA Competence Baseline[2] which breaks project management in 46 competences, or SHL Universal Competency Framework[3] which defines the "great eight" cross-domain competencies, in order to model and structure the competencies of their employees. The initial TARGET competency framework will use these frameworks. However, each TARGET user community will also be able to contribute to the competency framework. Thus, the set of competencies is very likely to become very versatile as the community of users represent different educational backgrounds, work history and business domains.

The competencies of an individual are characterised by a state of attainment (degree of mastery) which we call level, and which the system estimates by analysing the user's *performance*. Therefore we define a competency profile as a set of competency-level pairs. A learner in our system has assigned both a *current competency profile*, and a *targeted competency profile*.

In this work, we consider the system being deployed and used within enterprises, each TARGET instance having its own competency representation, imposed by the

---

[2] http://www.ipma.ch/certification/standards/Pages/ICBV3.aspx.

[3] http://www.shl.com/OurScience/Documents/SHLUniversalCompetencyFramework.pdf.

particular enterprise. The set of competencies is very likely to strongly differ among domains and communities. While the framework presented in this work could theoretically fit a Web-based online learning environment, an important research challenge would be to organise domain concepts and competencies so that they can deal with users of very different cultural background. One option would be the use of encyclopedic knowledge bases like DBpedia[4] to extract relations between concepts, and use this graph to create learning paths. Semantic Web technologies can be used to link the DBpedia concepts to the serious games annotated as learning objects metadata, according to [23]. For sake of generality, the only assumption we make about the competencies, is that from their representation, dependency (e.g. prerequisite) relations can be extracted, which would then be used to guide the learning plan creation.

The Learning Objects

The stories represent the personalised learning material that is generated for each learner and are part of the case base described in the next subsection. They are created starting from story templates by the TARGET game engine. These story templates, together with the competency-training situations are stored in the Learning Objects Repository. The TARGET game engine has the responsibility of creating stories from these "raw" learning objects (story templates) by selecting the required competency-training situations, player roles and level, non-player characters and narrative thread. While the TARGET game engine and its story creation mechanism are outside the scope of this paper, we give in section "Story Generation Toy Example" a brief example of a story template and its "child" stories.

The Case Base

At the core of any CBR system is the case-base, which in this context brings together all the experiences created by learners using the system. In a CBR system, a case denotes a problem-solution pair. In our system, the problem is represented by the goal, preconditions and learner model, as shown in Fig. 1. Still, depending on the solution, we have two kinds of cases: story cases, where the solution is a story, and plan cases where the solution is a plan. A plan is an ordered sequence of stories. Experiences are instances of stories created each time a learner plays a story, whereas trails are instances of plans, therefore sequences of experiences. Experiences and trails are used to evaluate the stories and plans respectively. On the basis of these definitions, we can formalise the case knowledge of the system as containing a set of knowledge assets with a story at the core. Each story holds references to the experiences it has seeded. The stories are interconnected into plans, which are associated with a set of trails that link together experiences. These knowledge assets have associated social data created by the community, such as feedback, ranking,

---

[4] http://dbpedia.org.

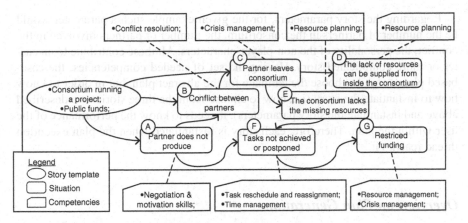

Fig. 2 Example of story template and potential situations

peer assessment, tags, etc. Section "Hierarchical CBP for Personalised Learning Plans" contains the details on case representation.

Other knowledge that such an integrated system would use are the social network and the game mechanics, but their description is outside the scope of this paper.

Story Generation Toy Example

Figure 2 illustrates an example of a story template with its corresponding possible situations, and the competencies trained and evaluated in each situation. The situations are labeled with letters A-G. The arrows which lead from one situation to another show the possible flows of situations. For example, situation A *"Partner does not produce"*, can lead to one or both situations B *"Conflict between partners"* and F *"Tasks not achieved or postponed"*. The dashed lines in the figure illustrate the links between situations and the related competencies. For example, situation B trains and evaluates *conflict resolution*.

For each story template, an instantiated story consists of one path through its graph of situations. The game engine will instantiate the story according to the requirements of the learner as stated by the CBP module. The story instantiations consists of: (i) selection of the story situations, (ii) instantiation of story parameters. Given the example in Fig. 2, we can consider a user who wants to train in conflict resolution, crisis management and resource planning. Then, a candidate story is created by switching on the situations B, C and D. To train in the required competencies, the learner chooses the role of project coordinator. During his experiences, the user is first evaluated on how he handles the conflict between the partners. Then he is evaluated on how he manages the situation where a partner leaves the consortium where other partners have sufficient resources to overcome the loss. Other candidate stories starting from the same template can be: $B \rightarrow C \rightarrow E$, or even $B \rightarrow C \rightarrow E \rightarrow F \rightarrow G$, which would suit a more experienced learner, or a learner who needs a more complex story.

Regarding the story parameters, for the given example such a parameter would be the number of partners in the consortium, the number of partners involved in the conflict, the personality of the non-player-characters. All these contribute to an easier or more complicated story. Having the set of needed competencies, the case-based planner might choose the template for the abstract plan, but in order to know how to instantiate the story (i.e, how to choose from the three stories we described above and instantiate the story parameters), it needs to know the performance of the user within the plan. Therefore, each story is instantiated when the plan execution thread reaches it.

Overview on Plan Generation

At the start of the process, the learner decides to achieve more competencies. A case for the case-based planner is derived from the plan goal (targeted competencies), by the set of possible intermediate goals (competency gap), and the plan preconditions (the learner model and his current competencies).

Drawing on this data and on the competencies knowledge, the system uses case-based planning to generate personalised plans for the learner. From a list of recommended learning plans, the learner chooses the one he prefers. As he or she plays, an experience is generated and added to his or her trail.

Depending on the learner's performance, the system decides if the intermediate competencies have been achieved. If the learner has failed to achieve them, the case-based planner identifies the situation as a failure and tries to recover in two ways: (i) the planner anticipated the problem and will have already assigned a recovery plan for a particular story. If this is the case, the planner will choose the recovery plan with highest eligibility value; (ii) otherwise the planner will undergo a CBR process to recommend other stories to the learner in order to bring him or her to the required standard in relation to the intermediate competencies. This is similar to the process suggested by variation theory of learning which states that a key feature of learning involves experiencing that phenomenon in a new light [34]. When all the goals of the plan have been achieved, the trail is saved and becomes part of the case base.

The plan generation described above uses a case-based planning approach based on 4 phases.

Plan Retrieve

Starting with the goals and preconditions, the planner searches the case base to find plans with similar descriptions, which yielded good results for the learner. In order to do this, the system must consider different types of knowledge and reasoning methods such as similarity metrics, utility metrics, statistical reasoning and collective filtering. An important focus of research related to this phase concerns the *new-student problem*. In this situation, the system will not yet hold enough information to be able to assign a learner model to the student. In this context, a conversational CBR (CCBR) approach might be used. A CCBR system is used when the problem is not completely known and, therefore, the traditional retriever has no data to match the cases to. The system starts a conversation with the user, asking him questions which discriminate between learner models by traversing a decision tree. As the learner model is drawn out from this conversation, and the other problem data are known, the system selects the suitable cases. An even more attractive direction would be to adapt CCBR so that, instead of using conversations to figure out the learner model, learners are given stories to play, where the stories are chosen in such a way that the user's actions lead the reasoner along the same discriminative decision tree.

Plan Reuse and Revise

The differences between the goals of retrieved plans and the goals of the current learner are identified and used to adapt the plan. If the goal competencies are not similar, the competencies to be removed are identified and the associated stories are removed from the plan. If the current targeted competencies usually entail the mastery of some new competencies, the plan is adapted so that it targets these competencies. The obtained plan and stories are then analysed using domain knowledge to make sure that they are coherent, and revised if needed.

Plan Retain

The plan and its trail are saved in a temporary storage after it has been played by the learner. Then, periodically these plans and trials are analysed and filtered. For the stories which failed (eg.: the learner did not achieve the related competencies), the planner updates its fail expectation, and saves the recovery plan which worked. The recovery plan is represented by the stories the learner played until they achieved those competencies. At this stage, if the plan is a new one, it is assigned a utility and eligibility value. If the plan is a reused one, these values are updated. When a contingency story has a better eligibility value than the story in the original plan, it replaces the story in the plan. An important challenge here is to filter out the plans and stories which are not considered relevant for future use.

Section "Hierarchical CBP for Personalised Learning Plans" discusses these stages in more detail, as well as case representation.

Learning Theory Principles

Game-based learning has pedagogical foundations in problem-based learning [42], experiential [28] and inquiry-based learning [3]. More-over, they are also able to support other types of learning strategies because the content of the learning material is highly customisable, simulating real life situations, and capturing the learners' actions when they are faced with various tasks. This section describes some learning principles inspired by modern learning theories, that can be supported by the case-based planner overviewed in the previous section.

Principles of Linking Stories in a Learning Plan

The learning plan must be created so that the flow of stories the user engages with, lead him to the targeted competencies. For the creation of the learning plan we must consider the fact that the way learning episodes relate to each other is very important in order to keep the learner motivated and on the flow. There are several aspects which we focus on in creating the learning plans. First of all, we have to consider if there exists a domain model where possible competencies are represented and have specific relations between them (e.g. decomposition, prerequisites, constraints). These relations are extracted from the Competencies Graph illustrated in Fig. 1 and they guide the ordering of the story templates in the abstract plan.

Secondly, it is important that the learning plan builds new competencies on top of existing ones. Following this principle, the competencies are developed both horizontally and vertically. By horizontally we mean the development and association of new competencies from existing ones, and by vertically we mean reaching higher levels of mastery in a competency. Thus, in the learning plan the story complexity and the difficulty will increase as the user performs.

The third principle is that learning needs practice, and often recursiveness and/or repetition. The *variation theory of learning* [34] and the *cognitive flexibility theory* [53] argue that practice of the same thing in different contexts, not pure repetition, leads to better learning outcomes. Following this principle, a learning plan should train the same competency in typical but varied situations until the learner reaches the desired level and also subject him to at least one atypical situation.

While in the case of case-based planning the plans are usually extracted from the case-base, these principles must be enforced (1). in the case of *data-sparsity* problem when plans must be built from scratch for example in a manner close to [26] and (2). when new learning plans are obtained as adaptations of existing ones, in the "revise" stage of the CBP process.

Principles for Personalised Story Recommendation

Besides plan generation, we use a case-based reasoner to recommend stories which might help the learner get over the stages where he or she gets stuck in the learning process. When the learner fails to achieve the supposed intermediate goals, the planner detects a fail. This failure might be interpreted by the planner as either an expectation failure or plan failure. A learner might get stuck in a game by not making any relevant progress, which can lead to frustration. The learner is assessed on-the-fly [45], his actions being evidences for competency assessment, as well as for his emotional state [4]. This embedded formative assessment can guide the story personalisation. In this case, the case-based reasoner suggests targeted stories or story episodes, starting from one which poses problems to the learner, but adapted based on the variation patterns from *variation theory of learning*.

The proponents of the variation theory of learning define four main patterns of variation that facilitate learning [33]: (i) *contrast*—experience the world with or without the property of interest; (ii) *generalisation*—experience various worlds containing the object of interest; (iii) *separation*—experience the property of interest by varying it while other aspects stay the same; (iv) *fusion*—experience related or dependent properties of interest simultaneously. Therefore, these dimensions of variation can be employed by the case-based recommender in the adaptation stage of the CBR process. A preliminary study on how variation theory can be implemented in a serious games scenario is presented in [40].

The case-base can be used to also recommend similar experiences of other learners. This enables the environment to integrate *case-based learning (CBL)*[5] [20]. CBL allows the students to view how others act, analyse and compare with their own actions and has already been successfully used in serious games.

In addition, the system should show the learner graphs and statistics on their performance and their learning patterns. In this way, learners have the chance to analyse their overall progress and how it was achieved, and thereby have facilitated *meta-learning* [35], a process of being aware and taking control of one's own learning.

Hierarchical CBP for Personalised Learning Plans

Reasoning with Abstraction to Build Learning Plans

In a game-based learning environment, a learning plan is an ordered list of stories meant to support the learner until he reaches the desired competency profile. The learning plan has to be adapted to the learner data like age, gender, cultural background. As well, it has to dynamically adapt based on the learner performances within the plan. This means that the planner does not have enough knowledge to create the whole plan in the initial stage of the planning. Therefore, at this stage several abstract plans are created, as sequences of story templates, and the learner can choose which one to execute. The story instances are created on-the-fly based on the story templates as the plan execution thread reaches them. At this stage the

---

[5] Please note that although case-based learning uses similar wording as case-based reasoning, we use it here to denote a human learning and teaching strategy, and has nothing to do with machine processes.

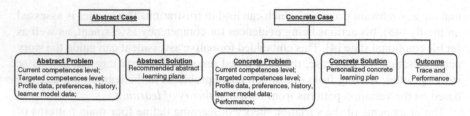

Fig. 3 Single case components

system has accumulated knowledge from the user's performances so far, and can individualise each story.

This methodology is inspired from the use of abstraction in case-based reasoning. By using abstraction, the less relevant features of a problem description are ignored in a first stage, leading to an abstract solution. Then, as the ignored features of the problem are being considered, the final concrete solution is derived from the abstract one [5]. In our case, the reasoner does not ignore features of the problem, but has to reason with an incomplete problem, which becomes complete as the solution is executed.

Following this hierarchical model, the abstract cases solve the problem requirements related to competency needs and learner profile data, by suggesting several abstract plans. The concrete cases have the problem enriched with the learner's performances, and therefore the solution is an iteratively created concrete learning plan. The two types of cases are represented in Fig. 3.

Hierarchical Case-Based Planning

For planning on several layers of abstraction, many terms have been used in literature, the most common ones being hierarchical case-based reasoning [49] and stratified case-based reasoning [9]. The basic idea is that in the hierarchy of cases, only the "leaf" cases are concrete, and all the other nodes are "abstract cases". The studies presented in [6, 9, 49], to name just a few, prove the advantages of this approach. Compared to classical case-based planning, it shows significant improvements in efficiency of retrieval and adaptation.

There are still differences in these approaches. In some of them, the abstract cases are created by abstraction and generalisation [1] of concrete cases. This is a bottom-up process which consists of merging concrete cases based on similar features. These are then discriminated based on their specific features, obtaining a hierarchical tree structure. In these systems the plans are retrieved entirely, and the new solutions are created by adapting them, e.g., in the PARIS system [6]. Other approaches create the abstract cases starting from task or goal decomposition. The concrete cases are the atomic actions which cannot be decomposed any more. The work described in [31] uses such an approach. In these type of systems, each planning step is retrieved individually and then they are integrated to form the adapted solution. Another system, Déjà-Vu [49], combines the two types of hierarchies.

In our research, each planning step (a story instantiation) is not retrieved individually but is adapted by the user's previous interactions. Hence in our approach plan instantiation and the final steps of plan adaptation occur together. Generated abstract plans are presented to the user and he makes the choice of which one to follow. Every story generation is directly followed by user execution and system evaluation. The results are used to create new tasks for the subsequent steps.

In our solution, there are two levels of abstraction. In the systems which use abstraction it is common that the depth of the hierarchy is flexible, as the abstract cases are generated dynamically as soon as new cases share common features. The results of [9] show a significant improvement in efficiency when 3–4 levels of abstractions are used. If this proves to be valid in our system too, we will consider the option of using dynamic abstraction within each of the two current layers.

Abstract Plans

Abstract Case Representation

In order to represent the abstract cases we have to consider that there can exist multiple learning plans achieving the same learning goals. Consequently, all the plans which have similar initial states and goals are grouped under the same root. Then a description node is created for each abstract plan. This description node contains the users who executed the plan in the past, and a summary of their experiences (the plan outcome). This abstract plan outcome includes information like the time the user needed to complete the plan, the average number of story repetitions, and the performances. It is important to note that this summary, although part of the abstract case representation, is extracted from the concrete layer. This way, we compensate for the loss of information which is inherent in reasoning with abstract cases [6]. Including this information in the description node gives us the possibility of combining CBR with collective filtering. In this scenario, collective performance information from similar learners will help in ranking candidate cases. The model also supports the inclusion in the description of learners who were recommended the plan but did not choose to execute it. This information lends itself to providing explanations (e.g. 8 out of 10 learners selected this plan, 6 out of 8 learners completed this plan).

The description nodes have as children the abstract plans they describe. This hierarchy is illustrated in Fig. 4. As mentioned in section "Overview", an abstract plan is a list of story templates. In Fig. 4, the abstract plan 1 is composed of the story templates $ST1 \rightarrow ST2 \rightarrow ST3$, and the abstract plan 2 is $ST4 \rightarrow ST3$.

The figure shows that the learners *Learner 1*, *Learner 2* and *Learner 3* have similar initial and goal competency states. Still, both *Learner 1* and *Learner 2* chose the *Abstract plan 1*, while *Learner 3* chose *Abstract plan 2*. Let us define the initial

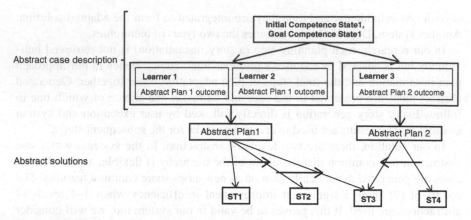

Fig. 4 Abstract case representation; ST—story template

competency state as *(conflict resolution, beginner), (negotiation, average), (crisis management, beginner), (resource planning, upper average)* and the goal competency state as *(conflict resolution, average), (crisis management, average), (resource planning, expert)*. Then, the story template illustrated in Fig. 2 is a good candidate for being part of the two abstract plans. Moreover, since it brings together all the goal competencies, it is a good candidate for being *ST3*.

Each story template in the abstract plan, has assigned the competencies it has to train and evaluate within that plan, and an initial set of tasks, based on the available knowledge about the learner. For example, let us consider the story template in Fig. 2 is labeled *ST3* in Fig. 4. Then, within the two abstract plans, the template is assigned the tasks to select situations which match *conflict resolution, negotiation, crisis management* and *resource planning*, since these are the competencies it was chosen for, even if it can support situations addressing other competencies as well.

This information is kept latent until the instantiation process, when the story is created. It can be seen as an explanation why the template is part of the abstract plan. Still, this data is not enough for a personalised story. To personalise the story, more tasks to fulfill are assigned to the template as described later in section "Planning on First Principles".

Abstract Plan Retrieval and Reuse

The retrieval of the abstract learning plan is a top-bottom traversal of the tree presented in Fig. 4. This consists of two main steps: during the first step the system matches the current problem's initial state and goal to existing cases in the case base. Considering Fig. 4, this stage retrieves a set of nodes from the first level.

During the second step the system first retrieves the child nodes of the nodes returned after the first step. Then, for each such child it computes a *suitability* value,

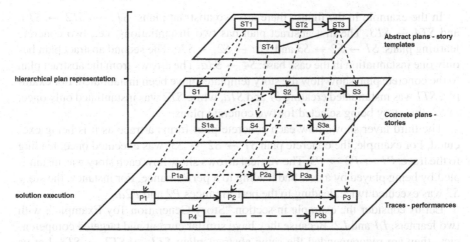

Fig. 5 Learning plans hierarchy; ST—story template; S—story; P—performance

rather than a similarity value. The suitability value takes into consideration the learner similarity, the plan outcome for him and as well adaptation complexity [48].

After the most suitable abstract plans are retrieved, they are adapted so that they fulfill all the problem's requests: they fit the learner, his current competency profile as well as his targeted competencies. The adaptation consists of adding/removing/replacing story templates from the original abstract plan. At this stage, the system has to make sure that the order of trained competencies and story templates respects the constraints described in section "Learning Theory Principles".

Concrete Cases

Concrete Case Representation

Concrete case representation inherits from hierarchical representation used by Smyth et al. in Déjà-Vu [49]. The similarity comes from the fact that stories are generated step by step, therefore the final concrete solution is obtained by integrating the individual stories. Still, our suggested planner executes each step before instantiating the next. Both approaches permit multiple case reuse, which means that each planning step can be retrieved and reused from multiple cases.

As described in Fig. 3, a component of the concrete problem is the set of previous user performances. Therefore, a learning plan that has been even partially executed by the learner is stored along with its performance score as a plan trace. The performances are analysed and depending on the result, the system selects and tailors the next story to play. Figure 5 shows the concrete plans layer, standing between the abstract plans layer and performance layer.

In the example in the figure, there are two abstract plans: $ST1 \to ST2 \to ST3$, and $ST4 \to ST3$. The first abstract plan has two instantiations, i.e., two concrete learning plans: $S1 \to S2 \to S3$ and $S1a \to S2 \to S3a$. The second abstract plan has only one instantiation in the case base: $S4 \to S3a$. The arrows from the abstract plan to the concrete plan show how the story templates have been instantiated. For example, $ST1$ was instantiated creating $S1$ and $S1a$, while $ST2$ was instantiated only once, in $S2$, this story being selected for two concrete plans.

The third layer shows how each concrete plan forms a trace as it is being executed. For example, the concrete plan $S1 \to S2 \to S3$, was executed once, leading to the trace: $P1 \to P2 \to P3$. The vertical arrows show how each story was instantiated by being played by a user and leading to a performance. For instance, the story $S2$ was executed twice, leading to the performances $P2$ and $P2a$.

Let us consider the example in section "Story Generation Toy Example", with two learners, $L1$ and $L2$. Because they have similar current and targeted competencies, they are recommended the same abstract plan: $ST1 \to ST2 \to ST3$. Let us further consider that the story template in Fig. 2 is labeled $ST3$ in Fig. 5. Before the instantiation of $ST3$, the learner $L1$ has executed two stories, $S1$ and $S2$, with performances $P1$ and $P2$. At the same stage, the learner $L2$ has executed the stories $S1a$ and $S2$ with performances $P1a$ and $P2a$, respectively. As the planner analyses the performances, $L1$ seems to make a good progress and successfully execute the tasks is short time. The planner can then decide to instantiate the $ST3$ template to a complex story, therefore creating story $S3$ as the flow of situations $B \to C \to E \to F \to G$. To make the story challenging, the planner also chooses to enforce a large consortium, with a spread conflict which determines a key partner to leave and cause a big resource gap. At the same time, if learner $L2$ has a slow progress, with blockages and long idle times, the system can decide to instantiate $ST3$ into $S3a$ as the flow of situations $B \to C \to D$. To make the story accessible, it defines a consortium of 4–5 partners with only two conflicting partners. A partner with a low contribution has to leave, and the lost resources can be covered from within the remaining consortium.

Planning on First Principles

The learning plan is created step by step, by instantiating the story templates of the abstract plan, at the moment they are needed or when the learner requests it.

In order to create the next story, the system needs to interpret the previous performances and modify the remainder of the plan accordingly. Algorithm 1 illustrates how this is done. It uses a task creation and distribution mechanism shown in Algorithm 2: after a performance has been analysed a list of tasks is created. If the learner failed to reach the level planned for the current story, the planner can recommend him to replay a variation of the same story with a different difficulty level. Otherwise, the planner sends the package of tasks to the first subsequent story template. The story template keeps for itself the tasks which it can achieve and sends the rest further to the subsequent template in the plan, and so on. In case a story template

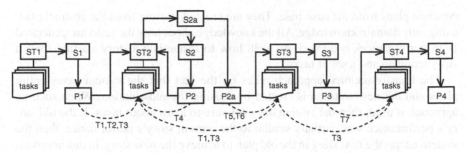

Fig. 6 Plan instantiation example

cannot satisfy any new task, it is considered that it needs no further personalisation, and it is instantiated based on its initial set of tasks, set by the abstract plan.

An example of the concrete-plan creation process based on the task distribution is presented in Fig. 6. The dashed arrows in the figure show how each performance triggers the delivery of tasks to the subsequent story template, which keeps for itself the tasks it can achieve and sends the rest forward.

As an example, let us consider that the story template *ST3* represents the story template illustrated in section "Story Generation Toy Example", Fig. 2. The template receives the tasks *T1* and *T3* due to the performance *P1*. *T1* states that the complexity of the story should be high, and *T3* requires that the *team management* competency should be approached so that it suits a beginner. *ST3* receives the two tasks but, because *T3* refers to a competency the story template cannot address, it can only keep *T1*. *T3* is sent further to the next story template. Due to previous performance *P2a*, *ST3* also receives tasks *T5* and *T6*. *T5* states that the competency *crisis management* should be approached so that it suits an average level learner. *T6* states that the set of competencies needed to successfully achieve the story mission must include the learner's targeted competencies, but not exclusively.

When *ST3* needs to be instantiated, it has to consider therefore the tasks *T1*, *T5* and *T6*. Because of *T1* and *T6*, the story is created so that it brings a large number of situations. Because of *T5*, the situations have to be chosen and adapted so that *crisis management* is required in many situations, but not very demanding. This requirements lead to the instantiation of story *S3* as the flow of situations $B \rightarrow C \rightarrow E \rightarrow F \rightarrow G$ with parameters instantiated so that situations *C* and *G* cannot be handled unless the learner has an average level of proficiency in crisis management (due to *T5*).

Using CBP Adaptation Techniques to Create Concrete Plans

The way the stories are created at this step from the story templates, can be either based on first-principles, or using one of the case-based-planning adaptation techniques like *derivational* or *transformational analogy* [12, 36, 52]. When the stories are generated on first-principles planning, then the system does not need to retrieve concrete plans from the case-base. They are created starting from the abstract plan, using only domain knowledge. All the knowledge about how the tasks are generated from performances is needed. As well, how to instantiate a story starting from a story template and a set of tasks.

The transformational approach relies on the fact that the system saves entire plans and the new solution is created by reusing the old solution. When such an approach is used, then the system does not care to learn about tasks. If the old story's performance was partially similar to the current story's performance, then the system adapts the next story in the old plan to achieve the new story. In this approach domain knowledge is needed to be able to adapt the old story to the new previous performance.

On the other hand, using the derivational analogy, the cases are adapted based on the way the old solution has been built. Here, the system does not save the entire plans, but the decisions taken which lead to the plan generation. In our case, this would mean that the system does not need to know the stories, it is only interested in the tasks which led to their generation. If the old story's performance was partially similar to the current story's performance, then the system adapts the old set of tasks and creates the new tasks. Using these tasks, it generates the story. Here, the system needs domain knowledge on how to integrate the tasks in the story creation.

The transformational approach can be used when the sequence of story templates in the new plan is similar to the old plan, and there is a high chance that the new learner performs similar to the previous learner. Because this situation is unlikely to happen too often, we suggest the derivational analogy as being more appropriate for our problem. Its proven advantage is that it provides more flexibility, because the planner can replay the derivational trace relative to the new problem [36]. In our case, the derivational trace is represented by the tasks, and because the tasks are not dependent on the next stories, they indeed can be applied to the new plan. Another advantage of derivational approach is that it can be used with introspective case-based planning in order to prune fruitless past tasks.

Still, research and evaluation of the possible approaches has to be done before the best fitted solution can be selected.

Discussion and Future Work

By now, we have presented how learning plans are created for the learners and adapted to match their needs and performances. Another crucial part of case-based systems is the retain phase, during which the system adds the new cases to the case-base. The case base should avoid redundancy and be kept at a size which does not negatively influence the retrieval and adaptation efficiency. For this, we propose to keep all the traces and experiences in a separate storage, and then periodically carry out maintenance analysis [46] to make sure that only the cases which bring value to the case-base are retained.

Keeping the traces of successful and failed plans allows us to analyse the features and feature weighting that are leading to unsuccessful retrievals. Introspective learning techniques for feature weighting are designed to increase or decrease the weights of selected case features on the basis of problem solving performance [7]. Such techniques have also been used to facilitate easier adaptation of cases [30]. Analysing the repository of plan traces using introspective learning should allow us to improve the retrieval of abstract cases and their adaptation to the learner context.

An important aspect of game-based learning that does not make the focus of this paper is related to user's performance assessment. This process is the focus of another component in the TARGET system, which models the relations between competencies and situations (i.e. the dashed lines in Fig. 2). The user's execution during a situation stands as evidence of his level of mastery of the related competencies. The way of automatically interpreting these evidences, assessing the user's competencies and finally student modelling is a challenging research direction on its own. One possible solution would be the use of dynamic belief networks, where the relations between competencies and situations are represented as probabilistic relationships, as suggested by Reye in [38].

Throughout this paper we mention the user data like age, gender and geographical details to be used for finding the suitable plan. Although it has been proven that cultural background, age and gender might influence a person's way of learning, we have to analyse if this data is relevant in our system. Therefore, we will use this data only for analysis during the early stages of the case base. If the analysis of cases proves any relation between learning and these parameters, we will consider them for plan retrieval.

Another aspect we have to consider when plans and stories are recommended is diversity [50]. We need diversity both for the learner and for the system. For the learner, it is important that recommended plans are varied and do not overlap with the user's already executed plans. For the system, it is important that it explores the efficacy of new plans as well, not only relying on old highly evaluated ones.

While the goal of this paper was to present a model of CBP and online learning using serious games, we should discuss our plans for implementation and evaluation. This work is being developed as part of the large European project TARGET, which contains academic and industrial partners and the case-based recommendation engine will be evaluated iteratively in small user trials, as well as fully integrated with the other components of the TARGET system.

Conclusion

We have presented a methodological framework for creating personalised learning plans based on serious games—interactive narratives designed to teach particular competencies. We justified our reasons for proposing a novel a case-based planning approach and described in detail our hierarchical case structure and our iterative retrieval and adaptation process. We proposed that the learning process can be continuously adapted for each individual learner. We showed how alternative plans which target the same goals can be represented, and retrieved based on their outcomes for different learners. The retrieved plans are then adapted on-the-fly, based on an evaluation of the learner's performance. We proposed a hierarchical planning methodology which enables the planner to retrieve and personalise the learning plan for each user. We also examined how plan traces from all learners can be exploited to improve the case-base of learning plans. This work is being developed as part of the European project TARGET and will be evaluated iteratively in small user trials.

Acknowledgements This work was partly supported by the TARGET project under contract number FP7-231717 within the Seventh Framework Program, and by the Lion II project funded by Science Foundation Ireland (SFI) under Grant SFI/08/CE/I1380.

References

1. Aamodt A, Plaza E (1994) Case-based reasoning: Foundational issues, methodological variations and system approaches. AI Comm 7(1):39–59
2. Adomavicius G, Tuzhilin A (2005) Toward the next generation of recommender systems: A survey of the state-of-the-art and possible extensions. IEEE Trans Knowl Data Eng 17(6): 734–749
3. Barab S, Thomas M, Dodge T, Carteaux R, Tuzun H (2005) Making learning fun: Quest atlantis, a game without guns. ETR D 53(1):86–107
4. Bedek M, Seitlinger P, Kopeinik S, Albert D (2012) Inferring a learner's cognitive, motivational and emotional state in a digital educational game. Electron J e-Learn 10(2):172–184
5. Bergmann R, Wilke W (1995) Building and refining abstract planning cases by change of representation language. J Artif Intell Res 3:53–118
6. Bergmann R, Wilke W (1996) On the role of abstraction in case-based reasoning. Advances in case-based reasoning. Lecture Notes in Artificial Intelligence, p 28–43
7. Bonzano A, Cunningham P, Smyth B, et al (1997) Using introspective learning to improve retrieval in CBR: A case study in air traffic control. Lect Note Comput Sci 1266:291–302
8. Boyle E, Connolly TM, Hainey T (2011) The role of psychology in understanding the impact of computer games. Entertain Comput 2(2):69–74
9. Branting K, Aha DW (1995) Stratified case-based reasoning: Reusing hierarchical problem solving episodes. In: IJCAI, p 384–390
10. Charles D, McAlister M (2004) Integrating ideas about invisible playgrounds from play theory into online educational digital games. Entertain Comput ICEC 2004, pp 598–601
11. Connolly TM, Boyle EA, MacArthur E, Hainey T, Boyle JM (2012) A systematic literature review of empirical evidence on computer games and serious games. Comput Educ 59(2):661–686
12. Cox MT, Munoz-Avila H, Bergmann R (2006) Case-based planning. Knowl Eng Rev 20(3): 283–287
13. de Freitas S (2008) Emerging technologies for learning. Technical report, Becta
14. Drachsler H, Hummel H, Koper R (2007) Recommendations for learners are different: Applying memory-based recommender system techniques to lifelong learning. In: Workshop on social information retrieval for technology-enhanced learning and exchange
15. Drachsler H, Hummel H, Koper R (2009) Identifying the goal, user model and conditions of recommender systems for formal and informal learning. J Dig Inform, 10(2):4–24
16. Druckman D, Bjork R (1991) National research council. In the mind's eye: Enhancing human performance. Washington DC: The National Academies Press

17. Gómez-Albarrán M, Jiménez-Diaz G (2009) Recommendation and students authoring in repositories of learning objects: A case-based reasoning approach. iJET 4(S1):35–40
18. Gómez-Martín M, Gómez-Martín P, González-Calero P (2004) Game-driven intelligent tutoring systems. In: Lecture Notes in Computer Science 3166. Springer, New York, p 108–113
19. Gómez-Martin P, Gómez-Martin M, Diaz-Agudo B, González-Calero P (2004) Opportunities for cbr in learning by doing. In: Proceedings of 6th international conference on case-based reasoning (ICCBR). Springer, New York
20. Hammond JS (1976) Learning by the case method. Harvard Business School Publishing Division, Harvard Business School, Boston, MA
21. Hammond K (1990) Case-based planning: A framework for planning from experience. Cognit Sci 14:385–443
22. Harzallah M, Berio G, Vernadat F (2006) Analysis and modeling of individual competencies: Toward better management of human resources. IEEE Trans Syst Man Cybern A Syst Hum 36(1):187–207
23. Hendrix M, Protopsaltis A, Dunwell I, de Freitas S, Arnab S, Petridis P, Rolland C, Llanas J (2012) Defining a metadata schema for serious games as learning objects. In: The fourth international conference on mobile, hybrid and on-line learning
24. IBM and Seriosity (2007) Virtual worlds, real leaders: Online games put the future of business leadership on display. Technical report, IBM and Seriosity
25. Jonassen DH, Hernandez-Serrano J (2002) Case-based reasoning and instructional design: Using stories to support problem solving. Educ Tech Res Dev 50(2):65–77
26. Karampiperis P, Sampson D (2005) Adaptive learning resources sequencing in educational hypermedia systems. Educ Tech Soc 8:128–147
27. Kebritchi M, Hirumi A, et al (2008) Examining the pedagogical foundations of modern educational computer games. Comput Educ 51(4):1729–1743
28. Kolb DA, Boyatzis RE, Mainemelis C (2001) Experiential learning theory: Previous research and new directions. Perspectives on Thinking, Learning, and Cognitive Styles, 227–247
29. Kolodner JL, Hmelo CE, Narayanan NH (1996) Problem-based learning meets case-based reasoning. In: Second international conference of the learning sciences
30. Leake D, Kinley A, Wilson D (1995) Learning to improve case adaptation by introspective reasoning and CBR. Lecture Notes in Computer Science, pp 229–229
31. Lee C, Cheg KYR, Liu A (2008) A case-based planning approach for agent-based service-oriented systems. In: Proceedings of the IEEE international conference on systems, man and cybernetics (SMC 2008), pp 625–630
32. Manouselis N, Drachsler H, Vuorikari R, Hummel H, Koper R (2011) Recommender systems in technology enhanced learning. In: Ricci F, Rokach L, Shapira B, Kantor PB (eds) Recommender systems handbook. Springer, New York, pp 387–415
33. Marton F, Pang MF (2006) On some necessary conditions of learning. J Learn Sci 15(2): 193–220
34. Marton F, Trigwell K (2000) Variatio est mater studiorum. High Educ Res Dev 19(3): 381–395
35. Meyer JHF, Shanahan MP (2004) Developing metalearning capacity in students: actionable theory and practical lessons learned in first-year economics. Innovat Educ Teach Int 41(4): 443–458
36. Munoz-Avila H, Cox MT (2008) Case-based plan adaptation: An analysis and review. IEEE Intell Syst 23(4):75–81
37. Pal S, Shiu S (2004) Foundations of soft case-based reasoning, vol 8. Wiley-interscience, Hoboken
38. Reye J (2004) Student modelling based on belief networks. Int J Artif Intell Educ 14:1–33
39. Richter MM, Aamodt A (2005) Case-based reasoning foundations. Knowl Eng Rev 20(3):203–207
40. Ruskov M, Seager W (2011) What can bits teach us about leadership: A study of the application of variation theory in serious games. In: Ma M, Fradinho Oliveira M, Madeiras Pereira J

(eds) Serious games development and applications, vol 6944 of Lecture Notes in Computer Science. Springer, New York, pp 49–60

41. Santos OC, Boticario J (2010) Modeling recommendations for the educational domain. Procedia CS 1(2):2793–2800

42. Savery JR, Duffy TM (1994) Problem based learning: An instructional model and its constructivist framework

43. Schank R, Abelson R (1977) Scripts, plans, goals and understanding: An inquiry into human knowledge structures. Lawrence Erlbaum Associates

44. Schank RC (1996) Goal based scenario: Case-based reasoning meets learning by doing. Case-based reasoning: experiences, lessons and future directions, pp 295–347

45. Shute VJ, Ventura M, Bauer M, Zapata-Rivera D (2009) Melding the power of serious games and embedded assessment to monitor and foster learning: Flow and grow. In: Ritterfield U, Cody MJ, Vorderer P (eds) Serious games: Mechanisms and effects. Routledge, NY, pp 295–321

46. Smyth B (1998) Case-base maintenance. In: Proceedings of the 11th international conference on industrial and engineering applications of artificial intelligence and expert systems

47. Smyth B (2007) Case-based recommendation. In: Brusilovsky P, Kobsa A, Nejdl W (eds) The adaptive web. Springer, New York, pp 342–376

48. Smyth B, Keane MT (1998) Adaptation-guided retrieval: questioning the similarity assumption in reasoning. Artif Intell 102:249–293

49. Smyth B, Keane MT, Cunningham P (2001) Hierarchical case-based reasoning integrating case-based and decompositional problem-solving techniques for plant-control software design. IEEE Trans Knowl Data Eng 13(5):793–812

50. Smyth B, McClave P (2001) Similarity vs. diversity. Lect Note Comput Sci 2080:347–361

51. Soh L-K, Blank T (2008) Integrating case-based reasoning and meta-learning for a self-improving intelligent tutoring system. Int J Artif Intell Educ 18:27–58

52. Spalazzi L (2001) A survey on case-based planning. Artif Intell Rev 16:3–36

53. Spiro RJ, Feltovich RP, Jacobson MJ, Coulson RL (1992) Cognitive flexibility, constructivism, and hypertext: Random access instruction for advanced knowledge acquisition in ill-structured domains. Constructivism and the technology of instruction: A conversation, pp 57–76

54. Tobias L, Dietrich A (2003) Identifying employee competencies in dynamic work domains: Methodological considerations and a case study. J Univers Comput Sci 9(12):1500–1518

An Approach for an Affective Educational Recommendation Model

Olga C. Santos, Jesus G. Boticario, and Ángeles Manjarrés-Riesco

Abstract There is agreement in the literature that affect influences learning. In turn, addressing affective issues in the recommendation process has shown their ability to increase the performance of recommender systems in non-educational scenarios. In our work, we combine both research lines and describe the SAERS approach to model affective educational recommendations. This affective recommendation model has been initially validated with the application of the TORMES methodology to specific educational settings. We report 29 recommendations elicited in 12 scenarios by applying this methodology. Moreover, a UML formalized version of the recommendations model which can describe the recommendations elicited is presented in the paper.

Keywords Affective computing • Educational recommender systems • Recommendation model • Semantic affective educational recommender systems

Introduction

Affective issues have been modeled to personalize systems that account for the affective states of users. Two competing modeling approaches exist to study the affect: (1) the categorical representation of discrete states in terms of a universal emotions model assuming that affective experiences can be consistently described by unique terms between and within individuals, and (2) the dimensional representation of affective experiences which assumes that the affect can be broken down into a set of dimensions. As to the former, several authors have proposed their own set of universal emotions, being probably Ekman's work the most popular [15]. Regarding the latter, the dimensional model was introduced by Mehrabian [26] as

O.C. Santos (✉) • J.G. Boticario • Á. Manjarrés-Riesco
aDeNu Research Group, Artificial Intelligence Department, Computer Science School,
UNED, C/Juan del Rosal, 16, Madrid 28040, Spain
e-mail: ocsantos@dia.uned.es

N. Manouselis et al. (eds.), *Recommender Systems for Technology Enhanced Learning: Research Trends and Applications*, DOI 10.1007/978-1-4939-0530-0_6,

the pleasure-arousal-dominance space, which describes each emotional state as a point in a three-dimensional space.

From the educational point of view, there is agreement in the literature that affect influences learning (see section "Related Research"). Moreover, from the recommender system field, several experiments have shown some improvements when considering affective issues in the recommendation process [2, 22, 32, 44, 49].

In a previous work [38] we introduced the discussions, from the modeling viewpoint, of how to deal with affective issues in the recommendation process in educational scenarios. The approach follows a generic and interoperable perspective by extending Semantic Educational Recommender Systems (SERS) so that they are able to deal with the emotional state of the learner. In this paper we deepen the modeling of affective recommendations and present the resulting formalized version of the recommendations model in UML, which has been improved to account for an experience focused on modeling affective recommendations elicited with TORMES methodology.

The paper is structured as follows. First, we present related research, commenting on how affective issues are managed in learning environments, introducing how emotions are considered in recommender systems, and finally reporting examples of recommender systems that deal with affective issues in educational scenarios. Then, we introduce the SEARS approach and its modeling issues, highlighting its interoperability features with existing e-learning services. Thereafter, we present the application of the TORMES methodology to elicit affective educational-oriented recommendations in several educational settings and present the feedback received by 12 educators who were asked to validate 29 recommendations elicited in 12 scenarios. Following, we present the UML description of the SAERS. Finally, we discuss the findings, present some conclusions and outline future work. This research is framed in the context of the MAMIPEC project [40].

Related Research

In the last decade, the feedback between e-learning and pedagogical research on the interplay between affect and learning has been of benefit to both [30]. The effectiveness of intelligent tutoring systems, which have traditionally focused on the diagnosis and amendment of cognitive errors of students while learning, can be improved by considering the affective dimension [12, 33, 42]. Tutoring systems have been enriched with e-learning materials that are pleasant, enjoyable, motivating, etc., in brief, designed to favor a positive affective attitude towards learning [5]. In this context, affective modeling [10], a sub-area of affective computing [29], involves detection of users' emotion and adaptation of the system response to the users' emotional state. Affect detection is usually the result of human observation [47] or analysis of hardware sensor data [3, 51]. Multidisciplinary research is thus an outstanding characteristic of this emerging and promising field, as illustrated elsewhere [7, 51].

Thus, affective e-learning systems face two complex tasks: detecting affective states in learners, and reacting appropriately to these states when intervention is suited to support the affective dimension of learning [43]. Ideally the reaction should be adapted both to the individual student and to the learning context, and should be consistent with a long-term instruction strategy [7] that considers students' evolving characteristics. Thereby, the literature about affective e-learning addresses mainly three topics.

The first one is detecting relevant emotions in educational settings. In affective e-learning, the student interactions with the e-learning platform have to be dynamically collected focusing on data relevant to the learning progress and on behaviors that can be seen as affect expressions (e.g. inappropriate task strategies, procedural errors, misconceptions, problem-solving behavior, questionnaire responses, time spent on hints, number of hints selected, etc.). Additionally, physiological parameters that can be disturbed by affective states can be monitored through technology common to other affective modeling areas (e.g. heart rate sensors embedded within office chairs [1]). In particular, physiological sensors can detect internal changes [28], eye positions and eye movement can be measured with an eye tracker [13], user physical actions can be observed in an unobtrusively manner, such as from keyboard and mouse interactions [16], facial and vocal spontaneous expressions [54] or gestures [24]. Combinations of multiple sources of data and contextual information have improved the performance of affect recognition [54]. In this context, machine-learning techniques can be used to discover correlations between affect (e.g. revealed in a post-survey) and observable behavior [20], such as correlations between either emotion indicators or learning attitudes [47] or between student behavior and emotional state [3, 51].

The second topic deals with integrating affective issues in learner models, which is an area that has received a great interest in recent years as a wide range of affective variables have been assessed within interactive learning environments, such as emotional valence (positive or negative emotions), Ekman's basic emotions (e.g. anger, happiness, and fear), cognitively complex states (e.g. joy and shame) or recently to more cognitive-affective states that are more specific to the educational domain (e.g. boredom, frustration, and uncertainty) [14].

Moreover, personality characteristics—commonly measured with the Five Factor Model FFM [18]—account for the individual differences of emotions in motivation and decision making [53]. For instance, students' personality characteristics impact on how students respond to attempts to provide affective scaffolding [33]. Moreover, the learner modeling has to be sensitive to the complex relationship among affect, meta-cognition and learning [45].

The third and last topic focuses on defining pedagogical interventions in response to student emotional states. Affective learning is still an open discipline, relying on general theories, such as constructivist theories, that provide no clear guidelines about instructional practice. It is difficult to determine how best to respond to an individual's affective state [33], so there are open issues to be investigated, such as at which emotion state will the learners need help from tutors and systems [44]. To answer this question, observational techniques on tutoring actions can be carried out to facilitate the externalization of the tutors' decision-making processes during the tutoring support [30]. Given the lack of solid and widely accepted theories, pedagogical interventions are normally based on heuristics that are defined ad-hoc for each particular tutor. These interventions do not only depend on the current emotional state of the student but are also customized for each student and each context via a learner model [30, 33]. Besides including general heuristics, affective e-learning systems often make use of machine learning optimization algorithms to search for strategies to give affective support adapted to individual students [4]. In this context, different pedagogical intervention approaches can be found in the literature: (1) Basing intervention on emotionally animated agents that play the role of affective mirrors or empathetic learning companions [5, 6, 9, 48, 52], or give realism to the interaction with a virtual tutor as in [27]; (2) Teaching meta-affective or meta-cognitive skills about emotion management strategies or affect awareness [7, 44]; and (3) Handling emotions by means of two strategies [7]: (a) emotional induction, when promoting positive emotions while engaged in a learning activity, and (b) emotional suppression, when the focus on an existing emotion disrupts the learning process.

In this context, to date there have been a few recommender systems in educational scenarios that have considered affective issues. They have been used to (1) recommend courses according to the inferred emotional information about the user [19], (2) customize delivered learning materials depending on the learner emotional state and learning context [43] and (3) provide the list of most suitable resources given the learner affective state, provided that the learner fills in (a) her current affective state (flow, frustrated, etc.) and (b) her learning objectives [23]. These systems are typical applications of recommender systems in the educational domain, which mainly focus on recommending courses or content [25, 37, 50]. Furthermore, as for interoperability issues are concerned, although most recommenders are stand-alone applications, the third system (i.e. [23]) shows recent efforts being made to integrate affective recommendation support with existing e-learning services. This is in line with the SAERS approach presented in the next section.

In summary, works in several related fields suggest that educational recommender systems (as part of e-learning systems) can benefit from managing learners' affective state in the recommendation process. From the aforementioned key research questions, in this paper we address how educational recommender systems can model the affective issues involved during the learning process, considering that this modeling has to be managed and integrated with the rest of existing e-learning services. Moreover, given the open issues in affective learning theories, the heuristic knowledge that is applied in everyday instruction practice in learning institutions might be of great importance. As for the current literature on this topic, large parts of this knowledge have not yet been collected. For this, we propose the involvement of educators in order to carry out an exhaustive and methodical compilation of heuristics concerning affective learning, as already suggested in the literature (e.g., see [30]), by applying a user-centered methodological approach combined with data mining techniques [39]. To this end, we are using the TORMES methodology [36], as described below.

Semantic Affective Educational Recommender Systems

To address the aforementioned key research issues, we have investigated the development of Semantic Affective Educational Recommender Systems (SAERS), which take advantage of existing standards and specifications to facilitate interoperability with external components. In particular, in this section we present the modeling issues involved in their development. To support the required semantic characterization and guarantee interoperability, existing standards and specifications should be used. Thus, the information exchanged by the different components involved in the SAERS approach can take advantage of existing standards and specifications from IMS, ISO and W3C, integrating meaningful stand-alone XML fragments from those specifications. In [35] it was discussed which standards and specifications are applicable to describe the different attributes defined in the SERS recommendation model. In addition to those already reported, to deal with the emotional information, the Emotion Markup Language (EmotionML) [43] proposed by the W3C can be used to allow a technological component to represent and process emotional data, and to enable interoperability between different technological components processing these data.

Thus, the SAERS approach [38] is an extension of SERS [35] to deal with affective issues in a multimodal enriched environment where sensors and actuators are key to collect and produce learners' interaction data. This extension involves issues that deal with: (1) user centered design of recommendations, (2) enrichment of the recommendation model and (3) definition of new services in the architecture to support new functionalities to cover the detection of emotions and the provision of emotional feedback in a multimodal environment. As in SERS, SAERS enriches the recommendation opportunities of educational recommender systems, going beyond the aforementioned typical course or content recommendations. In fact, in this approach, both passive (e.g. reading) and active (e.g. contributing) actions on any e-learning system object (e.g. content, forum message, calendar event, blog post, etc.) can be recommended to improve the learning performance, in as much as they are related to educational issues involved [39].

To support the required interoperability SAERS design follows the principles of a service-oriented architecture [11]. The different components involved in the architecture, shown in Fig. 1 using the UML syntax for component diagrams, encapsulate categories of functionalities to be offered as reusable services. The diagram shows the behavior of the main components defined in terms of both provided (symbol ◯) and required (symbol C) service interfaces exposed via ports (symbol ☐). Some of the components exhibit an internal structure where subcontracting of services is represented by means of delegation connectors. These components are: (1) **Learning Environment Interface**, concerning the interface through which the learner carries out the educational tasks with a certain interaction agent (i.e. a device) in an environment where there are information flows from sensors and actuators; (2) **Learner Profile**, responsible for modeling learner needs, interests, preferences, progress, competences, affective states, etc.; (3) **Interaction Agent Model**, responsible for modeling the capabilities and configuration information of the interaction agent used by the learner to access the course space; (4) **SAERS admin**, which supports the recommendations design; (5) **SAERS server**, which is the reasoning component and implements a recommendation knowledge-based system, and (6) **Learning context**, which gathers the interaction data from different sources, such as interaction agent, learning environment and emotional information gathered from sensors. In particular, the latter consists of the **Emotional Data Processor** with the

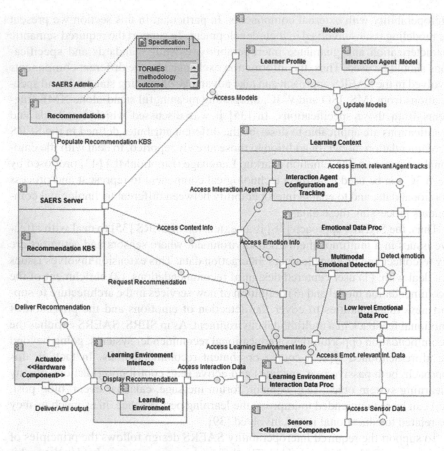

Fig. 1 Main components in the SAERS approach

following subcomponents: (a) **Low Level Emotional Data Processor**, which collects the input from emotional data available such as physiological data, eye positions and movements and physical interactions of the user (movements of the mouse, uses of the keyboard, voice or gestures) and (b) **Multimodal Emotional Detector**, which combines different sources of emotional data gathered to recognize the emotional state of the learner.

In the SAERS approach the learner of a course in an e-learning system is placed in a rich environment where sensors (defined in a general term) get data from her interactions and actuators provide personalized responses through a given interaction agent (e.g. PC, laptop, mobile, etc.), which might be combined with assistive technology (e.g. Braille line, speech recognition software, screen magnifier, among others) when the user requires some accessibility support.

To broadly understand the system dynamics let us assume that at a certain point during the learning process, a recommendation request is received by the *SAERS server* for a specific learner with details about her context in the learning environment, the interaction agent and affective state. To attend the request, the SAERS server requests additional data about the user and the capabilities of the interaction agent to the corresponding models (i.e. *Learner Profile* and *Interaction Agent*), as well as from the context of the user. This information is managed by the *Learning Context*, which processes the information about (a) the configuration and tracking of the interaction agent (b) the emotional state of the user, which is computed from the data received by the *Emotional Data Processor* and (c) interaction data in the learning environment. With this information, the reasoning component (SAERS server) selects the appropriate recommendations taking into account the current affective state of the learner. SAERS server consists of a knowledge-based recommender that store rules, which are managed according to their applicability conditions in order to recommend appropriate actions to be carried out for the current learner (with her individual features, preferences, affective state, etc.) in her current context (including course activity, course history, interaction agent used, etc.). Therefore, with that information, SAERS server looks for recommendations whose applicability conditions matches user features and emotions, interaction agent capabilities and educational context, and take into account predefined runtime restrictions (i.e. constrains). These recommendations are those that have been designed and properly modeled through the *SAERS admin* with the user-centered design methodology called TORMES (Tutor Oriented Recommendations Modeling for Educational Systems) [36]. The resulting selected recommendations that are instantiated for the given request are delivered to the learner by the corresponding actuator in the appropriate affective mode.

In order to facilitate the information exchange among the aforementioned components, a recommendation model is required to semantically characterize the recommendations and bridge the gap between their description by the educator and the recommender logic when delivering affective recommendations in the running course [38]. This recommendation model can be defined along the dimensions of "6 Ws and an H"—What, Where, How, Who, When, Why and Which—(inspired by Sundaresan's reporting of dimensions [46]):

- *What* is to be recommended, that is, the action to be done on the object of the e-learning service (for instance, to post a message in the forum).
- *How* and *Where* to inform the learner about the recommendation, which in a multimodal enriched environment, should describe the modality in which the recommendation has to be delivered to the learner (e.g. text or voice) as well as how the emotions are handled by the actuators when presenting the recommendations to the learner. For instance, a recommendation to be delivered by voice can be provided with a relaxed tone or with an angry tone. This emotional information can be described using the W3C EmotionML specification. In particular, the attribute 'expressed-through' for the modality and the element 'category' for the emotional output.
- *When* and to *Who* produce the recommendation, which depends on defining the learner features, interaction agent capabilities and course context that trigger the recommendation. It describes both the restrictions that may limit recommendation delivery as well as the applicability conditions that trigger the recommendations.

- *Why* a recommendation has been produced, providing the cognitive and affective rationale behind the action suggested.
- *Which* features characterize the recommendations themselves, such as (a) their classification into a certain category from a predefined vocabulary (e.g. active participation; technical support; communication; relevant information; accessibility; motivation, evaluation activities; course materials; progress in knowledge; profile), (b) their relevance (i.e. a rating value for prioritization purposes), (c) their appropriateness for a certain part of the course (e.g. getting used to the platform or if doing course activities), and (d) their origin, that is, the source that originated the recommendation (e.g. proposed in the course design, defined by the tutor during the course run, popular among similar users, based on user preferences).

As commented above, the goal behind this model is to facilitate the recommendation description among the actors involved, both educators and software components. As it is described in the next section, this recommendation model has been validated with some educators, who have applied the TORMES methodology to elicit affective recommendations for their scenarios. In section "Affective Recommendation Model for a Knowledge Based System Approach," we present the resulting UML structure for the affective recommendation model.

Application of the TORMES Methodology

TORMES methodology focuses on involving educators in identifying *when, who, what, how, where* and *why* emotional feedback needs to be provided to each particular learner in a given educational scenario, as well as on *which* features characterize the recommendations [38]. In particular, TORMES adapts the ISO standard 9241-210 to guide educators in eliciting and describing recommendations with educational value for their scenarios [36]. Four activities are defined in an iterative way: (1) understanding and specifying the context of use, (2) specifying the user requirements, (3) producing design solutions to meet user requirements, and (4) evaluating designs against requirements.

To validate the appropriateness of the affective recommendation model proposed in [38] three educators from the Psychology School and three educators from the Computer Science School of the Spanish National University for Distance Education (UNED) were asked to elicit affective oriented recommendations following TORMES methodology. The educators were chosen for several reasons. First, they have been teaching distance-learning courses for more than 10 years each. Second, these distance-learning instructors have also enough experience as classroom instructors. This matters for dealing with emotional aspects since, to date, affection has been neglected in distance learning and mainly addressed in face-to-face courses. However, there are distinctive and unique affective experience issues intricately linked to the computer interaction experience (supported by e-learning platforms).

In addition to that, these participants have been also involved in educational programs focused on dealing with educational innovation and functional diversity, where the pedagogical approaches integrate affective aspects.

Given the lack of straightforward information on student affective states in this context, information was obtained from various sources, such as forum and email messages, as well as occasional telephone calls that express emotions more or less directly. Frequency of learners' communications and interactions in virtual courses may also indicate hidden emotional states. There is no doubt that it is difficult to assess with certainty the emotions involved, their intensity, their permanency, etc. only from these information sources. Nevertheless, educators reported in the interviews that however the circumstances they are able to detect learners' emotional issues that let them react with the appropriate affective support to enhance learning.

TORMES methodology was applied to these six educators by two researchers. Educators completed the following activities of the TORMES methodology: 'Context of use,' 'Requirements specification' and 'Create design solutions.' As a result, an initial set of recommendations was elicited, identifying *when* a recommendation opportunity arises for a particular learner (*who*) in a representative educational scenario, *what* the appropriate recommendation has to be about, *why* it has been selected, *how* and *where* it has to be communicated to the learner, and *which* are the recommendation features.

As for the first activity of TORMES, in order to enrich the context of use educators took into account—apart from their own experience—data from a pilot experiment carried out in July 2012 [40] and the large scale experiment at the 2012 Madrid Science Week that took place in November 2012 [41]. Both experiments informed about the affective detection possibilities available. In these experiments participants were induced emotions while taking some mathematical activities with several levels of difficulty and varied time restrictions. Emotions were detected from their interactions in the e-learning environment through multiple sources, namely questionnaires to gather information about the user personality and sensors to get information about learners' interactions (i.e. eye movements from an eye tracker, face expressions from Kinect, video from a web cam, heart and breath parameters from physiological sensors, and mouse and keyboard movements). After each exercise they were asked to fill in the Self Assessment Manikin (SAM) scale [8] to measure their emotions in a dimensional space.

All that information was considered during the second activity of the elicitation methodology, where relevant educational scenarios were built according to the proposed scenario based approach [34] for the 'Requirements specification.' In this activity, the information obtained from the context of use (i.e. *when, who, what, how, where* and *why*) is used to build representative scenarios of the tutoring task in order to identify recommendation opportunities in them. Here there are two types of complementary scenarios: a problem scenario that identifies the situations where learners were lack of support, and a solution scenario built from the problem scenario that avoids or minimizes those problematic situations by offering appropriate recommendations.

After that, in the third activity, the recommendations proposed were validated in a focus group where educators and researchers were involved. In that process, the recommendations were redefined and described in more detail following the recommendation model, adding the recommendation features to be considered (*which*). Moreover, the resulting recommendations were also presented for evaluation to other educators. Details are provided next.

Some Scenarios and Recommendations Elicited

In this section we report some of the scenarios and recommendations elicited by the three Computer Science educators after applying TORMES as described above, as well as some qualitative outcomes from the evaluation carried out with additional educators who were not involved in the elicitation process. In this initial analysis, 12 affective scenarios were selected for evaluation and are compiled in Table 1. Note that different emotions are considered as responses to the same situations (e.g. Sc3a and Sc3b), proposing different recommendations either in tone or content when different emotions are involved, as shown in Table 2.

To illustrate the result of the elicitation process in terms of a particular recommendation, Tables 2 and 3 provide respectively description and modeling involved for one of the above recommendations. Thus, Table 2 illustrates the first of the above elicited recommendation (Rec-1). The output obtained from the educators' description pointed out the aforementioned key questions, i.e. *when*, *who*, *what*, *how* and *why* the recommendation is to be delivered.

Table 3 shows the above recommendation described in terms of the recommendation model after the focus group validation of the third activity. The attributes of the recommendations (i.e. those to answer the question '*which*') were also added. In order to describe the recommendations, the affective recommendation model proposed in [38] was used as a starting point. However, the practical experience suggested some minor changes in that structure (mainly naming issues), which turned into the up-to-date affective recommendation model presented in the next section in UML.

As introduced above, in the third activity, the scenarios and recommendations in Table 1 were evaluated by 12 educators (six men and six women; age range 30–55) of representative profiles, who have not taken part in the elicitation process. They were questioned to find out their feelings about the scenarios and recommendations elicited by the other three educators. They all had higher education qualifications and experience on both teaching through e-learning platforms and face to face teaching. Ten of them have also been distance learning students. The research field (Recommender systems in e-learning platforms) was well known by seven participants, while two of them had only a vague idea of it, and the remaining three never had heard of it. Their opinions about the relevance of providing affective support to students were diverse. In particular, four considered this issue of critical importance, while other four appreciated its importance but do not regarded it as crucial, and for

Table 1 Affective scenarios and recommendations elicited

ID	Situation addressed	Emotions involved	Recommended content	Tone
Sce 1	Getting used to the platform	Anxiety/frustration/ helplessness	**Rec-1**: Advise a presentation in the forum "Getting started." **Rec-2**: Point to the user manual. **Rec-3**: Technical assistance if required.	Kind, reassuring, understanding, patient, friendly, encouraging
Sce 2	Difficulties defining work plan	Anxiety/confusion/ frustration/ helplessness	**Rec-4**: Advise taking it easy and reassure about own capacities to manage learning. **Rec-5** Advise about planning in distance learning. **Rec-6**: Advise planning in the base of the course working plan.	Kind, calm, suggestive, friendly
Sce 3a	Where to start?	Distraction/indolence/ apathy	**Rec-7**: Point to working plan. **Rec-8**: Point to next learning objective uncovered.	Kind but firm & slightly critical
Sce 3b		Anxiety/confusion/ frustration/ helplessness	**Rec-9**: Point to appropriate learning objects.	Kind, reassuring, suggestive, friendly
Sce 4a	Exam imminence. Going from one learning object to another without focus or focus on inappropriate objects with regards to exam, knowledge & competencies	Anxiety/depression	**Rec-10a**: Point to appropriate learning objects focusing on gaps in knowledge & competencies, & exam objectives **Rec-11a**: Advise study plan review **Rec-12**: Highlight key learning objectives achieved	Empathetic, confident, convincing, encouraging
Sce 4b		Distraction/ detachment	**Rec-10b**: Point to appropriate learning objects focusing on gaps in knowledge & competencies, & exam objectives **Rec-11b**: Advise study plan review **Rec-13**: Highlight importance & imminence of exam	Kind, firm & slightly critical
Sce 5	The learner is critical either of organization, study materials or exam approach	Aggression/sarcasm/ disrespectfulness	**Rec-14**: Thank the criticism, give explanation **Rec-15**: Acknowledge the criticism foundation **Rec-16**: Respect the emotional expression **Rec-17**: Welcome future criticisms **Rec-18**: Ask for a serene tone in future criticisms	Kind but firm, confident, conciliating

(continued)

Table 1 (continued)

ID	Situation addressed	Emotions involved	Recommended content	Tone
Sce 6a	The learner is having problems dealing with certain instructional material. She has successfully completed a significant part of the course	Anxiety	**Rec-19a**: Point to lack of knowledge & misunderstandings underlying the blockage **Rec-20**: Point to appropriate learning objects of less difficulty/review notes/glossary **Rec-21**: Post question for teachers/class mates **Rec-22**: Advise changing activity **Rec-23**: Point to relaxing/amusing learning objects (ed. games)	Empathetic, understanding, cheering, affectionate
Sce 6b		Boredom	**Rec-19b**: Point to lack of knowledge & misunderstandings underlying the blockage **Rec-24**: Point to a more suggestive and entertaining appropriate learning objects addressing the same objectives (i.e. interactive, amusing, interesting, stimulating, inspiring)	Empathetic, confident, convincing, encouraging
Sce 6c		Despair	**Rec-19c**: Point to lack of knowledge & misunderstandings underlying the blockage **Rec-25**: Point to enjoyable appropriate learning objects of less difficulty addressing the same objectives **Rec-26**: Advise share worries with class mates in same situation	Firm, animating
Sce 6d		Impatience	**Rec-19d**: Point to lack of knowledge & misunderstandings underlying the blockage **Rec-27**: Point to more motivating, interesting and entertaining appropriate learning objects of less difficulty addressing the same objectives	Reassuring, critical
Sce 6e		Relaxation/confidence	**Rec-19e**: Point to lack of knowledge & misunderstandings underlying the blockage **Rec-28**: Advise persevere in challenging learning objectives **Rec-29**: Point to enjoyable, motivating, interesting appropriate learning objects of less difficulty addressing the same objectives	Determined, slightly critical, motivating

Table 2 Description of one of the recommendations elicited

ID	Rec-1
TITLE	Advise a presentation in the forum "Getting started."
DESCRIPTION	Foster the learner to send a message to the forum "Getting started" when is new to the platform, has a nervous personality and is anxious.
WHEN and WHO	The learner is getting used to the e-learning platform. She has had just a few sessions in it and has not contributed to any of the platform services. Seems to be a nervous person and appears anxious.
WHAT	Post a message in the forum "Getting started" to present yourself (a link to the forum e-learning service is provided).
HOW and WHERE	In a calm voice from an avatar integrated in the e-learning platform.
WHY	The learner is getting used to the platform, and appears to have much trouble with it. She has not yet used the available services. She seems to be a nervous person and is experiencing quite a lot anxiety. For all these reasons, she should calm down and carry an easy non-educational task (e.g. speak about herself) to practice with a simple task and get confidence with the platform usage before going to the course tasks.

Table 3 Rec-1 described in terms of the recommendation model (see section 6)

Recommendation attributes (which)	ID	Rec-1
	Description	Foster the learner to send a message to the forum "Getting started" when is new to the platform, has a nervous personality and is anxious.
	Category	Technical support
	Stage	Getting used to the platform
	Origin	Tutor
	Relevance	4.2
Recommendation rules (when and how)	Runtime constrains	Context Learning Environment inv self.e-learning services els → exists(els | (els.type = forum) &(els.name = Getting started))
		Context Interaction Agent Model inv self.standards supported std → exists(std | std.name = HTML 3.0)
	Applicability conditions	Context Deliver Recommendation(l: learner) post l.learner_behaviour_record.platform_sessions < 5 l.learner_behaviour_record.service_contributions = null l.learner_profile.personality = nervous l.learner_current_affective_state = anxious
Recommended action (what)	Content	Present yourself in the forum "Getting started"
	E-learning service	Context Deliver Recommendation post result = r | r.e-learning service.type = forum result = r | r.e-learning service.name = Getting started
	Action	Context Deliver Recommendation post result = r | r.e-learning service.action = Post a message

(continued)

Table 3 (continued)

Justification (why)	Message	You are new to the platform and you have not yet used the available services. Since according to your personality profile you trend to be a nervous person and appears to be experiencing some anxiety, you should calm down and carry out an easy non-educational task (e.g. speak about herself) to practice with a simple task and get confidence with the platform usage before going to the course tasks.
	Cognitive	Competence Progress = null
		Course Progress = null
	Affective	Personality = nervous
		Affective state = anxious
Format (how and where)	Emotional delivery (tone)	State = calm
		Actuator = platform avatar
	Output	Modality = voice

Constraints are described using the OCL constraint specification language

the remaining four it was considered dispensable. Moreover, five of participants stated that they were interested in the aims of the research, and two of them were particularly interested in developing strategies to integrate in their teaching practice.

This preliminary study has not shown any gender bias in the questionnaire answers, or any other correlation with the participants' profile.

Preliminary qualitative results showed that each of the 12 scenarios was identified by at least 4 of the educators as recurrent scenarios they often have to deal with in their common virtual teaching practice. Scenarios Sce-2 and Sce-3/b were scored with the highest occurrence rates, while scenarios Sce-4/, Sce-4/b and Sce-6/e were scored with the lowest occurrence rates. Nevertheless, an affective pedagogical intervention was judged as very important also in the later cases. The educators mainly pointed scenarios Sce-1, Sce-2, Sce-5, Sce-6/a and Sce-6/c as those that more clearly demanded pedagogical intervention.

Regarding the recommendations, most of them were considered quite valuable by the educators. The best rated were the recommendations Rec-2, Rec-19/a, Rec-19/b and Rec-14. These recommendations do not fully coincide with the most common interventions of the educators (Rec-2, Rec-19/b, and Rec-20 were identified as most practiced). In particular, educators appreciated very much Rec-14 but this recommendation only ranked third as practiced recommendation for the given scenario. With regard to Rec-8, Rec-7/a and Rec-9/a, some educators stated that they were beyond their capabilities given the lack of the knowledge of the students they required. The lower scores were for Rec-22, Rec-23 and Rec-27.

It is significant that the scenarios that were more familiar to the participants were related to difficulties of the students in learning management. This underlines important weaknesses of virtual courses currently delivered through the e-learning platform that recommender system research is addressing.

It is also remarkable that despite only four of the educators surveyed stated originally that they considered of crucial importance affective teaching, all of them made a fairly positive assessment of the proposed pedagogical interventions. Our analysis also suggests that distance learning educators might not intervene in certain valuable affective ways due to the lack of both resources to detect information about the student and knowledge on the appropriate intervention strategies considering the affective dimension. Furthermore, the educators interviewed considered it important to intervene mainly when the students experience negative emotions, while pedagogical studies show that attitudes involving either indifference or over-optimism can be just as detrimental for academic progress [17]. From the above it would appear that there is little awareness and little training regarding affective educational dimension but a latent sensibility to the issue. Integrating affective recommender systems in e-learning platforms could contribute to raising awareness and training for an affective teaching. Thus, an affective recommender system such as the SEARS proposed here could provide undoubtedly added value to e-learning platforms.

Affective Recommendation Model for a Knowledge Based System Approach

The initial recommendation model that deals with affective information was proposed in [38]. When trying to describe the TORMES elicited recommendations in terms of the recommendations features, some changes in the model structure were identified. The resulting recommendation model has been formalized in UML specification. This model is the formalization of the SAERS specification (based on reusable service oriented components) which considers the elicited knowledge from the affective recommendations. The aim for this formalization is to clarify the architectural issues involved towards the system development, thus specifying the system components, its functionalities and their interoperability. In fact, modeling decisions lie on the advantages of the system architecture, which in the SAERS approach involves standards-based interactions among the different components in an interoperable way.

In Figs. 2, 3 and 4 we present some extracts of this specification showing the more significant classes and associations. The 'when' and 'who' questions are addressed with the Learning Facts class—see Fig. 4. In turn, the 'which' question is

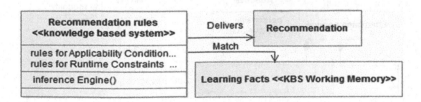

Fig. 2 Main model classes

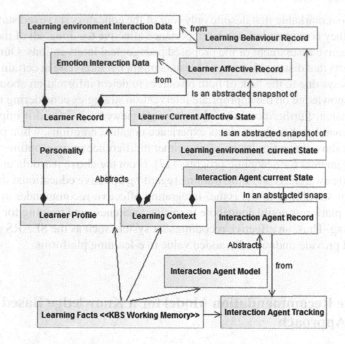

Fig. 3 Learning facts class diagram

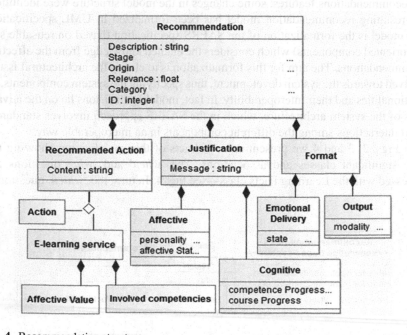

Fig. 4 Recommendation structure

addressed with the *Recommendation* class, the '*how*' and '*where*' questions with the *Format* class, the '*why*' question with the *Justification* class, and the '*what*' question with the *Recommended Action* class—see Fig. 3.

In Fig. 2, the class *Recommendation rules* is stereotyped as << *knowledge based system*>> (KBS) since it is implemented following the knowledge based system paradigm. The class *Learning Facts* is stereotyped as <<*KBS Working Memory*>>, meaning that the facts about the learner and the current learning context constitute the working memory of the *Recommendation Knowledge Based System*. Figure 3 highlights that the facts about the learner consist of a static part (*Interaction Agent Model* and *Learner Profile*) that can be actualized through the learning process, and a dynamic part (*Learning Context and Interaction Agent Tracking*) extracted from the online interaction records.

Black diamond links represent the aggregation relationships. Notice in Fig. 4 that *Recommended Action*, *Action* and *E-learning service* are liked by a ternary relationship, meaning that a customized exclusive action on a specific e-learning service and playing a particular role in a given recommendation is offered. The other two classes (*Justification, Format*) reflect the rest of elements identified.

If compared to the previous version [38], the recommended features are the attributes of the *Recommendation* class and subclasses, the type is described with the *Recommended Action* class and subclasses, the content is described by the *Format* class and subclasses and the applicability conditions and runtime restrictions are described in the *Recommendation rules* class and subclasses. The justification did not change the name but added a couple of subclasses, i.e. *Affective* and *Cognitive*.

This formalized version of the recommendations model in UML, which considers the elicited knowledge from the affective recommendations obtained with the modeling experience carried out with TORMES methodology, is meant to facilitate SAERS development in terms of the interoperable standards-based components presented in section "Semantic Affective Educational Recommender Systems."

Discussion, Conclusions and Future Work

This paper has provided some details of the issues to be considered when eliciting affective recommendations in educational recommender systems. In particular, the process proposed follows the SAERS approach, which is focused on bringing educators to the recommendations elicitation process and which is characterized by considering interoperability issues between recommendations and the rest of e-learning services. In particular, the paper provides an overview of the issues involved in such process and illustrates the main modeling aspects that are to be considered to design affective educational recommendations. These recommendations are elicited following the TORMES methodology, which deal with learners' affective traits in educational scenarios.

The paper has also provided some details of the elicitation process followed by six experienced educators, who were asked to fulfill the modeling issues involved, including the "6 Ws and an H" questions. TORMES has supported them throughout the whole process. Thus, following the scenario based approach recommendations were placed in relevant course situations aimed to emotionally support learners in their interaction within the learning environment. Afterwards, a focus group was used to refine the recommendations and describe them in a more structured way. For this, the recommendation model in [38] was used. Recommendations were properly designed provided that some adjustments were done to the model. The UML description of the model, which considers the elicited knowledge from the affective recommendations obtained with the modeling carried out with TORMES methodology, has been reported in section "Affective Recommendation Model for a Knowledge Based System Approach" to guide the SAERS development in terms of the interoperable standard-based components presented in section "Semantic Affective Educational Recommender Systems." Moreover, scenarios and recommendations elicited were evaluated by 12 additional educators. In general terms, they found them as valuable affective pedagogical interventions. However, in some cases, educators pointed out that applying them into real practice was beyond their capabilities given the difficulties involved in detecting them in real learning scenarios. This shows that distance learning educators might not intervene in certain valuable affective ways due to the lack of resources related to dealing with the student affective state and applying appropriate intervention strategies. As a result, it is expected that an affective recommender system, such as the SEARS proposed here, provides added value to e-learning platforms.

In the context of the MAMIPEC project we aim to progress on this research, mainly by carrying out a compilation of heuristics concerning affective learning by applying the TORMES methodology for eliciting educational recommendations, which later can be delivered in the learning scenarios with the SAERS. Given the lack of sound theories on affective learning, the heuristic knowledge that is applied in everyday instruction practice in learning institutions is of great importance. Judging from the current literature on this topic, large parts of this knowledge have not yet been collected. Several research questions can be posed in this respect, such as (a) "Does affect improve recommendation accuracy compared to a non-affective recommender systems?," (b) "Do affective recommendations improve student satisfaction?," or (c) "Do affective recommendations increase student performance?."

Regarding interoperability, we have considered the W3C EmotionML specification. However, there are other specifications that might be of interest, such as the Attention Profiling Mark-up Language (APML)[1] and the Contextualized Attention Metadata (CAM).[2]

A large scale experiment is to be carried out to evaluate the effects of the affective recommendations elicited when they are delivered in the e-learning system, as described in the fourth activity of the TORMES methodology (Evaluation of designs against requirements). The infrastructure provided in the experiment carried out in

---

[1] APML: http://apml.areyoupayingattention.com/

[2] CAM: https://sites.google.com/site/camschema/home

the 2012 Madrid Science Week to investigate the detection of changes in the emotional state of learners is being extended to deliver the recommendation support following the SAERS approach. In order to design the evaluation plan, user centered-evaluation frameworks [21, 31] are to be considered to explain the user experience.

In summary, open issues in the field deal with the detection of learners affective states while interacting with the e-learning platform, the elicitation of proper strategies to support learners in these situations and their automatic delivery through SAERS.

Acknowledgments Authors would like to thank the European Commission and the Spanish Government for funding the projects of aDeNu research group that have supported this research work. In particular, MAMIPEC (TIN2011-29221-C03-01), A2UN@ (TIN2008-06862-C04-01/TSI) and EU4ALL (FP6-2005-IST-5). Moreover, they would also like to thank the educators who were involved in the recommendations elicitation process, as well as in the corresponding evaluation.

References

1. Anttonen J, Surakka V (2005) Emotions and heart rate while sitting on a chair. In: Proceedings of the ACM conference on human factors in computing systems. ACM, New York, NY, pp 491–499
2. Arapakis I, Moshfeghi Y, Joho H, Ren R, Hannah D, Jose J, Gardens L (2009) Integrating facial expressions into user profiling for the improvement of a multimodal recommender system. In: Proceedings of the IEEE International conference on multimedia and expo. IEEE, Washington, DC, pp 1440–1443
3. Arroyo I, Mehranian H, Woolf BP (2010) Effort-based tutoring: An empirical approach to intelligent tutoring. EDM 1–10, 2010
4. Arroyo I, Cooper DG, Burleson W, Woolf BP (2010) Bayesian networks and linear regression models of students' goals, moods & emotions, 3rd International conference on educational data mining EDM 2010, Pittsburgh, PA, USA, June 11–13, 2010
5. Arroyo I, Woolf B, Cooper D, Burleson W, Muldner K (2011) The impact of animated pedagogical agents on girls and boys. Emotions, attitudes, behaviors and learning international conference of advanced learning technologies, ICALT 2011, Athens, GA, July 2011
6. Baldassarri S, Cerezo E, Seron FJ (2008) Maxine: a platform for embodied animated agents. Comput Graph 32(4):430–437
7. Blanchard EG, Volfson B, Hong YJ, Lajoie SP (2009) Affective artificial intelligence in education: from detection to adaptation. In: Proceedings of the 2009 conference on artificial intelligence in education: building learning systems that care: from knowledge representation to affective modelling (AIED 2009). Ios Press, Amsterdam, pp 81–88
8. Bradley MM, Lang PJ (1994) Measuring emotion: the self-assessment manikin and the semantic differential. J Behav Ther Exper Psychiatr 25(I):49–59
9. Burleson W, Picard R (2007) Evidence for gender specific approaches to the development of emotionally intelligent learning companions. IEEE Intell Syst 22(4):62–69
10. Carberry S, de Rosis F (2008) Introduction to special issue on affective modeling and adaptation. User Model User Adapt Interact 18(1):1–9
11. Channabasavaiah K, Holley K, Tuggle EM (2004) Migrating to a service-oriented architecture, IBM White paper, April 2004
12. Craig SD, Graesser AC, Sullins J, Gholson B (2004) Affect and learning: an exploratory look into the role of affect in learning with AutoTutor. J Educ Media 29(3):241–250
13. de Lemos J, Sadeghnia GR, Ólafsdóttir I, Jensen O (2008) Measuring emotions using eye tracking. Proceedings of measuring behavior. Noldus Information Technology, Maastricht, p 226

14. Desmarais MC, Baker RSJD (2012) A review of recent advances in learner and skill modeling in intelligent learning environments. User Model User Adapt Interact 22(1–2):9–38

15. Ekman P (1999) Basic emotions. In: Dalgleish T, Power T (eds) Handbook of cognition and emotion. Wiley, New York, NY

16. Filho J, Freire O (2006) On the equalization of keystroke time histograms. Pattern Recogn Lett 27(12):1440–1446

17. Goetz T, Frenzel A, Hall N, Pekrun R (2008) Antecedents of academic emotions: testing the internal/external frame of reference model for academic enjoyment. Contemp Educ Psychol 33(1):9–33

18. Goldberg LR (1993) The structure of phenotypic personality traits. Am Psychol 48(1):26–34

19. Gonzalez G, de la Rosa JL, Montaner M, Delfin S (2007) Embedding emotional context in recommender systems. In: Proceedings of the 2007 IEEE 23rd international conference on data engineering workshop (ICDEW '07). IEEE, Washington, DC, pp 845–852

20. Kabassi K, Alepis E, Virvou M (2011) Evaluating an affective e-learning system using a fuzzy decision making method. Smart Innov Syst Technol 11:177–186

21. Knijnenburg BP, Willemsen MC, Gantner Z, Soncu H, Newell C (2012) Explaining the user experience of recommender systems. User Model User Adapt Interact 22(4–5):441–504

22. Kuo FF, Chiang MF, Shan MK, Lee SY (2005) Emotion-based music recommendation by association discovery from film music. In: Proceedings of the 13th annual ACM international conference on multimedia (MULTIMEDIA '05). ACM, New York, NY, pp 507–510

23. Leony D, Pardo A, Parada Gélvez HA, Delgado Kloos C (2012) A widget to recommend learning resources based on the learner affective state. 3rd International workshop on motivational and affective aspects of technology enhanced learning (MATEL), Saarbrücken, Germany, September 18, 2012

24. Mahmoud M, Baltrušaitis T, Robinson P, Riek L (2011) 3D corpus of spontaneous complex mental states. In: Proceedings of the international conference on affective computing and intelligent interaction (ACII 2011), Lecture notes in computer science. Springer, Berlin

25. Manouselis N, Drachsler H, Verbert K, Duval E (2013) Recommender systems for learning. Springer briefs in electrical and computer engineering. Springer, New York, NY

26. Mehrabian A (1996) Pleasure-arousal-dominance: a general framework for describing and measuring individual differences in temperament. Curr Psychol 14(4):261–292

27. Neji M, Ammar MB (2007) Agent-based collaborative affective e-learning framework. AACE, Chesapeake, VA

28. Oehme A, Herbon A, Kupschick S, Zentsch E (2007) Physiological correlates of emotions. Workshop on artificial societies for ambient intelligence. Artificial intelligence and simulation of behaviour, in association with the AISB '07, New Castle, UK, 2–4 April

29. Picard RW (2000) Affective computing. MIT Press, Cambridge

30. Porayska-Pomsta K, Mavrikis M, Pain H (2008) Diagnosing and acting on student affect: the tutor's perspective. User Model User Adapt Interact 18(1–2):125–173

31. Pu P, Chen L, Hu R (2011) A user-centric evaluation framework for recommender systems. ACM, New York, NY, pp 157–164

32. Qing-qiang L, Zhu J, Kong T (2009) RSED: a Novel recommendation based on emotion recognition methods. In: International conference on information engineering and computer science (ICIECS 2009). IEEE, Washington, DC, pp 1–4

33. Robison JL, McQuiggan SW, Lester JC (2010) Developing empirically based student personality profiles for affective feedback models. Intell Tutor Syst 2010:285–295

34. Rosson MB, Carroll JM (2001) Usability engineering: scenario-based development of human computer interaction. Morgan Kaufmann, San Francisco, CA

35. Santos OC, Boticario JG (2011) Requirements for semantic educational recommender systems in formal e-learning scenarios. Algorithms 4(2):131–154

36. Santos OC, Boticario JG (2011) TORMES methodology to elicit educational oriented recommendations. Lect Note Artif Intell 6738:541–543

37. Santos OC, Boticario JG (eds) (2012) Educational recommender systems and techniques: practices and challenges. IGI Publisher, Hershery, PA

38. Santos OC, Boticario JG (2012) Affective issues in semantic educational recommender systems. In: Proceedings of the 2nd workshop on recommender systems for technology enhanced learning. CEUR-WS proceedings, vol 896. ACM, New York, NY, pp 71–82
39. Santos OC, Boticario JG (2013) User-centred design and educational data mining support during the recommendations elicitation process in social online learning environments. Expert Systems, doi:10.1111/exsy.12041, in press
40. Santos OC, Boticario JG, Arevalillo-Herraez M, Saneiro M, Cabestrero R, del Campo E, Manjarres A, Moreno-Clari P, Quiros P, Salmeron-Majadas S (2012) MAMIPEC - affective modeling in inclusive personalized educational scenarios. Bull Tech Comm Learn Technol 14(4):35–38, Previously called Learning Technology Newsletter (ISSN 1438–0625). Special Issue Articles: Technology-Augmented Physical Educational Spaces
41. Santos OC, Rodriguez-Ascaso A, Boticario JG, Salmeron-Majadas S, Quirós P, Cabestrero R (2013) Challenges for inclusive affective detection in educational scenarios. Universal access in human-computer interaction. design methods, tools, and interaction techniques for einclusion. Lect Note Comput Sci 8009:566–575
42. Sarrafzadeh A, Alexander S, Dadgostar F, Fan C, Bigdeli A (2008) How do you know that I don't understand? A look at the future of intelligent tutoring systems. Comput Hum Behav 24(4):1342–1363
43. Schröeder M, Baggia P, Burkhardt F, Pelachaud C, Peter C, Zovato E (2012) Emotion markup language (EmotionML) 1.0. W3C Candidate Recommendation 10, May 2012
44. Shen L, Wang M, Shen R (2009) Affective e-learning: using "emotional" data to improve learning in pervasive learning environment. Educ Tech Soc 12(2):176–189
45. Strain AC, Azevedo R, D'Mello SK (2010) Exploring relationships between learners' affective states, metacognitive processes, and learning outcomes. ITS 2012:59–64
46. Sundaresan N (2011) Recommender systems at the long tail. In: Proceedings of the fifth ACM conference on recommender systems (RecSys '11). ACM, New York, NY, pp 1–6
47. Tai M, Woolf B, Arroyo I (2011) Using the think aloud method to observe students. Help-seeking behavior in math tutoring software. In: International conference of advanced learning technologies ICALT 2011. IEEE, Washington, DC
48. Teeters A (2007) Use of a wearable camera system in conversation: toward a companion tool for social-emotional learning in autism. MIT MS Thesis, September 2007
49. Tkalcic M, Burnik U, Kosir A (2010) Using affective parameters in a content-based recommender system for images. User Model User Adapt Interact 20(4):279–311
50. Verbert K, Manouselis N, Ochoa X, Wolpers M, Drachsler H, Bosnic I, Duval E (2012) Context-aware recommender systems for learning: a survey and future challenges. IEEE Trans Learn Technol 5(4):318–335
51. Woolf B, Burleson W, Arroyo I, Dragon T, Cooper D, Picard R (2009) Affect-aware tutors: recognising and responding to student affect. Int J Learn Tech 4(3/4):129–163
52. Woolf P, Arroyo I, Muldner K, Burleson W, Cooper D, Dolan R, Christopherson RM (2010) The effect of motivational learning companions on low-achieving students and students with learning disabilities. Int. conference on intelligent tutoring systems, Pittsburgh, PA, 2010
53. Yik M, Russell JA, Ahn CK, Fernandez Dols JM, Suzuki N (2002) Relating the five-factor model of personality to a circumplex model of affect: a five-language study. In: McCrae RR, Allik J (eds) The five-factor model of personality across cultures. Kluwer Academic Publishers, New York, NY, pp 79–104
54. Zeng Z, Pantic M, Roisman GI, Huang TS (2009) A survey of affect recognition methods: audio, visual and spontaneous expressions. IEEE Trans Pattern Anal Mach Intell 31(1):39–58

The Case for Preference-Inconsistent Recommendations

Christina Schwind and Jürgen Buder

Abstract Critical thinking requires knowledge about the diversity of viewpoints on controversial issues. However, the diversity of perspectives often remains unexploited: Learners prefer preference-consistent over preference-inconsistent information, a phenomenon called confirmation bias. This chapter attempts to introduce how recommender systems can be used to stimulate unbiased information selection, elaboration and unbiased evaluation. The principle of preference-inconsistency and its role in supporting critical thinking is explained. We present our empirical approach, the experimental paradigm and a summary of our main findings. Taken together, the results indicate that preference-inconsistent recommendations are an effective approach for stimulating unbiased information selection, elaboration and evaluation. In conclusion, implications for research and practice are discussed.

Keywords Recommender systems • Critical thinking • Confirmation bias • Preference-inconsistency

Introduction

In a culture that values active citizenship and informed decision making, the ability to think critically about controversial societal issues has been hailed as a crucial twenty-first century skill for learners [43]. When people try to get informed about a controversial issue and form an opinion based on what they see, they often search the Web. But will this search activity be indicative of critical thinking? We believe that this is not generally the case, and therefore our research over the last few years has explored whether the development of critical thinking in these contexts can be facilitated by the use of technologies. In particular, we have investigated from a

C. Schwind (✉) • J. Buder
Knowledge Media Research Center, Tübingen, Germany
e-mail: c.schwind@iwm-kmrc.de

N. Manouselis et al. (eds.), *Recommender Systems for Technology Enhanced Learning: Research Trends and Applications*, DOI 10.1007/978-1-4939-0530-0_7,
© Springer Science+Business Media New York 2014

psychological perspective whether recommender systems—if properly adapted—can be powerful tools that lead towards critical thinking. This chapter charts our journey through this topic.

The chapter is structured as follows: First, we describe three steps that can be associated with critical thinking on controversial issues. We argue that there is a need to support these three steps in educationally meaningful ways, as human information processing of controversial topics is biased in ways that counteract the development of critical thinking. Second, we suggest a novel approach of how recommender systems—or more generally, recommendations—could have a beneficial impact on all three steps towards critical thinking. Third, we describe the experimental paradigm that we used to get an insight into the psychological mechanisms that play a role in the use of recommendations in critical thinking contexts. Moreover, we report findings from five experimental studies that we have conducted in order to test our assumptions. Finally, we will discuss implications for further research and practice.

The Three Steps Towards Critical Thinking

The learning context which is relevant for the current chapter focuses on informal adult learning, especially on critical thinking about controversial issues. Nowadays, this type of learning is almost ubiquitous: Whether through developments in politics, society, or science, or simply through personal experiences, we are frequently put in a situation in which we are confronted with issues that are both controversial and novel. In these situations, it is relevant how people form an opinion of whether to be in favor or against a specific viewpoint of the controversy. This opinion formation can be characterized in three steps: Individuals have to select information, then they should elaborate the information, and finally the information should be evaluated. Ideally these three steps result in critical thinking, meaning that learners should be able to evaluate thoughts and arguments without being influenced by their own opinion [41, 45].

The first step, information selection, refers to the type of information that people actively attend to. More and more frequently, people search the Web in order to receive and actively select information, as a multitude of opinions is publicly available on discussion forums, social networks, or other channels. Individuals have to inform themselves about the different perspectives at stake. Ideally, dealing with controversial information and committing oneself to one alternative starts with an unbiased information search [18]. That implies that information will be selected irrespective of one's previously held opinion, thus constituting an informal, spontaneous learning process that is driven by a mode of inquiry. The second step, elaboration, refers to the cognitive processing of information. For instance, an individual might select dissenting information, but subsequently processes this information in a very shallow manner. However, ideally learners should elaborate on both sides of a controversial issue, for instance by attempting to integrate multiple perspectives [40] or diverse information on the same subject matter [46]. The third step, evaluation, refers to the way in which information is judged, and this step goes beyond selection and elaboration. Ideally, when evaluating the merits of various arguments, individuals should reject weak arguments that are in favor of their viewpoint, and acknowledge strong arguments that run counter to their own viewpoint. Evaluating the merits of arguments independent from one's preferences would be a perfect display of critical thinking [41, 45].

However, this ideal process rarely occurs in everyday information search. "The availability of diverse information in an environment does not guarantee that a person's views will be equally diverse." [13]. Indeed, there is a considerable bulk of research in social psychology and communication science indicating that when facing arguments in a controversy, we exhibit a penchant for selectively turning to information that is consistent with our opinion and disregard information that runs counter to our preferences—even when such information is present [13, 17, 22, 35]. While the names for this phenomenon vary (selective exposure, confirmation bias, congeniality bias), the message is quite uniform: we are equipped with cognitive mechanisms that let us seek more of the same. From an educational viewpoint, this penchant for preference-consistent thoughts and arguments is somewhat problematic: Rather than being close-minded, biased information seekers, learners should be open-minded, informed decision makers who build their opinions and attitudes based on critical thinking [40].

This raises the question of how these biases can be overcome. Given that learners often search for controversial issues on the Web (an environment without guidance from a teacher), a technology is needed which supports learners in selecting, elaborating and evaluating information in an unbiased way. It is important that such a technology combines two characteristics: On the one hand, it should take the learner's perspective into account [5], meaning that it should be able to personalize the information for each learner. On the other hand, it should provide orientation to the learners and help them navigating through the crowded information space [11]. Quite obviously, recommender systems perfectly fit these two requirements, thus making them ideal candidates to support critical thinking.

However, there's the rub: Classical recommender systems are based on the principle of maximum similarity [28]. In other words, they are designed for preference-consistency, whether it is in accurately predicting users' tastes (in commerce) or in predicting prior knowledge (in contexts of technology-enhanced learning). By virtue of these properties, classical recommender systems would only bolster learners' tendencies of selectively attending to preference-consistent arguments. In other words, if the goal is to support learners in critical thinking about controversial issues, classical recommender systems are likely to fail. Therefore, the approach established in our research involves the use of systems that are not based on the principle of maximum similarity. Instead, the research takes the approach of testing systems that explicitly recommend preference-*in*consistent information.

The Pivotal Role of Preference-Inconsistency

Information can be inconsistent in many ways. For instance, information might be inconsistent to preconceptions about scientific topics [4, 44]; information might be logically inconsistent within an incoherent text section [2] or over multiple documents [19]; and information can be inconsistent to expectancies and stereotypes [34]. The current chapter, by contrast, focuses on *preference*-inconsistency. Evidence supporting the importance of preference-inconsistency for thinking, development, and innovation can be found across the psychology literature:

From a developmental psychology perspective, inconsistency of information with cognitive structures induces cognitive conflict which in turn triggers cognitive development. Piaget [32] characterizes conflict as a driving factor for learning. The basic assumption is that conflict, for example in the form of evidence that is inconsistent with expectations, destabilizes the equilibrium of the cognitive structures. This imbalance is a necessary requirement for the cognitive and intellectual progress of children [33]. While Piaget's conceptualization addresses intra-individual conflicts, Doise and Mugny [7] adapted the concept into the notion of socio-cognitive conflict by stressing the importance of the social situation in which the conflict takes place. Having different perspectives in a group creates preference-inconsistency as each learner is confronted with inconsistent information from the social environment. As preference-inconsistency and resulting conflict are associated with learning, methods have been developed to induce conflict in classrooms. For instance, "constructive controversy" is an instructional method for teaching controversial issues in social studies [15, 16]. It is argued that conflict helps to involve pupils in the subject matter and to arouse their epistemic curiosity [3]. As a result, learners are encouraged by the challenging views to transform their knowledge into argumentations. From a social psychological perspective, the role of preference-inconsistency was investigated in the social influence literature [47], as controversial topics often result in (perceived) majority and minority viewpoints. Whereas preference-inconsistency with a majority viewpoint might lead to a simple compliance of minority members, preference-inconsistency and dissent evoked by a minority is playing a cognitively stimulating role [29, 30]. For instance, when individuals are confronted with a dissenting minority, they exhibit divergent thinking patterns, i.e. they will search for more information and show more creative ways of dealing with different approaches and perspectives.

These examples highlight the pivotal role of preference-inconsistency for cognitive stimulation and development. Learning methods like structured controversy already demonstrate how preference-inconsistent information can be used to cause change and rethinking. However, these beneficial effects of dissent are typically investigated in research contexts in which people interact within real groups. Our approach tries to evoke similar effects by employing principles found in recommender systems. Therefore, the question arises whether conflicting information must originate from direct interaction with another person or whether a preference-inconsistent recommendation originating from a computer system may also stimulate conflict and foster deeper elaboration. One indication that computer-based recommendations can be efficient substitutes relates to the notion that users often ascribe human social categories to recommender systems [25, 48]. Empirical clarification is needed to investigate whether or not the "recommender personality" is sufficient to stimulate socio-cognitive conflict. However, we believe that by combining the benefits of recommender systems and the benefits of preference-inconsistency into a preference-inconsistent recommender system, we can create a powerful tool that facilitates critical thinking on controversial issues. In order to test this assumption, we carried out a research program that investigated the role of preference-inconsistent recommendations from a psychological perspective.

The Empirical Approach

Our research investigated how recommendations support learners in thinking critically about a controversial topic. Therefore, we analyzed the effects of preference-inconsistent recommendations on information selection, elaboration and evaluation. This class of interventions was compared to classical preference-consistent recommendations. The first step of our empirical investigation was focused on information selection. Thus, if the goal is to support unbiased information search, should recommendations then be matched with preferences—or not? We proposed that classical preference-consistent recommendations lead to biased information selection, whereas preference-inconsistent recommendations have a debiasing effect on information selection and thus reduce this selection bias.

Following the three steps towards critical thinking, we were then interested whether preference-inconsistent recommendations do generate effects which are indicative for learning. Therefore, we investigated elaboration measurements (i.e., free recall and opinion statements) as further dependent variables. We assumed that unbiased information selection will have its equivalent in the elaboration measurements: Participants confronted with preference-inconsistent recommendations are likely to experience dissent. Therefore they should exhibit deeper elaboration than participants confronted with preference-consistent recommendations.

And finally, we were wondering which boundary conditions should be taken into account when implementing preference-inconsistent recommendations for supporting critical thinking. To put it more concrete, we investigated the role of two possible moderators (low vs. high prior knowledge; cooperation vs. competition). Moreover, in our moderator studies we were not only interested in learners' abilities to select arguments, but also in their ability to evaluate arguments irrespective of their own preference. It was hypothesized that selection behavior and evaluation behavior will show the same result pattern: Preference-inconsistent recommendations should reduce biases only in two conditions, namely for learners with low prior knowledge, and when the learning context is characterized by cooperation.

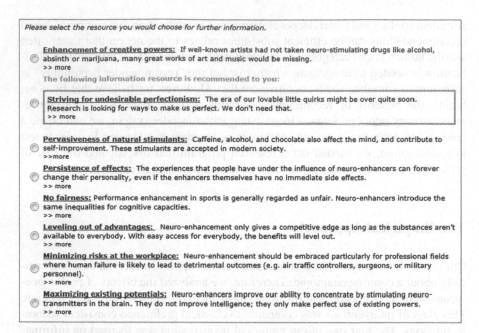

Fig. 1 Screenshot of the web search result list. Recommended argument and order of all arguments were randomized across trials

Experimental Paradigm

We used an experimental approach for testing our hypotheses. This approach comprises five studies, which were carried out as lab and/or online experiments. To conduct the experiments, a recommendation-based learning environment was developed. It should be noted that this environment did not involve an actual recommender system. It rather mimicked crucial recommender system capabilities by creating an experimental match or mismatch between a learner's preference (captured through a simple self-assessment) and a recommended piece of information. The learning environment was the same for all five studies and comprised a number of Web pages. All participants received an introductory text about the controversial topic of neuro-enhancement, referring to the facilitation of cognitive abilities through training or through medication. Then, participants were requested to indicate their prior preference on neuro-enhancement. The main page of the experiment consisted of a list of eight arguments, displayed as bogus Web search results (see Fig. 1). Four of these arguments supported and four of them opposed neuro-enhancement. Each argument consisted of a headline followed by two explanatory sentences.

For experimentally manipulating the recommendations, one of the arguments was highlighted by an orange-colored frame surrounding the text. This argument represented the recommendation. The caption above the frame stated: "The following information is recommended to you." Depending on experimental condition, the recommendation was either consistent or inconsistent with prior preference, thus mimicking the personalization part of recommender systems. The order of the arguments and the serial position of the recommendation were randomized across trials in order to minimize content and order effects.

The task of the participants was to select one of the eight arguments that they would like to read more about by clicking on an adjacent box. Information selection was measured in order to assess confirmation bias. A confirmation bias was present when more participants in one condition selected preference-consistent arguments than preference-inconsistent arguments. As we were interested in further reactions to preference-inconsistent recommendations (especially on elaboration and evaluation), participants were requested—depending on the study—to indicate their post-preference, to recall the arguments from the Web search result list, to state their opinion in an essay, or to evaluate all eight arguments regarding the perceived quality of the information.

Summary of the Main Results

Study 1 investigated information selection of participants who either received a preference-consistent or preference-inconsistent recommendation. In line with expectations, results showed that preference-consistent recommendations lead to confirmation bias while preference-inconsistent recommendations reduced confirmation bias [36]. Moreover, participants expressed more positive attitudes towards consistent recommendations compared to inconsistent recommendations. When confronted with consistent recommendations, participants ascribed this information to a majority opinion, whereas inconsistent recommendations were ascribed to a minority opinion. Taken together, the first study is an indication of the beneficial effects of preference-inconsistent recommendations. According to the results, preference-inconsistent recommendations support fostering unbiased information selection. However, this benefit comes at the expense of diminished popularity.

The empirical investigation thus far neither included a control condition without recommendation nor a measurement for elaboration. In order to detect whether a natural confirmation bias is present when no recommendation is given and whether the bias detected in the experimental conditions are enhanced or reduced in comparison to a natural confirmation bias, Study 2 and Study 3 employed a one factorial design with three conditions (no recommendation vs. consistent recommendation vs. inconsistent recommendation) [37]. These studies demonstrated that participants show natural confirmation bias when no recommendation was given, that this bias is present (but not enhanced) with preference-consistent recommendations, and that this bias is reduced with preference-inconsistent recommendations. Moreover, we investigated the cognitive consequences for participants confronted with preference-inconsistent recommendations. Study 2 showed that preference-inconsistent recommendations additionally led to a more moderate view on the controversial topic. Concerning elaboration, we found in Study 3 that preference-inconsistent recommendations stimulated less confirmation-biased recall, and evoked more elaborated opinion formation: Participants had the task to write an essay about the subject-matter and results show that participants confronted with inconsistent recommendations wrote a more comprehensive essay with more arguments generated by the participants (instead of arguments from the experimental material). Further, the perceived source of recommendation was identified as a mediating mechanism: Preference-inconsistent recommendations were perceived as minority viewpoints, which in turn led to the generation of more novel arguments in an opinion statement. To put it in a nutshell, preference-inconsistent recommendations can help to counteract biased information selection, to adapt preferences, and to stimulate elaboration.

So far, the ultimate question was whether consistent recommendations trigger different effects than inconsistent recommendations. Consequently, in Study 4 and Study 5 we further focused on the boundary conditions for the effectiveness of preference-consistent and preference-inconsistent recommendations [38]. Recommender systems are personalized filtering tools; thus, the adaptability to an individual's needs is fundamental for the functioning of such a system [8]. In other words, the same recommendation might work differently for different learners. As we are interested in recommendations in educational contexts, two moderating variables were relevant: Prior knowledge on the one hand and cooperation vs. competition on the other. Additionally, the set of dependent variables was extended to include evaluation of the perceived quality of all arguments. An evaluation bias is indicated if learners evaluate the quality of preference-consistent arguments higher than the quality of preference-inconsistent arguments [9, 12, 27]. The results of Study 4 show that preference-inconsistent recommendations reduced confirmation bias for low and high prior knowledge, whereas evaluation bias was only reduced for low prior knowledge. Further, it was found in Study 5 that preference-inconsistent recommendations led to less biased information selection under cooperation and under competition, whereas evaluation bias was only reduced under cooperation [38]. Put together, preference-consistent recommendations were largely ineffective in preventing confirmation bias or evaluation bias. In contrast, preference-inconsistent recommendations led to less confirmation-biased selection behavior in all conditions. Consequently, the application of preference-inconsistent recommendations in educational contexts should be encouraged. However, there are two limitations which should be considered: Preference-inconsistent recommendations were not able to reduce evaluation bias for learners with high prior knowledge (in contrast to learners with low prior knowledge) or for learners under competition (in contrast to learners under cooperation). However, the studies show that preference-inconsistent recommendations serve as a door opener for critical thinking under several conditions and are particularly effective for low prior knowledge and under cooperation.

Implications

So far, our endeavor into the role of recommendations in fostering critical thinking about controversial issues has brought about some promising results. We could show that all three steps towards critical thinking—information selection, elaboration, and evaluation—can be fostered by the use of preference-inconsistent recommendations. The results of our empirical work—mainly conducted in the laboratory under controlled and restricted conditions—invite us to think about the larger implications that this body of work might have on future research and practice. With regard to directions for future research, we see two interesting issues that deserve further empirical investigation.

The first issue refers to the generalizability of our results. While we found stable effects both in laboratory experiments and online experiments, and while we found stable effects for European vs. American participants (who actually differed in their average attitude about neuro-enhancement), we never addressed the role of recommendations in any other controversial domain. Though the topic of neuro-enhancement evoked strong reactions among some of our study participants, many participants have never heard about the topic before, or have given much thought about it. This raises the question of whether our findings can be generalized towards controversial domains or topics that participants have encountered before. Could we replicate our results in areas in which people have lots of prior exposure, for instance about topics that involve political partisanship? Of course, it is possible that in this case classical preference-consistent recommendations will exacerbate confirmation bias and lead to stronger attitudes, a finding that would mirror effects found in the psychological literature [6, 23] and postulated as "cyberpolarization" in the literature on social media [42, 49]. Moreover, the beneficial effects of preference-inconsistent recommendations might disappear. But even if we found serious limitations for the effectiveness of preference-inconsistency, this would open up interesting questions that could deepen our understanding about the role of recommendations. For instance, one could test whether lifetime exposure on a controversial topic, prior knowledge about arguments, or personal relevance of the controversy are the key factors that might inhibit the power of preference-inconsistent recommendations.

A second issue for further research refers to the source of a recommendation. Learning materials about controversial topics often explicitly list the pros and cons of the issue at hand. However, according to our findings it is not enough to confront people with the arguments of both sides of a controversial issue [37]. In addition, there needs to be an explicit endorsement of preference-inconsistent information in form of a recommendation to overcome confirmation bias. The open question is which type of endorsement is needed. Educational psychology research on constructive controversy [14–16] and social psychological research on minority dissent [29–31] show that endorsements should oppose the person's view in order to be constructive. However, it is also known that statements from an opposing camp might be disregarded only *because* they come from an opposing camp [20, 21]. Might it be possible that preference-inconsistent recommendations are even more effective when they originate from a support group? Research has shown that users prefer recommendations originating from friends [39], and the efficiency of recommender systems that are based on trust networks provides further evidence for the importance of social factors [24]. Moreover, our findings indicate that preference-inconsistent recommendations are perceived to stem from a minority. It would be interesting to see how people react if a preference-inconsistent recommendation is explicitly framed as originating from either a majority or minority source. It could also be investigated how people who know from prior experience that their own preference represents a majority or minority viewpoint in a controversy react to different types of recommendations.

Knowing more about the generalizability of our findings, and knowing more about how the actual or perceived source of information influences the way that recommendations are processed will have a great impact on the design of preference-inconsistent recommender systems. Of course, it would be premature to conceptualize a full-blown recommender system based on the current state of our research. Moreover, designing a workable preference-inconsistent recommender system is both beyond our expertise and our research interests as psychologists. Nonetheless, some tentative conclusions about the look of such a system can already be drawn. First, such a system would probably be based on user-generated arguments about controversial topics. A similar approach was already tested in the environment Opinion Space that visualizes citizen responses to a set of initial questions of political and societal relevance [10]. Second, a rating interface would be needed. For such a recommender system, the underlying rating scale should not necessarily be based on users' likes or dislikes; instead, it should be based on users' agreement or disagreement with arguments. Third, one would need algorithms to determine similarity or dissimilarity. Some classical recommender systems have employed the approach of user-based collaborative filtering [1] that defines a neighborhood of users with a similar rating profile. Based on this idea, it would be an open question whether a preference-inconsistent recommender system should employ an "anti-neighborhood" of highly dissimilar users. At the current state, our guess would be that one should avoid user reactance [26] and therefore use preference-inconsistent recommendations only intermittently and embedded within a set of preference-consistent recommendations. This would rather suggest using a neighborhood of similar users or even based on a trusted network of friends, and focally intersperse recommendations that systematically deviate from the preferences of the neighborhood. Fourth, if one would use a mixed set of consistent and inconsistent recommendations, it should be avoided that users interpret inconsistent recommendations as system failures. One solution to this problem could be to frame recommendations accordingly ("you might like this argument" for preference-consistent recommendations; "you might feel challenged by this argument" for preference-inconsistent recommendations). Finally, such a system would need algorithms about when to present consistent or inconsistent recommendations. The basis for such a decision could be the navigational behavior of a user. If someone exhibits a strong confirmation bias by mainly navigating towards preference-consistent pieces of information, he or she might be provided with inconsistent recommendations until a certain navigational balance between the dissenting viewpoints is achieved. Of course, all these crucial design issues would come on top of the regular challenges that arise in setting up workable recommender systems: cold-start problems, incomplete metadata etc.

This chapter has made the case for preference-inconsistent recommender systems. Of course, it does not imply that classical, preference-consistent recommender systems should be replaced. When the educational goal is to provide access to the best learning resources, employing the principle of maximum similarity to the needs and requirements of a learner is certainly commendable. However, our focus was less on providing resources, but rather to stimulate a particular type of thinking. In this regard, we envision recommender systems as thinking tools that assist learners in developing an open-minded stance towards controversial issues. Consequently, our approach explicitly violates the principle of maximum similarity and recommends information that learners likely wouldn't have selected by themselves. Our findings show some promising signs that preference-inconsistent recommendations might be a door-opener towards critical thinking. If these findings can be substantiated by further research, preference-inconsistent recommender systems might become powerful tools for dedicated activities, thus adding to an ever-increasing repertoire of learning technologies.

References

1. Adomavicius G, Tuzhilin A (2011) Context-aware recommender systems. In: Ricci F et al (eds) Recommender systems handbook. Springer, New York, NY, pp 217–253
2. Baker L (1989) Metacognition, comprehension monitoring, and the adult reader. Educ Psychol Rev 1:3–38
3. Berlyne DE (1960) Conflict, arousal, and curiosity. McGraw-Hill, New York, NY
4. Chinn CA, Brewer WF (1993) The role of anomalous data in knowledge acquisition: a theoretical framework and implications for science instruction. Rev Educ Res 63:1–49
5. Cronbach LJ, Snow RE (1977) Aptitudes and instructional methods: a handbook for research on interactions. Irvington, New York, NY
6. Ditto PH, Lopez DF (1992) Motivated skepticism: use of differential decision criteria for preferred and nonpreferred conclusions. J Pers Soc Psychol 63:568–584
7. Doise W, Mugny G (1984) The social development of the intellect. Pergamon Press, Oxford
8. Drachsler H et al (2008) Navigation support for learners in informal learning environments. Proceedings of the 2008 ACM conference on recommender systems. ACM, New York, NY, pp 303–306
9. Edwards K, Smith EE (1996) A disconfirmation bias in the evaluation of arguments. J Pers Soc Psychol 71:5–24
10. Faridani S et al (2010) Opinion space: a scalable tool for browsing online comments. Proceedings of the 28th international conference on human factors in computing systems. ACM, New York, NY, pp 1175–1184
11. Farzan R, Brusilovsky P (2005) Social navigation support in e-learning: what are the real footprints? In: Mobasher B, Anand SS (eds) Proceedings of the 19th international joint conference on artificial intelligence. Morgan Kaufmann Publishers Inc., San Francisco, CA, pp 49–80
12. Greitemeyer T, Schulz-Hardt S (2003) Preference-consistent evaluation of information in the hidden profile paradigm: beyond group-level explanations for the dominance of shared information in group decisions. J Pers Soc Psychol 84:322–339
13. Hart W et al (2009) Feeling validated versus being correct: a meta-analysis of selective exposure to information. Psychol Bull 135:555–588
14. Johnson DW et al (2000) Constructive controversy: the educative power of intellectual conflict. Change 32:28–37
15. Johnson DW, Johnson RT (1979) Conflict in the classroom: controversy and learning. Rev Educ Res 49(1):51–69
16. Johnson DW, Johnson RT (2009) Energizing learning: the instructional power of conflict. Educ Res 38:37–51

17. Jonas E et al (2001) Confirmation bias in sequential information search after preliminary decisions: an expansion of dissonance theoretical research on selective exposure to information. J Pers Soc Psychol 80:557–571
18. Jonas E, Frey D (2003) Information search and presentation in advisor–client interactions. Organ Behav Hum Decis Process 91:154–168
19. Kienhues D et al (2010) Dealing with conflicting or consistent medical information on the web: when expert information breeds laypersons' doubts about experts. Learn Instr 21(2): 193–204
20. Van Knippenberg D et al (1994) In-group prototypicality and persuasion: determinants of heuristic and systematic message processing. Br J Soc Psychol 33:289–300
21. Van Knippenberg D, Wilke H (1992) Prototypicality of arguments and conformity to ingroup norms. Eur J Soc Psychol 22:141–155
22. Knobloch-Westerwick S, Meng J (2009) Looking the other way: selective exposure to attitude-consistent and counterattitudinal political information. Commun Res 36:426–448
23. Lord CG et al (1979) Biased assimilation and attitude polarization: the effects of prior theories on subsequently considered evidence. J Pers Soc Psychol 37(11):2098–2109
24. Massa P, Avesani P (2007) Trust-aware recommender systems. Proceedings of the ACM conference on recommender systems. ACM, New York, NY, pp 17–24
25. McNee SM et al (2006) Making recommendations better: an analytic model for human-recommender interaction. In: Grinter R et al (eds) Proceedings of the ACM CHI conference on human factors in computing systems. ACM Press, New York, NY, pp 1103–1108
26. Miron AM, Brehm JW (2006) Reactance theory - 40 years later. Z Sozialpsychol 37(1):9–18
27. Mojzisch A et al (2010) Biased evaluation of information during discussion: disentangling the effects of preference consistency, social validation, and ownership of information. Eur J Soc Psychol 40:946–956
28. Munson SA et al (2009) Designing interfaces for presentation of opinion diversity. In: Olsen DR Jr et al (eds) Proceedings of the 27th international conference extended abstracts on human factors in computing systems. ACM Press, New York, NY, pp 3667–3672
29. Nemeth CJ (1995) Dissent as driving cognition, attitudes, and judgments. Soc Cogn 13(3): 273–291
30. Nemeth CJ (2003) Minority dissent and its "hidden" benefits. New Rev Soc Psychol 2:11–21
31. Nemeth CJ, Rogers J (1996) Dissent and the search for information. Br J Soc Psychol 35: 67–76
32. Piaget J (1976) Die Äquilibration der kognitiven strukturen. Klett, Stuttgart, Germany
33. Piaget J (1950) The psychology of intelligence. Routledge & Kegan Paul, London, England
34. Roese NJ, Sherman JW (2007) Expectancy. Social psychology: handbook of basic principles, vol 2. Guilford Press, New York, NY, pp 91–115
35. Schulz-Hardt S et al (2000) Biased information search in group decision making. J Pers Soc Psychol 78:655–669
36. Schwind C et al (2011) I will do it, but I don't like it: user reactions to preference-inconsistent recommendations. In: Tan D et al (eds) Proceedings of the ACM CHI conference on human factors in computing systems. ACM Press, New York, NY, pp 349–352
37. Schwind C et al (2012) Preference-inconsistent recommendations: an effective approach for reducing confirmation bias and stimulating divergent thinking? Comput Educ 58:787–796
38. Schwind C, Buder J (2012) Reducing confirmation bias and evaluation bias: when are preference-inconsistent recommendations effective–and when not? Comput Hum Behav 28(6):2280–2290
39. Sinha R, Swearingen K (2001) Comparing recommendations made by online systems and friends. Proceedings of the DELOS-NSF workshop on personalization and recommender systems in digital libraries. ACM, New York, NY
40. Spiro RJ, Jehng JC (1990) Cognitive flexibility and hypertext: theory and technology for the nonlinear and multidimensional traversal of complex subject matter. In: Nix D, Spiro RJ (eds) Cognition, education, and multimedia: exploring ideas in high technology. Erlbaum, Hillsdale, NJ, pp 163–205

41. Stanovich KE, West RF (1997) Reasoning independently of prior belief and individual differences in actively open-minded thinking. J Educ Psychol 89:342–357
42. Sunstein CR (2007) Republic. com. 20. Princeton University Press, Princeton, NJ
43. Trilling B, Fadel C (2009) 21st century skills: learning for life in our times. Jossey-Bass, San Francisco, CA
44. Vosniadou S (1994) Capturing and modeling the process of conceptual change. Learn Instr 4: 45–69
45. West RF et al (2008) Heuristics and biases as measures of critical thinking: associations with cognitive ability and thinking dispositions. J Educ Psychol 100(4):930–941
46. De Wit FRC, Greer LL (2008) The black-box deciphered: a meta-analysis of team diversity, conflict, and team performance. Academy of Management Best Paper Proceedings. AOM, Briarcliff Manor
47. Wood W et al (1994) Minority influence: a meta-analytic review of social influence processes. Psychol Bull 115:323
48. Yoo KH, Gretzel U (2011) Creating more credible and persuasive recommender systems: the influence of source characteristics on recommender system evaluations. In: Ricci F et al (eds) Recommender systems handbook: a complete guide for research scientists and practitioners. Springer, New York, NY, pp 455–477
49. Zuckerman E (2008) Homophily, serendipity, xenophilia, http://www.ethanzuckerman.com/blog/2008/04/25/homophily-serendipity-xenophilia/

Further Thoughts on Context-Aware Paper Recommendations for Education

Tiffany Y. Tang, Pinata Winoto, and Gordon McCalla

Abstract Simply matching learner interest with paper topic is far from enough in making personalized paper recommendations to learners in the educational domain. As such, we proposed the multidimensional recommendation techniques that consider (educational) context-aware information to inform and guide the system during the recommendation process. The contextual information includes both learner and paper features that can be extracted and learned during the pre- and post-recommendation process. User studies have been performed on both undergraduate (inexperienced learners) and graduate (experienced learners) students who have different information-seeking goals and educational backgrounds. Results from our extensive studies have been able to show that (1) it is both effective and desirable to implement the multidimensional recommendation techniques that are more complex than the traditional single-dimensional recommendation; (2) recommendation from across different learning groups (with different pedagogical features and learning goals) is less effective than that from within the same learning groups, especially when collaborative filtering technique is applied.

Keywords Paper recommender • Multidimensional recommendation • Contextual recommendation • User study

T.Y. Tang (✉) • P. Winoto
Department of Computer Science, Kean University, Union, NJ, USA
e-mail: yatang@kean.edu; pwinoto@kean.edu

G. McCalla
Department of Computer Science, University of Saskatchewan, Saskatoon, SK, Canada
e-mail: mccalla@cs.usask.ca

N. Manouselis et al. (eds.), *Recommender Systems for Technology Enhanced Learning:*   159
Research Trends and Applications, DOI 10.1007/978-1-4939-0530-0_8,
© Springer Science+Business Media New York 2014

Introduction

When there is an information flood, a successful personalization system would 'attempt' to understand its user by following the steps of its user, observing the interests of the group of similar users and picking items that best suit the users. A recommender system (RS) has been known to be capable of doing this based on either the liked items by the user (content-based recommendation) or implicit observations of the user's followers/friends who have similar tastes with the user (collaborative-filtering based recommendation, or CF in short) [1, 10, 12, 15]. The latter approach has gain more spotlight due to the recent popularity of social networking as a CF recommender would build a user profile through the group of the like-mindness [8, 21] and does not rely on delicate analysis on the content features of the target item (the item to be recommended) in an attempt to establish the relationship between what the user likes and the target item.

Both approaches have drawbacks. Since user profiles in the content-based approach are built through an association with the contents of the items, the approach tends to be quite narrowly focused and with a bias towards highly scored items. Thus, a user might be restricted to those items that are very similar to the ones he/ she has read before, which is known as the issue of over-specialization of the recommendations [1] or being trapped into a so-called similarity hole [16]. In addition, the approach only considers the preferences of a single user. CF-based approach also suffers from some major drawbacks. For instance, if an item has not received enough ratings from users, or if many users have not rated each item, correlation computations cannot be performed. These two problems, the first-item problem and the first-rater problem respectively, are collectively referred to as cold-start problems. A cold-start problem prevents users from seeking recommendation information on new items and serendipitous items (items that nobody or only a few users have rated). It can be challenging for the system to form neighbors when users have unusual tastes, since the correlation of ratings between these unusual users and 'mainstream normal' users could be low, resulting in poor recommendations. The performance of the CF-based approach relies heavily on finding neighboring users who have co-related enough items.

Hybrid recommendation mechanisms attempt to deal with some of these issues and smooth out the drawbacks of the CF and content-based approaches. A fourth type called 'knowledge-based filtering' or 'conversational' [3, 22] builds user profile gradually [3]. Such approaches include preference-based feedback and critiques [22]. Regardless of approach, the key idea is personalization of the recommendation and at the core of personalization is the task of building a model of the user. Content-based approaches build user models that link the contents of the information a user has consumed about the artifacts to be recommended to the preferences of the user concerning those artifacts; CF approaches build user models that link the information preferences of a user to those of other users with similar tastes or preferences; hybrid approaches use a mixture of CF and content-based modeling; and knowledge-based approaches construct user profiles more gradually using many 'interactive' forms of knowledge structure. In all approaches, the success of the item recommended is represented by the utility of the item, usually captured by a rating specified by the user based on how much the user liked the item [1].

Educational Recommendation Systems

Earlier research efforts on educational RS have largely focused making recommendations based on learners' interests. For example, Recker et al. [19] discuss recommending educational resources through Altered Vista. Brusilovsky et al. [4] provided "annotation-based" social navigation support for making personalized recommendations through Knowledge Sea III. McNee et al. [15] and Torres et al. [28] utilized document titles and abstracts to make recommendations. Other recommendation studies made use of data mining to construct user profiles [11]. These studies failed to consider whether the recommended paper is appropriate to support learning (goal-oriented RSs).

Recently, researchers have made efforts to identify and incorporate learners' pedagogical features (contexts) for recommendations. Nadolski et al. [17] considered a learner's competence level, study time, and efforts. Manouselis et al.'s study [14] differ from ours in that target users were not students, though the contexts considered are similar to ours. Other similar efforts include Lemire et al. [13]; Khribi et al. [11]; Gomez Albarran and Jimenez-Diaz [7]; Manouselis et al. [14] and Drachsler et al. [5]. Verbert et al. [29, 30] compares various open datasets for TEL, in terms of the algorithmic design and evaluations and points to future challenges not only in the TEL community but also the entire educational RS community. We are especially interested in the three challenges specified: evaluation, dataset sharing, and privacy. While we mostly agreed with the evaluation frameworks presented (mostly objective), we do believe that subjective evaluation techniques based on a careful understanding of the educational purposes and tasks for which the RS is to support are essential, since *'the bottom-line measure of RS success should be user satisfaction'* (page 6, [10]).

Data Mining Techniques for Personalization in Education[1]

Data mining is an interdisciplinary research area that is inspired by research from artificial intelligence, machine learning, neural networks, evolutionary computation, statistics, pattern recognition, information retrieval, psychology, etc. Due to its enormous success both in research and practice, data mining and web mining have penetrated into almost every area where information is needed, including in

---

[1] For a more complete discussion on educational data mining, readers can refer to [20].

education. A wide variety of data and web mining techniques have been used, among them, association rules mining, data clustering, classification (including K-nearest neighbor classification (KNN)) are three of the most popular.

KNN, one type of data classification methods, is characterized by the size of neighbors and the similarity between pairs of data. CF-based recommendation technique has used KNN at its core by establishing a set of neighbors of a target user with their similarity representing user ratings, preferences, mood, or other quantified data. Content-based recommendation approach has its roots in information retrieval (IR) and filtering. Thanks to the significant advances made by IR and information filtering researchers, the majority of current content-based techniques are able to associate the content aspect of items such as books, movies, documents, news articles etc., with the elements that are the most probably attractive to users (see among others, [2, 28, 33]).

Ha et al. [9] study the mining of learners' aggregate paths for the purposes of course customization as well as dynamic link recommendations. Zaiane [34] investigate the correlation between learners' on-line learning activities and the pages they have browsed, which could be utilized to recommend learners' future learning activities. Tang and McCalla [24] outline a large-generalized clustering algorithm that identifies clusters of students with similar learning characteristics based on their path traversal patterns and the content of each page they have visited. After student clusters are identified, the generalized paths mostly visited are also recorded, which can be used for group-based course content delivery and recommendations. Tang et al. [23] construct a personalized e-articles reading tree based on predetermined keyword(s), where the e-articles are mandatory reading materials for students. The system is much like text or keyword-driven information retrieval, because no students' learning characteristics (including learning activities, skills, learning patterns etc.) are considered, although the authors acknowledge that certain students' information should be included. Nevertheless, the system is capable of providing adaptive and personalized course contents to individual students.

Recommending educational resources is also not new. Recker et al. [19] study the recommendation of educational resources through Altered Vista, where teachers and learners can submit and review comments on educational web resources provided by learners who are pre-categorized into different 'pedagogical' groups. Brusilovsky et al. [4] reports a user study of Knowledge Sea III which provide 'annotation-based' social navigation support for making personalized recommendations to students engaging in learning a computer programming language. Reputation indicators like a 'question mark', 'thumbs up' and 'sticky note' were adopted to provide visual clues to students regarding to the specific elements. A number of researchers work on making paper recommendations. For instance, McNee et al. [15] investigate the adoption of CF techniques to recommend additional references for a target research paper. A similar study by Torres et al. [28] utilizes document titles and abstracts to make recommendations. Although these studies have focused on making paper recommendations, unfortunately, they failed to consider users' pedagogical factors when making recommendations. That is, whether or not the recommended paper is appropriate to enhance learning.

To deal with this issue, in our previous studies, we proposed a pedagogical paper recommender which incorporates learner and user features to make pedagogically appropriate papers and obtained potentially promising results [25, 27]. A pedagogical paper recommender use additional information (contextual information) instead of the pure numeric ratings to determine the closeness between users. Take an example, John does not like Cartoon movies, but likes to watch them during weekends with his kids. Therefore, he should be recommended "The Incredible" on Saturdays and Sundays. In the e-learning domain, for instance, student Steven's job is not related to UI design, but he found out that a paper on UI design and usability engineering is useful in understanding his Software Engineering course, hence, he still rate this paper high. In other words, his rating on the "usefulness" of this paper reflected the pedagogical value of it for those taking Software Engineering course.

Adomavicius et al. [1] argue that dimensions of the contextual information can include when, how and with whom the users will consume the recommended items, which, therefore, directly affect users' satisfaction towards the system performance. To deal with the multi-dimensional CF, they propose to use data warehouse and OLAP application concepts in slicing available database.

Pazzani [18] also studied an earlier 'version' of multi-dimensional CF through the aggregation of users' demographic information such as their gender, age, education, address, etc. In order to make predictions to a target user, the demographic based-CF learns a relationship between each item and the type of the people who tend to like it. Then, out of 'that' type of the people, the CF identifies the neighbors for the target user, and makes recommendations accordingly. Clearly, the difference between the traditional CF and the demographic based CF is that the preprocessing steps of 'grouping' similar users.

Lekakos and Giaglis [12] consider users' life styles in making recommendation. Lifestyle includes users' living and spending patterns, which are in turn affected by external factors (e.g. culture and family) and internal factors (e.g. personality, emotions, and attitudes). The system will then compute the Pearson correlation of users' lifestyles instead of ratings in the traditional CF: the chance that users with same lifestyle tend to have similar tastes will be higher. After this filtering process, the system will make predictions on items for the target user based on ratings from neighbors. In another paper [31], we proposed a mood-aware recommendation approach which consider user mood in finding the like-mindness group for recommendation. Essentially, our approach in this paper is similar to that in [12], [18] and [31]: use additional contextual information instead of pure ratings to determine the closeness between users. And our context is for paper recommendation wherein learners' pedagogical features are used to measure the similarity between them.

Our earlier study [27] explored the characteristics of pedagogical paper recommendation; that is to determine the factors that rank a paper high in terms of its pedagogical benefits (say whether the learner have gained knowledge from reading a paper will affect his/her rating on the paper) Three statistical methods were performed: partial correlation, Principal Components Regression (PCR) and Partial Least Squares Regression (PLS). Results show the importance of several features in making paper recommendation in this domain. In particular: (1) learner interest is not that important and not the only dimension for making recommendations; (2) other contextual information-seeking goals such as task- and course-related goals are related to learners' perceived value of the papers; (3) learners' willingness of further making peer recommendation on a paper depends largely on the closeness of its content topic to their job nature.

These observations can help tutors support the learner in making a decision as to which item(s) to select, and highlight the uniqueness of pedagogical recommendation when compared to other types of recommendation. In this paper, we detail the multidimensional recommendation algorithm and provide insights on the applicability of the system on different pools of learners. It is known that the performance of a RS is sensitive to users from different segments characterized by contextual factors such as demographic or socioeconomic status [12, 18], mood [31], pedagogical background and learning goals [27, 32] etc.

The Organization of the Paper

The organization of this paper is as follows. In section "Pedagogical Recommendation System: The Algorithms," we explain a variety of multidimensional pedagogical recommendation techniques. In subsection "General Comments on Performance of the Pedagogical Paper Recommender", through a series of empirical evaluation on two groups of learners, we discuss and compare the performance of these techniques under various learning contexts. Lessons learned from our extensive studies are also provided in this section.

Pedagogical Recommendation System: The Algorithms

Pedagogical Paper Recommendation Techniques: Motivation

Unlike the movie/music/book domains where both users and ratings tend to be more readily available, there lacks of users, and ratings in the education domain. Therefore, recommendation techniques (for example, content-based filtering, user-model based CF) that can cold-start the system should be considered. In additions, for rating-based CF we may not have enough co-rated items, hence we have to consider multidimensional ratings on each item in order to boost the number of co-ratings so that to find more accurate neighbors for a target user. In addition, we also take into consideration paper popularity in an attempt to start up the recommendation when there are not many ratings in the system.

Factors considered in our multi-dimensional CF to profile learners include papers' overall-ratings, popularity, value-added, degree of being peer recommended or peer_rec, and learners' pedagogical features such as interest and background

Table 1 A summary of the recommendation techniques for pedagogy-aware paper recommendations

Category	Name	Remarks
Content-based	ContentF	Content-based (User-item) filtering
CF-based	1D-CF	Uni-dimensional rating-based CF
	3D-CF	Multi-dimensional rating-based CF
	UM-CF (2D-CF)	User-model based CF
	5D-CF	Rating- and user-model-based CF
Hybrid	Pop3D	Non-personalized and rating-based CF
	Pop5D	Non-personalized and 5D-CF
	Pop2D	Non-personalized and User-model based CF
	PopCon2D	A combination of Non-personalized, user-item content filtering and 2D-CF
Other types	Manual rec.	
	Pop1D	Non-personalized method

knowledge. Overall rating represents the overall rating given to a paper by a user (e.g. in a Likert scale 1–4). Value-addedness represents the knowledge gained from a paper, and peer recommendation represents the user's willingness to recommend a paper to other learners.

Table 1 organizes and categorizes the various recommendation techniques that are discussed in this section. Generally, they fall into four main categories: content-based, CF-based, hybrid recommendation, and other techniques.

The Algorithms

Non-personalized Recommendation (Benchmark)

The inclusion of paper popularity (the average Overall ratings of a paper) is regarded as a non-personalized method. We treat all of the students in the same class as a group. In the context of this paper, the average rating of each paper k among all the learners with similar backgrounds, denoted by $\bar{r}^k$, will be labeled as the *paper's popularity*.

The introduction of $\bar{r}_k$ is very useful to tackle cold-start problems. We consider it as a best-case benchmark for other personalized recommendation techniques.

User-Item Content-Based Filtering (ContentF)

In the ContentF method, recommendation is achieved through a match between learner interest and minimal background knowledge needed to understand the paper. Each paper has been pre-categorized based on its topics and the minimal knowledge needed for understanding it, thus obtaining the paper model. User model (interest and background knowledge) is obtained through a pre-questionnaire; user interest contains topical keywords, while background knowledge refers to the necessary knowledge to understand the papers. We proposed seven variations of contentF which differs from each other regarding the treatment of paper appropriateness [26].

CF and Hybrid Recommendation Techniques

Traditional Collaborative Filtering (1D-CF)

Uni-dimensional rating-based CF is the traditional CF that has been used in the literature. First, we calculate the Pearson correlation between users a and b, which is given by:

$$P(a,b) = \frac{\sum_{k \in K}(r_{a,k} - \overline{r}_a)(r_{b,k} - \overline{r}_b)}{\sqrt{\sum_{k \in K}(r_{a,k} - \overline{r}_a)^2 \sum_{k \in K}(r_{b,k} - \overline{r}_b)^2}} \quad (1)$$

where $r_{i,k}$ is the rating by user i on item k, $\overline{r}_i$ is the mean rating by user i to all items, and K is the set of items co-rated by both a and b. The estimated rating for a target user a on paper j, $r_{a,j}^e$ is then computed through the target user's neighbors, denoted as B, using the following formula:

$$r_{a,j}^e = \frac{\sum_B P(a,b) \times r_{b,j}}{\sum_B P(a,b)} \quad (2)$$

In the education domain, not many papers (less than 30 for each student in one semester) are commonly assigned as part of a learning activity in a course, which is different from other domains such as movie, music and book. Thus, our research focus is for the case with a limited number of co-rated papers, i.e. $|K|$ less than or equal to 5 and the number of neighbors $|B|$ is from 2 to 15.

User-Model-Based Collaborative Filtering (UM-CF)

Suppose we have a target user a, who has not rated any item, and many other users who have rated some items. The Pearson correlation of user model a to its neighbor b is given by:

$$P_K(a,b) = \frac{\sum_K(r_{a,k} - \overline{r}_a)(r_{b,k} - \overline{r}_b)}{\sqrt{\sum_K(r_{a,k} - \overline{r}_a)^2 \sum_K(r_{b,k} - \overline{r}_b)^2}} \quad (3)$$

where K is the set of user model features $\{interest, backgrd\_knowledge\}$co-rated by both a and b; $r_{a,k}$ or $r_{b,k}$ is the rating given by user a or b to feature k; $\bar{r}_a$ and $\bar{r}_b$ are their average rating to features in K. Given two Pearson correlations, we can linearly combine them:

$$P_{2DStdModel}(a,b) = w_{interest} P_{interest}(a,b) + w_{backgrd\_knowledge} P_{backgrd\_knowledge}(a,b) \quad (4)$$

where $w_{interest}$ and $w_{backgrd\_knowledge}$ are the weights used in our linear combination. After that, we can then calculate the estimated rating of target user a on item j, denoted by r_j^{2D}:

$$r_j^{2D} = \sum_B P_{2D}(a,b) r_{b,j} \quad (5)$$

Combinations of Non-personalized Recommendation and User-Model-Based Collaborative Filtering (PopUM-CF)

PopUM-CF is a combination of UM-CF and non-personalized recommendation method. It is used to overcome rating-based CF's reliance on co-rated papers. The recommendation is obtained by:

$$r_j^{Pop2D} = r_j^{2D} + w_r n \tilde{r}_j \quad (6)$$

where r_j^{2D} is obtained from UM-CF in Eq. (5), n is the number of neighbors $= |B|$.

Multi-Dimensional Rating-Based Collaborative Filtering (3D-, 5D- and 6D-CF)

We first consider three rating dimensions to measure the closeness of a pair of users, i.e. the overall ratings, value-addedness and peer recommendations. Suppose P_d (a, b) is the Pearson correlation based on the rating r_d on dimension d, then, we can combine those three correlations into a *weighted sum* Pearson correlation as:

$$P_{3D}(a,b) = w_{overall} P_{overall}(a,b) + w_{valueadd} P_{valueadd}(a,b) + w_{peer\_rec} P_{peer\_rec}(a,b) \quad (7)$$

where $w_{overall} + w_{valueadd} + w_{peer\_rec} = 1$.

A combination of user-model based and rating-based CF might yield a more satisfying result. 5D-CF is one of this hybrid approaches. To compute it, we first compute the 2D-Pearson correlation between learners based on their student models using Eq. (4). The result is then combined with 3D-Pearson correlation from co-rated papers:

$$P_{5D}(a,b) = P_{3D}(a,b) + w_{2D} P_{2DstdModel}(a,b) \quad (8)$$

Table 2 Factors that are considered in our Multi-Dimensional CF

Dimension	Factors
3D	Overall rating, value-addedness, peer recommendations
5D	Overall rating, value-addedness, peer recommendations, Learner interest, Learner background knowledge
Pop3D	Overall rating, value-addedness, peer recommendations, $\tilde{r}$
Pop5D	Overall rating, value-addedness, peer recommendations, learner interest, learner background knowledge, $\tilde{r}$

We then use the following equation to calculate the aggregate rating of each paper:

$$r_k^{5D} = \sum_B P_{5D}(a,b) r_{b,k} \tag{9}$$

Finally we combine this rating with the average rating of each paper (i.e. paper's popularity $\tilde{r}$) to obtain a 6D-CF based rating for the papers:

$$r_k^6 = r_k^{5D} + w_{\tilde{r}} n\tilde{r} \tag{10}$$

where $w_{\tilde{r}}$ is the weight of paper's popularity.

Combinations of Non-personalized Recommendation
and Rating-Based Collaborative Filtering (Pop1D and Pop3D)

When a resulting estimated rating from either a 1D-CF or 3D-CF is combined with the average rating (*popularity*) given by all users in a group, we will have Pop1D and Pop3D respectively. Specifically, the recommendation is determined by linear combination of paper popularity. $\tilde{r}_j$, and a rating calculated from 1D- and 3D-CF, i.e. r_j^{1D} and r_j^{3D} respectively, which results in the following:

$$r_j^{Pop1D} = r_j^{1D} + w_r n\tilde{r}_j \tag{11}$$

$$r_j^{Pop3D} = r_j^{3D} + w_r n\tilde{r}_j \tag{12}$$

where $w_{\tilde{r}}$ is the weight of linear combination and is the control variable in our experiment.

Combinations of Non-personalized Recommendation and the Combined
Rating-Based and User-Model-Based Collaborative Filtering (Pop5D)

Combining the rating obtained from 5D-CF, we have a hybrid 5D recommendation (Pop5D) for the papers:

$$r_j^{Pop5D} = r_j^{5D} + w_r n\tilde{r}_j \tag{13}$$

Note that the Pop5D actually upgrades Pop3D, by injecting two aspects of student models into the recommendation process. Table 2 summarizes those factors considered in our multi-dimensional CF to correlate one user with another.

Combinations of Content-Based Filtering, Non-personalized Recommendation, and User-Model-Based Collaborative Filtering (PopCon2D)

Another hybrid method is to combine content-based filtering with non-personalized recommendation and user-model-based CF, namely PopCon2D (for Popularity + Content-based filtering + 2D user-model-based CF). However, we shall normalize the closeness value by dividing each value with max_B ($|closeness_b|$) so that our closeness value is always between $(-1, 1)$.

Suppose $\tilde{r}_j$ is the average rating of paper j and r_j^{2D} is the estimated ratings of neighbors in UM-CF, i.e. Eq. (5). The recommended paper(s) can be calculated by the following:

$$r_j^{PopCon2D} = r_j^{2D} + n\left(w_r \tilde{r}_j + w_c Closeness\right) \qquad (14)$$

where w_r is the weight assigned to paper popularity and w_c is a weight on the closeness value calculated from content-based filtering. Again, paper(s) with a higher rank will be picked up.

General Comments on Performance of the Pedagogical Paper Recommender

We carried out two series of user studies on both undergraduate and graduate students in 2 years. The first experimental study was conducted in an introductory software engineering course for Master's-level students, while the second experiment was conducted in a junior-level software engineering course for 45 undergraduates. Details of the experiments and results can be found at [32].

Overall, the experimental results are encouraging, especially in confirming that making recommendations to learners is not the same as making recommendations to users in commercial environments such as Amazon.com. In such learning environments, learners are willing to accept items that are not interesting, yet meet their learning goals in some way or another. For instance, our experimental results suggest that user-model based CF works well with content-based filtering and non-personalized methods (such as paper popularity) as in Pop5D. Although the computation in Pop5D is more sophisticated than the other CF-based approaches, under certain circumstances it helps inform the recommender and therefore improve the recommendations. The results also indicate that incorporating ratings from value-added-ness and peer recommendation can slightly improve the performance of CF-based RSs when the number of co-rated papers is small. Among the proposed multi-dimensional methods, 3D-CF demonstrated the most potential in terms of average Overall rating when the number of co-rated papers is small.

Our findings illuminate learner satisfaction as a complicated function of learner characteristics, rather than the single issue of whether the paper topics matched learner interests. The results lead us to speculate that if in the domain that there are limited number of both papers and learners; considering other features rather than

Table 3 A summary of recommended recommendation methods

Contexts		Appropriate recommendation method(s)	
		Top one	Top three
When there is enough ratings and papers	The learner is new to the course	PopCon2D	PopUM-CF
	The learner is half–way in the course	PopCon2D	PopUM-CF
	The learner is near the end of the course	PopCon2D	Pop5D
When there is not enough ratings and papers	The learner is new to the course	PopCon2D	PopUM-CF
	The learner is half–way in the course	1D-CF	Pop5D

relying on Overall rating and user interest can help inform the recommendation. Table 3 summarizes our recommendations on adopting appropriate mechanisms based on the system context.

Here, PopCon2D performs very well under four typical learning contexts for picking the best one paper, and the more complex CF algorithms including Pop5D, PopUM-CF work well for making the best three recommendations. Due to its characteristics, PopCon2D can not only be used to start up the recommendation but also to inform the recommendation (since it contains information such as paper popularity, paper content, user model on learner interest and knowledge background which can be used to generate recommendation without using paper ratings). In dimensions such as this, with a limited number of both papers and learners (and other constraints such as course syllabus), we can conclude that considering other features than just overall rating and user interest can help inform the recommendation.

When the system does not have enough data on paper and user models, a content-based filtering method is appropriate by matching the new user model and existing user and paper models. However, when there are not enough papers to perform the matching, some other features such as popularity need to be injected to inform the RS, as in PopCon2D and PopUM-CF. These methods characterize the features of the pedagogical paper recommendation and reflect that human judgments of scientific articles are influenced by a variety of factors including a paper's topical content, its content appropriateness and its value in helping users achieve their task. It also highlights the importance of appropriately incorporating such factors into the recommendation process.

Through extensive experimental studies, we discovered two key findings to answer the two broad research questions raised:

1. Incorporating contextual information to inform the recommendations is vital in the education domain. This can be achieved by adopting approaches such as PopUM-CF for a number of learning contexts.
2. Making recommendations from across different learning groups is less effective than making suggestions from within the same learning groups, especially with collaborative filtering.

The second finding is consistent with previous studies that RS tends to perform differently on users from different demographic, socioeconomic and pedagogical (in our domain) sections, which although seems to be trivial, it is, to the best of our knowledge, the first documented study in the educational domain.

Concluding Remarks

Obviously, finding a 'good' paper is not about the simple fact that the user will either accept the recommended items, or not; rather, it is a multiple-step process that typically entails the users navigating the paper collection, understanding the recommended items, seeing what others like/dislike, and making decisions. Therefore, a future research goal to proceed from the study here is to design for different kinds of social navigation in order to study the impact on user behavior, and how over the time, user behavior feeds back to influence the system performance. Additionally, we realized that one of the biggest challenges is the difficulty to test the effectiveness or appropriateness of a recommendation method due to a low number of available ratings. Testing the method with more students, say, in two or three more semesters, may not be helpful, because the results are still not enough to draw conclusions as strong as those from other domains where the ratings can be as many as millions. Hence, we are eager to see the collaborations from different institutions in using the system in a more distributed and larger-scale fashion (as it is very difficult to achieve it in using one class each time and in one institution). Through this broader collaboration, our ambition is to hope in educational domain, more *MovieLens*-like benchmark database would appear as a test-bed on which more algorithms can be tested (including ours), which has also been pointed by [29, 30]. Currently, there are some great efforts on exploring the use of datasets for Technology Enhanced Learning (TEL) [6, 29, 30]; some modified versions of both user- and item-based CF techniques have been applied on these datasets. However, one of the shortcomings of the experiments is the way the comparisons were made to show the effectiveness of the algorithms: the testing methods are largely objective which is similar to those in the traditional movie/book/music recommendation systems; however, we believed the task-oriented evaluation framework is more appropriate than most of the objective-evaluation techniques since it can in directly assessing user satisfaction and acceptance over the recommended items; *'the bottom-line measure of RS success should be user satisfaction'* (page 6, [10]).

References

1. Adomavicius G, Mobasher B, Ricci F, Tuzhilin A (2011) Context-aware recommender systems. AI Mag 32(3):67–80
2. Basu C, Hirsh H, Cohen W, Nevill-Manning C (2001) Technical paper recommendations: a study in combining multiple information sources. JAIR 1:231–252
3. Burke R (2002) Hybrid recommender systems: survey and experiments. User Model User Adapt Interact 12(4):331–370
4. Brusilovsky P, Farzan R, Ahn J (2005) Comprehensive personalized information access in an educational digital library. In: Proc. Of IEEE/ACM joint conference on digital libraries (ACM DL'2005), Denver, CA, USA, pp. 9–18
5. Drachsler H, Hummel HGK, Koper R (2007) Recommendations for learners are different: applying memory-based recommender system techniques to lifelong learning. In: Duval E, Klamma R, Wolper M (Eds) Creating new learning experiences on a global scale: second European conference on enhanced technology learning, EC-TEL, Crete, Greece, September 17–20, 2007, pp 1–9

6. Drachsler H, Verbert K, Manouselis N, Vuorikari R, Wolpers M, Lindstaedt L (2012) Datasets and data supported learning in technology-enhanced learning. International Journal of Technology-Enhanced Learning (IJTEL) 4(1/2)
7. Gomez-Albarran M, Jimenez-Diaz G (2009) Recommendation and students' authoring in repositories of learning objects: a case-based reasoning approach. Int J Emerg Technol Learn 4:35–40
8. Guy I, Zwerdling Z, Carmel D, Ronen I, Uziel E, Yogev S, Ofek-Koifman S (2009) Personalized recommendation of social software items based on social relations. In: Proceedings of the third ACM conference on recommender systems. ACM, New York, NY, pp 53–60
9. Ha S, Bae S, Park S (2000) Web mining for distance education. In: IEEE international conference on management of innovation and technology. ACM, New York, NY, pp 715–719
10. Herlocker J, Konstan J, Terveen L, Riedl J (2004) Evaluating collaborative filtering recommender systems. ACM Trans Inform Syst 22(1):5–53
11. Khribi MK, Jemni M, Nasraoui O (2009) Automatic recommendations for e-learning personalization based on web usage mining techniques and information retrieval. Educ Tech Soc 12(4):30–42
12. Lekakos G, Giaglis G (2006) Improving the prediction accuracy of recommendation algorithms: approaches anchored on human factors. Interact Comput 18(3):410–431
13. Lemire D, Boley H, McGrath S, Ball M (2005) Collaborative filtering and inference rules for context-aware learning object recommendation. Int J Interact Tech Smart Educ 2:179–188
14. Manouselis N, Vuorikari R, Van Assche F (2010) Collaborative recommendation of e-learning resources: an experimental investigation. J Comput Assist Learn 26(4):227–242
15. McNee S, Albert I, Cosley D, Gopalkrishnan P, Lam S, Rashid A, Konstan J, Riedl J (2002) On the recommending of citations for research papers. In: Proceedings of the 2002 ACM conference on computer supported cooperative work, New Orleans, LA, November 16–20, 2002, pp 116–125. New York, NY: ACM
16. McNee S, Riedl J, Konstan JA (2006) Being accurate is not enough: how accuracy metrics have hurt recommender systems. In: the Extended abstracts of the 2006 ACM conference on human factors in computing systems (CHI 2006), Montreal, QC, Canada, pp 1097–1101
17. Nadolski R, Van den Berg B, Berlanga A, Drachsler H, Hummel H, Koper R, Sloep P (2009) Simulating lightweight personalised recommender systems in learning networks: a case for pedagogy-oriented and rating based hybrid recommendation strategies. J Artif Soc Soc Simul 12(1):4
18. Pazzani M (1999) A framework for collaborative, content-based, and demographic filtering. Artif Intell Rev 13(5–6):393–408
19. Recker M, Walker A, Lawless K (2003) What do you recommend? Implementation and analyses of collaborative information filtering of web resources for education. Instr Sci 31:299–316
20. Romero C, Ventura S (2007) Educational data mining: a survey from 1995 to 2005. Expert Syst Appl 33(1):135–146
21. Shi Y, Larson M, Hanjalic A (2009) Exploiting user similarity based on rated-item pools for improved user-based collaborative filtering. In: Proceedings of the third ACM conference on recommender systems. ACM, New York, NY, pp 125–132
22. Smyth B, McGinty L, Reilly J, McCarthy K (2004) Compound critiques for conversational recommender systems. In: Proc of 2004 IEEE/WIC/ACM international conference on web intelligence (WI' 2004), Beijing, China. IEEE, Washington, DC, pp 141–151
23. Tang C, Lau RWH, Li Q, Yin H, Li T, Kilis D (2000) Personalized courseware construction based on web data mining. In: Proc. of the 1st international conference on web information systems engineering (WISE 2000), Hong Kong, China, vol 2. IEEE, Washington, DC, pp 204–211
24. Tang TY, McCalla G (2002) Student modeling for a web-based learning environment: a data mining approach (student abstract). In: Proceedings of 18th national conference on artificial intelligence (AAAI-2002). AAAI, Menlo Park, CA, pp 967–968
25. Tang TY, McCalla GI (2005) Paper annotations with learner models. In: Proceedings of the 12th international conference on artificial intelligence in education (AIED 2005), Amsterdam, The Netherlands. Ios Press, Amsterdam, The Netherlands, pp 654–661

26. Tang TY (2008) The design and study of pedagogical paper recommendation, Ph.D. Thesis, University of Saskatchewan, Department of Computer Science
27. Tang TY, McCalla G (2009) A multi-dimensional paper recommender: experiments and evaluation. IEEE Intern Comput 13(4):34–41
28. Torres R, McNee SM, Abel M, Konstan JA, Riedl J (2004) Enhancing digital libraries with TechLens. In: Proc. of IEEE/ACM joint conference on digital libraries (ACM/IEEE JCDL'2004), Tucson, AZ, USA, pp 228–236
29. Verbert K, Drachsler H, Manouselis N, Wolpers M, Vuorikari R, Duval E (2012) Dataset-driven research to support learning and knowledge analytics. Educ Tech Soc 15(3):133–148
30. Verbert K, Manouselis N, Ochoa X, Wolpers M, Drachsler H, Bosnic I, Duval E (2012) Context-aware recommender systems for learning: a survey and future challenges. IEEE Trans Learn Technol 5(4):318–335
31. Winoto P, Tang T (2010) The role of user mood in movie recommendations. Expert Syst Appl 37(8):6086–6092
32. Winoto P, Tang TY, McCalla GI (2012) Contexts in a paper recommendation system with collaborative filtering, International Review of Research in Open and Distance Learning, Special issue on technology enhanced information retrieval for online learning, 13(5):56–75
33. Woodruff A, Gossweiler R, Pitkow J, Chi E, Card S (2000) Enhancing a digital book with a reading recommender. In: Proc. of ACM conference on human factors in computing systems (ACM CHI'00), The Hague, The Netherlands, pp 153–160
34. Zaiane O (2002) Building a recommender agent for e-learning systems. In: Proceedings of the 7th international conference on computers in education (ICCE 2002). IEEE, Washington, DC

Part III
Platforms and Tools

Towards a Social Trust-Aware Recommender for Teachers

Soude Fazeli, Hendrik Drachsler, Francis Brouns, and Peter Sloep

Abstract Online communities and networked learning provide teachers with social learning opportunities, allowing them to interact and collaborate with others in order to develop their personal and professional skills. However, with the large number of learning resources produced every day, teachers need to find out what are the most suitable ones for them. In this paper, we introduce recommender systems as a potential solution to this. The setting is the Open Discovery Space (ODS) project. Unfortunately, due to the sparsity of the educational datasets most educational recommender systems cannot make accurate recommendations. To overcome this problem, we propose to enhance a trust-based recommender algorithm with social data obtained from monitoring the activities of teachers within the ODS platform. In this article, we outline the requirements of the ODS recommender system based on experiences reported in related TEL recommender system studies. In addition, we provide empirical evidence from a survey study with stakeholders of the ODS project to support the requirements identified from a literature study. Finally, we present an agenda for further research intended to find out which recommender system should ultimately be deployed in the ODS platform.

Keywords Recommender system • Collaborative filtering • Social data • Social networks • Sparsity • Trust • Trust network • Teacher • Learning object

S. Fazeli (✉) • H. Drachsler • F. Brouns • P. Sloep
Faculty of Psychology and Educational Sciences, Welten Institute – Research Centre
for Learning, Teaching and Technology, Open University of the Netherlands,
Heerlen, The Netherlands
e-mail: soude.fazeli@ou.nl; francis.brouns@ou.nl; peter.sloep@ou.nl;
hendrik.drachsler@ou.nl

N. Manouselis et al. (eds.), *Recommender Systems for Technology Enhanced Learning:*
Research Trends and Applications, DOI 10.1007/978-1-4939-0530-0_9,
© Springer Science+Business Media New York 2014

Introduction

The Internet provides teachers with a social space to interact and access resources in the form of either content or knowledgeable people outside their school [3, 4, 31]. However, with the increasing amount of user-generated content (e.g. in the form of learning resources, videos, discussion forums, blogs, etc.) produced every day, it becomes ever more difficult for teachers to find the most suitable content for their needs. Recommender systems have been introduced in the educational domain as a practical approach to solve information overload problems [21]. Generally speaking, recommender systems provide a user with the most suitable content based on their past behaviour. They have become popular because of their successful applications in the e-commerce world such as by Amazon[1] and eBay.[2] Fortunately, they can be adjusted and successfully used also in the educational domain as proven in the latest state of the art report by Manouselis et al. [21]. In this research, we investigate which recommender system algorithm suits the information overload problem of teachers best. The algorithm to be selected feeds on the activities of the teachers within an online social platform. The platform in this research is to be provided by the FP7 Open Discovery Space[3] (ODS) project. The ODS project aims to present a social network style platform that mainly aims to provide teachers with convenient accesses to approximately 1.550.000 learning resources from several content repositories and educational portals all over the Europe.

In general, two methods have been used in recommender systems: content-based filtering and collaborative filtering. Content-based methods recommend an item to a user based on the similarity between the item's content description and the user's preferences model [26]. Collaborative filtering algorithms try to find similar users based on the users' ratings and opinions. CF algorithms search for like-minded users that are introduced as neighbourhoods and they predict an item's rating for a target user based on collected ratings of the user's neighbours [14, 29]. In this research, we use collaborative filtering methods as we mainly focus on the interactions and collaborations between teachers within an online social platform. However, it is difficult to compute similarity of user profiles when users do not share a common set of ratings or when there are too few ratings available; this is known as the *sparsity problem* [11, 29]. Unfortunately, educational datasets suffer from this problem more often than commercial datasets [36]. Therefore, before we can even use recommender systems in learning, we need to find ways to overcome the sparsity problem.

Social trust has been introduced to many recommender systems as a response to the sparsity problem [11, 16, 17, 24, 39]. Trust has an important role in research areas as wide ranging as sociology, psychology, and computer sciences. Trust has many forms as it depends on many factors. In this research, we focus on trust in the

---

[1] http://www.amazon.com

[2] http://www.ebay.com

[3] Open Discovery Space is a 7th framework European project, http://opendiscoveryspace.eu/

context of social networks. In general, users prefer to receive recommendations from people they trust. Ziegler and Golbeck [39] show a strong connection between trust and user similarity. In previous work, we utilized this when forming ad-hoc transient groups of similar users as a means of collectively solving content-related questions that learners experience [10, 32, 35]. However, Golbeck [11] shows that trust captures not only simple overall similarity between users but also other features of the relationships between users. In recommender systems research, trustworthy users have been introduced as the users who have shared positive experiences in the past [11, 17, 18] and thus, trust is a value that reflects "a history of interactions rather than a history of similar ratings" [17].

Trust can help us to solve sparsity problem if it is assumed to be transitive; that is, if A trusts B and B trusts C, then A trusts C. Assuming that trust is transitive allows us to find a relationship between two users who have no common set of items but do have friends in common. Suppose we have two users: Alice and Carol who have no rated set of items in common. Therefore, it is not possible to compute similarity between them. As a result, there will no direct relationship between Alice and Carol even though they are already indirectly connected through another user Bob. However, Carol might be a useful source of information for Alice and *vice versa*. In this case, the transitivity of the trust relationship helps us to infer a relationship between Alice and Carol through their common friend Bob: if Alice trusts Bob in his recommendations on papers and Bob also trusts Carol in the same way then, Alice can trust Carol in her recommendations on papers. It is important to note that the trust value between two users is computed based on their history of interactions that shows to what extent a user can trust the other. The initially assigned trust value will be gradually adjusted on the basis of users' interactions. In this way, the potential recommenders who provided valuable information to a user are trusted with higher degrees of trust and the users who could not be sources of information will be downgraded [17]. So, *this is how we define "trust" in this research: trust is a transitive relation between users who share a history of interactions*. Although trust defined this way is different from many other, social or psychological definitions, it is sufficiently similar to them to be useful in realistic contexts.

In teachers' communities, teachers can perhaps be supported to find trustworthy resources as proxies for reliable sources of information. Such trustworthy resources enable teachers to feel more comfortable to share and interact within a closed and trustful community. To achieve this, we follow a trust-based recommender system proposed by Fazeli et al. [9] to create trust networks of users based on the rating information of user profile and item profile. Fazeli et al. proposed a concept called T-index to measure trustworthiness of users in order to improve the process of finding the nearest neighbours. The T-index is inspired on the H-index, which is used to evaluate the impact of publications [15]. In the present context, the higher the T-index value of a user, the more trustworthy that user becomes. Fazeli et al. showed how the T-index improves the structure of a generated trust network of users by creating connections to more trustworthy users [9]. Trust networks of users are described as a graph in which nodes represent the users and directed edges show the trust relationships [5, 9, 12]. Fazeli et al. created the trust relationships between users based on the ratings users gave to the items in their system [9]. Although user evaluations in the form of ratings is one of the important examples of users' activities within a social environment, other social activities of users should not be ignored up front. In general, the social activities of users describe each action of users within a social environment, for instance browsing a Web page, bookmarking, tagging, making a comment, giving rating, etc. We refer to the data that comes from the social activities of users, as *social data*. In this research, we aim to enhance the existing T-index approach of Fazeli et al. [9] by using social data of users. We intend to create trust relationship between users based on the collected social data from their activities within the ODS platform.

Therefore, the first research question is:

RQ1: Can the sparsity problem within educational datasets be solved by using inter-user trust relationships, which originally come from the social activities of users within an online environment, and, if so, how?

Moreover, we aim to study how the generated trust networks of users can be improved by social data of users. Therefore, we need to study the structure of trust networks for teachers and show how using trust relationships between users can have a positive effect on the generated trust networks of users. So, the second research question is:

RQ2: Can the use of the inter-user trust relationships that originally come from the social activities of users within an online environment, help teacher networks evolve?

The rest of this paper is organized as follows: section "State-of-the-Art" presents the state-of-the-art in recommender systems with the aim of exploring what characteristics should be taken into account when designing a recommender system. In section "Requirement Analysis," we describe the requirements analysis phase. We define a use case scenario as a practical example and then we validate the given use case with the collected data in a visionary workshop. Based on the requirements derived in section "Requirement Analysis," section "Ongoing and Future Research" presents an overview of on-going and future tasks in our research. Section "Conclusion" discusses our conclusions.

State-of-the-Art

Several reviews exist which detail how to study and classify recommender systems in terms of recommendation techniques, tasks, delivery mode, etc. However, each of these reviews focuses only on some of the dimensions to classify recommender systems and none of them present an integrated framework for the classification of recommender systems [21]. Manouselis and Costopoulou [20] propose a framework for categorizing the dimensions of recommender systems, which were identified in the related studies. We will use this framework to investigate the characteristics

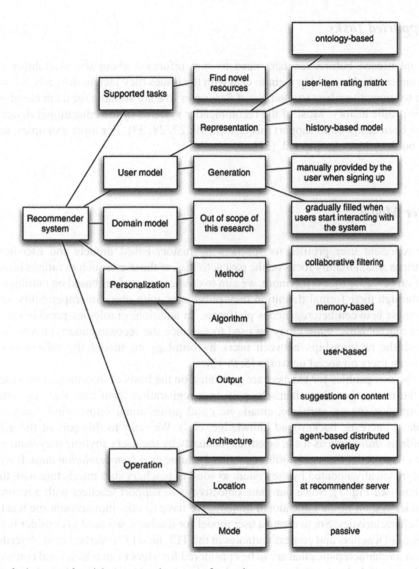

Fig. 1 A proposed social recommender system for teachers

that should be considered when designing a recommender system for teachers. As shown in Fig. 1, the proposed framework consists of five main categories of characteristics: (1) Supported tasks, (2) User model, (3) Domain model, (4) Personalization, and (5) Operation. We will now introduce each of the characteristics briefly and conclude with how the resulting framework could be applied to a recommender system for teachers.

Supported Tasks

As mentioned before, teachers need to stay informed about the availability of resources which may help them to deal with the issues they face in their job. So, we aim to support teachers to *Find Novel Resources* that are suitable for them based on their profile history. Most of the recommender systems in the educational domain have been designed to support this task [8, 19, 27, 28, 33]. For more examples, see the book by Manouselis et al. [21].

User Model

We represent user profiles for teachers by history-based models and user-item matrices which mainly focus on the past activities of the users, such as ratings information [19, 23, 28]. Furthermore, we aim to create user profiles based on ontologies as through their formal definition they provide us with more interoperability and openness between heterogeneous platforms. In addition, ontologies provide inference mechanisms, which may be used to enhance the recommender systems. We create the relationships between users by ontology to model the relationships between users on social networks [5, 9, 12].

The user profiles for teachers are generated on the basis of information provided by the users when they themselves fill in a registration form with their personal information (name, surname, email, etc.) and professional information (teaching subject, interests, background knowledge, etc.). We refer to this part of the user profile as *static data* as it can be edited manually by the users anytime they want to. The other part of the user profiles contains dynamic or *recommendation data*. It will be dynamically updated by the system as soon as teachers start interacting with the system (see Fig. 1). Since our main objective is to support teachers with a recommender system in the educational domain, we have to take into account the teachers' characteristics. So, to create a user model for teachers, we need to consider both actions of teachers and context variables in the TEL field [37]. Verbert et al. describe the main characteristics that are to be considered for users in an educational context, such as knowledge level, interests, goals and tasks, and background knowledge, in addition to the data regarding users' actions in terms of type and result of actions and the context in which an action has been taken [37].

As indicated, we intend to take advantage of social data of users to deal with the sparsity problem. To do so, we keep track of users' actions, so-called social activities, when they for instance rate, tag, bookmark, or share content in the ODS platform. In this way, the recommendations will be generated and improved based on the recorded actions of teachers while they interact with the ODS platform. As mentioned before, social data originally come from these recorded actions of users (teachers). To capture the social data, we intend to follow a standard specification to store and maintain users' actions. Several standard specifications to describe social data of users and guarantee their interoperability exist. They are:

- **FOAF**. The FOAF (Friend-of-a-Friend) vocabulary [13] describes user's information and their social connections through concepts and properties in form of an ontology using Semantic Web technologies [12]. The FOAF Vocabulary describes personal information and social relationships. The FOAF Vocabulary shows basic information of users (FOAF Basics) such as name, surname and also personal information about the people that a user "knows" and its interest area (Personal Info). In this research, we could extend the FOAF ontology to describe users by the concept of *FOAF:agent* that enables us to present our system in a distributed setting to provide more scalability. Several trust-based recommender systems have described the trust relationship between users by extending the FOAF ontology to model the social relationship between users [9, 12, 24].

- **CAM**. Contextualized Attention Metadata (CAM) is a format to capture observations about users' activities with any kind of tool [30, 38]. A CAM schema aims to store whatever has attracted users' attention while the users are working with the tool. It also stores users' interaction with the tool such as rating, tagging, etc. A CAM schema records an event and its details when a user performs an action within a tool. The metadata stored in the CAM format describe all types of users' feedback and, therefore, can be used to make recommendations for the users. Platforms that have been developed based on CAM schema, allow users to remove the tags they already assigned to a learning object, or to modify the ratings value they already gave to a learning object. Although this kind of information can be useful when generating recommendations, we prefer to provide users with the updated information of a learning object and not with the history of removed tags, modified ratings, etc. [25].

- **Organic.Edunet**. In the context of Organic.Edunet,[4] Manouselis and Vuorikari [22] developed a model to represent and store users' feedback, including rating, tagging, reviewing, etc. in a structured, interoperable and reusable format. This model is also based on the CAM format and aims to transfer the social data of users between heterogeneous systems. The social data of users are stored and retrieved by help of a so-called Social Navigation Module that is also in charge of making recommendations based on user profiles. At the moment, the Organic.Edunet schema does not support social data of users other than the ones already implemented by the Social Navigation Module in forms of tags, ratings and reviews.

We have also reviewed other standard specifications to describe social data such as Learning registry paradata[5] and NSDL paradata[6] but they have been designed to store the usage data of a learning object in an aggregated manner. In other words,

---

[4] http://portal.organic-edunet.eu/

[5] http://www.learningregistry.org/documents/starter-resources

[6] http://www.learningregistry.org/community/nsdl

they do not specifically keep track of the individual actions of each user. In our research, we need to store and retrieve every single action of the users in order to make recommendations for them. This is why we selected the standard specifications mentioned above, that is FOAF, CAM, and Organic.Edunet schemas.

Domain Model

Objects that are to be presented to teachers need to be represented somehow and need to be generated before they can be presented. This task is out of scope for the present research project. It will, parenthetically, be taken up by the ODS project, which aims to represent an integrated object repository containing several collections of learning objects hosted by the ARIADNE[7] infrastructure. (The ODS intends to provide the largest European learning object repository in the field of education in 2015 including approximately 1.550.000 learning resources from 75 content repositories and 15 educational portals.)

Personalization

Method. As we pointed out in section "Introduction," we use collaborative filtering methods because they purely depend on users' opinions and interactions and do not need the actual content descriptions required by content-based methods. We intend to enhance the trust-based collaborative filtering approach of Fazeli et al. [9] by using social data of users within the ODS platform.

Algorithm. CF methods are often categorized according to type or technique. *Type* refers to memory-based and model-based algorithms [20, 29]. Model-based algorithms use probabilistic approaches to develop a model of a user from the user's history and profile. Examples of model-based algorithms are Bayesian networks, neural networks, and algebraic approaches such as eigenvectors [16]. Although these algorithms are faster than memory-based algorithms, they require a full set of users' preferences to develop user models; such a set is often not available. Moreover, model-based algorithms are often very costly for learning and updating phases. Instead, memory-based algorithms are quite straightforward to use. They find correlations between users based on statistical techniques for measuring similarity, such as Pearson correlations or Cosine similarities [2]. As they are more straightforward, we use memory-based algorithms in this research. In case the pure memory-based algorithms do not scale well in real-life applications, we combine them with some pre-computation to reduce the run-time complexity [29].

---

[7] http://www.ariadne-eu.org/repositories

The *technique* of CF algorithms often refers to user-based and item-based algorithms [20, 29]. User-based algorithms try to find patterns of similarity between users in order to make recommendations, and item-based algorithms follow the same process but are based on similarity between items [29]. In this research, we are interested in user-based algorithms because we focus on users interactions and activities within an online social environment such as the ODS platform.

Output. The majority of the recommender systems generate recommendations in the form of suggestions on content or people, or sometimes ratings [1, 8, 28]. Another common output of recommender systems is predictions of a rating value that a user would give to an item [29]. In this research, we currently focus on recommending content to the teachers in the context of the ODS platform. As a further step, we aim to make suggestions on people as well.

Operation

In the TEL domain, most of the recommender systems follow a centralized architecture, in which a central recommender server provides access to a single learning object repository; only a few are based on a distributed architecture [21]. In this research, we intend to follow the agent-setting distributed approach by Fazeli et al. [9] to provide more scalability if the number of users were to increase. Fazeli et al. describe each user by extending the FOAF agent concept [5, 9, 12]. As a result, each user can be viewed as a peer in a distributed setting such as peer-to-peer networks.

The recommendations are to be made at the recommender server (location) and are to be sent to the users as a part of their natural interactions within the ODS platform, e.g. when a user browses a page or rates a learning object. In this way, users do not need to ask for recommendations explicitly; this is referred to as passive mode [29]. Thus, users receive recommendations on learning objects they make an action such as browsing, rating, tagging, etc. within the ODS platform.

Requirement Analysis

In this research, we follow the methodology described by Manouselis et al. for recommender systems in TEL [21]. We extended this methodology by first conducting a survey study with teachers in the context of the ODS summer school for European teachers in Greece, July 2012. We there asked them to fill in a questionnaire regarding the importance or usefulness of the activities within an online social platform and also regarding the use of recommender systems. The questionnaire consists of questions about the use of social data and recommender systems by teachers e.g. "Do you find sharing of content on Facebook, Twitter, etc. or by email important, useful or useless." Moreover, the designed questionnaire includes questions about how teachers think of recommender systems.

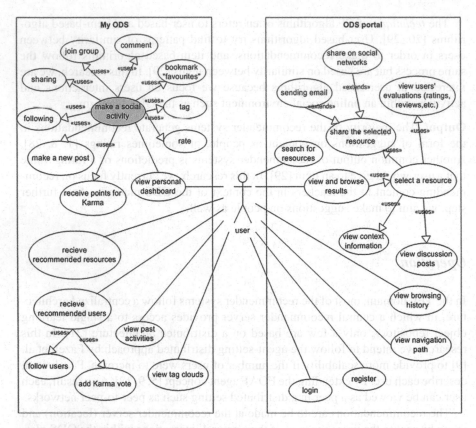

Fig. 2 Irma use case diagram

In the following subsections, we will first describe a use case scenario for a teacher called Irma, to identify the main requirements; then, we will discuss the results we achieved based on the Irma use case scenario. The results present a list of the most important needs and requirements of teachers within an online social environment such as the ODS platform.

Irma: A Teacher from the Netherlands

We created a use case scenario for a staring teacher in math and physics at a secondary school in the Netherlands [6]. We call her Irma. Figure 2 shows a UML use case diagram to describe her activities within the ODS platform.

Irma has just started to work as a teacher and as a new teacher she faces several challenges every day at her school. An official mentor was already assigned to her to have weekly meetings but she still does not feel confident. She would like to get in touch with other teachers, mentors, experts, and novices, to share her concerns with them. Sometimes it is not even clear to her what the problem is and how she can formulate it when she has official meetings with her mentor. So, she needs to hear how things went with the other teachers, what were their main challenges when they started their job, and how they tackled those issues. She is quite curious to know if there is somebody out there who is in a situation similar to hers and, if so, whether they could exchange information. Moreover, she is very interested to know how she could innovate her teaching in her classroom to attract and motivate the pupils and to make the atmosphere of the classroom more entertaining. Irma has just seen an advertisement about a social platform for teachers called the ODS platform. She decides to check it out and she first uses the search mechanism by entering a few keywords to explore the available learning resources related to her teaching subject. She browses the results and selects a couple of them that look interesting to her. If she so wishes, the platform allows her to share the interesting ones with others on the social networking sites such as Facebook or Twitter, or simply by sending emails to them.

Whenever Irma happens to find a learning resource, she can see the evaluations of other users (ratings, reviews, etc.) and the discussion posts connected to the selected learning resource. Irma finds several groups related to the discussion posts that attracted her and she feels quite motivated to participate in discussions because that is exactly what she has been looking for. To do so, Irma has to become a member first, to be allowed to go to the "My ODS" (shown in Fig. 2). So, she fills a registration form and becomes a member. Now, she can join groups of her interest and participate in discussions. She can rate, tag, bookmark the learning resources and make comments as part of her activities within the ODS as a social platform (note that this we referred to as *social activities* of a user). The more she contributes to the social activities, the more points she receives for her 'Karma,' that shows her potential for being a trustworthy user. Furthermore, Irma sees a personal dashboard on the "My ODS" page where she receives recommendations on learning resources that might be of interest to her. That is particularly useful when she is not quite sure about the exact keywords she has to enter when searching for learning resources. Irma becomes even happier when she sees a list of recommended people for her based on her past activities and profile. She browses the list and finds experts, mentors, and other novices among them with whom she would like to get in touch. So, she chooses to "follow" them in order to see what kind of social activities they have been engaging in within the ODS platform e.g. if they rated, bookmarked, tagged resources and if they posted a new discussion in a particular group. Based on their activities, Irma can add to their Karma vote. After checking out the ODS platform, Irma now feels much more confident to see that there is much suitable content and there are many interesting people in the ODS for her (For a more detailed use case scenario, please refer to the ODS deliverable 8.1 [6]).

Validation of Irma Use Case

To validate the Irma use case, we took advantage of a summer school for European teachers that was held in Greece, July 2012 in the context of the ODS. We first presented the Irma use case to the participants of a visionary workshop, and followed

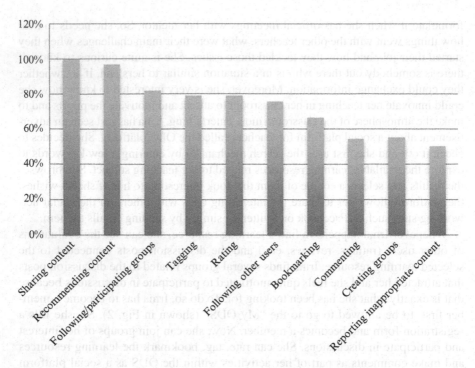

Fig. 3 How much the teachers find the online social activities important/useful

that up with discussions on the use case. Then, we asked the participating teachers to fill in a questionnaire consisting of statements about social activities and recommender systems. The intention was to find out if the participating teachers would find them useful or important for their personal and professional development. In total, 33 teachers participated in the survey study; they came from 14 countries (Portugal, Germany, France, Finland, Greece, Austria, Poland, Lithuania, Spain, Hungary, Romania, Cyprus, Ireland, Serbia and the US). From each country two teachers participated except for Spain and Hungary with five and four participants, respectively. The majority of participants were secondary school teachers (73 %) while there were also representatives from primary schools (6 %), teacher trainers (6 %) and trainees (27 %), university lecturers (6 %), museum educators (6 %), curriculum developers (3 %) and educational policy makers (6 %). Some of the participating teachers indicated that they had more than one role. Eighteen female and fifteen male teachers participated. Participants came from different age ranges: 20–30 years old teachers (25.2 %), 31–40 years old (33.4 %), 41–50 years old (22.2 %) and over 50 years old (19.2 %).

Figure 3 shows the degree to which the participating teachers found it useful or important that the social activities displayed on the horizontal axis be provided within a social platform like the ODS. All of them agreed that the possibility to *share content via social networks* such as Facebook or Twitter is very important. In the second place, around 97 % of the teachers found *recommending content to*

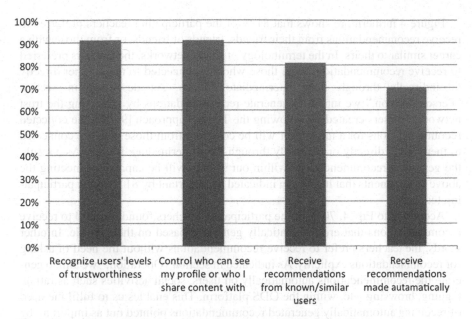

Fig. 4 How much teachers find the detailed requirements important/useful

somebody like a friend or colleague quite useful. Moreover, almost 80 % of the participants thought that it is important to be able to *tag the content* by keywords, to *rate the content*, to *follow other users*, and *to follow/participate existing groups* in an online social platform. For around 65 % of participating teachers *bookmarking* content seemed to be a useful activity. On average, 53 % of the teachers thought that it is useful to *comment*, to *create groups*, and to *report inappropriate content or a broken link*.

In total, more than 50 % of the participants found most of social activities important or useful. It shows how much the teachers are interested in the social features that the ODS platform is to provide to them.

In addition to the results shown in Fig. 3, we asked the teachers some more detailed questions about receiving recommendations, as well as about privacy issues in a an online social platform. Figure 4 presents the results of what the participating teachers found important or useful and the degree to which they thought so. It shows that privacy issues are quite important for most of the teachers. They want to know with whom they share content and information, and also who can see their profile. Therefore, they need to be able to control their privacy settings in an online social platform. Moreover, 91 % of the participating teachers found it important to recognize how much they can trust the other users e.g. with respect to the content other users shared with them. The planned extension of the trust-based recommender (section "Personalization") will ensure that some user is introduced to the other users in trust networks by the assigned T-index, which bases itself on that user's contributions and history. This will then also enable us to address these requirements.

Figure 4 furthermore shows that 81 % of the participating teachers preferred to receive recommendations from their friends, friends of friends, or from those with a career similar to theirs. In the terminology of social networks, the teachers preferred to receive recommendations from those who are connected to them either directly or indirectly through their intermediate friends. As described in section "Personalization," we intend to generate recommendations by traversing the trust networks of users created by following the T-index approach [9]. So, the collected recommendations for a target user will be collected from those who are connected to them either directly or indirectly through their intermediate friends. As a result, the generated recommendations within our system will be capable of meeting the above requirements that have been indicated as important by 81 % of the participating teachers.

According to Fig. 4, 70 % of the participating teachers found it useful to receive recommendations that are automatically generated based on their profile. In other words, the teachers prefer to receive recommendations without the need of asking for recommendations explicitly. As indicated in section "Operation," we aim to generate the recommendations automatically on users' social activities such as rating, tagging, browsing, etc. within the ODS platform. This enables us to fulfil the need of receiving automatically generated recommendations pointed out as important by 70 % of the teachers.

Ongoing and Future Research

Section "Requirement Analysis" described our requirements analysis as the first step of our research method. This section now presents next steps that should be taken.

Data Study

The main goal is to find a recommender system algorithm that best covers the requirements for teachers derived in section "Requirement Analysis." To uncover what is best, we will conduct an offline empirical study of different recommender system algorithms on a selected collection of representative datasets. The study will be in terms of the metrics that are most often used to evaluate the performance of recommender systems, such as prediction accuracy of the generated recommendations. In addition, we aim to study the structure of the trust networks of users when using the trust-based recommender system [9]. The network's structure will be evaluated in terms of indegree distribution (for some node on a network, the indegree describes the number of incoming edges to that node). In this research, we can interpret the indegree of a user within a network, as the number of users that already trusted the user. In general, we are interested in a balanced indegree distribution that can have a positive effect on users' mutual interactions and their contributions.

Initial results will indicate which of the recommender algorithms suits teachers best and if the trust-based recommender system can indeed help to deal with the problem of sparse data exhibited by the datasets used.

Based on the requirement analysis described in section "Requirement Analysis," we selected the following educational datasets as our candidate datasets to be studied [36]: Travel well, MACE, OpenScout, MERLOT. The planned study will evaluate a set of different classical CF algorithms next to the trust-based algorithm [9] on a variety of educational datasets. An issue with the educational datasets is that most of them are not publicly available. Moreover, unfortunately, there is no golden standard dataset in the educational domain such as is the MovieLens dataset[8] in the e-commerce world. For instance, for the Travel well dataset, different versions are available. In fact, no unique version has been singled out for running the experiments, nor for making a comparison in the recommender system community. To address these issues, the dataTEL project proposed to establish a set of representative datasets as a reference for running data-driven studies in the educational domain [7].

User Evaluation Study

Having identified the most promising recommendation algorithms based on the data study, we will develop the initial recommender system for the ODS project. We will run a user evaluation study at one of the upcoming ODS summer schools to study usability of the prototype by evaluating users' satisfaction. Through a questionnaire the end-users will be asked to provide feedback on the prototype. Questions asked will be how interesting the end-users find the recommended content and how recommended content can help users to gain new knowledge or improve their current knowledge [34].

Based on the outcomes, the prototype will be customized and improved so as to be able to deploy an improved release for an extended pilot study with a large number of European teachers as the ODS real users. Initial feedback by end-users on usability of the prototype is the outcome we expect.

Pilot Study

Ultimately, we aim to deploy a stable release that will be tested under realistic and standard operational conditions with the end-users. To do so, we compare the performance of a proposed recommender system based on our presented framework with classical collaborative filtering algorithms. Furthermore, we aim to study the

---

[8] http://www.grouplens.org/node/73

structure of the teachers' networks to investigate how networks of teachers will evolve by the use of social data. To evaluate the effectiveness of the proposed recommender system, we will compare the results in terms of the total number of learning objects which have been visited, bookmarked, rated, etc. for two groups of users:

- Those who are aided by recommender systems to access learning objects
- Those who access learning objects directly from the repository, without the help of a recommender system.

We will measure prediction accuracy, coverage and F1 measure of the generated recommendations, effectiveness in terms of total number of learning objects visited, bookmarked, or rated, as well as indegree distribution. The last will be used to study how the structure of the networks changes. Once the results are in, we expect to find out whether our proposed recommender system outperforms the classical CF algorithms. An important concomitant outcome will be the visualization of teachers' networks, to show how the network's structure evolves when relying on inter-user trust relationships that come from the social data of users.

Conclusion

In this paper, we introduced recommender systems as a potential way to support teachers in finding content that matches their needs and interests. We also argued that we likely need to overcome the sparsity problem, which hinders recommender systems in the educational domain. Therefore, we presented two research questions and research method that mainly focus on ways to tackle the sparsity problem. Social trust is a key concept here. The results of a requirement analysis presented in this paper were consistent with the main requirements described by a use case scenario. The results indicated that the majority of the teachers are interested in online social activities such as rating, tagging, bookmarking, sharing the content, commenting, following other users, etc. Moreover, the results show that teachers prefer to receive recommendations from trustworthy users in particular. This requirement underscores the use of social trust when designing a recommender system for teachers.

Besides recommending the most suitable content to teachers, we plan to support teachers to find the peers with whom they can share their concerns and, in general, exchange knowledge.

Acknowledgment This paper is part of a doctoral study funded by NELLL (the Netherlands Laboratory for Lifelong Learning at the OUNL) and the Open Discovery Space project. Open Discovery Space is funded by the European Union under the Information and Communication Technologies (ICT) theme of the seventh Framework Programme for R&D. This document does not represent the opinion of the European Union, and the European Union is not responsible for any use that might be made of its content.

References

1. Beham G, Kump B, Ley T, Lindstaedt S (2010) Recommending knowledgeable people in a work-integrated learning system. Proc Comput Sci 1:2783–2792
2. Breese JS, Heckerman D, Kadie C (1998) Empirical analysis of predictive algorithms for collaborative filtering. In: Proceedings of the 14th conference on uncertainty in artificial intelligence (UAI 1998). Morgan Kaufmann, San Francisco, CA, pp 43–52
3. Brown JS, Adler RP (2008) Minds on fire: open education, the long tail, and learning 2.0. EDUCAUSE Rev 43(1):16–32
4. Dawson S (2008) A study of the relationship between student social networks and sense of community. Educ Tech Soc 11:224–238
5. Dokoohaki N, Matskin M (2008) Effective design of trust ontologies for improvement in the structure of socio-semantic trust networks. Int J Adv Intell Syst 1:23–42
6. Drachsler H, Greller W, Fazeli S, Niemann K, Sanchez-Alonso S, Rajabi E, Palmér M, Ebner H, Simon B, Nösterer D, Kastrantas K, Manouselis N, Hatzakis I, Clements K (2012) D8.1 Review of social data requirements. Open discovery space project. http://hdl.handle.net/1820/4617
7. Drachsler H, Verbert K, Sicilia M-A et al (2011) dataTEL - Datasets for technology enhanced learning - White paper
8. Drachsler H, Pecceu D, Arts T, Hutten E, Rutledge L, Van Rosmalen P, Hummel HGK, Koper R (2009) ReMashed – recommendations for mash-up personal learning environments. In: Cress U, Dimitrova V, Specht M (eds) Learning in the synergy of multiple disciplines. Proceedings of the 4th European conference on technology enhanced learning (EC-TEL 2009). Springer, Berlin, pp 788–793
9. Fazeli S, Zarghami A, Dokoohaki N, Matskin M (2010) Elevating prediction accuracy in trust-aware collaborative filtering recommenders through T-index metric and top trustee lists. J Emerg Tech Web Intell 2:300–309. doi:10.4304/jetwi.2.4.300-309
10. Fetter S, Berlanga AJ, Sloep PB, Van der Vegt W, Rajagopal K, Brouns F (2012) Using peer-support to connect learning network participants to each other: an interdisciplinary approach. Int J Learn Technol 7(4):378–399. doi:10.1504/IJLT.2012.052212
11. Golbeck J (2009) Trust and nuanced profile similarity in online social networks. ACM Trans Web 3(4):1–33. doi:10.1145/1594173.1594174
12. Golbeck J (2005) Computing and applying trust in web-based social networks. University of Maryland at College Park, College Park, MD
13. Graves M, Constabaris A, Brickley D (2007) FOAF: connecting people on the semantic web. Spec Iss Knitt Seman Web 43:191–202. doi:10.1300/J104v43n03_10
14. Herlocker JL, Konstan JA, Terveen LG, Riedl JT (2004) Evaluating collaborative filtering recommender systems. ACM Trans Inf Syst 22:5–53
15. Hirsch JE (2005) An index to quantify an individual's scientific research output. Proc Natl Acad Sci U S A 102(46):16569–16572
16. Kamvar SD, Schlosser MT, Garcia-Molina H (2003) The Eigentrust algorithm for reputation management in P2P networks. Proceedings of the twelfth international conference on World Wide Web - WWW'03. ACM Press, New York, NY, p 640
17. Lathia N, Hailes S, Capra L (2008) Trust-based collaborative filtering. Trust management II, IFIP advances in information and communication technology, vol 263. Springer, Boston, MA, pp 119–134. doi:10.1007/978-0-387-09428-1_8
18. Lee DH, Brusilovsky P (2009) Does trust influence information similarity? In: Proceedings of the workshop on recommender systems and the social web (RSWEB'09). ACM, New York, NY, pp 3–6
19. Lemire D, Boley H, McGrath S, Ball M (2005) Collaborative filtering and inference rules for context-aware learning object recommendation. Interact Tech Smart Educ 2:179–188
20. Manouselis N, Costopoulou C (2007) Analysis and classification of multi-criteria recommender systems. WWW Int Web Inform Syst 10(4):415–441

21. Manouselis N, Drachsler H, Verbert K, Duval E (2012) Recommender systems for learning. Springer, New York, NY, pp 1–61. doi:10.1007/978-1-4614-4361-2
22. Manouselis N, Vuorikari R (2009) What if annotations were reusable: a preliminary discussion. In: Spaniol M (ed) Proceedings of the 8th international conference on advances in web-based learning - ICWL 2009. Springer, Berlin, pp 255–264
23. Manouselis N, Vuorikari R, van Assche F (2010) Collaborative recommendation of e-learning resources: an experimental investigation. J Comput Assist Learn 26:227–242
24. Massa P, Avesani P (2007) Trust-aware recommender systems. Proceedings of the ACM conference on recommender systems - RecSys'07. ACM Press, New York, NY
25. Niemann K, Scheffel M, Wolpers M (2012) A comparison of usage data formats for recommendations in TEL. Proceedings of the 2nd workshop on recommender systems in technology enhanced learning (EC-TEL 2012), Saarbrücken, Germany, September 18–19 2012
26. Pazzani MJ, Billsus D (2007) Content-based recommendation systems. The adaptive web, vol 4321, Lecture notes in computer science. Springer, Berlin, pp 325–341. doi:10.1007/978-3-540-72079-9_10
27. Rafaeli S, Dan-Gur Y, Barak M (2005) Social recommender systems: recommendations in support of e-learning. IJDET 3(2):30–47. doi:10.4018/jdet.2005040103
28. Recker MM, Walker A, Lawless K (2003) What do you recommend? Implementation and analyses of collaborative information filtering of web resources for education. Instr Sci 31:299–316. doi:10.1023/A:1024686010318
29. Schafer JB, Frankowski D, Herlocker J, Sen S (2007) Collaborative filtering recommender systems. The adaptive web, vol 4321, Lecture notes in computer science. Springer, Berlin, pp 291–324. doi:10.1007/978-3-540-72079-9_9
30. Schmitz H, Scheffel M, Friedrich M et al (2009) CAMera for PLE, vol 5794. Springer, Berlin, pp 507–520
31. Schuck S (2003) Getting help from the outside: developing a support network for beginning teachers. J Educ Enqu 4:49–67
32. Sloep PB (2009) Fostering sociability in learning networks through ad-hoc transient communities. In: Purvis M, Savarimuthu BTR (eds) Computer-mediated social networking, ICCMSN 2008, LNAI 5322. Springer, Berlin, pp 62–75
33. Tang T, McCalla G (2003) Smart recommendation for an evolving e-learning system. Workshop on technologies for electronic documents for supporting learning, International conference on artificial intelligence in education (AIED 2003), Sydney, Australia, July 20–24, 2003
34. Tang TY, McCalla G (2009) The pedagogical value of papers: a collaborative-filtering based paper recommender. J Digit Inf 10(2):1–12, Social Information Retrieval for Technology Enhanced Learning
35. Van Rosmalen P, Sloep PB, Brouns F et al (2008) A model for online learner support based on selecting appropriate peer tutors. J Comput Assist Learn 24:483–493. doi:10.1111/j.1365-2729.2008.00283.x
36. Verbert K, Drachsler H, Manouselis N et al (2011) Dataset-driven research for improving recommender systems for learning. Proceedings of the 1st international conference on learning analytics and knowledge. ACM, New York, NY, pp 44–53
37. Verbert K, Manouselis N, Drachsler H, Duval E (2012) Dataset-driven research to support learning and knowledge analytics. Educ Tech Soc Spec Iss Learn Knowl Anal 15:133–148
38. Wolpers M, Najjar J, Verbert K, Duval E (2007) Tracking actual usage: the attention metadata approach. Educ Tech Soc 10:106–121
39. Ziegler C-N, Golbeck J (2007) Investigating interactions of trust and interest similarity. Decis Support Syst 43:460–475. doi:10.1016/j.dss.2006.11.003

ALEF: From Application to Platform for Adaptive Collaborative Learning

Mária Bieliková, Marián Šimko, Michal Barla, Jozef Tvarožek,
Martin Labaj, Róbert Móro, Ivan Srba, and Jakub Ševcech

Abstract Web 2.0 has had a tremendous impact on education. It facilitates access
and availability of learning content in variety of new formats, content creation,
learning tailored to students' individual preferences, and collaboration. The range
of Web 2.0 tools and features is constantly evolving, with focus on users and ways
that enable users to socialize, share and work together on (user-generated) content.
In this chapter we present ALEF—Adaptive Learning Framework that responds to
the challenges posed on educational systems in Web 2.0 era. Besides its base functionality—to deliver educational content—ALEF particularly focuses on making
the learning process more efficient by delivering tailored learning experience via
personalized recommendation, and enabling learners to collaborate and actively
participate in learning via interactive educational components. Our existing and
successfully utilized solution serves as the medium for presenting key concepts that
enable realizing Web 2.0 principles in education, namely lightweight models, and
three components of framework infrastructure important for constant evolution and
inclusion of students directly into the educational process—annotation framework,
feedback infrastructure and widgets. These make possible to devise and implement
various mechanisms for recommendation and collaboration—we also present
selected methods for personalized recommendation and collaboration together with
their evaluation in ALEF.

Keywords Personalized recommendation • Web 2.0 • Collaborative learning •
Adaptive learning • Educational platform

M. Bieliková (✉) • M. Šimko • M. Barla • J. Tvarožek • M. Labaj • R. Móro
I. Srba • J. Ševcech
Institute of Informatics and Software Engineering, Faculty of Informatics
and Information Technologies, Slovak University of Technology in Bratislava,
Ilkovičova, 842 16 Bratislava, Slovakia
e-mail: maria.bielikova@stuba.sk; marian.simko@stuba.sk; michal.barla@stuba.sk; jozef.
tvarozek@stuba.sk; martin.labaj@stuba.sk; robert.moro@stuba.sk; ivan.srba@stuba.sk;
jakub.sevcech@stuba.sk

N. Manouselis et al. (eds.), *Recommender Systems for Technology Enhanced Learning:*   195
Research Trends and Applications, DOI 10.1007/978-1-4939-0530-0_10,
© Springer Science+Business Media New York 2014

Introduction

Technology has shaped the way people learn for decades. A particularly great influence of technology on learning came with the emergence of the Web in 1990s. But it was the next generation of Web, so called Web 2.0, which significantly shifted the existing paradigm of learning.

In general, Web 2.0 made the experience more interactive, empowering users with easy-to-use tools. It enabled user-based authoring of content (by utilizing blogs and wikis) and facilitated organization and sharing of knowledge (by annotating and tagging content, discussing content). It also simplifies collaboration and interaction between users. Users in web-based systems are no longer only content consumers, they have become content creators themselves and indeed they have started to actively contribute to the Web's content as envisioned by Berners-Lee [2].

An important implication is that Web 2.0 reflected into improved user experience during learning in web-based educational environments. A user—*learner*—gains more competences that result into greater autonomy for the learner. The traditional role of a teacher changes and distinction between teacher and student blurs [11].

Together with the increasing popularity and spread of the Web, we witness significant growth of educational materials available online. In order to allow effective learning techniques for adaptive navigation and content presentation adaptive web-based educational systems were devised almost two decades ago [1]. A common example of adaptive navigation is *recommendation* of learning objects. The recommendation methods tailor the presented content to a particular learner and/or support a learner by providing adaptive navigation. Most current adaptive web-based educational systems attempt to be more intelligent by advancing towards activities traditionally executed by human teachers—such as providing personal advices to students [4].

We see both collaboration and adaptation as key concepts facilitating learning in current web-based educational systems. Opportunities introduced by emergence of Web 2.0 imposed new requirements for adaptive web-based learning that should respond for constant change and inclusion students directly into educational process. The requirements shifted to the following criteria [40]:

- Extensible personalization and course adaptation based on comprehensive user model, which allows for simultaneous use of *different adaptive techniques* (such as recommendation) to enhance student's learning experience.
- Student *active participation* in learning process with the ability to collaborate, interact and create content by means of the read-write web vision. In particular, we exploit different types of annotations as a suitable way to allow for rich interactions on the top of the presented content.
- *Domain modeling* that allows (i) automation of domain model creation, and (ii) collaborative social aspect and the need to modify or alter domain model by students themselves.

In order to address the challenges posed on educational systems in Web 2.0 era and beyond, we developed ALEF—Adaptive LEarning Framework [40]. We have followed up on the prior research on adaptive learning at the Slovak University of Technology including adaptive learning applications ALEA [18] and FLIP [46]. ALEF now constitutes both a framework for adaptive collaborative educational systems and an instantiated system created primarily for research purposes, but used successfully in educational process at the Slovak University of Technology. After several years of research, ALEF became a base for various autonomous components, some of which present standalone applications, so now ALEF can be viewed rather as a platform for adaptive collaborative web-based learning.

The ALEF platform offers recommendation on various levels. The recommendation is not only on the level of course parts as a whole (learning objects), but also content outside of the integrated course material is recommended through annotation with information gathered from external sources. Content and information within the learning objects is recommended through summarizations.

In this chapter we present Adaptive Learning Framework ALEF. We focus on recommendation and collaboration in ALEF, which aims at delivering tailored learning experience via personalized recommendation, and enabling learners to collaborate and actively participate in learning via interactive educational components. We present not only functionality realized in ALEF, but also an infrastructure for providing this functionality, which facilitates personalized recommendation and active collaboration—domain model, user model and unique framework components: annotation framework, feedback infrastructure and widgets. Core part of this chapter discusses recommendation, which is performed in ALEF on several levels—on the learning objects level and on the content of learning objects where we provide also summarization which recommends particular parts of learning objects for effective repeating. Next, we present a concept of implicit and explicit collaboration in ALEF. This part is related to the recommendation as during collaboration several decision points exist where recommendation is useful concept. We conclude this chapter with short summarization and future directions.

Related Work

Adaptive and intelligent web-based educational systems address the new challenges related to impact of Web 2.0 on education in various ways. The same way as a good teacher adapts instruction to individual student's needs the adaptive and intelligent web-based educational system provide adaptive features (e.g., adaptive content presentation and navigation support) and intelligent features (e.g., problem solving support and solution analysis). The emergence of Web 2.0 technologies with its focus on user also changed user expectations. Users now expect that a learning system adapts according to their previous interactions, they expect to be able to actively participate in communities, collaborate and share their work.

Consequently, modern adaptive and intelligent web-based educational systems incorporate collaborative aspects such as knowledge sharing and organization (e.g., annotation and tagging of learning content, discussion forums), synchronous and asynchronous group work, and user-oriented content authoring (e.g., wikis).

User participation via Web 2.0 tools that enable creation, rating and sharing learning content drives the emergence of learning networks [17], which provide methods and technology for supporting personal competence development of lifelong learning, typically in an informal setting. Learning networks are structured around tags and ratings, which are often only sparsely provided by users, raising additional strain on recommendation methods in this setting. TENcompetence project is the largest EU-driven initiative that studies bottom-up approaches of knowledge creation and sharing.

There are two possible ways to take when building a modern adaptive learning system: (1) integrate adaptive features into an existing Learning Management System (LMS) such as Moodle, or (2) design and build an adaptive learning system from scratch. Some authors argue that the adoption rate of adaptive technologies in learning remains low mostly due to limited feature set of existing adaptive learning systems [23]. The learning systems are usually experimental prototypes designed and developed from scratch and not used beyond the university departments of their authors. Consequently, Meccawy et al. propose the WHURLE 2.0 framework that integrates Moodle's Web 2.0 social aspects with adaptation features. Their design follows the typical service-oriented architecture of other adaptive learning systems such as the distributed architecture of KnowledgeTree proposed by Brusilovsky [3]. KnowledgeTree architecture is based on distributed reusable learning activities that are provided by distributed activity servers, while other types of servers provide the remaining services which are required in every adaptive learning system: domain modeling, student modeling, and adaptation engine. The service-oriented architectures facilitate reusability of learning content and learning analytics across different services provided by the learning system.

Modern adaptive and intelligent web-based educational system is expected to provide diverse learning content and services to students. The content can range from non-interactive course material, simple quizzes and exercises to highly interactive synchronous collaborative learning. The basic services include the generic LMS services such as course administration, and automatic quiz/exercise evaluation services. Additional services result from the adaptive and social properties of the learning system. Each bit of the learning content is

1. adapted in various ways (e.g., student's needs, preferences or knowledge, teacher's requirements), and is
2. socially enabled by providing knowledge sharing, group work and user content authoring facilities. These services are typically backed by methods based on artificial intelligence and presented within a user interface that is continuously recording each user action providing back the data for analysis by the adaptation methods. Examples include methods for course material personalization and recommendation according to student's knowledge or time constraints.

Recommendation in education brings about additional requirements compared to methods of generic recommendation such as books or movies recommendation [22]. The typical recommendation scenarios apply (e.g., predicting link relevance, finding good (all) items, recommending sequence of items, finding novel resources, finding peers/helpers) with the additional consideration of relevancy to learning goals and learning context. The recommendation must also account for various pedagogical rules.

Recommendation differs substantially based on the type of corpus used. Closed corpus recommendation systems can take advantage of detailed metadata description and/or ontological representation of the learning objects. Consequently, the recommendation systems can effectively personalize the learning process through adapting the learning content and/or the learning sequence. The recommendation methods can take into account the various learning goals, contexts and pedagogical rules. As examples we can mention an approach for semantic recommendation in education settings called SERS [31] or XAPOS system [37].

Open corpus recommendation, on the other hand, does not require preexisting metadata descriptions. The objects are often preprocessed with automatic metadata extraction methods, and the recommendation itself typically relies on collaborative filtering methods that are robust to noisy input. The recommendation results improve when more user/item data is provided over the course of the recommendation systems lifetime.

Personal learning environments (PLE) enable even more personalized experience by providing facilities to build and personalize their own learning environment. The concept of PLEs and recommendation has been extensively studied in the ROLE project, approaches for recommendation specific to personal learning environments are outlined by Mödritscher [29].

Adaptive and intelligent web-based educational systems are based upon domain and user models. User model often follows overlay student modeling that represents student knowledge and other characteristics on top of domain model. Several reference models for adaptive web-based systems have been proposed, such as Adaptive Hypermedia Application Model (AHAM) [10], Munich reference model [16], and LAOS [6] and its social extension SLAOS [7]. When considering domain modeling in these reference models, they often suffer from tight coupling between conceptual description of subject domain and content. Also, support for Web 2.0 paradigm on the level of domain modeling is limited in these models. Although there are attempts to incorporate social collaborative aspects (e.g., content annotations, tagging, rating, commenting) into adaptive web-based systems at abstract level, it has limitations in extendibility of interaction and collaboration in domain model and ability to support interaction and collaboration on top of user-generated entities [7].

Adaptive Learning Framework ALEF

ALEF's primary goal is to provide an infrastructure for developing adaptive collaborative educational web-based systems [40]. Besides its base functionality—to deliver educational content—it particularly focuses on making the learning process more efficient by (1) delivering *tailored* learning experience via recommendation/ personalization, and (2) enabling learners to *collaborate* and *actively participate* in

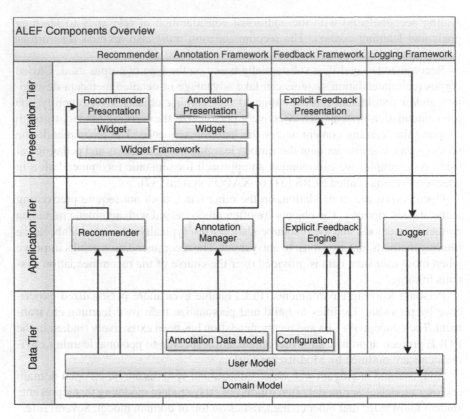

Fig. 1 ALEF components overview—three tiers architecture: data, application and presentation tier. Particular framework components spread across all of these tiers

learning via interactive educational components. To facilitate both aims ALEF's architecture incorporates two core models and framework components:

- *domain model*—rich yet lightweight domain model semantically describes resources within a course,
- *user model*—overlay user model represents current state of user's knowledge and goals,
- *framework components*—extendable components such as annotations framework and widgets provide fundamental functionality related to adaptive web-based systems.

Models can be used easily in any learning domain, and together with extendable framework components they allow developers to build custom framework extensions, that is, shifting the notion of ALEF from a framework for adaptive web-based educational systems towards a modern web-based educational platform.

Overview of different framework components together with their close connection to domain and user model is displayed on Fig. 1. Individual models and frameworks are discussed in more details in the following sections.

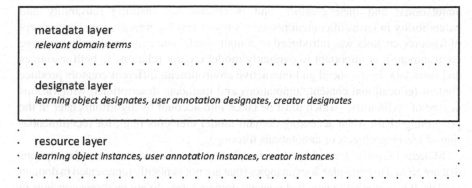

Fig. 2 Domain model scheme: metadata layer over designate layer. Resource instances are not a part of domain model (*solid line*) [39]

Domain Model

In domain modeling, ALEF leverages the so-called lightweight semantics and proposed a lightweight domain model for adaptive web-based educational courses [39]. We consider modern educational courses to consist of educational content[1] authored by teachers, and user-generated content (e.g., comments, tags) provided by students. The various types of user-generated content are represented uniformly as *annotations*—an abstraction representing user-generated content in ALEF.

Learning resources are not described using complex domain descriptions such as ontologies, instead, resources are described by *domain relevant terms*. The terms, relationships between terms, and their associations to resources constitute the core domain conceptualization that forms a basis for user modeling and is utilized by the adaptation engine. We take advantage of multilayer design that explicitly differentiates between resources, their abstractions and semantic descriptions (see Fig. 2) and clearly separates content from conceptualization.

Domain model consists of:

- designate layer, and
- metadata layer.

These two layers represent a conceptual abstraction over resource instances (both learning objects and annotations) that are created and modified by content authors. Resource instances form the actual learning content presented to learners (e.g., a learning object *Recursion basics* in a programming course).

Designate layer is further divided into *resource designates* and *creator designates*. Designate layer represents an abstraction of resources (learning objects,

---

[1]A basic component for education delivery is a learning object. For learning object we adopt a broader definition by IEEE, which defines a learning object as any entity, digital or non-digital, that may be used for learning, education or training [15].

annotations) and their creators, and is crucial for ensuring reusability and extendibility in terms of content resource's lower level representation. The concept of resource creators was introduced to domain model since in social and interactive environment it is important to explicitly model creator relations to both resources and metadata. In the social and interactive environment, different creators produce content (educational content, annotations and metadata descriptions) with various degree of "reliability," which must be taken into account by algorithms later in the processing chain when accessing domain model elements (e.g., for recommendation of learning objects or annotations filtering).

Metadata layer is formed by domain relevant terms—easy to create descriptions that are related to particular domain topics (that are not explicitly represented in domain model). It is important to note that relevant domain terms do not represent concepts in strict ontological definition, cf. [8]. They rather represent lexical reference to non-explicit topics or concepts, which form the domain model. Examples of relevant domain terms in the domain of programming involve *recursion*, *cycle* or *comment*.

Learning content is comprised of various types of learning objects such as explanations, exercises and questions. These elements are interconnected via various types of relationships that represent different forms of relatedness between domain model elements. In ALEF's domain model, we distinguish three (high level) types of element relationships:

- relationship between designates,
- relationship between designates and relevant domain terms,
- relationship between relevant domain terms.

Relationships between resource designates typically reflect relationships between resource instances (e.g., hypertext links or hierarchical book-like structure of learning objects), or creators and resources (authorship relation).

Relationships between resource designates and relevant domain terms represent lightweight semantic descriptions of resources. Such relationships arrange relevant domain terms in a lightweight semantic structure that is necessary to perform reasoning tasks. We refer to all these types of relationships as resource-metadata relationships. Note that each relationship type can be assigned arbitrary attributes, e.g., a relation weight.

A basic example of a relationship between resource and metadata is the relationship that associates resources with relevant domain terms representing its content. Examples of relationships between relevant domain terms include similarity relationship (e.g., *recursion* is-similar-to *cycle*), composition relationship (*comment* is-part-of *program*), and hierarchical relationship (*printf* is-a *function*).

When considering domain model in general, it is important to point to the issue of domain model authoring. Conceptual description of even a small domain typically contains hundreds of concepts—domain knowledge elements—and thousands of relationships. Providing conceptual descriptions manually is a very demanding task that teachers (adaptive content authors) can accomplish only with difficulties. ALEF benefits from the proposed lightweight domain modeling, which open doors for methods that can automatically create lightweight semantic descriptions, while preserving acceptable quality of personalization.

We devised such methods and showed that *automated* creation of domain model—ranging from relevant domain terms extraction [42] to various types of relationships discovery [43, 44]—is to a great extent comparable to manual creation in terms of quality of produced domain descriptions as well as their suitability for learning object recommendation [24]. Though our methods do not replace a teacher (which is hardly possible), they can be used with advantage to support her/him when authoring adaptive courses.

User Model

User model employed in ALEF is based on principles of overlay user/student modeling, that is, it adds several user-related layers on top of the domain model. The most basic layer is used to store interaction of users with domain elements, and contains mainly information about:

- which learning object student visited, how much time he/she spent reading it
- which questions and exercises student solved and how successful he/she was (e.g., whether he/she answered correctly right away or was forced to request a hint or did not manage to answer correctly despite of the hint provided)
- which additional resources (via annotations) student interacted with

This layer is basically representing the students' interaction history. On top of this layer sits an additional one that is used to store student characteristics (mainly knowledge of domain concepts (relevant domain terms) related to relevant learning objects).

Each such characteristic apart from its value (scalar from 0 to 1) and a timestamp contains:

1. *confidence* representing the level of certainty that a student does have this characteristic at this value, and
2. *source* of the characteristic (such as "self-reported" in case of a questionnaire, or discovered by a particular user model inference agent).

When a user model is updated, the update spreads through relationships among concepts using standard spreading activation algorithm [9]. This ensures that any gain or loss of knowledge is appropriately distributed to all relevant parts of the overlay model following lightweight representation of domain model.

Framework Components

ALEF's architecture comprises the following easily reusable and extendable pivotal components:

- Annotation framework,
- Feedback infrastructure,
- Widgets

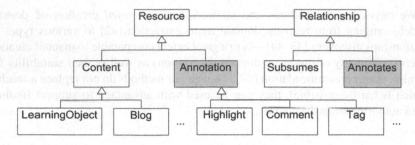

Fig. 3 Extensibility of resource annotations [41]

Annotation framework constitutes a robust framework for creating, updating, accessing and sharing annotations as a fundamental means for educational content enrichment and interaction. *Feedback infrastructure* streamlines and unifies the process of feedback collection and evaluation for various components and methods deployed within the educational system. *Widgets* represent building blocks of user interface. They are active learning and collaboration-supporting components and act as gateways for accessing learning content and annotations.

Annotation Framework

Students get more involved in the educational process through the possibility of adding different kinds of annotations to the content; they can create both new content and metadata. The *annotation framework* is designed to provide means and encourage this kind of participation [41].

ALEF's annotation framework aims to support and standardize interaction with various types of annotations and to ease the development of new annotation types by providing a common software infrastructure. In order to achieve a high degree of reusability and extendibility, content and annotations share common representation within the framework.

Content and annotation are defined as the same entity—*Resource* (see Fig. 3). In this representation, *Resources* can be connected with *Relationships* of various types (e.g., *Annotates*). This allows not only to assign annotations to the content, but even to interconnect annotations with each other. It also allows to easily add a new annotation type by extending the *Annotation* entity, as well as to add a new content type, which is immediately annotable by existing set of annotation types.

Every annotation is defined by its *content* and *context*. Content is a piece of textual information added by a student in a form of annotation, such as a comment or URL of an external source. In a special case, it can also be empty (e.g., in case of a highlight). Context represents an association (binding) of the annotation to a learning object and in some cases also to the text, where the annotation has been originally inserted by the student. Whether an annotation has been assigned to the learning object as a whole or only to a specific fragment of its text (i.e., a word, a

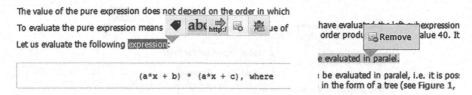

The value of the pure expression does not depend on the order in which

To evaluate the pure expression means ...ue of

Let us evaluate the following expression:

have evalua... ...expression order produ... ...alue 40. It

(a*x + b) * (a*x + c), where

e evaluated in paralel.

be evaluated in paralel, i.e. it is pos: in the form of a tree (see Figure 1,

Fig. 4 In-text pop-up menu for creating a new annotation (*left*): tag, highlight, external source, comment and error report (icons in order from *left* to *right*); and removing an existing one (*right*); content in Slovak

phrase, or a paragraph) differentiates two distinct types of annotations on the conceptual level: *per-text-annotations* and *per-content-annotations*.

Students can access annotations and navigate among them using both content and context: by context (*access-by-context*), i.e., directly in the text, where the annotation has been assigned in case of the per-text-annotations; by content (*access-by-content*), i.e., separately from the text (usually using a specialized *widget*).

We designed four distinctive user interface elements as a means for creating and accessing both the content and the context information of annotations:

- in-text interaction and presentation,
- sidebar,
- annotation browsers,
- annotation filter.

In order to create (using in-text pop-up menu, see Fig. 4, left), access and remove (by hovering the mouse over the text, see Fig. 4, right) per-text-annotations, students use *in-text interaction and presentation*, which represents the fastest access to annotations with no significant interruption of the learning process.

Sidebar represents another type of access-by-context navigation element. Annotations which are contextually close, i.e., were inserted in close proximity within each other in the text, are grouped into regions visualized on the sidebar. Hovering over a region shows a list of inserted annotations and highlights them in the text. Hovering over a particular annotation shows a tooltip with annotation's content; it also enables students to edit or remove the selected annotation (see Fig. 5).

Access-by-content navigation is provided by the *annotation browser*, which lists all annotations (of a specific type) related to the currently displayed learning object. Thus, students can interact with annotations regardless of their position in the text; however, selection or interaction with an annotation inside the browser invokes in-text visualization to indicate context of the annotation, if any. Annotation browsers are implemented as widgets located on the side of the screen, not distracting students from the main text in the central part. We provide more detailed description and examples of specific annotation browsers thereinafter in section on "Implicit Collaboration."

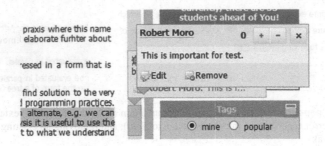

praxis where this name
elaborate furhter about

·essed in a form that is

find solution to the very
1 programming practices.
1 alternate, e.g. we can
rsis it is useful to use the
t to what we understand

Fig. 5 Sidebar with a region of grouped annotations and a tooltip showing detail of a selected annotation with other interactive elements; content in Slovak

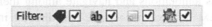

Fig. 6 Annotation filter with all the annotation types set to be displayed

Annotation filter allows users (students as well as teachers) to select types of annotations to be displayed in the text as well as on the sidebar (Fig. 6). Users can therefore focus their attention on selected types of information, resulting in more effective navigation among annotations. The filter contributes to adaptability of the learning environment towards learners' preferences and actual needs.

Feedback Infrastructure

The feedback infrastructure in ALEF was devised to alleviate two tasks: (1) monitoring student actions and building models, especially the user model, through the *logging framework*, and (2) evaluating personalization methods through *evaluation feedback engine*.

Logging framework. ALEF combines many experimental methods implemented through multiple components. User (student) feedback gathered in any part of the educational system (e.g., commenting on a selected part of the learning content through annotations, solving an exercise) implies student's knowledge and interests. Therefore both implicit actions and explicit ratings from students are integrated into a common user model layer storing interaction with domain elements. This is ensured through logging framework, which acts as a proxy intercepting any action made by a student: (1) *before it is processed*—when it is being sent to the framework, e.g., the student clicked a button to evaluate the solution, (2) *after it was processed*, e.g., the solution was evaluated as correct and additional information to be logged can be included while processing, this is then collected by the logging framework.

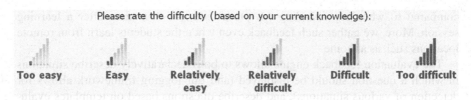

Fig. 7 Difficulty rating options displayed after student has finished a question or an exercise

Vast numbers of basic relationships to domain elements are created from both pre-processing and post-processing logging, including both implicit feedback, e.g., a student has looked on a fragment of a learning object [19], and explicit feedback, e.g., a student has rated difficulty of an exercise (Fig. 7) or rated learning object usefulness through a personalized rating scale. Advantage of this centralized logging pipeline is that one particular type of activity is always evaluated uniformly, regardless of a component which triggered the activity.

If any needed feedback or a new type of feedback from a new component is not yet logged, it can be easily added by creating a declarative description (processed by the logging framework) describing which relationship is to be created from which actions.

Evaluation feedback engine. ALEF has served and serves as a test bed for many experimental methods and often needs to collect diverse types of feedback. A rule-based *explicit feedback engine* was designed and developed in order to provide flexible feedback options. Besides generic question facility, it allows to display personalized questions instantiated from question templates.

An example of a typical problem in adaptive systems is when users do not use a newly added adaptive tool. If a recommended learning object is visited, we can easily evaluate the recommendation method on whether the student liked it or not and what knowledge did they gain after using it. However, when the recommendation facility is not used at all, we can only guess what is wrong with it (were the recommendations completely wrong so a student did not click on any recommended item or they simply overlooked them?). The evaluation feedback engine can help resolve such issues. Consider a scenario, which we realized in ALEF: a student is considering visiting a learning object from a list of recommendations presented to him (i.e., he looks on it, which we detect via gaze sensors) but then decides to use the menu instead. Right after the student makes the user interface action (mouse click on the menu item) the engine can ask a question about why the student chose the menu item rather than the recommendation. Gaze, as one of the indicators, is estimated either through mouse movement or through a commodity webcam by analyzing shape of the eye in the image feed in the browser. Using a simple low-resolution camera source or mouse movements brings smaller or larger errors to the gaze estimation, however these sources are sufficient for estimation of widget usage.

By personalizing the evaluation questions to the current context and asking them in appropriate situations, the engine can collect feedback of a better quality compared to when e.g., handing out predefined questionnaires after a learning session. More, we gather such feedback even when the students learn from remote locations such as at home.

The evaluation feedback engine allows to both declaratively describe situations in which a question should be displayed (and our logging framework allows for detection of various situations), and describe questions based on templates evaluated within student's current context.

Widgets

Annotation browsers, navigational and other components providing specific functionality (e.g., presentation of current student's score) are implemented within ALEF in the form of *widgets*. The main goal of our widget framework is to provide modular approach for designing and implementation of various functions for supporting students during their learning process and expose them in a uniform manner within the user interface. The widget framework provides standard functionality to all widgets (initialization, display of a widget, asynchronous state transitions, content refreshes, etc.), thus ensuring reusability and extendibility. It means that a developer can focus on design and implementation of widget's primary functions instead of solving various integration issues.

Widget framework is dynamic and flexible. It makes it easy to add a new type of widget, to change its default behavior, etc. It can even provide a gateway towards external systems, e.g., we have applied this widgets' framework to integrate ALEF with the PopCorm extension that is used for collaborative learning.

An example ALEF's user interface consisting of widgets is depicted on Fig. 8. The ALEF user interface is divided into three major parts: *navigational part*, *content part*, and *supporting components* providing specific functionality presented as widgets. Navigation through sets of learning objects is provided by navigational widgets such as hierarchical menu or list of recommendations. Various forms of interactions are enabled by incorporating annotations and interaction/collaboration widgets. Annotations constitute both a means for learners to better organize their own learning space, and also an interface for enrichment (contributions) to the learning content (the implementation of read/write web). We discuss specific widgets' usage (as annotation browsers) in section on "Implicit Collaboration."

Recommendation

The objective of recommendation in the domain of adaptive educational systems is to help students choose a topic which is best according to a combination of various factors: student's current state and goals, the actual available materials, assignments, etc. Recommendation approaches and presentation can vary according to typical workflow in given system. Are students given possibility to move through

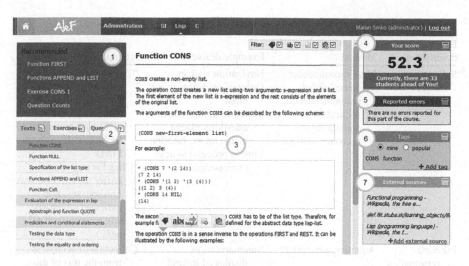

Fig. 8 Screenshot of ALEF user interface. It is divided to three vertical parts (*left* to *right*): (a) navigational part containing learning objects recommendations (*1*) and learning objects hierarchical menu (*2*); (b) educational content containing selected learning object (*3*); and (c) learning and collaboration supporting widgets: system activity score (*4*), error reporter (*5*), tagger (*6*) and external resource inserter (*7*); content in Slovak

the course(s) on their own? Or is the system used as a support for courses being taught offline? Nevertheless, the recommendation should be personalized, as each student has different knowledge in various topics (both prior and during the learning), different learning pace, goals, etc.

The recommendation in ALEF is performed on several levels. First, learning objects (e.g., course material, programming exercise, quiz question) are recommended. Second, the content of learning objects (at any stage of completeness) is not usually everything that is known about a given topic, and students can take advantage of studying about it from external resources, for example information available on the open Web. ALEF recommends such information to students via automatic creation of annotations within learning objects.

Third, students may benefit from personalized summaries of learning objects. In the same way in which students can make use of additional content to the learning objects, other students may need only the most important pieces of information, some overview or quick reference to given learning objects. ALEF recommends the most important or relevant information within learning objects in the form of personalized summarizations.

The described levels are complementing each other. The recommendation of learning objects helps selecting a learning object to focus on. The summarization helps picking the most useful information within the selected learning object, while their augmentation by annotations expands the available information (extending the volume even beyond the scope of authored content). Examples of different recommendations delivered to the user are shown in Table 1.

Table 1 Examples of recommendations within ALEF platform

Event description	Method	Example delivery	Example recommendation
Selecting an object	Meta-recommender (time-limited recommendation, sequential walkthrough recommendation, …)	Navigation widget Order of exercises in the menu Selection of exercises/ questions placed inside an explanation Link to proceed to next exercise/question	"Try the following exercises now to learn the most in the remaining time (1:31 h): Lambda REMOVE-IF, Scheme FIND" "Click for next exercise" (After the exercise was finished. It is not indicated which one will be displayed as next.)
Filtering information within the object	Adaptive summarizer	Summarization displayed instead of the object (quick reference) Summarization displayed after the object (repeating)	Collection of sentences from the text of the learning object
Accessing information outside the object	Automated annotation creation	In-text annotations Sidebar	"Construction of <u>software</u> includes transformation of detailed module specifications to <u>program</u> realization." (Term <u>program</u> is annotated with definitions and excerpts from external sources for "computer program," "programming language," and "process.")

In general, recommendations in ALEF are made based on information stored and maintained in user and domain models. User characteristics related to domain concepts (such as concept knowledge) represented by relevant domain terms are considered to select appropriate resources that are a subject of recommendation via relationships between domain model's metadata and designate layers. Relationships within metadata layer (connections among relevant domain terms) are typically used to update and spread information about student inferred from her/his actions. However, particular utilization of models depends on a recommendation method used.

Recommending Learning Objects

For recommending learning objects, the ALEF supports multiple recommendation methods, which can be easily added. They are selected or combined on-the-fly for a given student by the means of meta-recommender, which is effectively a hybrid recommender system. ALEF uses weighted (recommenders are given weights and results are combined), switching (a recommender is selected for the given user at the current time), and mixed (multiple recommenders present their results at once) hybridization methods. Also where multiple domain or user models exist, a recommender can operate on any of them and the model to serve as a source for recommendation to the given user is personalized.

The methods supported within ALEF include traditional approaches found in adaptive web-based systems. One recommendation approach offered in ALEF—the sequential course walkthrough—is based on traditional recommendation principles of content similarity. Current student's learning interests are considered and based on them, several learning objects (LOs) are recommended in order to both (1) advance current subject further through course advancement in Explanations, and (2) refine knowledge being gained in the current subject through exercising in Exercises and Questions.

ALEF was used to experiment with a novel time-limited recommendation. The time spent learning is very important in the domain of learning—it is a form of currency that students "pay" for selecting items (here, learning objects) and of which each student has only a limited amount available. The proposed method for time-limited exercise and question recommendation is briefly described below.

The basic function of the time-limited recommendation is to help students in selecting appropriate assignments for learning the most and meeting the learning goals. In this method, assignments (Questions and Exercises) are recommended based on the student's knowledge of related topics, the target topics (e.g., knowledge required for a mid-term exam), together with time that the student has available for learning. The time limit is either determined externally by time remaining to an event (e.g., exam), or a student can allocate his/hers own available time. The learning targets were set by the domain expert (a teacher giving the exam), but can be also self-imposed by the students or set automatically.

The recommendation itself supports the recommendation task *find good items* (recommend a list of N most suitable assignments). Exercises are each composed of a task definition, a hint and a sample solution. Students can take various paths through the exercise (requesting the hint or not) and even when the student does not solve the exercise completely, he/she may or may not understand the sample solution. This is also being considered in the recommendation. Each available assignment in the course is assigned a scalar value of *appropriateness* computed from three criteria on a given assignment.

- *Appropriateness of related domain terms for the student*. Following three criteria apply to all domain terms related to the assignment which is being evaluated: (1) The domain term must be a member of the learning targets. (2) The student's

Table 2 Results of recommendation experiment using time-limited recommendation

	Pre-test (%)	Post-test (%)	Difference
Group A: recommendation, automatic model	50.2 (±21.2)	70.5 (±15.2)	+20.2 (±15.2)
Group B: recommendation, manual model	42.4 (±21.0)	58.3 (±20.4)	+16.0 (±13.8)
Group C: no adaptive navigation support	48.2 (±25.4)	59.2 (±17.6)	+11.0 (±17.6)

knowledge of the domain term must be less than the estimated optimal value. The estimated optimal knowledge levels suppress further overlearning of domain terms which are already mastered at a satisfying level, to allow better learning of other domain terms, where current knowledge is still lacking. The optimal level is estimated by student's current progress (increment of knowledge over time) extrapolated to the end of learning session and evaluated against current knowledge level using sigmoid function. (3) The knowledge requirements of domain term prerequisites must be met. That is, some domain terms may be required to be mastered by the student before learning another domain term. These requirements are represented by weighted prerequisite relations in the domain model.

- *Appropriateness of difficulty.* In order to prevent the student from being discouraged, difficulty of the assignment to be recommended should match student's knowledge. Difficulty appropriateness for a given assignment is computed based on a Gaussian function with its peak set at the current aggregated knowledge level of all domain terms related to the assignment. Steepness of the curve is based on difficulty distribution among the assignments.
- *Time passed from last attempt to solve.* In order to prevent repeating the same assignment after a short interval, a time period from previous attempt to solve such assignment is considered. Immediately after visiting an assignment, appropriateness for this parameter drops to zero and gradually returns to 1 over time via hyperbolic function using time from previous attempt and student's feedback on the previous attempt, which determines function steepness.

All of these criteria are supposed to be satisfied; therefore the appropriateness of an assignment is the minimum of the partial values. The assignments to be recommended are selected as those with largest appropriateness.

Evaluation. We evaluated the time-limited recommendation method in two experiments using Functional and Logic Programming course. In the first experiment, the students took a pre-test, studied for 60 min and then took a post-test. We divided 66 students into three groups: (1) a group with recommendation-based adaptive navigation using automatically generated domain model, (2) a group with recommendation-based navigation using manually created domain model, and (3) a group without adaptive features, all students navigated on their own. In the second experiment, the third group was provided with navigation using random recommendations and a 50-min learning session was followed by a post-test. Results of the first experiment are shown in Table 2. Both experiments [24] had shown groups with personalized recommendation outperforming control groups (third group).

Summarization of Learning Objects

Automatic summarization can be useful for students in various scenarios. By providing a short summary containing the main points of a learning object it can help them to navigate in the learning object space; another scenario is revising before an exam by providing a longer summary explaining important concepts contained in learning objects. Thus, it can be framed as a recommendation problem: we want to recommend fragments of a document which are the most relevant (e.g., interesting, useful) for students in a given situation.

Conventional (generic) summarization methods summarize the content of a document without considering differences among users, their needs or characteristics. However, in adaptive learning systems we usually have many information sources that can be used to adapt summaries. We identified these three main sources in the educational system ALEF:

- *Domain conceptualization*—we use information contained in the domain model to extract fragments that explain key concepts of the document more accurately.
- *Knowledge of users*—using the modeled user knowledge, we can filter fragments that explain concepts that are too difficult for a user or those which a user already understands very well (depending on our scenario, whether we want to help users revise what they have already learned or help them find and comprehend concepts which are new for them).
- *User-added annotations*—when a user highlights a fragment of a text (by adding highlight annotation), we assume that the fragment contains information deemed important or interesting by the user; when many users highlight the same (or similar) fragment of text, we assume that the fragment contains important and valuable information in general.

We proposed a method of personalized text summarization based on a method of latent semantic analysis [13, 36]. Our method consists of the following three steps [26]:

1. Pre-processing during which terms are extracted from the document and the document's text is segmented to sentences.
2. Construction of a terms-sentences matrix which represents an input to singular value decomposition [13].
3. Selection of sentences; we select sentences with the highest score using approach proposed by Steinberger and Ježek [36].

In order to adapt summaries we apply information from identified sources during a construction of a terms-sentences matrix, thus constructing a personalized terms-sentences matrix. Instead of a conventional weighting scheme based on tf-idf, we use our proposed weighting scheme based on a linear combination of multiple raters:

$$w\left(t_{ij}\right) = \sum_{k} \alpha_k R_k\left(t_{ij}\right) \tag{1}$$

where $w(t_{ij})$ is the weight of term t_{ij} in the matrix and α_k is the linear coefficient of rater R_k.

We designed a set of generic and personalized raters which positively or negatively affect the weight of each term. In order to produce baseline generic variants of summarization we designed *Terms frequency rater* and *Terms location rater*, which have been inspired by Luhn [21] and Edmundson [12] respectively. Our personalized raters take into account various sources of personalization and adaptation, i.e., *Relevant domain terms rater*, *Knowledge rater*, and *Annotations rater*. They determine which terms are important based on a source of information and assign increased weights to terms from selected sources.

Evaluation. The personalized summarizer is integrated with ALEF using a summarization widget based on the existing widget infrastructure. We carried out two experiments on the *Functional and Logic Programming* course. In total, 17 students took part in the first experiment and 27 students in the second.

Students' task was to evaluate a presented summary on a five-point Likert scale. After each summary rating, students were asked follow-up questions to further evaluate quality of the summary (e.g., whether sentences selected for the summary were representative, whether the summary is suitable for revision etc.). Moreover, we selected a comparison group of five students who were presented both variants in random order to decide which variant is better or whether they are content equivalents.

In the first experiment we compared generic summarization to the summarization considering the relevant domain terms [26]. The summarization considering the relevant domain terms gained on average approximately 7.2 % higher score than the generic variant; it was also evaluated as better or equal by the experts in 69 % of the cases. In the second experiment we compared generic summarization to the summarization considering user-added annotations [27]. We got results similar to the previous experiment, when the experts evaluated the variant considering the user-added annotations as better in 48 % of the cases as opposed to the 24 % when it was considered as worse.

Our results suggest that considering the relevant domain terms as well as user-added annotations in the summarization process leads to better summaries compared to the generic variant and can be of higher value to the students in the learning process.

Recommending Web Resources

ALEF contains a collection of learning objects available for students. However, great amount of quality resources are available on the Web. We were looking for the possibility to enrich content of ALEF by these resources. While reading a document, a student often encounters a word or a phrase, he/she may not understand or may require additional information to understand it sufficiently.

To provide more information about important parts of learning objects in ALEF, we proposed a method for automatically extending the content of learning objects by attaching annotations to selected terms in the text. Such annotations provide further explanations, links to related resources and other types of information retrieved using multiple publicly available services for information retrieval. The method is designed to be able to insert annotations into the text written in Slovak language with a potential to be language independent. It consists of three steps:

1. search for candidate words to attach annotations,
2. search for information to fill the annotations, and
3. adaptation and visualization of annotations.

To find locations to which it is appropriate to assign the annotation, various algorithms for keyword extraction or approaches from the field of natural language processing can be used. However, satisfactory results are currently achieved for English texts only. To overcome this problem it is possible to use machine translation to translate source text into English. Based on our experiments we believe that existing, although far from being perfect translation mechanisms are sufficient for this task, as we attach annotations mainly to nouns and verbs and these are translated correctly in most cases.

To solve the problem of linking extracted keywords from translated text to the original text, we proposed a method for mapping equivalent words between text translations based on a dictionary and comparing words using Levenshtein distance [38]. This method is the key element for annotation acquisition for various languages. We primarily consider Slovak language, which is an inflecting language with many various words forms and represents (considering its syntax) rather large group of languages.

Information for the annotations is retrieved from multiple publicly available services for information retrieval, where the query used to retrieve additional information consists of keywords extracted from the processed documents.

The final step of our method for automatic annotating the content of learning objects is the adaptation of the annotation content and the annotation visualization. For annotation adaptation we used implicit feedback from user interaction with annotations to sort annotation elements by their relevance for users. For finding the relevance of annotation elements we considered clicks on these elements as indication that an element is more relevant than other elements within the annotation. The clicks being the edges of a graph with vertices being elements, we apply PageRank algorithm to determine relevance of individual elements. Elements are then sorted according to this relevance. The annotation is visualized in a form of a tooltip that is displayed after clicking on a highlighted word within the text of the learning object.

Evaluation. We evaluated automatic annotating within the *Principles of software engineering* course in ALEF. We attached annotations to keywords in every learning object of the course, and the order of the links to related resources in these annotations was adapted according to the implicit feedback created by students while studying materials of this course. The recommendation of web resources was evaluated in two steps: (1) the evaluation of the method for mapping equivalent words between text translations, and (2) the evaluation of the method for information retrieval from multiple sources [38]. Our method for mapping equivalent words while taking into account adjacency of words in sentences, and stemmed lexicon used in the process of mapping achieved precision at 92.46 % with recall of 58.79 % which gives F-measure of 71.88 %.

Quality of added annotations heavily depends on the quality of a particular service for information retrieval. In our experiments we used Google Search, DBpedia, DictService and SlideShare. Relevancy of gathered information ranged from 70 % for Google Search to only 26 % for the SlideShare service. It can be improved mainly by adding personal context to the process of gathering information to fill the annotation, i.e. including information on users' interest to the query.

Collaboration

Collaboration among students is an important element of learning. Support of effective and successful collaboration during the learning process represents an important concept in ALEF. Collaboration can occur in different forms. The types of collaboration can be divided according to various dimensions: according to the form of mediation (i.e., face-to-face vs. computer-mediated), according to students' perceptions ranging from implicit (indirect) to explicit (direct) collaboration, and according to the formality of education ranging from formal to informal collaboration. ALEF focuses on computer-mediated formal collaboration in learning, and provides support for both implicit and explicit collaboration.

Implicit Collaboration

The process of annotating textual content represents an indirect form of collaboration. Students comment fragments of text for future reference, highlight important or interesting parts, report errors in text (factual or grammatical) etc. In doing so they do not help only themselves, they help other students as well: they can read comments inserted by others and respond to them, thus creating a form of discussion thread; they see which parts of texts were deemed important by their peers, can browse and navigate through the popular tags; and corrections made thanks to their error reports are beneficial to all of the students.

ALEF implements the annotation functionality within collaborative adaptive content creator components. The components are implemented using the aforementioned annotation and widget infrastructure. Each annotation widget introduces different goals for collaboration; it implements the whole lifecycle of an annotation type—creation of annotations, accessing (browsing) the annotations within the learning content, editing and optionally removing the annotations.

Tagger. The *Tagger* [28] is a simple annotation widget that allows assigning user-defined tags to content (i.e., learning object as a whole); a tag can be a word or a multiword phrase. While the motivation behind tagging may differ among users, the result is usually the same: users add tags that describe the content of a learning object, or their opinion (e.g., *important, funny*), or intention (e.g., *todo, toread*). Users can assign private tags as well as public anonymous tags, and can navigate through their own set of tags or through popular tags. We encourage this kind of motivation (i.e., better navigation as a result of tagging) by letting students filter exercises and questions using tags accompanied by the autocomplete feature.

Besides providing additional style of navigation within a course, tags can be utilized for maintaining course metadata, as they represent a form of collaborative semantic descriptions and quickly converge into folksonomy—a vocabulary shared by the community (students within the particular course).

Highlights. Highlights represent the simplest type of (per-text) annotation. The *Highlighter* aims to mimic common behavior of students when working with the printed text. They can simply select the desired part of text which they deem important or interesting, and choose to highlight it from the in-text pop-up menu without the need to insert any additional content of annotation.

Commentator. Sometimes highlighting the text is not enough; a student would like to insert additional information to the selected fragment of text for future reference. For this purpose serves the *Commentator* [41]. Students can add private, public, or anonymous public comments to any part of any learning object. It also supports replying to other users' comments, thus resulting into discussion threads on arbitrary topics, typically related to misconceptions or learning problems.

Error reporter. The *Error reporter* is a specialized version of the commentator widget [41]. It serves for reporting errors (factual or grammatical) found in the text by students. Reported errors are evaluated by a teacher resulting into improved content and thus better learning. This process supports collaboration between students and teacher or course documents maintainer.

External source linker. Important feature of ALEF is to let students get involved into the process of learning by finding new potentially interesting and relevant sources of information. This provides the *External source linker* by enabling students to add links (URLs) to these sources [25]. There are two ways to add a link: either as a per-text-annotation, using the in-text menu, or through the external source widget. The widget also serves as a means for accessing the inserted sources associated with the current learning object. The sources are displayed sorted according to their quality, with high quality sources (based on other users' ratings) on top of the widget.

Question creator. Understanding of an educational material comes with the ability to explain it to others and pose questions about it. This is the motivation behind the *Question creator* widget, which provides students with an interface for creating questions and for answering questions created by their peers [45]; thus students themselves become partly authors of the curricula. Students may add questions with five possible types of answers: (1) single choice question, (2) multiple choice question, (3) simple free text answer question, (4) sorting question (the task is to re-order the lines into correct order), and (5) text complement question where user is asked to fill missing words into dedicated fields within the text, e.g., completing missing commands in a program code.

Answers of peer students are automatically evaluated by the question creator and students can thus receive an instant feedback. Students can also rate questions in order to determine the question's perceived quality.

Evaluation. We carried out multiple experiments evaluating separate parts of the annotation framework. We analyzed tags added by users and their capability in helping domain experts to create and refine the domain model; we found out that students were able, in a short period of time, to find almost half (49.8 %) of all the concepts in the domain model, while the domain model covered only 17 % of the tags added by the students [28]. Similarly, we experimented with deriving new relations among learning objects and concepts in the domain model using the external sources added by students [25]: the method identified concepts with 74.8 % precision and managed to find also new relations not present in the current domain model. These experiments confirm that annotations created by students can be used as a valuable source of information for domain model construction.

We evaluated the usefulness of our error reporting feature as well [41]: 20 % of the most advanced students provided 82 % of all error reports; altogether students found one error per 1.46 learning objects, thus managing to significantly increase the quality of the educational materials for other students.

In the experiment with the Question creator we assessed quality of student-generated questions [45]. Results showed that 37.5 % of questions provided by students could have been used directly as new educational material with no need of teacher to intervene. Experiment also assessed automatic recognition of quality questions, which achieved accuracy of 70.1 %.

Explicit Collaboration

According to Soller [33] there are two approaches how to support effective collaboration in adaptive and personalized learning systems. The first approach is focused on collaboration at group level, namely how to support students to exchange information in the appropriate circumstances (group composition, context, level of detail etc.). The second approach is aimed to support collaboration at community level, i.e., how to share and discover common knowledge in online communities. In ALEF the focus is on supporting collaboration at group level, especially the *group formation* and *collaboration support*. Group formation is aimed to offer recommendations to students on how to create successful and effective groups, or alternatively, how to recommend peer help (another student which can participate on common collaboration). Collaboration support is aimed to support students during and after finishing collaboration. It is based on users' and groups' models which are

Table 3 Group formation experiment results

Groups created	Avg. score	Feedback	p-value A	B	C
A. By the proposed method	0.459	4.01	N/A	0.0006	0.0071
B. By the reference method (k-means)	0.392	3.55	0.0006	N/A	0.0987
C. Randomly	0.422	3.29	0.0071	0.0987	N/A

compared with models of ideal collaboration. Based on the mentioned models we can provide students recommendations how to achieve more successful collaboration.

Group Formation

We consider group composition as one of the most important precondition of effective and successful collaboration. There are many existing methods which solve group formation problem such as the jigsaw method of Hinze et al. [14], particle swarm optimization of Lin et al. [20], and ontology based methods of Ounnas et al. [30]. They are not suitable for all domains and scenarios. For instance, they are static and do not consider student's actual context and are limited in employing different information sources about students. Also, the methods assume that it is possible to decide which aspects make collaboration really effective and successful. However, this has not been sufficiently determined by current research.

Improving upon the previous approaches to group formation we propose a method which automatically creates small short-term dynamic groups [35]. Our method can consider any personal or collaborative user's characteristics. Collaborative characteristics can describe students' behavior during collaboration process or relationships between students [34].

Our method is inspired by the optimization approach called Group Technology [32]. Group Technology approach is rooted in optimization in industry area and solves the problem how to effectively produce different parts by set of machines. This problem can be adapted to our educational domain, but we have students instead of machines and students' characteristics instead of parts.

The method is applied to the same set of students iteratively. The collaboration process is evaluated after each group finishes solving a particular task. This allows us to continually improve the understating of which characteristics should be combined together based on score representing evaluation of how effective and successful collaboration was achieved. In addition, it is possible to automatically determine students' collaborative characteristics.

Evaluation. We evaluated the proposed method in two steps. First, we evaluated the preconditions of the method. Then we performed a long-term experiment where we compared the collaboration between groups created by our method and groups created by a reference method (we employed k-means clustering). Hundred and six participants were iteratively assigned to 254 groups. The results of this experiment

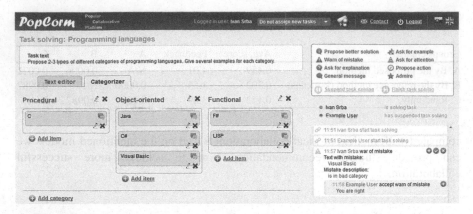

Fig. 9 Screenshot of ALEF's collaborative extension—PopCorm user interface. Categorizer tool is displayed on the *left side*. Semi-structured discussion is available on the *right side*

are displayed in the Table 3. Statistical significance testing yielded a p-value of 0.0048, producing statistically significant results.

Collaboration Support

The collaboration support in ALEF is based on a structured collaborative environment. Students can communicate by means of semi-structured discussion. It provides 18 different types of messages (e.g., propose better solution, accept proposal, ask for explanation, provide explanation). These different message types allow us to automatically identify student's activities.

Recorded activities are used to measure the collaboration by a set of seven dimensions the design of which is rooted in psychology studies: sustaining mutual understanding, information exchanges for problem solving, argumentation and reaching consensus, task and time management, sustaining commitment, shared task alignment and fluidity of collaboration [5]. We added one more dimension which represents teacher's evaluation of results correctness.

The computed value in each dimension of collaboration is presented to students after finishing each task. Students can self-reflect their collaboration and improve their activities in the subsequent collaboration. In addition, we provide recommendations for each dimension.

The collaborative environment consists of a set of tools which are suitable to solve collaborative tasks, which can be of several types (e.g., group discussion, list advantages/disadvantages, list pros/cons) while each type can be solved with one or more of the available tools: Text editor, Graphical editor, Categorizer, and Semi-structured discussion facility. These tools are available via ALEF's collaborative extension Popular Collaborative Platform (PopCorm). Students are able to ask for collaborative task assignment whenever during their individual study in ALEF. As soon as the collaborative task is assigned to them, they are able to solve this task in PopCorm besides searching for learning objects in ALEF (see Fig. 9).

Text Editor. The text editor is an interactive tool which is suitable for collaborative writing of free text. It provides functionality for parallel editing of written text by several users at the same time together with conflict resolution in the case when two users edit the same part of the text. Basic text formatting is sufficient for our purpose.

Graphical Editor. The graphical editor provides opportunity to collaborate visually by sketching. Its functionality includes drawing of vector shapes, importing raster images, adding text notes, etc.

Categorizer. The categorizer is a tool used to solve tasks involving one or more lists of items. Students are able to dynamically create, edit and remove categories (lists) and their items. In addition, it is possible to rearrange the items in the particular category, and even to move items from one category to another. All these changes are synchronized in real time among all group's members.

Semi-structured discussion. The semi-structured discussion facility represents a generic communication tool independent of a particular type of task being solved. Discussion is partially structured by employing sentence openers.

Future Directions and Conclusions

Higher demand for web-based learning gave rise to an increase of students who learn online and the expanding amount of educational material available online poses new challenges to web-based educational systems. To meet the challenges and to leverage the trends established by Web 2.0, we devised adaptive learning framework ALEF. ALEF builds on three pillars: (1) extensible personalization and adaptation, (2) student active participation in learning process and collaboration, and the underlying (3) lightweight domain modeling.

Started as a small adaptive learning web application, ALEF became a platform for adaptive collaborative learning, where new methods supporting both education and education research can be easily created, covering wide range of applications with a particular focus on personalization and collaboration.

Modeling of students' knowledge using our logging and feedback infrastructure enabled us to deliver personalized recommendation of learning objects to our students and thus to make the learning process more efficient. Recommenders in ALEF not only ensure that a sequence of learning objects respects all known prerequisites, but also that a minimal required level of knowledge is attained by a student in a given time limit.

Text summarization methods enabled ALEF to recommend relevant fragments of texts to students (as opposed to whole learning objects). It seems promising to also use the summaries to help students revise their knowledge, and to navigate more efficiently in the learning object space.

Recommendation during learning with ALEF reaches beyond the learning content contained within the educational system. Web resources, are automatically linked to the course content, not only provide increased detail on topics and ensure the content is more up-to-date, but also put topics into broader context and thus contribute to overall comprehension of the domain by our learners.

Students' annotations of educational material proved to be useful on various levels: students get more involved into the learning process, quality of learning materials improve over time thanks to student generated error reports, links to external resources etc. and finally, student annotations bring novel insight to the model of the domain, revealing relationships, important parts etc. as well as to the student model, refining student's interest and knowledge. On the other hand, it opens up new research problems of automatic maintenance of annotations in the changing environment and filtering (recommendation) of those quality annotations, which can be helpful to others.

ALEF can furthermore take advantage of implicit collaboration among students when dealing with tasks related to authoring and assessment of particular domain model parts, which cannot be solved easily by computers, such as providing and validating free-text answers to quiz questions.

In contrast with individual learning, explicit collaboration facilitates practicing social and communication skills. As a result, students learn more efficiently and successfully. In fact, we observed improvement mainly for weak students. We believe that recommendation and collaboration together with smart scoring of students' activities are key issues that make ALEF successful.

There are many possibilities how to continue in the research in almost all mentioned areas. Considering recommendation, we still have not fully covered all important decision points where a recommendation can improve learning experience both individual and collaborative. For example, various types of learning objects (explanations, exercises, questions) can be better distinguished thereby the recommendation is tailored for particular learning objects. We incorporated into our recent study on ALEF logs also external sources of valuable information on students such as manual assessment outside ALEF or personality traits, which represent valuable sources for the recommendation.

We already started work on improving interconnection of ALEF with resources on the open Web. We plan to extend our external source linker by direct support of a student exploring the Web for additional learning resources. We proposed client-side use modeler BrUMo,[2] which can be used for this task. In particular, we plan employing the BrUMo framework for improving recommendation outside ALEF by considering all the student knowledge already captured in ALEF. We realized BrUMo framework as a browser plugin. It provides low-level mechanisms to index and efficiently represent various user characteristics captured from visited web

---

[2] Browser-Based User Modeling and Personalization Framework, http://brumo.fiit.stuba.sk

pages in an efficient manner on the client-side. BrUMo mechanisms are powerful enough to support both collaborative and content-based filtering approaches.

Another promising area is explicit collaboration of students such as providing collaborative support on the community level (in addition to small group level as outlined in this chapter), and improving methods for groups formation and task selection according to the individual user models or group models. Our current research on collaborative validation of question-answer learning objects is also along this line. We propose a method that utilizes students' correctness estimations of answers provided by other students. Our preliminary results show that student estimations are comparable to teacher's evaluations of provided answers.

Not less important than research results is the impact of ALEF for real-world education. ALEF is actively used at the Slovak University of Technology in Bratislava. Currently it supports studies in the three undergraduate courses in Informatics and Computer Engineering: *Functional and logic programming*, *Procedural programming*, and *Principles of software engineering*. Together it contains more than 1,875 learning objects and since summer term 2009/2010, it has successfully served more than 1,000 university students.

Acknowledgements This chapter is based on publications that present partial results of our research in the field of adaptive and intelligent web-based educational systems, all mentioned in References. It was partially supported by the grants VEGA 1/0675/11/2011-2014, KEGA 028-025STU-4/2010, APVV-0208-10 and it is the partial result of the Research & Development Operational Programme for the project Research of methods for acquisition, analysis and personalized conveying of information and knowledge, ITMS 26240220039, co-funded by the ERDF.

The authors wish to thank colleagues from the Institute of Informatics and Software Engineering and all students (in particular members of PeWe group, pewe.fiit.stuba.sk) for their invaluable contributions to the work presented in this chapter either by discussions or participating in ALEF implementation and experiments. Special thanks deserve former members of ALEF team Pavol Michlík, Vladimír Mihál and Maroš Unčík for their direct contribution to ALEF design and implementation.

References

1. Beaumont I, Brusilovsky P (1995) Adaptive educational hypermedia: from ideas to real systems. In: Maurer H (ed) Proc of ED-MEDIA '95 – World Conf on educational multimedia and hypermedia, Graz, Austria, pp 93–98
2. Berners-Lee T (2005) Berners-Lee on the read/write web. http://news.bbc.co.uk/2/hi/tech-nology/4132752.stm. Accessed 27 Jan 2013
3. Brusilovsky P (2004) KnowledgeTree: a distributed architecture for adaptive e-learning. In: Proc of the 13th Int World Wide Web Conf, WWW'04. ACM Press, New York, NY, pp 104–113
4. Brusilovsky P, Peylo C (2003) Adaptive and intelligent web-based educational systems. Int J Artif Intell Educ 13:156–169
5. Burkhardt J, Détienne F, Hébert A, Perron L, Safin S, Leclercq P (2009) An approach to assess the quality of collaboration in technology-mediated design situations. In: Proc of European Conf on cognitive ergonomics: designing beyond the product (ECCE '09). VTT Technical Res. Centre of Finland, VTT, Finland

6. Cristea AI, de Mooij A (2003) LAOS: layered WWW AHS authoring model and their corresponding algebraic operators. In: Proc The 12th Int World Wide Web Conf WWW'03. Alternate track on education, Budapest, Hungary

7. Cristea AI, Ghali F, Joy M (2011) Social, personalized lifelong learning. In: E-Infrastructures and Tech for lifelong learning (ETLL). IGI Global, Hershey, PA, pp 90–125

8. Cimiano P (2006) Ontology learning and population from text: algorithms, evaluation and applications. Springer, New York, NY

9. Crestani F, Lee PL (2000) Searching the web by constrained spreading activation. Inf Process Manag 36(4):585–605

10. De Bra P, Houben GJ, Wu H (1999) AHAM: a Dexter-based reference model for adaptive hypermedia. In: Proc. of ACM Conf. on Hypertext and Hypermedia. ACM, New York, NY, pp 147–156

11. Downes S (2005) E-learning 2.0. ACM eLearn Maga 10:1

12. Edmundson HP (1969) New methods in automatic extracting. J ACM 16(2):264–285

13. Gong Y, Liu X (2001) Generic text summarization using relevance measure and latent semantic analysis. In: Proc of the 24th ACM SIGIR. ACM, New York, NY, pp 19–25

14. Hinze U, Bischoff M, Blakowski G (2002) Jigsaw method in the context of CSCL. In: Proc. of world Conf. on educational multimedia, hypermedia and telecommunications. Association for the Advancement of Computing in Education, Norfolk, VA, pp 789–794

15. IEEE (2002) LTSC draft standard for learning object metadata. IEEE Standard 1484.12.1

16. Koch N, Wirsing M (2002) The Munich reference model for adaptive hypermedia applications. In: Adaptive hypermedia and adaptive web-based systems. Lecture notes in computer science, vol 2347. Springer, Heidelberg, pp 213–222

17. Koper R, Rusman E, Sloep P (2005) Effective learning networks. Lifelong Learn Europe 1: 18–27

18. Kostelník R, Bieliková M (2003) Web-based environment using adapted sequences of programming exercises. In: Proc. of Inf. systems implementation and modelling, ISIM 2003, MARQ Ostrava, Brno, pp 33–40

19. Labaj M (2011) Web-based learning support based on implicit feedback. Inform Sci Tech Bull ACM Slovakia 3(2):76–78

20. Lin Y, Huang Y, Cheng S (2010) An automatic group composition system for composing collaborative learning groups using enhanced particle swarm optimization. Comput Educ 55(4): 1483–1493

21. Luhn HP (1958) The automatic creation of literature abstracts. IBM J Res Dev 2(2):159–165

22. Manouselis N, Drachsler H, Vuorikari R, Hummel H, Koper R (2010) Recommender systems in technology enhanced learning. In: Rokach L, Shapira B, Kantor P, Ricci F (eds) Recommender systems handbook: a complete guide for research scientists & practitioners. Springer, New York, NY, pp 387–415

23. Meccawy M et al (2008) WHURLE 2.0: adaptive learning meets web 2.0. In: EC-TEL '08 Proc of the 3rd European Conf on Tech enhanced learning: times of convergence, vol 5192, Lecture Notes in Computer Science. Springer, Heidelberg, pp 274–279

24. Michlík P, Bieliková M (2010) Exercises recommending for limited time learning. Proc Comput Sci 1(2):2821–2828

25. Mihál V, Bieliková M (2011) Domain model relations discovering in educational texts based on user created annotations. In: Proc of 14th Int Conf on interactive collaborative learning and 11th Int Conf Virtual University. IEEE, Piscataway, NJ, pp 542–547

26. Móro R, Bieliková M (2012) Personalized text summarization based on important terms identification. In: Proc of DEXA 2012 workshops (TIR 2012), 23rd Int workshop on database and expert systems applications. IEEE Computer Society, Los Alamitos, CA, pp 131–135

27. Móro R (2012) Combinations of different raters for text summarization. Inform Sci Tech Bull ACM Slovakia 4(2):56–58

28. Móro R, Srba I, Unčík M, Bieliková M, Šimko M (2011) Towards collaborative metadata enrichment for adaptive web-based learning. In: Proc of IEEE/WIC/ACM Int Conf on web

intelligence and intelligent agent technology – workshops. IEEE Computer Society, Los Alamitos, CA, pp 106–109

29. Mödritscher F (2010) Towards a recommender strategy for personal learning environments. Proc Comput Sci 1(2):2775–2782
30. Ounnas A, Davis H, Millard D (2008) A framework for semantic group formation. In: Proc of the 2008 eighth IEEE Int Conf on advanced learning technologies (ICALT '08). IEEE Computer Society, Washington, DC, pp 34–38
31. Santos OC, Boticario JG (2011) Requirements for semantic educational recommender systems in formal e-learning scenarios. Algorithms 4(2):131–154
32. Selim HM, Askin RG, Vakharia AJ (1998) Cell formation in group technology: review, evaluation and directions for future research. Comput Indust Eng 34(1):3–20
33. Soller A (2007) Adaptive support for distributed collaboration. In: Brusilovsky P, Kobsa A, Nejdl W (eds) The adaptive web, vol 4321, Lecture Notes in Computer Science. Springer, Heidelberg, pp 573–595
34. Srba I, Bielikova M (2010) Tracing strength of relationships in social networks. In: 2010 IEEE/WIC/ACM Int Conf on web intelligence and intelligent agent technology. IEEE, Washington, DC, pp 13–16
35. Srba I, Bieliková M (2012) Encouragement of collaborative learning based on dynamic groups. In: Proc of EC TEL 2012, 7th European Conf on technology enhanced learning, vol 7563, Lecture notes in computer science. Springer, Berlin, pp 432–437
36. Steinberger J, Ježek K (2005) Text summarization and singular value decomposition. In: Proc advances in information systems (ADVIS 04), vol 3261, Lecture notes in computer science. Springer, Berlin, pp 245–254
37. Šaloun P, Velart Z, Nekula J (2013) Towards automated navigation over multilingual content. In: Semantic hyper/multimedia adaptation, vol 418, Studies in computational intelligence. Springer, Berlin, pp 203–229
38. Ševcech J, Bieliková M (2011) Automatic annotation of non-English web content. In: Proc of IEEE/WIC/ACM Int Conf on web intelligence and intelligent agent technology – workshops. IEEE Computer Society, Los Alamitos, CA, pp 281–283
39. Šimko M (2012) Automated acquisition of domain model for adaptive collaborative web-based learning. Inform Sci Tech Bull ACM Slovakia 4(2):1–9
40. Šimko M, Barla M, Bieliková M (2010) ALEF: a framework for adaptive web-based learning 2.0. In: Proc of IFIP, vol 324, Advances in information and communication technology. Springer, Berlin, pp 367–378
41. Šimko M, Barla M, Mihál V, Unčík M, Bieliková M (2011) Supporting collaborative web-based education via annotations. In: ED-MEDIA 2011: Proc of World Conf on educational multimedia, hypermedia & telecommunications. AACE: Association for the Advancement of Computing in Education, Chesapeake, VA, pp 2576–2585
42. Šimko M, Bieliková M (2009) Automated educational course metadata generation based on semantics discovery. In: Proc of European Conf on technology enhanced learning, EC TEL 2009, Nice, France, vol 5794, Lecture notes in computer science. Springer, Berlin, pp 99–105
43. Šimko M, Bieliková M (2009) Automatic concept relationships discovery for an adaptive e-course. In: Barnes T et al (ed) Proc of educational data mining 2009: 2nd Int Conf on educational data mining, EDM 2009, Cordoba, Spain, pp 171–179
44. Šimko M, Bieliková M (2012) Discovering hierarchical relationships in educational content. In: Proc of 11th Int Conf on web-based learning, ICWL, vol 7558, Lecture notes in computer science. Springer, Berlin, pp 132–141
45. Unčík M, Bieliková M (2010) Annotating educational content by questions created by learners. In: Proc of SMAP 2010. IEEE Signal Processing Society, Washington, DC, pp 13–18
46. Vozár O, Bieliková M (2008) Adaptive test question selection for web-based educational system. In: Proc of SMAP 2008 – 3rd Int workshop on semantic media adaptation and personalization Prague CR. CS IEEE Press, Washington, DC, pp 164–169

Two Recommending Strategies to Enhance Online Presence in Personal Learning Environments

Samuel Nowakowski, Ivana Ognjanović, Monique Grandbastien, Jelena Jovanovic, and Ramo Šendelj

Abstract Aiming to facilitate and support online learning practices, TEL researchers and practitioners have been increasingly focused on the design and use of Web-based Personal Learning Environments (PLE). A PLE is a set of services selected and customized by students. Among these services, resource (either digital or human) recommendation is a crucial one. Accordingly, this chapter describes a novel approach to supporting PLEs through recommendation services. The proposed approach makes extensive use of ontologies to formally represent learning context that, among other components, includes students' presence in the online world, i.e., their online presence. This approach has been implemented in and evaluated with the OP4L (Online Presence for Learning) prototype. In this chapter, we expose recommendation strategies devised for OP4L. One is already implemented in OP4L, it is based on the well-known Analytical Hierarchical Process (AHP) method. The other one which has been tested on data coming from the prototype is based on the active user's navigation stream and used a Kalman filter approach.

Keywords Web-based learning • Social presence • Online presence • Ontology based resource recommendation • Kalman filter • Learning trajectories • AHP • CS-AHP

S. Nowakowski (✉) • M. Grandbastien
LORIA, Université de Lorraine, Campus Scientifique-BP 239,
54506 Vandoeuvre les Nancy Cedex, France
e-mail: Samuel.Nowakowski@loria.fr; Monique.Grandbastien@loria.fr

I. Ognjanović • R. Šendelj
Faculty of Information technology, Mediterranean University, Podgorica, Montenegro

Institute of Modern technology, Podgorica, Montenegro
e-mail: Ivana.Ognjanovic@unimediteran.net; Ramo.Sendelj@unimediteran.net

J. Jovanovic
FOS-Faculty of Organizational Sciences, University of Belgrade, Jove Ilica 154, Belgrade, Serbia
e-mail: jeljov@gmail.com

N. Manouselis et al. (eds.), *Recommender Systems for Technology Enhanced Learning:*   227
Research Trends and Applications, DOI 10.1007/978-1-4939-0530-0_11,
© Springer Science+Business Media New York 2014

Introduction

Web-based Personal Learning Environments (PLEs) have been increasing adopted by the TEL research community as a mean to support and facilitate online learning practices [1]. From the technical perspective, a PLE is a customizable set of tools and services aimed at enhancing students' learning experiences and learning outcomes. Among these services, resource (either digital or human) recommendation is a crucial one, given the number and the diversity of available resources on the Web. Various approaches have been proposed to improve the recommendation of resources and adapt them to the learners' needs [2–4]. They all rely on a learner profile and include a more or less rich description of the learning context, often based on ontologies.

In the last few years, we are witnessing a steady increase in the students' use of Web-based social software tools. This has lead to the emergence of novel forms of social presence in online learning environments, PLEs being no exception. Hence, the dominant forms of establishing and maintaining social presence become online status updates, online visibility, availability for online communication and the like. Semantic Web technologies, ontologies in particular, allow for taking these forms of social presence into account when generating recommendations for students.

This chapter reports on the recommendation strategies that have been implemented in the OP4L (Online Presence For Learning) [5] framework and evaluated using the data coming from the students' use of the framework. The first approach is based on the well-known Analytical Hierarchical Process (AHP) method and its adoption for handling conditionally defined preferences, named Conditional Stratified AHP (CS-AHP) method. The *PeerRec* service is developed based on the adoption of prioritization algorithms in a PLE. Based on the students' preferences about some important features of the learning process, the service offers recommendation of peers to communicate and/or collaborate with.

The second approach is based on the active user's navigation stream: we consider that users browsing the Web can be seen as objects moving along trajectories in the Web space. Having this assumption, we derive the appropriate description of the so-called recommender space to propose a mathematical model and state estimate based on a Kalman filter describing the behaviour of the users along the trajectories of the recommender space.

We present the theoretical background, and report on the obtained results and performances. The chapter concludes with perspectives for further developments and prospective evolution studies.

Background

In her "vision" paper on the design of social learning environments [6], Vassileva identifies three main roles that should be performed by PLEs: (1) support the learner in finding the right content (right for the context, particular learner, specific purpose of the learner and pedagogically), (2) support learner to connect with the right people (...) and (3) motivate/incentivize people to learn. To devise PLEs with such features, TEL researchers and developers rely on the body of knowledge and experiences originating from several interrelated research domains. The discovery and retrieval of learning resources is one of those domains, and has been widely investigated, beginning with the work on metadata interoperability, then going on with the use of ontologies to better match the learners' needs and context. As social web applications, such as collaborative tagging, became available, solutions mixing both ontology- and folksonomy-based approaches were proposed. Meanwhile, the recommender systems community developed powerful algorithms for the e-commerce sector, and PLE developers tried to adapt them to e-learning purposes [2–4].

Social presence is another relevant research field. It has been identified as a crucial success factor in e-learning for many years [7–9]. At the beginning of e-learning practices, social presence was mostly implemented through online forums and Instant Messaging tools that allowed for establishing and maintaining social presence in online learning settings. The wide adoption of social web applications, such as online social networks, resulted in the inclusion of these applications and connections that students had established in them into online learning environments. Though in theory students can interact with their entire social network, in practice they do not get any indicator about who is really available in the given moment and who is really capable of helping in the current task. Although recommending knowledgeable people for performing a given task is not new, it has been mostly investigated in company settings such as reported, for instance, in [10]. The OP4L framework brings solutions for the two aforementioned challenges in the manner described in the following sections.

OP4L Framework

Background and Objectives

The OP4L project was running between 2010 and 2012. Its aim was to explore the use of Web-based tools and services for supporting social presence in online learning environments, and thus lead to an improvement in the students' learning experience. In this chapter, we use the term OP4L to name both the project and the developed prototype.

OP4L defines online presence as a temporary description of a user's presence in the online world. It can be considered as an image that a person projects about him/herself into the online world. We explored online presence in the context of DEPTHS [11], a PLE customized for the domain of Software Design Patterns. It makes use of ontologies as a common foundation for the integration of different systems, services and tools in a common environment for collaborative learning of software design patterns. OP4L extends the set of services offered by DEPTHS, by processing online presence data at the semantic level.

Functional Description

A complete technical description of the OP4L framework can be found in [12] and [13], as well as in deliverables available on the project's web site.[1] Therefore, in the following we give just a brief overview of the OP4L framework in order to draw an overall picture of the services it offers and the ontologies that make possible the provided services.

From a functional perspective, the primary goal behind the OP4L framework was the development of a *context-aware* PLE through integration of *learning context* data from different learning systems/tools/services, using a flexible *ontology-based* model [14]. We define learning context, i.e., the context of a given learning situation as an interplay of the following main components:

- the learning activity that was performed or the learning-related even that occurred,
- the content that was used and/or produced during the learning activity,
- the individual(s) involved (e.g., learners, teachers, experts) and their respective on line presence statuses,
- the (online) environment where the learning activity took place,
- the time when the learning activity took place.

The notion of learning context is formally modeled through an interlinked set of ontologies collectively named LOCO (Learning Object Context Ontologies) framework [11]. Within the OP4L project, the notion of learning context is extended to include the notion of Online Presence. Accordingly, links have been established between the existing LOCO ontologies and the Online Presence Ontology (OPO) [15] to allow for explicitly defining the semantic of this extended notion of learning context. These ontologies served as the foundation for the development of the OP4L prototype with the following main features:

- Integration of data and resources from diverse learning applications that students interact with;
- Context-aware recommendation of resources on software design patterns from online repositories, learning artifacts produced and shared by peers, software projects, discussion threads, chats, etc.;
- Context-aware recommendation of other students, experts and/or teachers to offer help in the given situation.

These services make use of learners' overall learning context, including his/her online presence data, when providing them with recommendations about whom to ask for help or collaborative work. These data are periodically "pulled in" the OP4L system by specific software modules developed for that purpose. Within the online presence data, a key indicator is the "online status" [16] as declared by the user. For instance, a peer whose online status indicates that he/she is busy in the given moment will not be recommended; on the other hand, the system would recommend a face-to-face study session with a peer who has just checked in the same building and whose status indicates that he/she can be freely contacted.

---

[1] http://op4l.fon.bg.ac.rs/

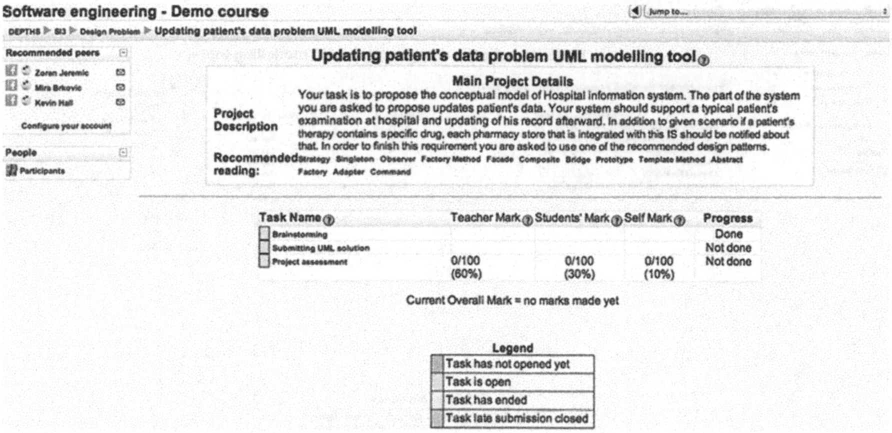

Fig. 1 Inside the prototype with recommended peers on the *left*

For course designers, one of the main challenges is to adapt interactions to the students' state of presence and to provide services so that interactions can be established smoothly among the participants.

Main Features of OP4L Prototype

OP4L services are accessible through a dedicated Moodle platform. The services become available after a student selects a course to study (e.g., the Design Pattern course) and a learning activity (e.g., updating patient's data problem using the UML modeling tool). Figure 1 shows the OP4L online presence services as presented to the student in the user interface. Specifically, they appear in the form of an online presence box in the upper left side of the screen. The box indicates who is competent for the given problem and available online for help or collaboration. It also indicates how to contact potential helper(s)/collaborator(s), either on the Moodle platform itself, or via Facebook or Twitter.

Services linking Moodle to Facebook and Twitter have been developed so that each student can remain using his/her current application, for instance, Moodle for the student looking for help/collaboration and Facebook for the student being contacted. Based on the online statuses declared by the peer students, the learner who is looking for help/collaboration will know in which manner he/she can communicate with the peers. In the case presented on Fig. 1, all of the peers can be contacted on Facebook and by email. The system offers several other services as described below.

The system recommends appropriate contents related to the topic of the course (Fig. 2). Its originality is to augment the course digital library with resources brought in and built by the students during the course.

For enhancing collaboration, students are also given a brainstorming tool where ideas can be annotated and rated. Finally, students can upload their work and benefit

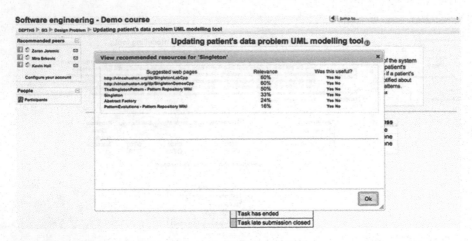

Fig. 2 Interface illustrating recommendation of digital resources

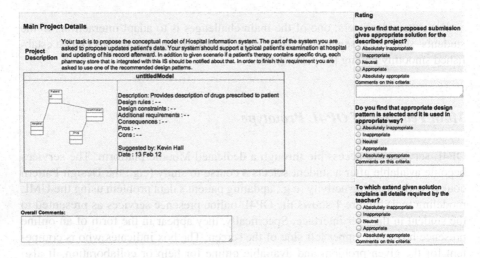

Fig. 3 Interface illustrating evaluation of other students' work

from peer evaluations, as shown in Fig. 3. They can assess solutions proposed by fellow students only after uploading their own solution.

Recommendations Strategies

To support students through recommendation of digital and human resources, the OP4L framework needs to implement recommendation algorithms. In this section, we present the algorithm that has been implemented to recommend peers and digital content. We also present a complementary approach based on the students' learning trajectories.

Recommendation Algorithm Based on the Conditional Stratified Analytic Hierarchy Process

In a learning environment each individual student has different characteristics, motivation and performance, which all together indubitably should be considered when designing and/or adapting the learning process. It has been well recognized that there is a need to move away from the 'one size fits all' paradigm, and to offer personalized learning experience to learners [17]. Most of the approaches aimed at adapting the learning process to individual learners or learning groups have been based on the learners' level of knowledge [18, 19]. Other learner features taken into account are background, hyperspace experience [20], preferences and interests, as well as learning styles and their effect on learning achievements [21]. However, despite interests in exploring these diverse learners' features, in recent years, modeling of adaptive systems has still revolved around acquiring and representing learners' knowledge. This orientation does not properly reflect real life situations where each learner has a variety of selection criteria and requirements over them when choosing other learners for collaboration and cooperation [22].

Representation and analysis of preferences have been studied in many fields such as economics, especially in project and risk management, decision theory, social choice theory, with further developments and applications in areas such as operational research, databases, security analysis, and artificial intelligence [23]. Modeling of user preferences is a great challenge, as it is difficult to express human opinion in a way that can be easily processed by computers [24]. The adoption of user preferences in the design of a PLE brings in additional challenges in coordination of the flow of information among the learners involved in a learning process, and in encouragement of interactions across learning systems/tools/services. In particular, communication between peers may be induced by different needs and expectations (e.g., general questions about the course organization, help needed in learning and understanding of some course topics, etc.). In some cases, urgent response is needed, while in others, only answers of good learners or good senior learners are useful. The following problems emerge from this observation: (*i*) characterization of peers for communication related to the selection criteria, and (*ii*) definition of specific requirements and preferences over them. Furthermore, it is reasonable to expect that appropriate peers are not available all the time for each learning topic, or the most appropriate peers are not there when a specific learner needs their assistance. Having all this in mind, the *PeerRec* service, developed as a part of the OP4L framework, integrates: (i) the aforementioned semantic representation of online presence data (see section "Functional Description"); (ii) two-level hierarchical structure of concerns and qualifier tags for semantic representation of selection criteria proposed in [25]; and (iii) the CS-AHP prioritization algorithm for presentation and ranking of users' preferences [25].

CS-AHP Algorithm

CS-AHP (Conditional Stratified Analytic Hierarchy Process) adopts Analytical Hierarchy Process (AHP) technique [26] for different kinds of preferences using a two-level hierarchical structure of concerns and qualifier tags. Concerns are a set of quality characteristics that represent important matters of interest for learners such as fields of professional specialization, spoken languages or preferred message response time. Qualifier tags represent possible values for each concern (e.g., qualifier tags for spoken languages could be *goodLevel*, *mediumLevel*, *lowLevel*, *unknownLanguage*).

Following the well-known AHP framework for expressing and ranking user requirements, the *PeerRec* service enables learners to express their requirements by defining relative importance between concerns, and between qualifier tags of each concern. Relative importance is typically defined with odd numbers ranging from 1 (equal importance) to 9 (extreme importance of one concern over the other). The options available to learners in respect to their online presence (i.e. peers for collaboration) are also associated with qualifier tags. Once the relative importance is set between all pairs of concerns, the AHP algorithm performs a tuned pair-wise comparison of the learners' requirements. The outcome of this process are ranks $\{r_1, \ldots, r_n\}$, which provide values from the $[0,1]$ interval over the set of available options. The process is done in two main steps: (i) the set of concerns and their qualifier tags are locally ranked with (ii) rank of each available option is calculated based on the ranks of the qualifier tags associated with that option.

CS-AHP also allows for setting conditional preferences. For example, learners are often aware that requirement of expertise is hard to meet, so they may define a compromise: they are only prepared to wait for response from a learner with expert knowledge, if the waiting time is kept at a very minimum; otherwise, they are willing to contact learners with lower level of expertise but with medium delays in response. CS-AHP is simple to perform, and requires quadratic number of comparisons, which brings linear time complexity to the number of available options [25].

Applying the CS-AHP Algorithm in a PLE

In order to develop a user-friendly service for the implementation of CS-AHP in a PLE, a structure of concerns and qualifier tags is built on the Preview framework related to learning environments [22]. The following three categories of concerns are recognized from the aspect of definition and management issues [27]: statically defined concerns, concerns dynamically defined for each conversation, and concerns with dynamic updates.

Statically defined concerns present general information about a learner who is looking for another peer appropriate for conversation; examples include the known language(s), preferred subject area, and availability for F2F contact. The recognized concerns are defined as attributes in the learner's profile developed for the *PeerRec* service. Information in the profile may be changed upon a learner's request;

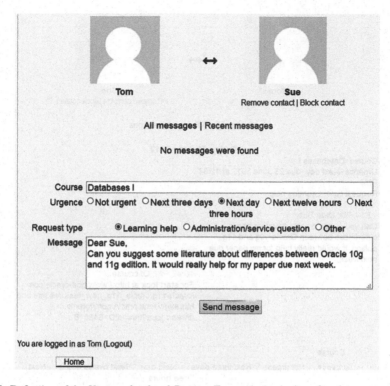

Fig. 4 Definition of the *Urgence level* and *Request Type* at the beginning of each conversation

otherwise, it remains unchanged, representing the learner's characteristics that are used in each call of the service.

On the other side, some concerns are directly related to the context of the upcoming conversation (i.e. concerns dynamically defined for each conversation), and, thus learners are enabled to define them explicitly. For example, a learner may define the type of conversation (e.g. the help in understanding, etc.) and/or the urgency level (e.g. extra urgent) (see Fig. 4).

Contrary to the concerns defined in the learner's profile (with qualifier tags statically defined and changeable only on the learner's explicit request), concern defined as ConversationRate should be updated for each completed conversation. To this end, the PeerRec service asks learner to rate each peer after communication (see button Rate conversation on Fig. 5), and based on the learner's feedback updates the values to be used in further communications with the same peer (see attributes Response speed and Response relevancy on Fig. 6). In cases when learner is not interested in setting rates (from different personal reasons ranging from current disengagement, lack of time or interests), he/she may select the N/A option meaning that experience from the latest conversation does not bring any change to the aggregated rates. Furthermore, if no rate is previously aggregated, initial selection of N/A represents indifferent and undeclared learner (neither positive nor negative rate is specified).

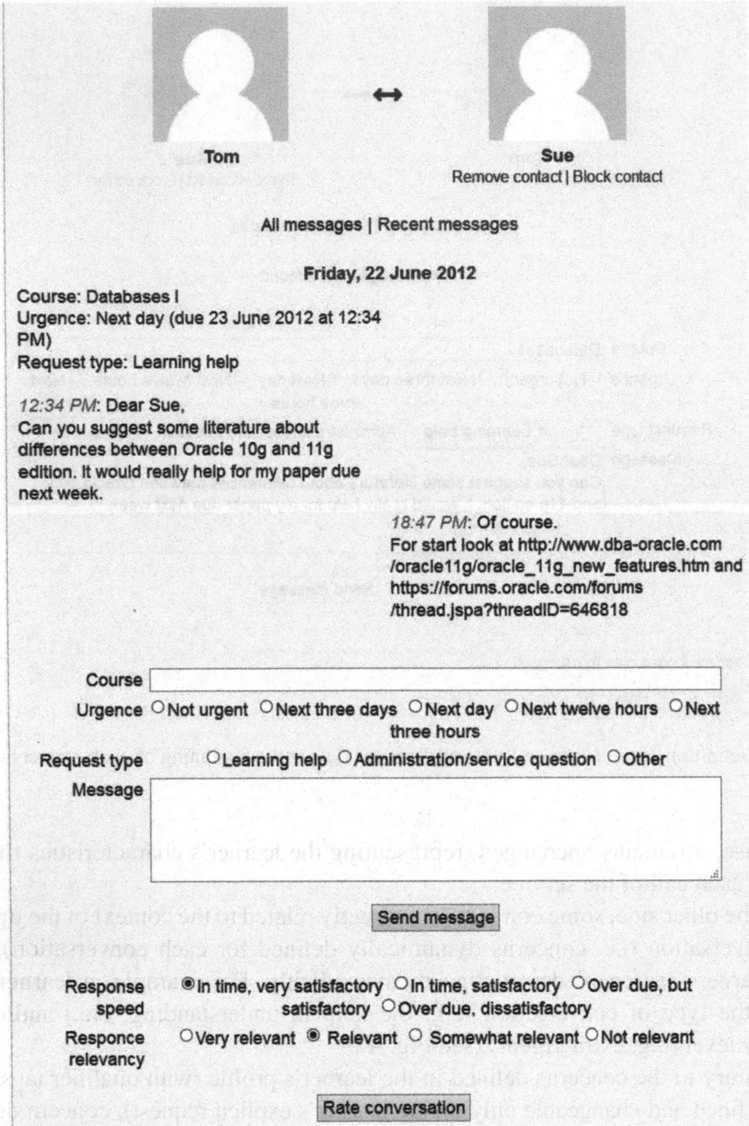

Tom   **Sue**
                                  Remove contact | Block contact

All messages | Recent messages

Friday, 22 June 2012

Course: Databases I
Urgence: Next day (due 23 June 2012 at 12:34
PM)
Request type: Learning help

12:34 PM: Dear Sue,
Can you suggest some literature about
differences between Oracle 10g and 11g
edition. It would really help for my paper due
next week.

> *18:47 PM*: Of course.
> For start look at http://www.dba-oracle.com
> /oracle11g/oracle_11g_new_features.htm and
> https://forums.oracle.com/forums
> /thread.jspa?threadID=646818

Course [   ]
Urgence ○ Not urgent ○ Next three days ○ Next day ○ Next twelve hours ○ Next
                                  three hours
Request type   ○ Learning help ○ Administration/service question ○ Other
Message [   ]

[Send message]

Response   ● In time, very satisfactory ○ In time, satisfactory ○ Over due, but
speed   satisfactory ○ Over due, dissatisfactory
Responce   ○ Very relevant ● Relevant ○ Somewhat relevant ○ Not relevant
relevancy

[Rate conversation]

You are logged in as Tom (Logout)

[Home]

Fig. 5 Rating conversations based on *Response speed* and *Response relevancy*

After invoking the PeerRec service, all currently available peers are ranked in decreasing order (based on the results obtained from applying the CS-AHP algorithm), and the learner can decide with whom to start a conversation (see Fig. 7).

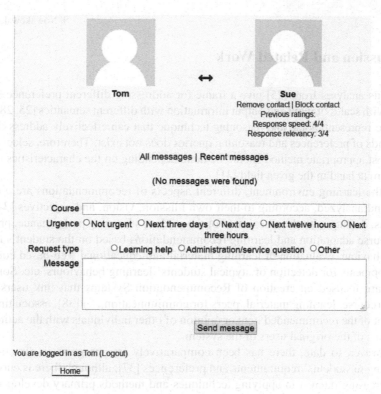

Fig. 6 Aggregated conversation ratings (*Response speed & Response relevancy*)

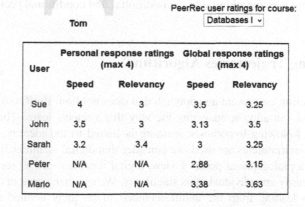

Fig. 7 The *PeerRec* service invocation and ranking of all peers available for communication

Discussion and Related Work

Previous analyses from [25] give a frame for addressing different preference structures with scales of input and output information with different semantics [25, 28–33]. Unique representational and reasoning technique that can effectively address different kinds of preferences and reasoning queries does not exist. Therefore, selection of the most appropriate method should be done depending on the characteristics of the problem at hand in the given field [31].

In the learning environment, different aspects of recommendations are considered and analyzed, according to their own mission, vision, and objectives [34–37] such as, dealing with the assessment of the student's learning performance, providing course adaptation and learning recommendations based on the student's learning behaviour, evaluation of learning material and educational web-based courses, developments for detection of atypical students' learning behaviours, etc. Some of them are focused on creation of Recommendation Systems that link users with items (course, learning material, peers for communication,...) [38], associating the content of the recommended item or opinion of other individuals with the actions or opinions of the original users of the system.

However, to date, there has been comparatively less progress in direction of focusing to students' requirements and preferences [37], although there is currently an increasing interest in applying techniques and methods primary developed and used in other fields to the educational environment [39]. In this context, recently developed CS-AHP algorithm extends well-known Analytical Hierarchical Process (AHP) proposed by Saaty [26] which is a widely adopted multi-criteria decision making method to make complex decisions [40, 41]. Also, the use of two-layered structure of concerns and qualifier tags has several explanations, sufficient expressiveness (according to [24]) and analogous to the concept of attributes in all developed techniques for addressing unconditional and conditional preferences [42].

Learning Trajectories Algorithm

In this section we present an approach that does not limit itself to the content recommendation, but aims at analyzing the way that students learn. This approach starts from the following hypothesis: learning is linked to the identity; so, when digital learning environments are used, we consider that digital identities have to be studied.

From a philosophical point of view, digital identities can be seen as the "sèmes" which identify an individual in its singularity. We can then speak of "individuation" as a process leading from the undifferentiated to uniquely defined and personalized. Consequently, we can identify someone by his/her personal trajectory in the cyberspace. To validate this approach, we have implemented a service (using Matlab) with input data from the OP4L learning framework. The following sections show the theoretical background of our approach, as well as some numerical results and perspectives.

Input Data

The input data we consider is made up of traces that users have left (log files and users' ratings) when interacting with the system (intranet, Web site, etc.). These data are first used to discover patterns of usage, and then to perform recommendations. In our case, data are coming from the log files of the OP4L prototypes. They show (for each user) the pages visited in the learning environment.

Markov Model

One well-known approach to making use of users' online history is to compute predictions by using Markov models. The use of Markov models in the frame of the Web has been first dedicated to the reduction of access time by pre-fetching and caching pages [43]. With the same goal, Box and Jenkins in [44] estimated conditional probabilities of transitioning directly from one page to another within a given time. First order Markov models are not very accurate in predicting the user's browsing behavior since these models do not look far in the past to efficiently discriminate different histories [45]. Pirolli and Pitkow in [46] and [47] showed that the prediction accuracy is increased when using a longer history. Higher order Markov models, also called kth order Markov models, are used to capture longer histories. Given the navigation history of size k, the probability of each resource is computed, and the resources with the highest conditional probability are recommended. The use of kth order Markov models lead to a high accuracy.

Let us notice that kth order Markov models are similar to frequent contiguous patterns of fixed size k + 1 in the case when support and confidence thresholds are set to 0. One drawback of kth order Markov models is the storage requirements; indeed, in a kth order Markov model a huge number of states are handled (this number increases according to the order of the model) [43]. Moreover, as with previous approaches, we are faced to a reduced coverage due to the problem of matching the active history and training data. Many approaches can overcome coverage limitation. For example, we can mention the development of Markov models of orders varying from 1 to k called the all kth order Markov model [48]. However such a model dramatically increases the complexity and storage space drawbacks.

When using Markov models, the order of navigation is taken into account and the sequences are strictly contiguous, hence, these models are not permissive. If a given user performs parallel navigations or goes to an unwanted resource (noise), the model cannot correctly handle such a behaviour and will thus reduce the size of the history considered. Such situations are handled by association rules and sequential patterns as resources are not contiguous. Moreover, when the model does not match the complete history, the most distant consulted resources are discarded for computing predictions. Thus, the most recent resources are always considered while some of them may be not important or may be navigation mistakes and should be discarded.

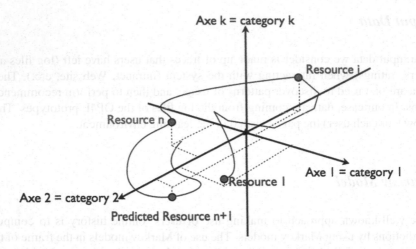

Fig. 8 Learning trajectory

In the following section, we show how we can derive from Markov model an approach based on Kalman filtering and target tracking. In our approach, we based our recommendation strategy on a transformation of the web space.

Principles

Kalman filter is an optimal state estimator of a linear system [49]. It can estimate the state of the system using a priori knowledge of the evolution of the state and the measurements. Kalman filter has main applications in control systems and target tracking.

Target Tracking in the Cyberspace [53]

We consider a user who browses Web pages or online resources. Each page/resource belongs to a category (categories are related to the classification of the available resources). We then consider that one category corresponds to one dimension of a space. And the aggregation of all the dimension builds a space having as dimensions as there are categories of resources. Then, all possible categories define the geometrical structure of the space.

Knowing that to see one resource corresponds to a specific position in the space i.e., a specific vector. Successive vectors $(\vec{v}_1$ to $\vec{v}_n)$ give successive "positions" in the space. In the context of online learning, these "positions – learning positions" define the trajectory of a user in the recommender space (Fig. 8).

Each vector has the following dimensions:

$m \times 1$, m is the number of categories; each seen page belongs to one or more categories. In our case, i.e., the analysis of the learning processes on the OP4L platform, each page coming from the tested site is classified (courses, exercises, ...). The structure of each vector will be as follows. Considering that we have m possible categories for the resources, to see one specific resource is to have a vector containing "1" in the corresponding row, and "0" elsewhere.

$$\begin{bmatrix} cat-1 \\ cat-2 \\ \dots \\ cat-i \\ \dots \\ cat-m \end{bmatrix} \leftarrow correspondingcategory \begin{bmatrix} 0 \\ 0 \\ \dots \\ 1 \\ \dots \\ 0 \end{bmatrix} = \vec{v}_k \tag{1}$$

Kalman Filter: Equations

Hypothesis
Our main hypothesis is the following: considering that users are moving along a trajectory defined by a set of vectors, we assume that the user can be considered as a target which is described by three components in the state space, i.e., position, speed and acceleration. These three components will completely describe the dynamics of the moving users [44, 49, 50]. Thus, we choose to represent the state vector by concatenating these three components. The state vector has the following form [51]:

$$X_k = \begin{bmatrix} x \\ v \\ \gamma \end{bmatrix}_k \tag{2}$$

where: $\dim(X_k) = 3m \times 1$

- x contains the components of the position vector, dimensions $m \times 1$
- v contains the components of the speed vector, dimensions $m \times 1$
- γ contains the components of the acceleration vector, dimensions $m \times 1$.

The dynamic of this state vector is modeled by a state space model of the following form:

$$\begin{cases} X_{k+1} = AX_k + w_k \\ Z_k = HX_k + v_k \end{cases} \tag{3}$$

Matrix A includes the relationship between the position, its first and second derivations will inform us on the geometrical characteristics of the trajectory. This is the matrix form of the cinematic equation linking position to speed and acceleration. T is a parameter that introduces time in the equation. In our case, we consider T equal to 1 because time is fixed each time the user goes to another webpage. The results of the algorithm are not sensitive to T.

$$A = \begin{bmatrix} \alpha & T & \frac{1}{2}T^2 \\ 0 & \alpha & T \\ 0 & 0 & \alpha \end{bmatrix} \quad (4)$$

Where: $\dim(A) = 3m \times 3m$

Many values of parameter α have been tested. The chosen value does not influence our numerical results.

w_k and v_k (Eq. (3)) are random noises (their properties will be given in the next section) which take into account unexpected variations in the trajectories.

Matrix H (Eq. (3)), called the measurement matrix, is structured to obtain the values of the positions in the recommender space. Thus, H will have the following structure:

$$H = \begin{bmatrix} 1 & 0 & .. & 0 & 0 & 0 & .. & 0 & 0 & .. & 0 & 0 \\ 0 & 1 & .. & 0 & 0 & 0 & .. & 0 & 0 & .. & 0 & 0 \\ .. & .. & 1 & 0 & 0 & .. & .. & .. & .. & .. & .. & 0 \\ 0 & 0 & 0 & 1 & 0 & 0 & .. & 0 & 0 & .. & 0 & 0 \end{bmatrix} \quad (5)$$

Where: $\dim(H) = m \times 3m$

General Equations of the Filter

Having the state space model (Eq. 3) and the structure of the state vector, we can derive the equations of the filter. First, we present some important properties of the Kalman filter:

- Information about X and Z is given as a Markov model i.e., Z is a linear combination of the components of X;
- Estimations of X are obtained from any initial instant;
- Estimations can be obtained for non-stationary process i.e., time-varying models.
- w_k and v_k are uncorrelated white noises where $w_k \approx N(0, Q)$ and $v_k \approx N(0, R)$.

The Kalman filter equations comprise the following equations [5, 54]:
Prediction: it is the predicted state knowing past values:

$$\begin{cases} \hat{X}_{k+1/k} = \hat{X}_{k/k-1} + K_k \left(Z_k - H\hat{X}_{k/k-1} \right) \\ \quad\quad = \left(A - K_k H \right) \hat{X}_{k/k-1} + K_k Z_k \end{cases} \quad (6)$$

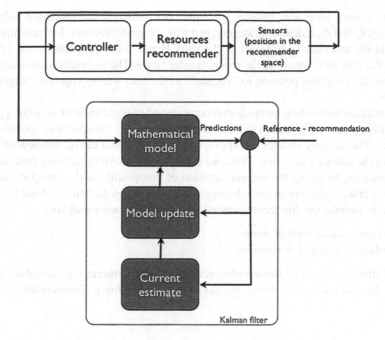

Fig. 9 Control loop for recommendation

Kalman gain: it describes the dynamic of the filter. The dynamic takes into account the variations of the moving target.

$$K_k = AP_{k/k-1}H^T \left(HP_{k/k-1}H^T + R\right)^{-1} \tag{7}$$

The evolution of the uncertainty on the estimation is then given by the following Riccati equation:

$$P_{k+1/k} = AP_{k/k-\&}A^T - AP_{k/k-1}H^T \left(HP_{k/k-1}H^T + R\right)^{-1} HP_{k/k-1}A^T \tag{8}$$

where the initial conditions (which initialize the filter) are given by:

$$\hat{X}_{0/-1} = X_0 \; P_{0/-1} = P_0 \tag{9}$$

and the state prediction is given by: $\hat{X}_{k+1/k}$

The Kalman predictor will predict the future position in the recommender space i.e. the most possible category knowing the past of the user.

Recommendation Strategy

The user profile is built from the list of pages visited on the platform. Each page/resource is defined by a subset of categories such as "modelling," "courses," etc.

Our new recommending strategy is based on the control loop shown in Fig. 9.

This control loop will observe the difference between the estimated value of the category and the calculated category, and will integrate the controller/recommender to build the most accurate model of the user. Hence this configuration can predict where the user will "move" in the recommender space. The recommendation strategy will use the predicted position to "suggest" to the user the appropriate category of content.

Conversely to existing methods that recommend specific content items to a given user, this method performs on the macroscopic level, i.e., subspaces of specific categories. The strategy isolates the appropriate subspace and the recommendation is done in the related categories. Then, we can imagine providing a more precise recommendation by doing the second iteration of computing on the subspace (target tracking in the trajectory in the subspace and positions prediction)—a kind of zoom effect. To summarize, the recommendation is based on two arguments:

- the user's actual state of mind
- a subset of retained dimensions

We then have a set of items to be recommended. Furthermore, according to the pages the user has visited during the day, we can refine our recommendation.

Results

In order to model the trajectories, we have to identify categories of pedagogical resources that define the recommender space. Based on the extensive log analysis, we propose the following basic description:

- assessment (MA)
- courses (C)
- resources (R)
- forum (F)
- modelling workgroup (MW)
- modelling brainstorm (MB)
- modelling (M)

Each position vector is built using relation Eq. (1). We obtain position vectors containing only "0" and "1" on the appropriate dimension.

Thus, we consider that users are moving in a 7 dimensions space. Using our approach and algorithms, we obtain the following results for a specific user (Figs. 10 and 11). In the following figures, we show one learner's trajectory along specific dimensions of the space (Dimensions MA, C and R). In both figures, X-axis represents time and Y-axis represents the seen item thus it is "0" or "1."

Combining all these evolutions, we obtain trajectories in 7-dimensions space. Applying our tracking algorithm, we can compute the next viewed category of contents. For example, we can show the results in one dimension, dimension R (Fig. 12).

Figures 10 and 11 show the evolution of the trajectory along the dimensions of the recommender space. Figure 12 shows the predicted trajectory to the real

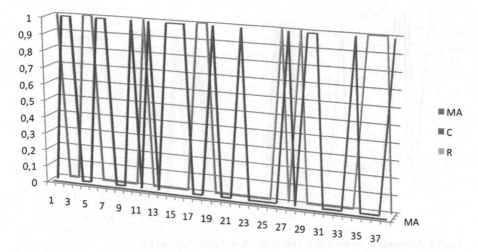

Fig. 10 Evolution in MA, C and R dimensions

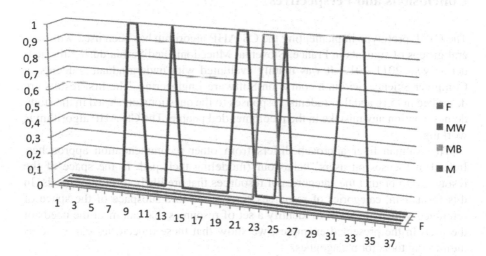

Fig. 11 Evolution in F, MW, MB and M dimensions

trajectory relatively to one dimension of the recommender space—dimension R. We can see that the prediction PR follows the real trajectory R. Having this prediction (PR), we can now derive a specific recommender system based on these categories. For example, using the information given by the prediction, the system can recommend specific content items to the student.

Thus, the strength of our approach is in its capability to make recommendations that consider the users' habits, i.e. give the main directions to follow knowing the trajectory in the space and not to suggest specific resources.

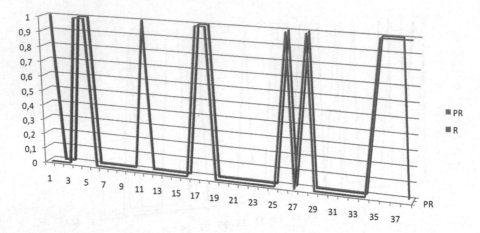

Fig. 12 Comparison between Real Dimension R and predicted one PR

Conclusions and Perspectives

The OP4L prototype implementing the CS-AHP algorithm has been used with several groups of students in France, Slovenia, Macedonia and Serbia during the academic year 2011–2012. It was mainly evaluated with undergraduate students in Computer Science, within a course on Software Engineering. The first results are described in [52], and the students' responses to the questionnaires used in the study do not mention any mistake in the recommended people. The CS-AHP algorithm is working.

The Kalman filter approach differs from other recommendation approaches. Indeed, it focuses on users' behaviour (modeling their path in the space of the resources) to predict the categories of resources that are likely to fit their needs. In this formalism, categories of resources correspond to a subspace of the space of reference, which allows us to identify a set of resources that can meet the needs of the user. In the presented examples, we show that these trajectories can serve as monitoring tools for pedagogues.

We are thus able to describe behaviours by learning trajectories and predict what types of resources a learner is likely to access.

We would like to conclude with the perspectives offered by the learning trajectories algorithm. In particular, the approach based on learning trajectories allows one to:

- model learning process, i.e. to understand how someone learns
- recommend content items more accurately, i.e. knowing about someone's learning process we can recommend exercises, courses, self-assessment, …
- develop a recommender system based on different levels of analysis, i.e. to identify the accurate subspace and then re-compute in a zoom effect to identify precisely the concerned dimensions.

Moreover, this geometrical approach opens a new field of research focused on the geometrical description of the recommender space, and how this geometry could lead to better recommendation and dynamics understanding. In the OP4L context, this approach of learning trajectory analysis will enable a better understanding of all the experiments done or to be done with students. Thus, the results obtained in the studies done in France, Macedonia, Serbia and Slovenia could be enforced and enriched by learning trajectories modelling. Moreover, this combined methodology will help us to identify the appropriate functionalities, those which are important, those which are not used, and will lead our research on the integration of others social networks (technically and also by recommending to students, some resources coming from the social network), and the definition of new ontologies related to other disciplines.

Acknowledgements This work was supported by the SEE-ERA Net Plus program, contract no 115, from the European Union.

References

1. Atwell G (2007) Personal learning environments – The future of eLearning? eLearning papers 2(1), ISSN: 1887-1542, www.elearningpapers.eu
2. Vuokari R, Manouselis N, Duval E (eds) (2009) Special issue on social information retrieval for technology enhanced learning, J Dig Inform 10(2), ISSN: 1368-7506
3. Manouselis N, Drachsler H, Vuorikari R, Hummel H, Koper R (2010) Recommender systems in technology enhanced learning. In: Ricci F, Rokach L, Shapira B, Kantor PB (eds) Handbook of recommender systems. Springer, Secaucus, NJ, pp 387–415
4. Santos OC, Boticario JG (2012) Educational recommender systems and technologies. Practices and challenges. IGI Global, Hershey, PA
5. OP4L project's website: http://op4l.fon.bg.ac.rs/
6. Vassileva J (2008) Towards social learning environments. IEEE TLT 1(4):199–214
7. Aragon SR (2003) Creating social presence in online environments. New Dir Adult Contin Educ 100:57–68
8. Cob SC (2009) Social presence and online learning: a current view from a research perspective. J Interact Online Learn 8(3):241–254
9. Lowenthal PR (2010) Social presence. In: Dasgupta S (ed) Social computing: concepts, methodologies, tools, and applications. IGI Global, Hershey, PA, pp 129–136
10. Beham G, Kump B, Ley T, Lindstaed SN (2010) Recommending knowledgeable people in a work-integrated learning system, 1st RecSysTEL workshop. Proc Comput Sci 1(2):2783–2792, Elsevier
11. Jovanovic J, Knight C, Gasevic D, Richards G (2007) Ontologies for effective use of context in e-learning settings. Educ Tech Soc 10(3):47–59
12. Jeremic Z, Milikic N, Jovanovic J, Radulovic R, Brkovic M, Devedzic V (2011) OP4L: online presence enabled personal learning environments, IEEE – ERK'2011 conference, Portoroz, Slovenia
13. Milikic N, Radulovic R, Devedzic V (2011) Infrastructure for exchanging online presence data in learning applications, IEEE – ERK'2011 conference, Portoroz, Slovenia
14. OP4L D3.1, OP4L models, http://op4l.fon.bg.ac.rs/sites/default/files/OP4LD3.1.pdf
15. Jovanović J, Gašević D, Stanković M, Jeremić Z, Siadaty M (2009) Online presence in adaptive learning on the social semantic web. In: Proceedings of the 1st IEEE international confer-

ence on social computing - workshops (Workshop on social computing in education), Vancouver, BC, Canada. IEEE, Washington, DC, pp 891–896

16. Stankevic M (2008) Modeling online presence, In: Proceedings of the first social data on the web workshop, Karlsruhe, Germany, October 27, 2008, CEUR workshop proceedings, ISSN 1613-0073, online CEUR-WS.org/Vol-405/paper1.pdf

17. Dagger D, Wade V, Conlan O (2005) Personalisation for all: making adaptive course composition easy. Educ Tech Soc 8(3):9–25

18. Popescu E, Trigano P, Badica C (2007) Adaptive educational hypermedia systems: a focus on learning styles. In: Proc of the international conference on computer as a tool (EUROCON), Warsaw, Poland. IEEE Computer Society, Washington, DC

19. Stash N De Bra P (2004) Incorporating cognitive styles in AHA! The adaptive hypermedia architecture. In: Proceedings of the international conference web-based education (IASTED), Innsbruck, Austria, pp 378–383

20. Brusilovsky P (2001) Adaptive hypermedia User modeling and user adapted interaction. In: Alfred Kobsa (ed.), Tenth year anniversary issue 11(1/2): 87–110

21. Mustafa A, Sharif S (2011) An approach to adaptive e-learning hypermedia system based on learning styles (AEHS-LS): implementation and evaluation. Int J Lib Inform Sci 3(1):15–28

22. Ognjanović I, Šendelj R (2012) Teachers' requirements in dynamically adaptive e-learning systems. In: Proceedings of 4th international conference on education and new learning technologies (EDULEARN12), Barcelona, Spain

23. Ognjanović I, Gašević D, Bagheri E, Asadi M (2011) Conditional preferences in software stakeholders' judgments. In: Proceedings of the 26th annual ACM symposium on applied computing, Taichang, Taiwan. ACM, New York, NY, pp 683–690

24. Yu Z, Yu Z, Zhou X, Nakamu Y (2009) Toward an understanding of user-defined conditional preferences. In: Proceedings of the 8th IEEE international conference on dependable, autonomic and secure computing. IEEE, Washington, DC, pp 203–208

25. Ognjanović I, Gašević D, Bagheri E (2013) A stratified framework for handling conditional preferences: an extension of the analytic hierarchy process. Expert Syst Appl 40(4):1094–1115

26. Saaty TL (1980) The analytic hierarchy process. McGraw-Hill, New York, NY

27. Ognjanović I, Šendelj R (2011) Making judgments and decisions about relevant learning resources. In: Proceedings of the 20th international electrotechnical and computer science conference, Portoroz, Slovenia (ERK 2011), pp 409–412

28. Boutilier C, Brafman RI, Domshlak C, Hoos HH, Poole D (2004) CP-nets: a tool for representing and reasoning with conditional ceteris paribus preference statements. J AI Res 21(1):135–191

29. Brafman RI, Domshlak C (2002) Introducing variable importance tradeoffs into CP-nets. In: The proceedings of the eighteenth conference on uncertainty in AI, Canada. AAAI, Menlo Park, CA, pp 69–76

30. Wilson N (2011) Computational techniques for a simple theory of conditional preferences. Artif Intell 175(7–8):1053–1091

31. Zavadskas EK, Kaklauskas A, Peldschus F, Turskis Z (2007) Multi-attribute assessment of road design solutions by using the COPRAS Method. Baltic J Road Bridge Eng 2(4): 195–203

32. Chen S, Buffett S, Fleming MW (2007) Reasoning with conditional preferences across attributes. In: Proceedings of the 20th conference of the Canadian society for computational studies of intelligence on advances in AI, Montreal, Canada. Springer, Berlin, pp 369–380

33. Berander P, Andrews A (2006) Requirements prioritization. Engineering and managing software requirements. Springer, Secaucus, NJ, pp 69–94

34. Hanna M (2004) Data mining in the e-learning domain. Campus Wide Inf Syst 21(1):29–34

35. Merceron A, Yacef K (2005) Educational data mining: a case study. In: Proc Int Conf Artif Intell Educ, Pittsburgh, PA, 2005

36. Baker R, Yacef K (2009) The state of educational data mining in 2009: a review and future visions. J Educ Data Mining 1(1):3–17

37. Romero C, Ventura S (2010) Educational data mining: a review of the state of the art. IEEE Trans Syst Man Cybern Part C Appl Rev 40(6):601–618

38. Schafer JB (2005) The application of data-mining to recommender systems. In: Wang J (ed) Encyclopedia of data warehousing and mining. Hershey, PA, Idea Group, pp 44–48
39. Lazcorreta E, Botella F, Fernández-Caballero A (2008) Towards personalized recommendation by two-step modified apriori data mining algorithm. Expert Syst Appl 35(3):1422–1429
40. Büyüközkan G, Çifçi G, Güleryüz S (2011) Strategic analysis of healthcare service quality using fuzzy AHP methodology. Expert Syst Appl 38(8):9407–9424
41. Chen MK, Wang S (2010) The critical factors of success for information service industry in developing international market: using analytic hierarchy process (AHP) approach. Expert Syst Appl 37(1):694–704
42. Ognjanović I, Gašević D, Bagheri E, Asadi M (2011) Conditional preferences in software stakeholders' judgments. In: Proceedings of the 26th annual ACM symposium on applied computing (SAC 2011), Tunghai University, Taichang, Taiwan. ACM, New York, NY
43. Padmanabhan V, Mogul J (1996) Using predictive prefetching to improve World Wide Web Latency. Comput Commun Rev 28(4):22–36
44. Box GEP, Jenkins GM (1970) Time series analysis: forecasting and control. Holden Day, San Francisco, CA
45. Despande M, Karypis G (2004) Selective Markov models for predicting web pages accesses. ACM Trans Internet Technol 4:163–184
46. Pirolli P, Pitkow J (1999) Distribution of surfer's paths through the World Wide Web: empirical characterizations. WWW J 2(1–2):29–45
47. Pitkow J, Pirolli P (1999) Mining longest repeating subsequences to predict World Wide Web surfing. In: Proceedings of the 2nd conference of USENIX symposium on internet technologies and systems. USENIX Association, Berkeley, CA, pp 139–150
48. Nakagawa N, Mobasher B (2003) Impact of site characteristics on recommendation models based on association rules and sequential patterns. In: Proceedings of the IJCAI'03 workshop on intelligent techniques for web personalization, August 9–10, 2003, Acapulco, Mexico
49. Anderson B, Moore JB (1977) Optimal filtering. Prentice Hall – Information and system sciences series. Prentice Hall, Englewood Cliffs, NJ
50. Gevers M, Vandendorpe L (2011) Processus stochastiques, estimation et prediction, http://www.tele.ucl.ac.be/EDU/INMA2731/
51. Nowakowski S, Boyer A, Bernier C (2011) Automatic tracking and control for web recommendation. New approaches for web recommendation. Conference SOTICS 2011, October 2011, Barcelona, Spain
52. Grandbastien M, Loskovska S, Nowakowski S, Jovanovic J (2012) Using online presence data for recommending human resources in the OP4L project. Conference RecSysTel, September 2012, Sarrebrück, Germany
53. Gibson W (1988) Neuromancien. Collection J'ai Lu, Paris
54. Söderström T (1994) Discrete-time stochastic systems estimation and control. Springer, Secaucus, NJ

Recommendations from Heterogeneous Sources in a Technology Enhanced Learning Ecosystem

Alejandro Fernández, Mojisola Erdt, Ivan Dackiewicz, and Christoph Rensing

Abstract A Technology Enhanced Learning (TEL) ecosystem is a kind of Digital Ecosystem formed by independent platforms combined and used by learners to support their learning. Related work shows that recommendations in TEL can support learners and that in TEL ecosystems, learners do use different platforms. We therefore pursue the goal to enable recommendations across different platforms by exploiting the synergies between them to benefit learners. However, building such cross-platform recommender systems poses new and unique technological challenges for developers. In this paper, we discuss the challenges faced and present a framework, with a running example, for the development of cross-platform recommender systems for TEL ecosystems. The framework decouples the development of the recommender system from the evolution of the specific platforms and allows the integration of different recommendation algorithms by combining graph-based algorithms. As proof of concept, the framework was effectively applied and evaluated to develop a cross-platform recommender system in a TEL ecosystem comprising Moodle as the Learning Management System, and MediaWiki customized as Learning Object Repository. For future work, the integration of different recommendation algorithms and a user study on the benefits of recommendations from different sources in a learning scenario is planned.

Keywords Recommender systems • Technology enhanced learning • Heterogeneous data sources • Graph based recommender systems

A. Fernández (✉)
LIFIA, CIC/Facultad de Informática. UNLP, La Plata, Argentina. Also at UCALP
e-mail: alejandro.fernandez@lifia.info.unlp.edu.ar

M. Erdt • C. Rensing
Multimedia Communications Lab, Technische Universität Darmstadt, Germany
e-mail: Mojisola.Anjorin@kom.tu-darmstadt.de; Christoph.Rensing@kom.tu-darmstadt.de

I. Dackiewicz
LIFIA, Facultad de Informática. UNLP, La Plata, Argentina
e-mail: idackiewicz@lifia.info.unlp.edu.ar

N. Manouselis et al. (eds.), *Recommender Systems for Technology Enhanced Learning:*   251
Research Trends and Applications, DOI 10.1007/978-1-4939-0530-0_12,
© Springer Science+Business Media New York 2014

Introduction

A Technology Enhanced Learning (TEL) ecosystem is a form of Digital Ecosystem [6] inhabited by elements from various platforms used in parallel by learners and teachers. Such a simultaneous use of platforms is often found in communities of practice [27], also known as learning networks, where learning is mostly self-directed. Take as a running example a TEL ecosystem with three platforms: a Learning Management Systems (LMS), a Social Networking Service (SNS), and a Learning Object Repository (LOR). An LMS offers activities as well as discussion forums and shared workspaces. Activities rely on learning objects (LOs) such as lesson notes and presentations. The visibility of a LO is normally limited to an activity. However when an LMS is used to support self-directed learning, it becomes particularly important that learners are aware of all activities, resources and peers they could potentially gain from. Nowadays, many learners participate in social networks connecting to other learners via Facebook,[1] or posting learning tasks and following other learners on Twitter.[2] Contacts the students have on platforms such as an LMS are disconnected from the online social networks they belong to outside the classroom. It is therefore up to the students to replicate in each of these worlds the relationships they have built in the other. The potential to share knowledge and find valuable contacts across these platforms therefore remains unexploited. Initiatives such as the MIT OpenCourseWare[3] or the Ariadne Foundation[4] with its LOR demonstrate the increasing interest in collecting and sharing high quality learning material. LORs however are isolated from the LMS and SNS. There therefore exists an opportunity to provide learners with information across multiple platforms by considering the synergies between them.

In a previous article [1], we initiated the discussion on the provision of cross-platform recommendations in TEL Ecosystems and presented general guidelines for the design of a framework to support its construction. In the following sections, we further elaborate on the requirements, and provide details about the framework's architecture and design.

Recommendations from Heterogeneous Sources in a TEL Ecosystem

Feature rich LMSs such as Moodle[5] support numerous forms of interaction and a wide variety of resource types. Lightweight approaches focus only on the most common subsets of interactions and resources. That is the case of the systems that

---

[1] http://facebook.com (last accessed 25/2/2013).

[2] http://twitter.com (last accessed 25/2/2013).

[3] http://ocw.mit.edu/index.htm (last accessed 25/2/2013).

[4] http://www.ariadne-eu.org/ (last accessed 25/2/2013).

[5] http://www.moodle.org (last accessed 25/2/2013).

the most popular MOOC (Massive, Open, Online Learning services) use (e.g., Coursera[6]). We interpret *resource* as any (digital) object that can be used in, or is the result of learning. Instructional material such as lecture videos, slides, lecture notes, articles, or ebooks are common examples of resources. Chat transcripts, forum discussions, thesauri, glossaries, simulations, taxonomies, and data-sets are also resources. Authors can design and package certain resources to support reuse. The goal of the Learning Objects movement is to foster these practices of reuse.

During the life-time of a learner, a person will need to interact with several different platforms. For example, a student will use an LMS at school (or possibly several, if each department provides its own system), and yet again a different one if he or she participates in MOOCs. Students usually do not find all resources they need in a single LMS. Sometimes they have to look for resources elsewhere; for example, in digital repositories, wikis, reference managers, or portfolio managers. This means that a student's resources (both used and required) are spread across various systems. As resources are a central element in learning, students face the daily challenge of finding the right ones.

Learning commonly occurs in the context of activities. Courses, classes, workshops, tutorials, projects, assignments, and individual learning goals, are common organizational structures that help students, in both formal and informal learning, to progress in their learning process. These organizational structures are ubiquitous in LMSs. In formal learning, it is still common that institutions organize learning; that is, they define the structure of activities that students must adhere to with more or less flexibility. In contrast, informal learning imparts to the student the responsibility of deciding what activities to take. Although not as often as it occurs with resources, students regularly need to find and select activities.

Social interaction is important in learning [21]. We learn in a social context while being part of a supporting team; when we engage with others in a learning activity; and when cultural artifacts support our learning. Sometimes, artifacts mediate our interaction with others (e.g., using our team's best practices catalogue). Sometimes, social interaction is more direct and obvious, for example when we complete an assignment with a group, or when we participate in a community discussion. LMSs, that realize the value of collaborative learning, support all these forms of interaction. They provide the means to form groups, and associate activities and resources to groups. They provide means for collaborative knowledge construction such as various forms of online conversations, and collaborative editing. Reference managers (e.g., Mendeley[7]) acknowledge the importance of social interaction and provide support for the creation of communities, social networks, and shared catalogs. Recent studies [15] on the use of SNSs such as Facebook show that despite being widely used by students, they have little educational use. However, Ellison [14] found empirical evidence of a strong connection between Facebook usage and indicators of social capital, which could support students while moving from one learning community to another.

---

[6] http://www.coursera.org/(last retrieved 25/2/2013).

[7] http://www.mendeley.com/(last accessed 25/2/2013).

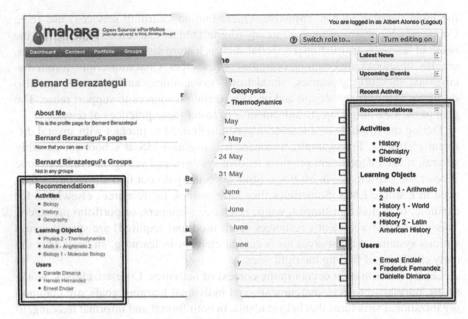

Fig. 1 Recommendation of activities, learning objects and users in Mahara and Moodle

Learners regularly require resources, activities and opportunities for social interaction. In current days, these resources, activities, and opportunities are scattered in a digital ecosystem. Recommender systems tackle similar scenarios. They help users find useful content they search for, and propose useful content that is available, even when users are not explicitly looking for it. However, recommender systems are commonly an internal component of one larger system (such as Amazon,[8] Netflix,[9] etc.). In our TEL scenario, recommendable objects reside in multiple, heterogeneous systems. Moreover, learners expect recommendations as they use any one of these systems. For example, they expect recommendations of interesting videos while they perform activities in the LMS, while interacting with friends in the SNS, or while they browse the contents of the digital repository.

A TEL ecosystem is a dynamic entity. It evolves when new components (e.g., new systems) are included. Even if we choose to focus only on three types of objects (resources, activities, people) every change in the constitution of the ecosystem brings new data and relationships between objects. Recommendation strategies must evolve to accompany the evolution of the ecosystem.

From the user's perspective, each platform should produce a recommendation list. Figure 1 illustrates how this could work for Mahara (an e-portfolio and social networking platform)[10] and Moodle. The recommendation list is shown in Mahara (left side) and in Moodle (right side). The recommendations are personalized considering the user's current focus. For example, in Fig. 1 recommendations are

---

[8] http://www.amazon.com (last accessed 25/2/2013).

[9] http://www.netflix.com (last accessed 25/2/2013).

[10] http://www.mahara.org (last accessed on 25/2/2013).

provided in Mahara for the user Albert Alonso taking into account that he is currently focused on viewing Bernard Berazategui's user profile. Depending on the recommendation strategy, the recommendation lists might include other users that Bernard has befriended, activities that he has completed, and resources that he frequently uses. Consequently, the recommendation lists contain items (i.e., activities, LOs and users) from any of the platforms that compose the ecosystem.

In summary, the core requirements to provide recommendations in a scenario like the one we have described are: (a) offer recommendations in all components of the TEL ecosystem; (b) recommend elements from all these systems (i.e., from heterogeneous sources), and (c) support the evolution of recommendation strategies. In the following sections we present an approach to tackle these challenges.

Related Work

Recommender Systems in TEL

Recommender systems based on approaches such as content based and collaborative filtering (CF) techniques have been shown to be very useful in TEL scenarios, especially in informal learning [17]. Collaborative filtering approaches use community data such as feedback or ratings from other users to make recommendations. Graph-based recommender techniques [3] can be classified as neighborhood-based collaborative filtering approaches [11]. A graph is used to represent the users or items as nodes and the edges as the transactions between them. PageRank [8] is an example of a graph-based approach based on a random walk similarity. Extensions to PageRank in learning scenarios are proposed in [19] and [3]. Content based approaches are used for example in [23]. All these different approaches are justifiable depending on the concrete learning scenario, the goals which are pursued with a recommendation (recommending similar or diverse resources) and the role the learner has (recipient of information or producer of data) in the pedagogic theory [9]. Therefore, with our framework, we aim to achieve a high flexibility regarding the integration of different recommendation algorithms and the combination of their results in a TEL ecosystem.

Learning Object Repositories and Federated Search

Learning Object Repositories are platforms which provide learners and teachers with so-called learning objects. Their main goal is to support the reusability of learning objects, that are provided mainly by teachers to the repositories. For a long time there have been discussions on how a learning object should look like [18, 20]. This discussion shall not be deepened here. Nevertheless it can be assumed that objects stored in LORs can be useful for learners and should be regarded as candidates when recommending resources. In order to search for objects from different repositories, interoperability mechanisms have been developed and engines for federated search in different repositories have been built. The Simple Query Interface (SQI) offers methods to facilitate interoperability between LORs by providing interfaces to the repositories [10]. The interface is supported by different repositories and allows the implementation of a federated search interface [25]. Query interfaces have disadvantages in scalability when a lot of requests for resources are made quite often, which is a typical characteristic of recommender systems. Whereas harvesting approaches support this type of request behaviour much better by offering all existing metadata in one request and providing incremental updates. Harvesters for collecting information from different LORs exist based on the OAI Protocol for Metadata Harvesting (OAI-PMH) [25].

Recommending Objects in Different Components of a TEL Ecosystem

Recommender systems are often implemented as components of a platform of a TEL ecosystem. This holds also for recommendations of learning objects in LORs [4, 7], for the recommendation of learning resources in learning networks or Personal Learning Environments [2, 12, 13] and for the recommendation of learning resources in LMSs [22]. All these approaches do not support the recommendation of objects from different sources in different platforms of the ecosystem. Exceptions are seldom. Sosnovsky et al. [24] for example describe an application that recommends resources from the Web, which is seen as an open corpus of learning materials, during the learning process. In contrast, we propose a framework to recommend activities, users and LOs across multiple platforms of the TEL ecosystem, thus pointing the learners to other valuable sources of information found on these different platforms.

Architectural Approaches for the Realization of Recommender Systems in TEL

Recommender systems are often implemented as closed, internal components of larger TEL platforms, usually having tightly coupled components. An exception is APOSDLE [5], which follows the SOA approach providing web services to publish knowledgeable person recommendations. Web services decouple the generation of recommendations from its presentation to the users. Santos and Boticario [22] decouple the recommendation engine from the LMS and a third component, managing the user model, by using web services as part of an SOA architecture. This architecture allows to integrate recommendations in different LMSs. Our framework uses a similar approach, but is not focused on LMSs and allows, in addition, the use of different recommendation algorithms.

Approach Overview

Figure 2 illustrates the key elements of our approach. On the right side of the figure, there is a simplified form of a TEL ecosystem. It consists only of one LMS, one SNS and one LOR. These platforms are independent of each other. They hold the objects the system will recommend. They produce most of the information that is needed to calculate recommendations (e.g., interaction between users and objects; additional information about objects, etc.). Moreover, they also present recommendations to users. We are focusing on ecosystems that might integrate platforms that already exist (e.g. Moodle). Therefore, we have to customize them. These customizations should neither increase coupling between platforms, nor require intrusive changes that will hinder their maintenance. Moreover, the choice of platforms to be integrated must remain flexible, allowing us to introduce new alternatives as a replacement for any of them or as a complement (i.e., there could be more than one LMS, SNS or LOR).

The *Recommender*, on the left side in Fig. 2 is implemented as a standalone component. It relies on data generated by all platforms in the ecosystem to recommend objects located in any of these platforms. Regardless of this dependency, coupling between the recommender and the other elements of the ecosystem must be kept low. The recommender provides a parametrizable implementation of a graph-based recommender algorithm (1). The algorithm takes as input a graph with nodes representing items in each of the platforms and links representing relationships between them (2). The values given to the nodes and the weights for the edges influence how the algorithm ranks the elements. A service publishes a function that the

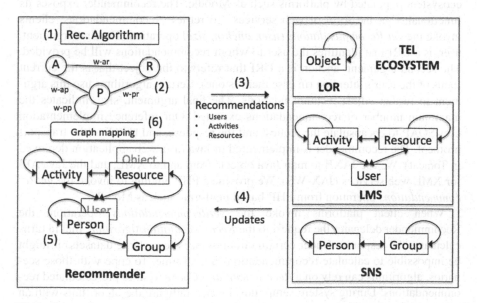

Fig. 2 Approach overview diagram

platforms can call to retrieve recommendations (3). This service encapsulates one of the dependencies between the recommender and the platforms.

Each platform presents recommendation lists to users in line with its own interface design. The response they receive from the recommender contains basic data for each element: a title, a type, and the object's URI in its hosting platform. If a user chooses to accept one of the recommendations, the URI will lead him to its location.

The recommender periodically polls the platforms for all changes that are relevant to compute recommendations (i.e., to build the graph) (4) and stores them in its data model (5). The data model is also the basis for exchanging relevant data between the platforms and the recommender. Each platform publishes a service that the recommender invokes to retrieve changes. These services encapsulate a second dependency between the recommender and the platforms.

Finally, there is a mapping (6) to generate the graph (i.e.,the nodes and edges) from the data model. The mapping allows for the introduction of links that did not exist in the data model (e.g., links connecting semantically related resources or links that connect users belonging to the same group). This mapping additionally represents the extension point to hook other forms of hybrid recommendation algorithms.

The Design of the Recommender

Figure 3 provides a high level view of the design of the recommender system. The top component models the recommender; the bottom component models the TEL ecosystem populated by platforms such as Moodle. The recommender exposes its functionality in the form of web services. To retrieve recommendations, clients invoke the *get Recommendations (user, anchor, size)* operation. The first argument, user, is a URI that identifies the user to whom recommendations will be provided. The second argument, anchor, is a URI that refers to the object that is the current focus of the user's attention (in case there is one). Certain algorithms use this argument to further adjust recommendations. The final argument, size, indicates the maximum number of recommendations expected. Our reference implementation uses SOAP to encapsulate the request and the response, and HTTP as the transport protocol. The recommender is implemented in Java (as a web application deployed in Tomcat). We use JAXB to map Java objects from and to XML, and the Java API for XML web services (JAX-WS). We provide a PHP binding to invoke the *getRecommendations* operation from PHP-based platforms such as Moodle.

When client platforms invoke the *getRecommendations* operation, the Recommender delegates the request to the *RecommendationAlgorithm*, that in turns calculates the response. Under certain circumstances (e.g., large datasets) it might be impossible to calculate recommendations in real time. To cope with those scenarios, algorithms can rely on a *RecommendationCache* to store pre-calculated recommendations. During system setup, developers configure the algorithms with an adequate update strategy.

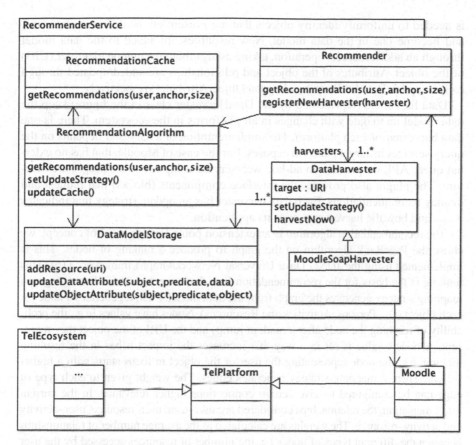

Fig. 3 High-level design

Recommendation algorithms work on the data available on the *DataModelStorage*. The data model serves two key purposes: first, it is used to create the graphs that feed the recommender algorithm. Second, it provides basic information about the objects that each of the platforms displays to the user. This approach has to remain generic enough to accommodate not only the platforms that we choose for our proof of concept (Moodle and Mediawiki) but other alternatives as well. The data model is stored in the form of triples. Each object has a unique id (a URI). Relationships between objects (objectURI, relationship, subjectURI) as well as object attributes (objectURI, attribute, value) are stored as triples. We currently use MongoDB,[11] a non-SQL, highly scalable database to store triples. A specific object attribute relates the object to its type (e.g, a user object to the URI of the Person type). The data model aggregates information that would otherwise be disconnected, e.g, it connects LOs from the LOR to users and activities in the LMS. Therefore the definition of a common unique identifier (e.g, primary email for persons) across all platforms

---

[11] http://www.mongodb.org (last accessed 25/2/2013).

is needed to uniformly identify objects that are present on the different platforms, and become one in the data model. New resources are added to the data model through an addResource() operation, taking as argument the unique identifier (URI) of the object. Attributes of the object and relationships are added/updated through calls to updateDataAttribute() and updateObjectAttribute() respectively.

Data harvesters (represented by the DataHarvester class in the figure) keep the data model up to date with changes in all platforms in the ecosystem. There is one data harvester for each platform. The implementation of a harvester depends on the query services its target platform exposes. For the case of Moodle, that has no external query API, we provide an ad-hoc web service using Moodle's plugin architecture. The plugin also provides the interface components (blocks) that request and display recommendations. Each data harvester has an update strategy that indicates when and how the harvester queries its application.

The recommendation algorithm is an extension point. For our proof of concept, we chose the PageRank algorithm on the graph to produce a ranking of nodes. This is implemented using the JUNG (Java Universal Network/Graph) framework [16]. This ranking is the basis for the recommendation lists that are returned to clients. A graph mapping strategy generates the graph from the data model. First, it generates a node for each object (i.e., Persons, Activities and Resources). Nodes have values (e.g., the probability of reaching the node after a random jump) and the URI of the object they represent. A node's value is set in a way that increases the impact it has in the resulting ranking, e.g. the node representing the user or the object in focus starts with a higher weight. Then, a mapping strategy generates edges. The weight given to each type of edge can be configured to give certain connections higher relevance. In the current implementation, the relationships considered are user–user, user–resource, user–activity and activity–resource. The weights are calculated as the average number of relationships between the different types of nodes i.e. the number of resources accessed by the user divided by the number of resources that have been accessed by any user.

Evaluation

To prove our concept and to obtain basic indicators for the performance of the reference implementation of the proposed architecture, we took existing usage data from a small TEL ecosystem and used it to simulate a realistic scenario. It consists of Moodle as LMS, and a Mediawiki customized as a LOR [26]. We studied how the characteristics of the architecture and the choice of domain model impacted the following: frequency and response time for recommendation requests; storage requirements for the model and resulting recommendations; and effort to harvest updates in the participating systems and consequently re-calculate recommendations.

Moodle and Mediawiki were deployed on virtual servers on the same network. We focused only on a subset of the available data related to an undergraduate course that ran in the second semester of 2012. Each student has one username to access both Moodle and the Mediawiki. The dataset includes information from enrolled users, course sections, forum discussions, resources uploaded to the course, learning objects (pages) available in the Mediawiki, and tags applied both to resources in Moodle and to Mediawiki pages. In total there are 421 students enrolled in the course. The course consists of 8 topics, includes 112 forum discussions, and publishes 31 resources. The Mediawiki contains 40 pages, each representing a learning unit. Thirteen different labels tag Mediawiki pages and resources uploaded to Moodle. The dataset additionally records connections from users to the discussions they read, comment, and create, to resources in the Mediawiki that they read, comment or rate, and to resources in Moodle that they access. It also includes connections from tags to the resources they are attached to, and from Moodle resources to the course sections they belong to. In summary, the dataset contains 625 unique elements, and 11.928 connections. For the current MongoDB implementation of the DataModelStorage, each model element requires a maximum of 1 Kb of storage space whereas each relationship requires 700 bytes. This adds up to a maximum total of 8.6 MB approximately.

To compute recommendations, the system reads the whole model into memory and transforms it into a graph using the JUNG framework. According to the framework's documentation there is no limit to the size of the graphs it can handle (other than that set by the hardware). Once in memory, the PageRank algorithm computes the score for each of the nodes in the graph. An entry in the RecommendationCache (which is also implemented using MongoDB) stores the resulting ranked list of resources. In our scenario, users receive recommendations that are customized to their focus of attention (the focus corresponds to the *anchor* argument of the *getRecommendations* operation). The focus can be the course in the case of Moodle, or the current page in the case of the Wiki. As explained in section "Approach Overview", we achieve such a customization by assigning a higher initial weight to the graph node that represents the desired focus. Therefore, we run the PageRank algorithm once for the course, and once for each wiki page. Following this approach, the number of times the PageRank algorithm needs to run grows linearly in relation to the number of expected anchors. The RecommendationCache stores each of the resulting ranked lists using the anchor as the search key.

In our evaluation, reading the model, building the graph once, running PageRank once for each context (i.e., 41 times), and caching the recommendations took 2 min. On a regular day, there are 1,060 page views in Moodle, with peeks of 100 visits around 8 A.M., 4 P.M. and 11 P.M. One hundred and ninety of the total visits are forum visits, and 450 are resource views. A popular resource receives 125 views in a day (e.g. a recently published assignment). The system displays recommendations for each visit, which means that the aforementioned quantities are an indicator of the number of requests that the recommender service must attend to in a realistic scenario (i.e., 100 requests an hour from one of the client systems). For each request, the system retrieves recommendations from the RecommendationCache using the anchor as the key. As we implemented the RecommendationCache as a wrapper to MongoDB, the system's performance (maximum load and response time) regarding recommendation requests is that of the database. We observed an average response time for recommendation requests of less than 15 ms.

User actions result in model updates (for example, the model records forum participation as a connection between the user node and the forum node). Therefore, we can infer that in peek hours of our scenario, Moodle generates 100 new connections that the system needs to add/update in the data model.[12] There is a DataHarvester for each of the systems that provide data for the model. They have an update strategy that schedules how often the harvester polls the target system for updates. If the harvester polls the target system only sporadically, more update data will be transmitted and persisted each time. The scenarios we currently aim for (having less than 1,000 events in an hour) pose no challenge in this regard for the database or network traffic. On the contrary, polling too often presents an additional load on the target systems, and brings no value if it occurs much more often than recommendation updates (i.e., it makes no sense to poll more than once between PageRank runs).

In summary, from this evaluation of our reference implementation of the proposed architecture we have learnt:

- The response time for recommendation requests is mainly given by the response time of the technology used to cache recommendations. The same is true for the maximum load the service can sustain.
- Storage requirements for the data model, using MongoDB as the supporting technology, has a ceiling that follows the function 1024 bytes * N + 700 bytes + R, where N represents the number of entities that will be used by the recommendation algorithm (i.e., users, recommendable resources, and other non-recommendable resources that could be used to infer relationships), and R represents the number of relationships between entities.
- Storage requirements for cached recommendations, using MongoDB as the supporting technology, follow the function NC * NRPC * 500 bytes. NC represents the number of different contexts (anchors) that will provide recommendations. NRPC represents the number of recommendations per context that we want to cache.
- The frequency for data polling and updates to recommendations are a function of the number of changes the systems generate, and of the time it takes for the recommendation algorithm to complete a single run. The former depends on the amount of activity in the TEL ecosystem, and the latter depends mainly on the number of different contexts/anchors, and to a smaller degree on the size of the dataset, and the complexity of the model.

We will continue evaluations on this reference scenario. The goals of this second evaluation stage are to better characterize the dynamics of the scenario (e.g., regarding usage), and to assess the students' perception regarding cross-platform recommendations.

---

[12] The Mediawiki was just available when the course was about to end (as it was being prepared for the 2013 edition of the course) therefore usage data for the Wiki does not reflect the activity of the scenario and we did not take it into account.

Conclusion and Future Work

In this paper, we propose to take advantage of the synergies that arise across multiple platforms in order to generate recommendations, aiming to further enhance the learning effort of the learners. We present the concept of a TEL ecosystem, and illustrate it with an example comprising Moodle as LMS, Ariadne as LOR, and Mahara as SNS. We discuss a general strategy to provide recommendations in each of the platforms that integrate the ecosystem. Our strategy separates and encapsulates the calculation and provision of recommendations in a standalone system. We present the architecture and high-level design of our reference implementation of the proposed approach. Although we focus on graph-based recommendations, the proposed design abstracts from the recommendation algorithms and the data harvesting strategies. This allows the adoption of other hybrid recommendation approaches, and lowers the effort required to integrate new platforms. To demonstrate the flexibility of such a framework, a proof of concept implementation and evaluation was made with Moodle as LMS, and MediaWiki customized as a LOR in a real student course. Future work will be to further evaluate this scenario.

A further application scenario would be to investigate recommending learning resources from a LOR like ARIADNE in a resource-based learning platform like CROKODIL[13] [2]. CROKODIL supports the collaborative acquisition and management of learning resources found on the Web. It offers a hierarchical activity structure to help learners structure their tasks and learning goals. The learners attach resources found on the Web to these activities. Learners can also collaboratively tag these resources, thereby forming a folksonomy. Many learners only search on the Web for learning resources and do not explicitly know of or bother to access LORs, although these are often freely accessible. It would therefore be beneficial for a learner, especially when working on a specific activity, to have additional relevant learning resources recommended from an external source like a LOR. CROKODIL already has a graph-based recommender system implemented based on the hierarchical activity structures [3]. The recommender system could thus easily be extended using our cross-platform recommender framework to incorporate the external LOs from the LOR. Challenges will be identifying duplicate learning resources and integrating the new learning resources in CROKODIL's folksonomy. The available metadata from the LOs, the tags and activity descriptions in CROKODIL could be leveraged to solve this. The evaluation of such a recommender system will also be a challenge as the recommendations of learning resources from external sources can not be evaluated using historical data [3] but must rather be evaluated by asking the learners. This scenario would provide us with new insights needed to further improve the design of our framework.

---

[13] http://www.demo.crokodil.de (last accessed 25/2/2013).

Acknowledgements This work was partially funded by the Argentinean Ministry of Science and Technology and the German Academic Exchange Service as part of the bi-national cooperation project "Semantic support for collaborative learning and knowledge management".

References

1. Anjorin M, Dackiewicz I, Fernandez A, Rensing C (2012) A framework for cross-platform graph-based recommendations for TEL. In: Manouselis N, Drachsler H, Verbert K, Santos OC (eds) Proceedings of the 2nd workshop on recommender systems in technology enhanced learning 2012. Sun Site Central Europe, pp 83–88. URL http://ceur-ws.org/Vol-896/paper7.pdf
2. Anjorin M, Rensing C, Bischoff K, Bogner C, Lehmann L, Reger AL, Faltin N, Steinacker A, Lüdemann A, García RD (2011) Crokodil - a platform for collaborative resource-based learning. In: Kloos CD, Gillet D, Garcia RMC, Wild F, Wolpers M (eds) Towards ubiquitous learning, Proceedings of the 6th European conference on technology enhanced learning, EC-TEL 2011, LNCS 6964. Springer, Berlin, pp 29–42
3. Anjorin M, Rodenhausen T, García RD, Rensing C (2012) Exploiting semantic information for graph-based recommendations of learning resources. In: Andrew Ravenscroft Stefanie Lindstaedt CK, Hernández-Leo D (eds) 21st century learning for 21st century skills. Proceedings of the 7th European conference on technology enhanced learning, EC-TEL 2012, vol 7563. Springer, Berlin/Heidelberg, pp 9–22
4. Avancini H, Straccia U (2005) User recommendation for collaborative and personalised digital archives. Int J Web Based Communities 1(2):163–175
5. Beham G, Kump B, Ley T, Lindstaedt S (2010) Recommending knowledgeable people in a work integrated learning system, Procedia Comput Sci 1(2):2783–2792
6. Boley H, Chang E (2007) Digital ecosystems: principles and semantics. In: Inaugural IEEE Int. conf. on digital ecosystems and technologies. Cairns, Australia
7. Bozo J, Alarcón R, Iribarra S (2010) Recommending learning objects according to a teachers contex model. Sustaining TEL: From innovation to learning and practice, pp 470–475
8. Brin S, Page L (1998) The anatomy of a large-scale hypertextual Web search engine. Comput Networks ISDN Syst 30:107–117
9. Buder J, Schwind C (2012) Learning with personalized recommender systems: A psychological view. Comput Hum Behav 207–216
10. CEN Members National Standard Bodies: A Simple Query Interface Specification for Learning Repositories (2005) URL ftp://ftp.cenorm.be/PUBLIC/CWAs/e-Europe/WS-LT/cwa15454-00-2005-Nov.pdf. European Committee for Standardization
11. Desrosier C, Karypis G (2011) A comprehensive survey of neighborhood-based recommendation methods. In: Ricci F, Rokach L, Shapira B, Kantor P (eds) Recommender systems handbook. Springer, New York, pp 107–144
12. Drachsler H, Hummel H, Koper R (2007) Recommendations for learners are different: Applying memory-based recommender system techniques to lifelong learning. In: 1st Workshop on social information retrieval for TEL and exchange
13. Drachsler H, Pecceu D, Arts T, Hutten E, Rutledge L, van Rosmalen P, Hummel HGK, Koper R (2009) ReMashed - recommendations for mash-up personal learning environments. In: Cress U, Dimitrova V, Specht M (eds) EC-TEL, LNCS, vol 5794. Springer, New York, pp 788–793
14. Ellison N, Steinfield C, Lampe C (2007) The benefits of Facebook friends: Social capital and college students use of online social network sites. J Comput Mediat Commun 12(4):1143–1168
15. Hew KF (2011) Students' and teachers' use of Facebook. Comput Hum Behav 27(2): 662–676
16. Madadhain J, Fisher D, Smyth P, White S, Boey Y (2005) Analysis and visualization of network data using jung. J Stat Software 10:1–35

17. Manouselis N, Drachsler H, Vuorikari R, Hummel H, Koper R (2011) Recommender systems in technology enhanced learning. In: Ricci F, Rokach L, Shapira B, Kantor P (eds) Recommender systems handbook. Springer, New York, pp 387–415
18. Polsani P (2006) Use and Abuse of Reusable Learning Objects. Journal Of Digital Information, 3(4). Retrieved from http://journals.tdl.org/jodi/index.php/jodi/article/view/89/88
19. Zaldivar VAR, García RMC, Burgos D Kloos CD, Pardo A (2011) Automatic Discovery of Complementary Learning Resources., in Carlos Delgado Kloos; Denis Gillet; Raquel M. Crespo García; Fridolin Wild & Martin Wolpers, ed., 'EC-TEL', Springer, pp 327–340
20. S3 Working Group (2002). Making sense of learning specifications & standards: A decision maker's guide to their adoption. Industry report, e-Learning Consortium of The MASIE Center, Saratoga Springs NY. URL http://www.staffs.ac.uk/COSE/cosenew/s3_guide.pdf
21. Salomon G, Perkins D (1998) Individual and social aspects of learning. Rev Res Educ 23:1–24
22. Santos OC, Boticario JG (2011) Requirements for semantic educational recommender systems in formal e-learning scenarios. Algorithms 4(2):131–154
23. Schmidt S, Scholl P, Rensing C, Steinmetz R (2011) Cross-lingual recommendations in a resource-based learning scenario. In: Towards ubiquitous learning, Proceedings of the 6th European conference on TEL, EC-TEL 2011, LNCS 6964. Springer, Heidelberg, pp 356–369
24. Sosnovsky S, Hsiao IH, Brusilovsky P (2012) Adaptation "in the Wild": ontology-based personalization of open-corpus learning material. In: 21st Century learning for 21st Century skills, pp 425–431
25. Ternier S, Verbert K, Parra G, Vandeputte B, Klerkx J, Duval E, Ordoez V, Ochoa X (2009) The ariadne infrastructure for managing and storing metadata. IEEE Internet Comput 13(4):18–25
26. Vidal JI, Fernandez A, Diaz A (2012) Thinking semantic wikis as learning object repositories. In: Dietze S, D'Aquin M, Gašević D (eds) Proceedings of the 2nd international workshop on learning and education with the web of data, held at the World Wide Web Conference (WWW 2012), CEUR Workshop Proceedings, vol 840, 2012. CEUR-WS.org
27. Wenger E, Communities of Practice: Learning, Meaning, and Identity. Cambridge University Press, 2000

COCOON CORE: CO-author REcommendations Based on Betweenness Centrality and Interest Similarity

Rory L.L. Sie, Bart Jan van Engelen, Marlies Bitter-Rijpkema, and Peter B. Sloep

Abstract When researchers are to write a new article, they often seek co-authors who are knowledgeable on the article's subject. However, they also strive for acceptance of their article. Based on this otherwise intuitive process, the current article presents the COCOON CORE tool that recommends candidate co-authors based on like-mindedness and power. Like-mindedness ensures that co-authors share a common ground, which is necessary for seamless cooperation. Powerful co-authors foster adoption of an article's research idea by the community. Two experiments were conducted, one focusing on the perceived quality of the recommendations that COCOON CORE generates and one focusing on the usability of COCOON CORE. Results indicate that participants perceive the recommendations moderately positively. Particularly, they value the recommendations that focus fully on finding influential peers and the recommendation in which they themselves can adjust the balance between finding influential peers and like-minded peers. Also, the usability of COCOON CORE is perceived to be moderately good.

Keywords Social network analysis • Science 2.0 • Co-authorship • Research network • Informetrics • Recommender systems • Scientometrics

R.L.L. Sie (✉)
D.L.Hudigstraat 64, 1019 TR Amsterdam, The Netherlands
e-mail: rory.sie@gmail.com

M. Bitter-Rijpkema • P.B. Sloep
Open Universiteit Nederland, Valkenburgerweg 177, 6419 AT Heerlen, Netherlands

B.J. van Engelen
Dandelion Group BV, Hoogstraat 53b, 3011 PG Rotterdam, Netherlands

N. Manouselis et al. (eds.), *Recommender Systems for Technology Enhanced Learning:*
Research Trends and Applications, DOI 10.1007/978-1-4939-0530-0_13,
© Springer Science+Business Media New York 2014

Introduction

One of the main aims of a researcher, besides developing knowledge and understanding, is to strive for success and a solid reputation. Approaches to measure scientific successfulness such as the h-index [1] and the g-index [2] exist, but it is still difficult for scholars [3], journals [4] and agencies [5] to determine reputation and research success. Also, scholars are often unaware of the skills that they typically should attain to become successful. Indeed, being successful does not merely depend on performing high quality research, but also depends on the ability to reach out and convince others of the quality of a research idea. Researchers need to know what the main drivers for success are and they need to be made aware of these.

Lambiotte and Panzarasa [6] draw attention to the fact that cohesive relationships in a topic-driven community foster researcher success. Articles need to be written, typically with co-authors, and these articles are subject to review. This requires a form of persuasion that involves knowledgeability and reputation. Leydesdorff and Wagner [7] argue that power lies within a core group of network members. Also, they suggest that members in the periphery of the network can profit from more central members, consistent with Kotter's guiding coalition to lead organisational change [8]. Abbasi, Altmann and Hossain [9] find that degree centrality, efficiency, tie strength and eigenvector centrality are indicators for a high g-index.

Current approaches to measure scientific success, such as the Hirsch spectrum tool [10], take the distribution of the h-index of the journal's authors to measure the quality of a journal. Kim, Yoon and Crowcroft [11] use network analysis to identify respected journals and proceedings. Particularly, they use node centrality and temporal analysis to provide insight into the emergence of scientific communities. SCImago [12] provides an overview of a journal's impact, such as the h-index, number of citations, cited versus non-cited documents, etc. The widely known Publish or Perish tool uses Google Scholar to measure an author's h-index or g-index [13]. Yet, none of these tools aims at strategically bringing researchers into contact with co-authors to improve scientific success, as suggested by Lambiotte and Panzarasa [6] and Leydesdorff and Wagner [7].

The COCOON CORE tool aims to inform researchers about their personal quality and the strategically relevant researchers whom they should connect to. Its main functionality, presented in the current article, is the recommendation of candidate co-authors, which is based on two main principles: (1) co-author reputation (and power), which in turn is based on a central network position, and (2) interest similarity between a candidate co-author and the target user (common ground and shared intention), reflected by an overlap between keywords that two authors use to describe personal documents. It searches the open repository DSpace (http://dspace.ou.nl) to aggregate and analyse the social network of individuals who co-authored documents. It has been built after the COCOON tool that generates co-author recommendations [14]. COCOON CORE caters to effective cooperation by finding candidate co-authors with a common ground and a shared intention. It does so by identifying peers in the network who have similar interests. Also, it caters to successful cooperation, by matching the target user with powerful, influential peers; peers who have authority, and are able to (indirectly) persuade others (e.g. reviewers).

The current article investigates what the opinion of the COCOON CORE user is toward the generated recommendations. As the recommendation calculation can be adjusted by the user by moving sliders, thus allowing one to focus on either influential peers or like-minded peers, it does not suffice to merely ask opinions about a recommendation that users can adjust themselves. To see how they value the two mechanisms, we also ask the users to focus fully on either mechanism. Hence, our research questions are as follows:

Research question 1: How do users value COCOON CORE's recommendation when the algorithm fully focuses on influential peers?

   Research question 2: How do users value COCOON CORE's recommendation when the algorithm fully focuses on like-minded peers?

   Research question 3: How do users value COCOON CORE's recommendation when they can adjust it to their personal preference?

Asking the user about the value of a recommendation can be influenced by the usability of the tool. To account for this, we conduct a standardised and widely established usability test called *SUS* [15]. The research question that follows from the usability test is as follows:

Research question 4: How do users experience the usability of COCOON CORE?

We start off the article with a discussion the workflow of COCOON CORE, what data it uses and what calculations it performs ("COCOON CORE"). We provide the method used to investigate the research questions ("Methodology") and the results and discussion ("Results and Discussion"). We draw this paper to a close by providing our conclusion and a brief outlook on future improvements ("Conclusion").

COCOON CORE

Co-authorship Network Data

The data that we use to compute comes from a university's local publication database. The database, called DSpace (http://www.dspace.org), supports the open archives initiative, and its protocol, the OAI-PMH makes it possible for software to automatically extract metadata from the publications in the database. Documents are submitted to this database by (former) employees of the university. Table 1 provides an overview of the employees, departments, and publications that submitted to the database.

The data that we use to compute the centrality of co-authors is extracted from this database. For each document in the database, we extract its authors. These authors inherently form a co-authorship relationship. The aggregation of all authors

Table 1 Overview of the database (snapshot as of April 2012)

Publications	2,924
Book chapters, articles and conference papers	1,113
Presentations	904
Other	907
Authors	1,361
Keywords	3,680
Departments	9

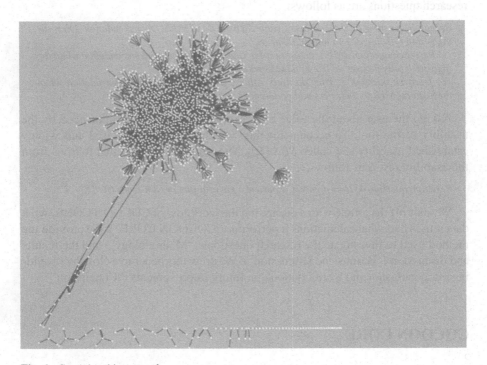

Fig. 1 Co-authorship network

of all publications forms a network in which the co-authors are represented by the nodes, and their co-author relationships are represented by the edges between the nodes (Fig. 1). As only (former) employees of the university submit documents to this database, the method of data collection is quite similar to that of an *ego-centric network*: a network as perceived from individuals' perspectives. Also, each document makes a *clique*; all authors of one document are interconnected through a bidirectional relationship. It is important to note that only (former) employees submit their articles to this database. Therefore, the population available for testing is relatively small, namely 89. We will elaborate on this in the "methodology" section.

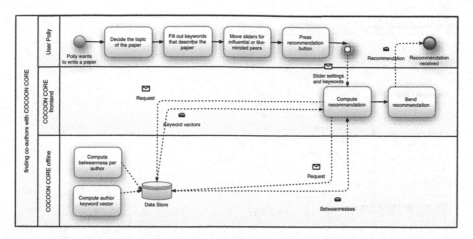

Fig. 2 Workflow for a COCOON CORE recommendation

Calculations

The principal aim of COCOON CORE is to recommend candidate co-authors. Its algorithm employs two types of calculations to arrive at the recommendation. First, for every author in the social network, it computes the power, or reputation of an author; to what extent other authors are dependent on the target author in terms of disseminating ideas within the network. It does so by taking the number of times a target author is on the shortest path between any two other authors in the network relative to the total number of shortest paths, also known as *betweenness centrality* [16, 17].

Second, the algorithm computes similarity between authors. High similarity, in gender for instance, is found to be an indicator for good relationships [18], and this is supported by research on homophily and friendships [19, 20]. Stahl [21] argues that cooperation between any two authors be guided by a common ground. To measure similarity, we first have to identify individuals within the network. For each author, we look at her submissions and the keywords that she has used in these submissions, and construct a keyword vector. The distance between authors' keyword vectors defines the similarity between authors (*vector similarity*).

Recommendation Workflow

The workflow of COCOON CORE is depicted in Fig. 2. The workflow commences with user Polly, who wants to write a new paper. A new paper requires a topic, so Polly starts defining the paper's topic or main research idea.

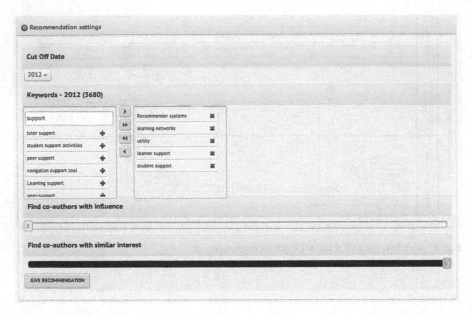

Fig. 3 Keyword input and example slider setting that focuses on finding authors with similar interest

Next, Polly fills out the keywords that describe her paper's topic (Fig. 3) and decides whether COCOON CORE should favour like-minded peers or influential peers. For instance, if Polly is exploring a topic in which she has relatively low authority, she may decide to focus on finding influential, powerful peers. She does so by moving the sliders to her preference. Figure 3 shows slider settings that favour like-minded peers (bottom slider), which reflects the situation that Polly already has some authority in the research field. Finally, she presses the button 'GIVE RECOMMENDATION' and COCOON CORE starts computing a recommendation. Thus, the main user interactions with COCOON CORE comprise (1) filling out keywords, (2) moving sliders to preference, and (3) pressing the 'give recommendation' button.

As indicated, Polly put in keywords that describe the topic of the new paper. These keywords, together with keywords that already exist in her personal keyword vector, are used to compute and find authors that are like-minded. Also, the slider settings define how much focus should be put on the similarity between authors by the recommendation engine. In detail, this is achieved by sending a request to the COCOON CORE backend, which already computed the keyword vector. The backend replies by sending the author keyword vectors, and now the similarity between authors can be computed.

Next, a request for influential peers is sent to the backend data store. The backend data store replies by sending back the betweenness centrality of each author. The slider setting now define to what extent the betweenness (influential peers) and keyword similarity (like-minded peers) should be taken into account to compute the final

Recommended Autors - 2012

Show 10 entries Search:

Score	Author	Betweenness 2012	Normalized Betweenness 2012	keyword similarity 2012
89.8622494477	Peter Dolog (dspace)	24429	0.817780111755	0.952517416291
89.3679355411	Paul A. Kirschner (dspace)	93773	0.926653085784	0.871696868496
89.2675333072	Wim Westera (dspace)	15245	0.779615301282	0.968048687599
88.9495411085	George Sielis (dspace)	11098	0.753917908376	0.979880412892
87.6052139781	Dirk Börner (dspace)	6852	0.714886637642	0.983495807873
87.5434463186	Renate De Groot (dspace)	53329	0.880970778275	0.87174358646
86.1654937193	Bert Hoogveld (dspace)	34806	0.846434420705	0.871801948186
86.1614753084	Davinia Hernández-Leo (dspace)	34813	0.84645069731	0.8717241236
85.7448849309	Wolfgang Greller (dspace)	17874	0.792492507114	0.900753077438
85.4038929965	Argyris Kouloumbis (dspace)	3712	0.665272822431	0.979883001654

Fig. 4 COCOON CORE recommendation result. The *first column* shows the final score, the *second* shows the recommended authors and their dspace link. The *third, fourth* and *fifth column* show intermediate computation results

score per peer. For instance, if the slider for influential peers is set to 20, then the normalised betweenness score (between 0 and 1) will be multiplied by 0.20, whereas the normalised keyword similarity will be multiplied by 0.80. A typical recommendation result is shown in Fig. 4. The authors (Fig. 4, column 2) are sorted by their calculated score (Fig. 4, column 1). Besides, authors can be sorted using their betweenness (Fig. 4, columns 3 and 4) and keyword similarity (Fig. 4, column 5).

Methodology

Participants

Participants in this experiment were 24 employees from the investigated university that hosts the DSpace repository in question ($N=24$, *total population* $=89$). All participants were selected based on their use of DSpace; they were active as a researcher at the target university and had uploaded at least one document. Therefore, the total population size is relatively small, namely 89. The group consisted of 13 male and 10 female participants with a tenure ranging from 1 to 35 years ($M=9.48$; $SD=7.84$). Their occupation ranged from Ph.D. researcher to full professor. Participation was voluntary and beside homemade pastry, no inducement was offered.

Materials

'Find Your Co-author' Task

The participants had to perform three tasks for which they had to evaluate the recommendation corresponding to the research question in point (cf. "COCOON CORE"). First, they were asked to set the slider for influence to 100 %. The slider for interest similarity was automatically set to zero percent. Second, they were asked to set the slider for interest similarity to 100 %. The slider for influence was automatically set to zero per cent. Finally, they were asked to adjust both sliders to their individual liking.

Task Instruction

Before the start of the task, participants were provided with a detailed briefing document that showed the basic functionality of the tool. The briefing showed how to login, how the dashboard functioned, and how they should put in keywords in order to generate a recommendation. One of the researchers was present either in person or online to support remote participants, but no serious issues arose. The task instruction lasted 10 min in total.

Recommendation Questionnaire

Participants were asked to answer three questions on a five-point Likert scale (1 = very bad, 5 = very good), corresponding to the three tasks for their individual recommendation and for the default user recommendation, respectively (Appendix A). These questions correspond to research questions 1–3.

System Usability Scale (SUS)

Next to testing the quality of the recommendations generated by COCOON CORE, we wanted to receive feedback on its user-friendliness (research question 4). The standardised and widely used System Usability Scale (SUS) was used to evaluate the usability of COCOON CORE. SUS conforms to the ergonomics of human-computer interaction DIN EN ISO 9241, part 11. Overall, it measures the perceived usability of the tool at hand and sub-scales include usability (questions 1–3 and 5–9) and learnability (questions 4 and 10). SUS is an industry standard with over 5,000 users and 500 reported studies. In detail, it contains ten questions that can be answered using a five-point Likert scale (1 = strongly disagree, 5 = strongly agree) (Appendix B). The final SUS score ranges from 0 (bad usability) to 100 (good usability) points. On average, systems evaluated using the SUS usability test score 68 points.

Table 2 Task sequence for two participant groups

Group 1: *DS* condition (*N*=12)	Default user recommendation *D*	Individual recommendation *S*
Group 2: *SD* condition (*N*=11)	Individual recommendation *S*	Default user recommendation *D*

Design and Procedure

Each participant has a different profile in the DSpace repository, which is dependent on the frequency of uploads and the keywords that they use to describe the document. For reasons of comparability, the experiment therefore included an evaluation of a recommendation for a default user's profile in DSpace besides the evaluation for the participants' individual profile. The default user profile consisted of one the author's profiles, whose articles were present in the database as well.

A between-subjects design was used, in which participants had to perform the three tasks for a default user (*D*), and for themselves (*S*). The main reason for this was to overcome a sequence bias in evaluation of COCOON CORE. Group 1 started with task *D*, and subsequently performed task *S*. Group 2 started with task *S*, and subsequently performed task *D* (Table 2). The participants were randomly assigned to Group 1: *DS* (*N*=12) or Group 2: *SD* (*N*=11).

Data Analyses

Difference between groups were tested for statistical significance using an independent samples *t*-test for each of the questions regarding the individual and default user recommendation (six in total). No significant difference between these groups would mean that there is no effect in the sequence in which these tasks are performed.

Note that the rating is reversed for each subsequent question in the SUS questionnaire; the odd-numbered questions' scores are calculated by the scale position minus one (e.g. 5 is a good rating, and results in a score of 4), and the even-numbered questions' scores are calculated by 5 minus the scale position the participant gave (e.g. 1 is a good score, and results in a score of 4). Next, the scores are multiplied by 25 to arrive at a scale between zero and 100.

Results and Discussion

Recommendation Questionnaire

Table 3 shows the significance tests for each of the six questions regarding the recommendations. It shows that the two groups do not significantly differ from one another for all except questions 1b and 2a. This means that there is no sequence

Table 3 Results of Levene's
independent samples *t*-test.

Question	t	DF	Sig.
1a	.000	22	.737
1b	-,924	22	.371
1c	-1.999	22	.653
2a	3.924	22	.177
2b	-.705	22	.707
2c	.240	22	.736
N=24			

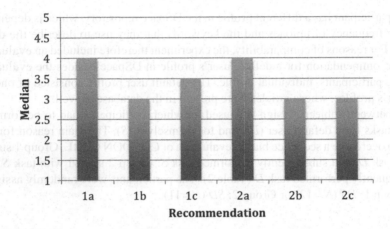

Fig. 5 Median for each recommendation question

effect between the two groups for questions 1a, 1c, 2b, and 2c. Furthermore, the text
For example, Levene's test shows that with respect to question 1a, the two groups
do not significantly differ ($t(22) = .737, p > 0.05$).

The medians for each recommendation question (Fig. 5) show that participants
are moderately positive toward the recommendations generated.

With respect to the individual recommendations, we can conclude that participants score the recommendation in which the influence slider is set to 100 (research
question 1, recommendation 1a) scores moderately positive. The individual recommendation in which the interest similarity slider is set to 100 (research question 2,
recommendation 1b) scores neutral. The individual recommendation in which participants can adjust the sliders themselves (research question 3, recommendation
1c) scores moderately positive. This implies that participants particularly value the
recommendations that either fully focus on finding influential peers, or the recommendation that they can adjust to their personal preference.

When compared with the default user's recommendations (recommendations 2a,
2b, and 2c), the ratings of the individual recommendations score slightly higher.
For example, the individual recommendation in which the influence slider is set to
100 (question 1a) scores equally high compared to the same recommendation for

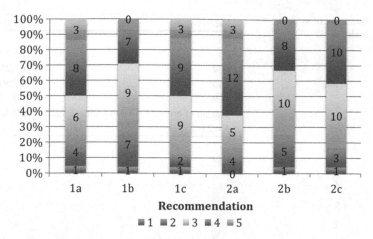

Fig. 6 Proportion of responses for each recommendation question

the default user (question 2a). Also, the individual recommendation in which similarity is set to 100 (question 1b) scores equally high compared to the same recommendation for the default user (question 2b). However, individual recommendation in which the sliders are set to personal preference (question 1c) scores slightly higher than the same recommendation for the default user (question 2c). This discrepancy may be due to the users' lack of familiarity with the default user's work. For example, we quote one participant: "*harder to judge, as this is not really my topic, than when searching with my keywords. But looks good.*"

A closer look at the proportion of responses (Fig. 6) reveals that participants are especially positive toward the recommendation that focuses entirely on influential peers (1a and 2a) and the recommendation in which participants could set the sliders to their personal preference (1c).

Thus, a recommendation that is based on successfulness and effective cooperation satisfies the users to a moderately positive extent. Regarded from a more algorithmic level, a combination of betweenness centrality to identify powerful, influential peers in the network, and vector similarity to identify like-minded peers satisfies the participants, and shows to have potential.

Our recommendation results are partly in contrast with research by Abbasi, Altmann and Hossain [8], who found no significant effect of betweenness centrality on the g-index. This disparity can be explained as follows. COCOON CORE focuses on successful and effective cooperation, rather than increasing the g-index. In other words, COCOON CORE aims at finding influential co-authors for papers, but also agreeable cooperation between co-authors. Numerous papers are rejected, and the reason for this is not always clear. Naturally, a paper should be rejected on the basis of lack of quality, and this could have been due to a lack of common ground among authors. The g-index is based on accepted papers that are highly cited, and does not reflect the actual successfulness of cooperation between authors. Furthermore, the

Table 4 Summary of system usability scale (SUS)

Measure	Value
Min	25
M	65.27
GM	65.25
Mdn	67.50
Max	90
Margin of error (90 % confidence level)	50.40–84.60
N=23	

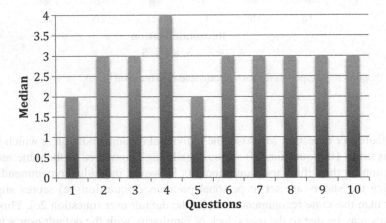

Fig. 7 Median score for each question of the system usability scale (SUS)

nature of Abbasi *et al.*'s g-index is different from the current study, which measures user satisfaction and usability.

System Usability Scale (SUS)

The SUS usability test brings forward that COCOON CORE scores fairly positively on a normalized scale of 0–100 (*Mdn*=67.50, Table 4). At a confidence interval of 90 % and a sample size of 23 (and total population of 89), this means that the average usability value is likely to fluctuate between 50.40 and 84.60.

Figure 7 shows that participants are especially positive about the learnability of COCOON CORE (questions 4 and 10, Figs. 7 and 8), for instance not needing a technical person to use COCOON CORE (question 4). Also, when looking at the proportions of responses (Fig. 8), participants think that there are few inconsistencies in COCOON CORE (question 6) and that COCOON CORE is not unnecessarily complex (question 2).

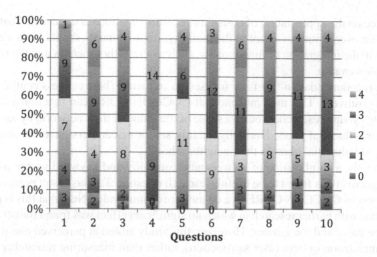

Fig. 8 Proportion of responses for each question of the system usability scale (SUS)

A closer look at Fig. 8 reveals that the most notable shortcoming lies in the integration of several functions (question 5). The proportion of responses for question 5 show that fourteen out of 24 participants (58 %) rated the integration of functions neutral to negative. This was expected, as functions such as author metrics and recommendations were distributed among several pages. Nevertheless, a future version of COCOON CORE should focus more on the integration, or at least the visual integration of functionality.

Conclusion

The tool presented here (COCOON CORE) recommends co-authors based on power and influence of peer co-authors (betweenness centrality), and a common ground between prospective co-authors (keyword vector similarity). It strives to simulate the intuitive process of a senior researcher to find new co-authors that are influential and knowledgeable, respectively. The nature of research questions was twofold. Firstly, we measured the perceived quality of recommendations, both from participants' individual perspective and default user's perspective. Secondly, we measured the usability of COCOON CORE by means of the standardised and widely used System Usability Scale (SUS), arguing that a low usability would influence the quality score negatively.

Participants perceive the usability of COCOON CORE as moderately positive. Especially the learnability of COCOON CORE (no technical assistance required) scores high and users do not face too much inconsistency. Therefore, no negative influence on the appreciation of co-author recommendations is expected. That said, next to an overall improvement of the usability, improvements should be made with respect to the integration of functionality, such as the author metrics and the recommendation engine.

The recommendation that fully focuses on influence (betweenness centrality) is valued positively. This may indicate that COCOON CORE can function as a tool that helps young researchers build a sense of the value of their network, by identifying their influential peers. Normally, mainly senior researchers have this intuitive feeling of influential peers in their neighbourhood.

Crucially, a combination of betweenness centrality and keyword vector similarity, respectively, is found to be useful (research question 3). This result points to the usefulness of COCOON CORE as a co-author recommender. Note that this is partly out of line with earlier research in which no significant effect was found for betweenness centrality and the g-index. However, this study aimed at perceived quality of a recommendation system (user satisfaction), rather than measuring researcher quality based on longitudinal data, thus explaining the discrepancy.

Future work should focus on longitudinal analysis of the successfulness of these recommendations. That is, it should investigate whether recommended co-authorships lead to higher researcher performance. To make such analyses possible, the authors plan to implement additional functionality that allows COCOON CORE users to directly or indirectly (through gatekeepers or the 'system as a mediator') approach a candidate co-author.

Acknowledgments The authors thank Dr. Lora Aroyo from the VU University Amsterdam for her insightful comments during the design and implementation phases of COCOON CORE.

Appendix A: Questions Regarding Quality of Recommendations

1a. Individual Recommendation: How do you value the recommendation that is generated if the slider for influence is set to 100?
1b. Individual Recommendation: How do you value the recommendation that is generated if the slider for interest similarity is set to 100?
1c. Individual Recommendation: How do you value the recommendation that is generated if you control the sliders yourself?
2a. Default User Recommendation: How do you value the recommendation that is generated if the slider for influence is set to 100?
2b. Default User Recommendation: How do you value the recommendation that is generated if the slider for interest similarity is set to 100?
2c. Default User Recommendation: How do you value the recommendation that is generated if you control the sliders yourself?

Appendix B: SUS Questionnaire

1. I think that I would like to use this system frequently.
2. I found the system unnecessarily complex.
3. I thought the system was easy to use.
4. I think that I would need the support of a technical person to be able to use this system.
5. I found the various functions in this system were well integrated.
6. I thought there was too much inconsistency in this system.
7. I would imagine that most people would learn to use this system very quickly.
8. I found the system very cumbersome to use.
9. I felt very confident using the system.
10. I needed to learn a lot of things before I could get going with this system.

References

1. Hirsch JE (2005) An index to quantify an individual's scientific research output. Proc Natl Acad Sci U S A 102(46):16569–16572. doi:10.1073/pnas.0507655102
2. Egghe L (2006) Theory and practise of the g-index. Scientometrics 1(2006):1–31
3. Linton JD, Tierney R, Walsh ST (2011) Publish or perish: how are research and reputation related? Ser Rev 37(4):244–257. doi:10.1016/j.serrev.2011.09.001
4. Gardner WL, Lowe KB, Moss TW, Mahoney KT, Cogliser CC (2011) Scholarly leadership of the study of leadership: a review of The Leadership Quarterly's second decade, 2000–2009. Leadersh Q 21(6):922–958. doi:10.1016/j.leaqua.2010.10.003
5. Feuer MJ, Towne L, Shavelson RJ (2002) Scientific culture and educational research. Educ Res 31(8):4–14. doi:10.3102/0013189X031008004
6. Lambiotte R, Panzarasa P (2009) Communities, knowledge creation, and information diffusion. J Informetr 3(3):180–190
7. Leydesdorff L, Wagner CS (2008) International collaboration in science and the formation of a core group. J Informetr 2(4):317–325. doi:10.1016/j.joi.2008.07.003
8. Kotter JP (1996) Leading change. Harvard Business, p 208
9. Abbasi A, Altmann J, Hossain L (2011) Identifying the effects of co-authorship networks on the performance of scholars: a correlation and regression analysis of performance measures and social network analysis measures. J Informetr 5(4):594–607. doi:10.1016/j.joi.2011.05.007
10. Franceschini F, Maisano D (2010) The Hirsch spectrum: a novel tool for analyzing scientific journals. J Informetr 4(1):64–73. doi:10.1016/j.joi.2009.08.003
11. Kim H, Yoon JW, Crowcroft J (2012) Network analysis of temporal trends in scholarly research productivity. J Informetr 6(1):97–110. doi:10.1016/j.joi.2011.05.006
12. Falagas ME, Kouranos VD, Arencibia-Jorge R, Karageorgopoulos DE (2008) Comparison of SCImago journal rank indicator with journal impact factor. FASEB J 22(8):2623–2628. doi:10.1096/fj.08-107938
13. Harzing A, van der Wal R (2008) Google Scholar as a new source for citation analysis. Ethics Sci Environ Polit 8:61–73. doi:10.3354/esep00076
14. Sie RLL, Drachsler H, Bitter-Rijpkema M, Sloep PB (2012) To whom and why should i connect? Co-author recommendation based on powerful and similar peers. IJTEL 1(2):121–137
15. Brooke, J. (1996). SUS: a "quick and dirty" usability scale. In P. W. Jordan, B. Thomas, B. A. Weerdmeester, & A. L. McClelland. Usability Evaluation in Industry. London: Taylor and Francis

16. Brandes U (1994) A faster algorithm for betweenness centrality. J Math Sociol 25:163–177
17. Freeman LC (1977) A set of measures of centrality based on betweenness. Sociometry 40(1):35–41
18. Ibarra H (1992) Homophily and differential returns: sex differences in network structure and access in an advertising firm. Science 37(3):422–447
19. Lazarsfeld PF, Merton RK (1954) Friendship as a social process: a substantive and methodological analysis. In: Berger M, Abel T, Page CH (eds) Freedom and control in modern society, Van Nostrand, New York, NY, 18:18–66, http://www.questia.com/PM.qst?a=o&docId=23415760
20. McPherson M, Smith-Lovin L, Cook JM (2001) Birds of a feather: homophily in social networks. Annu Rev Sociol 27(1):415–444. doi:10.1146/annurev.soc.27.1.415
21. Stahl G (2005) Group cognition in computer-assisted collaborative learning. J Comput Assist Learn 21(2):79–90. doi:10.1111/j.1365-2729.2005.00115.x

Scientific Recommendations to Enhance Scholarly Awareness and Foster Collaboration

Jan Petertonkoker, Wolfgang Reinhardt, Junaid Surve, and Pragati Sureka

Abstract Recommender systems have become an essential part of the web user's life. Whether it is recommended books or movies, friends on social networks or mobile phone contracts, service providers have realized that personalized recommendations and ads increase customer retention and satisfaction. Last but not lease, recommender systems can help selling more goods. Scientific recommender systems, on the other hand, have the goal to recommend useful scholarly objects such as publications, conferences or researchers to the interested researcher in order to make them aware of them and to foster collaboration and scientific exchange. In this paper we introduce PUSHPIN, a social network for researchers and its recommender approach. PUSHPIN is based on an eResearch infrastructure that analyzes large corpora of scientific publications and combines the extracted data with the social interactions in an active social network.

Keywords Scientific recommender systems • Research networks • Research 2.0 • Social media • Social networks • Visualization • Semantic similarity • Community mining

Introduction

"There is too much to read" [28].

This quote by Paul Otlet (1868–1944) and his insight is all but new and the outcry reoccurs in waves whenever a new technology is introduced. In fact, *information overload* has been documented for more than 2,300 years and scholars throughout

J. Petertonkoker • W. Reinhardt (✉) • J. Surve • P. Sureka
Department of Computer Science, University of Paderborn,
Fürstenallee 11, 33102 Paderborn, Germany
e-mail: janp@mail.upb.de; wolle@upb.de; jsurve@mail.uni-paderborn.de;
pragatisureka@gmail.com

N. Manouselis et al. (eds.), *Recommender Systems for Technology Enhanced Learning:*   283
Research Trends and Applications, DOI 10.1007/978-1-4939-0530-0_14,
© Springer Science+Business Media New York 2014

the periods criticized new technologies for the abundance of publications that it became impossible to have an overview of [3, 5]. The rise of the Internet, the widespread adoption of the WWW and, lately, the proliferated application of Web 2.0 technologies, tools and techniques on research lead to a tremendously increasing amount of published scientific content. Priem and Hemminger (2010) point out that today too much work is being published, which not only hinders the work of tenure and promotion committees, but also the daily work of any other researcher [30, 33]. Potentially relevant content is scattered in workshop, conference and journal publications, books, in blogs and wikis. The content is being shared, liked and mixed on social media, recommended and commented on in social networks and in focussed online communities of lifelong learners. On the one hand, this leads to the necessity of updated metrics of measuring impact of scientific publications [30, 31] and on the other hand it calls for awareness support and scientific recommendations [33, 36].

Researchers that try to get conspectus of the relevant literature and key authors in a given research subject face the issue of a comprehensive, socially augmented publication landscape, in which pathfinding is a very challenging task. Moreover, when looking for scholars that are interested in similar topics or when searching for help by peers, most researchers are limited to their established professional network because they are not aware of qualified scholars outside their own circles [35]. On top of that, much research is repeated multiple times by different groups because they lack knowledge of the work of others or cannot repeat their studies [20].

As Rayward (1994) points out, Otlet not only suggested to map published documents against the existing scientific domains as this mapping would *"assist exploration by reducing unnecessary voyages over already discovered terrain"* [32]. He also envisioned some semi-automatic document summarization that would give the reader an easy-to-grasp overview of the facts, interpretation of facts, statistics and sources of a document. This way, the reader would easily be able to compare one document to another, see what they have in common and then follow the link to the common object in order to be able to explore it and its connections. Otlet described an scholarly information science system, in which the scholars collaboratively organize existing knowledge into an open encyclopedia by using cards to describe the content of each item. Moreover, he speculated about some kind of international hypertext system that would allow the reader to move from one bibliographic reference to its full text, to images and charts within the document to author indices, similar documents and their authors indices [32]. In twenty-first century terms, Otlet was describing an open *Research 2.0* [20, 40, 41] system in which scholars could work together, following trails between each other and between scientific publications. Collaboratively, they would enrich the existing information and add links to relevant similar documents. The system would bypass large distances and help the scholars to get a better overview of the scientific domains and the knowledge within.

In this paper we introduce PUSHPIN,[1] a Research 2.0 service that is built on the ideas of Paul Otlet [28] and Vannevar Bush [7] and that takes into consideration Clay Shirky's elaborations on information overload versus filter failure [39].

---

[1] PUSHPIN is available as a free service at http://pushpin.cs.upb.de.

PUSHPIN is a social network designed for scholars that aims to enhance their awareness as well as to foster scholarly collaboration [33]. Being a social network, PUSHPIN connects people that are connected by a shared social object [13, 24]. The central social objects in PUSHPIN are (1) users, (2) publications, (3) authors, and (4) institutions. As MacLeod (2007) outlines, *"the Social Object, in a nutshell, is the reason two people are talking to each other, as opposed to talking to somebody else. Human beings are social animals. We like to socialize. But if think about it, there needs to be a reason for it to happen in the first place. That reason, that node in the social network, is what we call the Social Object"* [24]. Users of PUSHPIN can tag, bookmark, rate and share the existing social objects within the service and recommend publications to other users. Through the analysis of publications in the system, research networks of citations, publications and authorships are extracted, visualized and used for recommending similar objects to users.

The remainder of this paper is structured as follows: in section "State-of-the-Art in Scientific Recommender Systems" we will discuss the state-of-the-art in recommender systems and compare several existing scientific recommender solutions. Following, in section "PUSHPIN's General Approach for Enhancing Scholarly Awareness", we will introduce PUSHPIN's general approach for enhancing scholarly awareness and for providing added value to its users. The recommender approach that we implemented in PUSHPIN will be introduced in section "PUSHPIN's Recommender Approach" before we will conclude this paper with a summary and outlook on future enhancements of PUSHPIN in section "Conclusion and Outlook".

State-of-the-Art in Scientific Recommender Systems

Recommender Systems are well-known elements of e-business services[2] and leisure applications[3] and most users of the WWW are familiar with receiving recommendations for which goods to buy or music to listen. For being able to suggest such recommendations to their users, the service providers track and analyze the shopping/browsing behavior of their customers and are able to identify patterns in their behavior or interest. Such, they are able to predict that people who buy product A also often buy product B or that people that buy books from author X or movies with actor Y, tend to also buy books from author Z or to like music of this and that genre.

In this section we introduce general recommender techniques and present a selection of existing scientific recommender solutions. Finally, we compare the features and recommender techniques applied in those solutions.

---

[2] For example, http://amazon.com.

[3] Such as http://netflix.com, http://last.fm or http://spotify.com.

General Recommender Techniques

Recommender systems are commonly classified into three categories: content-based, collaborative and hybrid recommender systems [2, 19, 23, 25, 26, 37]. In the following sections these categories and their corresponding recommender techniques are described.

Content-Based Recommender Systems

In content-based recommender systems, items are recommended based on the items a user has expressed a preference for in the past [25, 26, 37]. On the basis of certain attributes, similar items to the previously preferred ones are computed [23]. Usually, such a recommender system works with user and item profiles. These profiles are represented by vectors, which contain the attributes characterizing the user or item. For example, in a recommender system working with text documents, the item vectors could contain weights that denote how often specific keywords are used in the document. The user profile is calculated using the items he previously rated. Creating a recommendation then means calculating a score between the user profile and various candidate item profiles. Typically, the items with the highest scores gets recommended.

There are a few problems and limitations with content-based recommender systems. The most obvious drawback of content-based recommenders, which results directly from their definition, is that they heavily depend on the type of items in the system. Only for text-based items the attributes (e.g., keywords) can be parsed by the computer automatically; for other kind of items the attributes need to be set manually (e.g., by tagging them). Additionally, two different items are equal for the recommender system if their profile is identical. There is no way to distinguish between these items, although one might be a good article and the other one might be a bad written article about the same topic (so the used terms are identical).

Another problem in content-based recommender systems is overspecialization [27]. Since items are recommended that have a high score with the user's profile, these are similar to the items the user rated before. For example, if a user only rated science-fiction movies in a movie recommender system, he would never get a recommendation for a historical movie (even if it would be one of the best movies ever created). The opposite case is a problem as well: recommendations of a content-based recommender can be too similar. A user does not necessarily want to read several different news article about the same event. One possible solution for this problem would be to implement some randomness in the recommendation calculation [1].

The last problem that is presented here is the so-called *New User Problem*. Users that are new to the system and have not rated a certain amount of items cannot be given good recommendations or any at all, because the system does not have enough data in their profile [2].

Collaborative Recommender Systems

Collaborative recommender systems recommend items that other users with similar tastes have preferred in the past [2, 19, 25, 26, 37]. The recommender technique used is also called *collaborative filtering*. A famous example of these recommender systems can be found on Amazon.com: new items are recommended to a user based on the history of which other items other people have viewed that have viewed the same items as the user before [19].

The problems with collaborative recommender systems are a bit different from the problems of content-based recommender systems. The problem that only similar items are recommended does not exist, because other people's ratings are used to create recommendations and they could have rated a wide range of different items. However, the *New User Problem* still exists. To be able to determine similar users, the system first needs to learn about the users tastes and this can only be achieved if the user has rated a sufficient amount of items.

Similar to the *New User Problem*, another limitation is the *New Item Problem*. New items that are added to the system would not be able to be recommended for some time (until they get rated by a certain amount of users), because the recommendations of a collaborative recommender system are only based on the ratings given by other users. Strongly connected to the *New User/Item Problem* is the *Cold Start Problem*: When a new system is started, a certain amount of users, items and ratings is needed to make any accurate recommendations at all [38].

Another problem is sparsity; on the one hand, the number of actual user ratings in the system is usually very small compared to the number of ratings the system needs to predict. On the other hand, even the most popular items (which are rated frequently by many different users) have a small number of ratings compared to the users in the system. One approach to overcome this problem would be the use of certain user characteristics. Then, similar users could be found according to certain attributes (e.g., age, language) and not solely based on ratings given to items.

The last problem of collaborative recommender systems presented here is scalability. Since, usually, the amount of users, items and ratings of such a recommender system is big, large computational power is needed to calculate recommendations.

Hybrid Recommender Systems

A hybrid recommender system is a combination of content-based and collaborative methods. Basically, there are four different kinds of hybrid recommenders [2, 25, 26, 37]:

1. separate content-based and collaborative recommender systems; results get combined somehow,
2. collaborative recommender system with some added aspects of content-based methods,

3. content-based recommender system with some added aspects of collaborative methods,
4. a single recommender system which unifies content-based and collaborative methods from the beginning.

The big advantage of hybrid recommender systems is that through the combination several limitations and problems of content-based or collaborative recommender systems alone can be reduced or completely avoided.

Existing Scientific Recommender Solutions

Recommender systems are not only used in e-business and leisure solutions but have also found their way into scientific practice. Researchers use scientific recommender systems to explore research domains, to find similar researchers or colleagues to start joint projects. In the last years, a number of scientific recommender solutions have been created that are, just like PUSHPIN, often embedded in a social networking application. In the following sections, we briefly introduce and compare some existing scientific recommender systems, their recommendation approaches and core publication analysis features.

Scienstein

Scienstein[4] was one of the first hybrid recommendation systems tailored to research papers [15]. It was also considered to be a dominant alternative for the existing scholarly search engines. Scienstein provided four different approaches for recommending scientific articles: (1) citation analysis, (2) author and source analysis, (3) text mining and (4) document rating. Although discontinued in the meantime and succeeded by SciPlore[5] and Docear,[6] the recommendation approaches in Scienstein have been novel for the field of scientific recommender systems.

Through Scienstein's citation analysis, research articles could be recommended on the concepts of in-text citation frequency analysis (ICFA) and in-text citation distance analysis (ICDA) [15]. The frequency with which a research paper has been cited in a publications gives a value of ICFA, whereas the distance between references within the document gives a value of ICDA, which is used to measure the degree of similarity between the references.

Scienstein's author and source analysis was a practically unapplied method [15]. In this method, only those articles were considered relevant, which were either from the same authors or sources for instance a journal. In addition, this method also ranked publications based on their impact factor.

---

4 http://www.scienstein.org/.
5 http://sciplore.org/.
6 http://www.docear.org/.

Using Scienstein's text mining method, recommendations are calculated bases on collaborative annotations [15]. Collaborative annotations (also known as group tagging) is a formal technique similar to assigning tags to an item. Currently, Scienstein allowed users to annotate documents in three different categories such as (1) field of research, (2) research method, and (3) research details. The content of these annotations later used to recommend articles with similar annotations.

Using Scienstein's document rating, recommendations were generated by keeping track of the user actions and behaviors with in the system. Such users actions could vary from bookmarking, downloading, following recommendations and many others [15]. The user's actions give an estimate about the user's interest for different types of publications. Later, this estimate is be used to recommend publication to a certain user.

CiteSeer

CiteSeer[7] is an *"autonomous citation indexing system, which understands how to parse citations, identify citations in different format and identity the context of citations in the body of articles."* [8]. Moreover, CiteSeer is a publication and citation database in which given the input document, citation analysis, co-citation analysis and bibliographic coupling are applied to get similar documents [8, 21]. This set of similar documents is later recommended to the users of the system.

Google Scholar

Google Scholar[8] is a scholarly search engine, which enables researchers to search for keywords, authors, and titles of scientific publications. It uses text mining and citation count as an indicator to list searched results against a search query [15].

Recently, Google Scholar started a recommendation service for its users [9]. Google Scholars recommendation system, which is backed by powerful Google search algorithms, helps users to discover new publications and to make new connections. Google Scholar recommendations are driven by the philosophy of "making new connections". It implements a hybrid recommendation system but has a clear focus on a content-based recommendation approach.

The process of recommending research documents starts with authors adding their own publications to their profile. Google Scholar then searches their index of scholarly content for relevant articles and papers that match the given publications. Relevance and recommendations of similar research articles, books and papers are determined using a statistical model that incorporates citations and co-authorships [4, 9]. Google Scholar also keeps track of the user profile data, which may include current interests, affiliations, areas of research, etc. and provides personalized recommendations for new articles and papers to the user.

---

[7] http://citeseerx.ist.psu.edu.

[8] http://scholar.google.com.

Mendeley

Mendeley[9] is a social network that helps organize research, collaborate and discover new research [18]. Mendeley implements a powerful hybrid recommendation system [17]. In Mendeley's content-based approach, recommendations are calculated using scientific articles uploaded in the library. Relevant information from all the articles in the library like title, authors, keywords, citations, etc. are extracted and processed. Various similarity metrics and matching algorithms are used to compute recommended articles. Also, the collaborative filtering approach used in Mendeley is quite powerful, as personalized recommendations are generated for every user. Mendeley uses many types of user-generated data in calculating its recommendations [18]. The data includes user profile data, interests of a similar researcher and other activities of the user on their site. The recommendations are calculated and updated every 24 h.

ResearchGate

ResearchGate[10] is another social networking platform for researcher like Mendeley. In ResearchGate, recommendations of documents is also calculated by using an hybrid recommendation approach. Besides recommendations, ResearchGate also allows users to request the full texts of publications of other users and they calculate a publicly visible RG score, which can be used as an indicator of the authors activity on the platform and the interest in his publications and user profile.

PUSHPIN's General Approach for Enhancing Scholarly Awareness

PUSHPIN is a research project at the University of Paderborn (Germany) that aims to provide awareness support for researchers through the integration of social networking and big data analysis features [33, 34]. PUSHPIN builds upon the success of social networks in the recent years. It is essential for a research idea to reach a wide audience; the social layer in PUSHPIN provides many features that engages users in a rich social environment increasing awareness and enabling collaboration. PUSHPIN implements many popular features of todays social networking: users can maintain their *profile page*, where they can provide information about their research interests, affiliations and disciplines. Users can *tag* other users and publications that may define certain characteristic. A user can form direct connections with other users by *following* this. This enables user to see activities (profile updates, publication uploads, tagging information, etc) of other user on their personal dashboard (see Fig. 1).

---

[9] http://www.mendeley.com/.
[10] https://www.researchgate.net/.

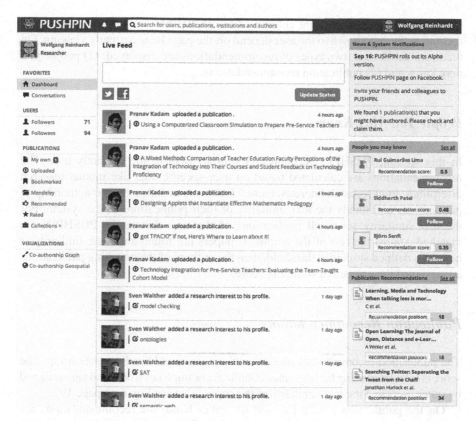

Fig. 1 Dashboard of PUSHPIN for the user 'Wolfgang Reinhardt'

Users of the service can also engage in many other social activities. They can share any information as a *status update* and others are free to comment on it. If users have connected other social media accounts (e.g., their Facebook or Twitter accounts) to their PUSHPIN account, they are enabled to share status updates with all their other social accounts with just one click. Users can exchange private messages and engage in conversations with multiple users. PUSHPIN users can also upload publications from any page just by a simple drag-and-drop feature. Users can also interact with uploaded publications, they can bookmark a publication for easier access, organize publications in collections or recommend publication to other users via PUSHPIN or email.

The structured analysis of uploaded scientific publications provides useful data that—in conjunction with user-generated data stemming from active participation in social interactions—can be used to find yet unknown facts. For example, this data is used to discover new relations between users and publications and thus provides awareness support for the PUSHPIN users.

Using all the data, PUSHPIN provides a powerful recommendation system. The service offers three different kinds of recommendation approaches, which are shown to the user in the right column of his PUSHPIN dashboard (Fig. 1). The recommendations shown to the user depend on the page he is currently viewing. On the users' dashboard, two types of recommendations are displayed: (1) people you may know and (2) publication recommendations.

People You May Know

In this section, PUSHPIN recommends similar users to the currently user. The recommendations are calculated based on user-specific data like mutual research disciplines, joint research interests, mutual followers or followees, co-authorship of publications and finally the text similarity of their publications in the system. For the text similarity score, all publications of the user that are in PUSHPIN are matched against the rest of the corpus. If papers are found and their similarity is beyond a defined similarity threshold, then the authors of the matching publications are assigned the respective similarity score.

Publication Recommendations

The publication recommendations are based on a user-publication relationship. The score is calculated using bibliographic coupling, common keywords and tags assigned by other users and the text similarity of the paper (also see Fig. 6 on page 19).

On the publication profile page on the other hand, the recommendations are based on a publication-publication relationship. The recommendations are calculated using the metadata of publications like co-citations, co-authors, bibliographic coupling, and the full text similarity (also see Fig. 5 on page 18). The calculated recommendations can be manipulated on-the-fly. Users can individually give more weight to the similarity based on metadata or full-texts, the recommendation scores are instantly updated and the recommendations are updated immediately.

For all three approaches, the common denominator is the full-text similarity of the publications. Besides these approaches, PUSHPIN also allows users to recommend a publication to other users of the system. If the user is not part of the system then the recommendation will be mailed to external recipients.

Technologies Used in PUSHPIN

In modern web-based (social) applications, users create huge amounts of data what in conclusion might require massive computational power to analyze the user-generated content. PUSHPIN makes use of a scalable e-research infrastructure that relies on the latest technologies used in big data analysis in order to analyze uploaded scientific papers and calculate recommendations.

In detail, PUSHPIN makes use of well-known and massively scalable frameworks like Apache Hadoop[11] and Twitter Storm[12] for batch-processing, handling large datasets and for real-time analysis [6, 42]. Both frameworks are designed to be fault-tolerant and highly optimized for parallel computation. Storm is a distributed realtime computation system, which is used to analyze uploaded publications in real time. Hadoop is a distributed processing framework for processing large datasets across clusters of computers. In PUSHPIN, Hadoop forms the backbone for calculating similarity between tens of thousands of papers. Moreover, it is used for disambiguating millions of authors extracted from the publications. Mahout[13]—a machine learning and data mining library for big data—is used for collaborative filtering in recommendation calculations and for calculating similarity between texts [29]. The analysis of publications results in huge amounts of data. To store these data sets PUSHPIN makes use of HBase,[14] often referred to as database for Hadoop. HBase is a distributed, scalable and non-relational database for storing "big data" and provides efficient ways to store and query very large sparse datasets [11, 14]. In PUSHPIN, HBase is used as the primary database for storing publication related information.

Metadata Extraction

When a publication is uploaded to PUSHPIN, it is first checked for duplicates at file level using a MD5 checksum. If the uploaded publication is not already in the system, the publication is assigned a UUID and saved in HBase. The assigned UUID is then added to a queue, to be delivered to Storm cluster for processing.

Storm keeps listening to a message queue for any new publications. If it receives UUID of a publication from ActiveMQ,[15] Storm then fetches the corresponding file from HBase. Once the document is inside Storm, ParsCit[16] and GROBID[17] are used to extract metadata and references. Metadata here refers to title, author names, author affiliations, author address, author email, abstract and keywords of the publication [10, 22]. Similar information is also extracted from all the referenced publications such as author names, year of publication, journal, range of pages, or conference. The extracted data from both parsers are combined to get a more refined set of metadata. The condensed metadata is then used to check for potential duplicates at reference level.

---

[11] http://hadoop.apache.org.
[12] http://storm-project.net/.
[13] http://mahout.apache.org.
[14] http://hbase.apache.org.
[15] http://activemq.apache.org.
[16] http://wing.comp.nus.edu.sg/parsCit/.
[17] http://grobid.no-ip.org.

Fig. 2 Author name
deduplication

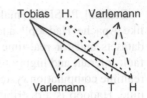

Publication De-Duplication

For finding duplicate publications in the database, first the titles are checked for
similarity. If any two publications have the same or a very similar title (based on
Levenshtein distance, [12]) they are further analyzed for their author similarity.
When checking for similar authors PUSHPIN has to take into account different
ways a name can be written and the probability that the automatically extracted data
is at least partially incorrect. For example, the author *Tobias H. Varlemann* can also
be written as *Varlemann, T H* within a reference string. Hence, just matching first
names with first name and last names with last names produces unsatisfactory
results. In PUSHPIN, all parts of author names are matched with each other as
shown in Fig. 2 and the identity of two authors is determined using a defined similarity threshold. If the calculated similarity values of the publication title and its
authors is above a defined threshold, the two publications are deemed duplicates.
The duplicate publication is not dropped entirely, but any new metadata extracted
from the publication is merged with the existing publication, thus increasing quality
of data in PUSHPIN.

Author Name Disambiguation

As the number of uploaded publication increases, the list of authors extracted from
the papers grows rapidly. Authors are extracted both from the header of uploaded
publications as well as from the extracted references. There is no straightforward
way to determine that two extracted authors are in fact the same person. Extraction
using algorithms and pre-defined models may not be entirely correct, as some of the
extracted information such as author email, affiliation or parts of author name could
be wrong. The process of finding identical authors cannot be accomplished immediately when a publication is uploaded. Every newly extracted author has to be
matched against all the existing authors in the potentially very big database. Thus,
the calculation is done separately as a batch process on PUSHPIN's Hadoop cluster
using a cron job.

To find same authors first the names are matched using same technique as
explained in section "Publication De-Duplication". Additionally, if authors with the
same name are found, then all their co-authors are matched using the same technique. Overlaps in the authors' co-authors are a good indicator that the matched
authors may in fact be same. The next step is to calculate the similarity of the

authors' publications' abstract and full text. If the similarity scores are above a defined threshold, this is an indicator for papers stemming from the same domain or dealing with a similar research topic, hence adding to the probability the two compared authors are in fact the same one.

Text Similarity

One of the parameters used for recommendations in PUSHPIN is text similarity. For calculating the text similarity between all publications in the PUSHPIN corpus, the full texts of any two publications is compared pairwise using the algorithms provided by Mahout. This process consumes very much memory (RAM and HDD) and is CPU intensive. Therefore, the calculation of text similarities in PUSHPIN is done in a batch process using a series of map-reduce jobs in Hadoop.

PUSHPIN's Recommender Approach

The users of PUSHPIN are provided with two type of recommendations: users and publications. For each type, two different kinds of recommendations are computed: General recommendations that are the same for all users and show similar items on each item's profile page and personalized recommendations that are personalized for each user and are shown on the user's dashboard or are delivered in weekly emails.

User Recommendations

User recommendations are computed based on several criterias that are categorized into two categories, the score for each category is calculated and then combined into a single resulting recommendation score in the end: The metadata score which consists of several criterias based on the extracted metadata of the uploaded publications and the social interactions of the users and the similar paper score which is computed based on the textual similarity between the users' publications. Both, the general and the personalized recommendations, use the same underlying model. In the user recommendations, content-based recommender techniques are used.

General Recommendations

Figure 3 shows the general user recommendations on the user profile. For each recommended user a table is shown which contains the metadata score, the similar papers score and the resulting combined recommendation score. The metadata score is further explained with a table of all components that contribute to it.

Fig. 3 General user recommendations on a user profile (detail view)

The metadata score takes into consideration several criterias based on the extracted metadata of the uploaded publications into account: The number of common authored publications, the number of times users' publications were cited together and the number of common referenced publications. Additionally, the contents of the user's profile are incorporated: Common research disciplines, common research interests and affiliations to common institutions. The third part of the metadata score consists of criteria based on the social interactions on PUSHPIN: Common followees, common followers and the number of common tags that were assigned to the user by other users.

The metadata score is then computed as a weighted sum of the common count of the different criterias. In the calculation, a weight of 20 % is assigned to the number of common citations, common referenced publications and common institutions. A weight of 15 % is assigned to common authorship of publications and the remaining 5 % is assigned to all the other criterias.

In the end, the metadata scores are divided by the highest metadata score any other user gets for similar users. As a result of this, the highest metadata score in the user recommendation list is always 1. This is done to be able to combine the metadata score with the similar publications score, because the similar publications score is always given as a percentage value. The metadata score and the included criteria are recomputed every 4 h, because the recalculation currently takes a few seconds. In the future, when there are more users and publications in the database, the period between recalculation might be increased (like in the publication recommendations).

The similar papers score is computed based on the textual similarity between the uploaded publications as described in section "Text Similarity". For each of the user's publication other publications that have a textual similarity > 10 % are searched for in all the publications that are available in PUSHPIN. If a publication is found with a similarity score of more than 10 % with more then one of the user's publications, the textual similarity values are summed up and divided by the number of the user's publications it is similar to. The result is a list of publications that are similar to the user's publications, each with a similarity percentage value. The next step is to search for the users that have authored the publications in this list. Similarly to the previous step, if there is one user found that has authored several of the publications in the list, the similarity values are summed up and divided by the count of authored publications in the list. The end result is a list of users that have written publications that have textual similarity with the publications of a user which we are searching similar users for, each with a similarity percentage value. The textual similarity between the uploaded publications on PUSHPIN is recalculated every night.

The resulting similar papers score will be a value between 0 and 1 which represents a percentage value of similarity calculated as described before. In the end, the metadata score is combined with the similar papers score. Each score accounts for 50 % of the final combined recommendation score the list of similar users are ordered by.

Personalized Recommendations

Figure 4 shows the personalized user recommendations. The underlying model for these kind of recommendations is the same as that of the general user recommendations. The only difference is that the users that the logged in user already follows no longer appear in the recommendation list. Since the same underlying model is used, these recommendations are recomputed at the same time as the general user recommendations.

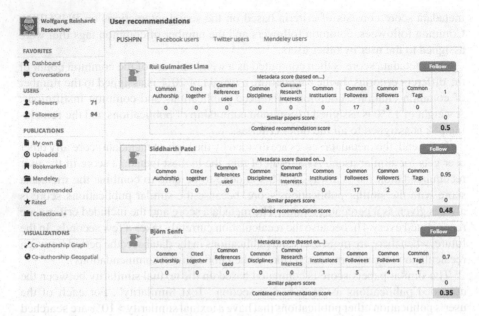

Fig. 4 Personalized user recommendations (detail view)

Handling of Typical Recommender Problems

Since only content-based techniques are used in the user recommendations, the problems presented in section "Content-Based Recommender Systems" occur here. However, the system is designed in a way to handle the problems to various degrees: PUSHPIN uses metadata extractors, which automatically extracts metadata from uploaded publications, so it is not needed to enter the data manually and it can directly be used as some of the criterias to find similar users.

To weaken the effect of the other problems, the system is designed in a way that it takes a wide range of different criterias into consideration: The user's profile, the social interactions, the publication metadata and the textual similarity between publications.

The *New User Problem* is still present, but very little action from the user is usually needed to start receiving personalized recommendations: it is usually enough to claim a few own publications or to start following a few users to receive recommendations. However, to receive more accurate recommendations more actions or authored and claimed publications are needed.

Publication Recommendations

Similar to the user recommendations, similar publications are recommended on every publication profile page and they are personalized publication recommendation based on the publications' similarity with the users publications and the user's actions on PUSHPIN. The general and personalized recommendations share some criteria, but (in contrast to the user recommendations) some different criterias are used as well.

General Recommendations

Figure 5 shows the general publication recommendations on the publication profile. For each publication a table is shown which contains a metadata score, a textual similarity score and resulting combined recommendation score. Like in the user recommendations, the metadata score is further explained with a table containing all of its components. This recommender takes into account purely content-based aspects.

The metadata score takes into consideration several criterias based on the extracted metadata of the uploaded publications such as bibliographic couplings, co-citations, common authors between the publications and common keywords that were extracted from the uploaded publications. Additionally, common research disciplines and common tags that were assigned to the publications by users which result from user actions on PUSHPIN are also taken into account.

The metadata score is then computed as a weighted sum of the count of the different criterias. In the calculation, a weight of 40% is assigned to bibliographic couplings and co-citations. A weight of 5% is assigned to all the other criterias. As in the user recommendations, all metadata scores get divided by the highest metadata score any publication gets with the one similar publication. The result is that the highest possible metadata score in the recommendation table is 1. This is done to be able to combine this score with the textual similarity score.

The textual similarity score is the percentage value that is calculated as described in section "Text Similarity". Initially, the metadata score and the textual similarity score are combined to one single recommendation score with an equal weight of 50%. However, there is a slider widget at the top of each publication profile recommendation page which lets the user decide how each of the two scores should be weighted in the recommendations that are shown to the user. This allows the user to view only recommendations based on textual similarity or only recommendations based on metadata criteria or something in between.

Additionally, at the top of the list of recommended publications there is a visualization which is a bar chart which shows the number of recommended publications subdivided by their combined recommendation score. This visualization changes dynamically to the slider position. The general publication recommendations and the textual similarity values are recomputed in a nightly run.

Personalized Recommendations

Figure 6 shows the personalized publication recommendations that can be reached from the PUSHPIN dashboard. These recommendations are computed differently than the general publication recommendations. Some of the similar criterias are taken into account, but in a different context.

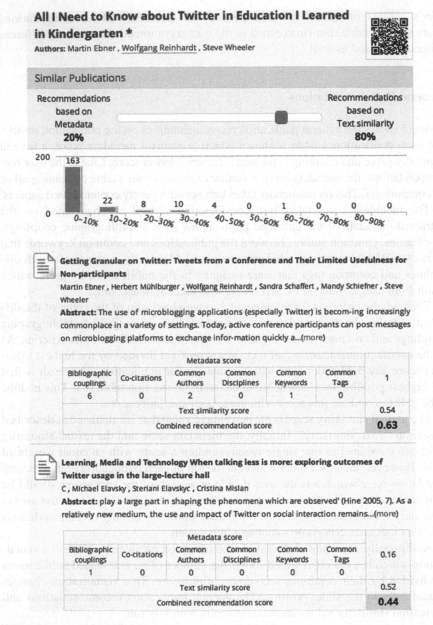

Fig. 5 General publication recommendations on a publication profile (detail view)

Basically, three different recommenders are executed, which produce three different lists of recommendations. In the end these three lists are combined. Two of these recommenders are content-based and take into account the publications that are authored by the user, recommendations are calculated on similar publications which are based on metadata criteria and the other based on textual similarity.

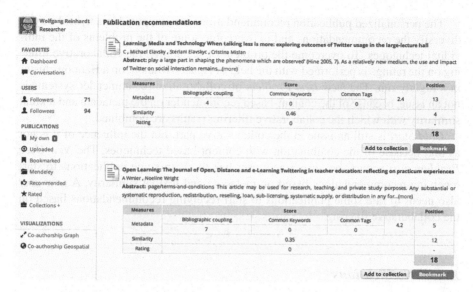

Fig. 6 Personalized publication recommendations (detail view)

The metadata recommender takes bibliographic couplings, common keywords and common tags given to the user's publications into account. The textual similarity of possible recommendations to the user's publications is computed in the same way as it is for the user recommendations in section "General Recommendations". Additionally, a third recommender performs a collaborative filtering on the basis of the ratings that the users have assigned to the publications in PUSHPIN. Here publications with higher ratings are recommended based on users with similar preferences.

The three resulting publication lists are then combined based on the publication's position in the respective lists. For every publication the corresponding positions in the three lists are summed up and the resulting combined list is ordered by on the basis of this sum. If a publication is not included in any of the lists, a value greater then the number of publications in the respective list is added to its position sum.

Recommendations are excluded from the list when a user bookmarks it or adds it to one of his/her collections. Like the general publication recommendations, these personalized recommendations are recalculated every night.

Handling of Typical Recommender Problems

The general publication recommendations are computed solely with content-based techniques. Like for the user recommendations, the system is designed to weaken the effects of the problems by using several different criterias (some of which can be extracted automatically from the uploaded publications and some result from user actions) to compute recommendations.

The personalized publication recommendations are computed in a hybrid way to diversify the recommendations and to overcome some of the problems of the individual techniques. To overcome the problem of scalability, the collaborative filtering on the ratings is performed with the help of Apache Mahout on a Hadoop cluster in a nightly run. The *New Item Problem* of collaborative recommender systems is not an issue, because of the content-based recommender on the metadata and textual similarity with which the collaborative filtering results are combined.

Cold Start is still an issue in the collaborative part, but the influence of it is not as big, because of the combination with content-based techniques. The *New User Problem* also occurs, because a new user has to claim some publications to start receiving recommendations based on metadata and textual similarity. A new user also needs to rate some publications to start receiving recommendations based on the collaborative filtering.

Email Notifications

PUSHPIN makes extensive use of emails in order to keep users motivated and up-to-date. Besides emails, to inform users about new followers, tags and ratings of their papers, PUSHPIN sends weekly newsletters to all users that contain a recap of the last weeks activities in PUSHPIN. Moreover, the newsletter contains personalized user and publication recommendations. The recommendations in the newsletter are the same that can be found on the dashboard but items that have already been recommended via email wont be recommended again.

Conclusion and Outlook

The widespread adoption of the Internet and satellite technologies has enabled us to share and publish large amount of data. And, though we now have websites that do allow us to share, and publish papers and also provide semantic analysis of these papers based on their own algorithms, they still leave us wanting more. The algorithms provide by these services are often not aligned with the user needs [16]. What they miss is a rich social layer that fosters social interaction and collaboration. Also, generally one's knowledge of the publication activities of co-authors or researchers working in the same domain is limited and there are not many resources available to expand this knowledge [33]. Moreover, even with this knowledge there is no platform to socially interact with these authors and researchers. PUSHPIN provides a platform for researchers to combine the powerful features of social networks with the structured analysis of scientific publications. In a nutshell, PUSHPIN recommends similar users and relevant publications based on one's co-authorship, research interests, publications, institutions and other parameters.

Another strong point of focus in PUSHPIN is the *publication*. Normally, during any research, one comes across hundreds of papers, articles, journals or publications that might or might not be relevant to one's research. Firstly, it is highly impossible to get 100 % relevant data in the search results and secondly, it is very difficult to go through every search result in order to judge its relevance. However, PUSHPIN helps users to acquire knowledge by providing the (automatically) extracted data, such as the title and abstract of publications, for the user to read and, if interested, to download the full text. PUSHPIN also recommends publications to users on the basis of bibliographic coupling, co-citation, text similarity of every paper, written by one particular user, with other publications, and other parameters.

Now, we know for a fact that every social networking website is designed with clearly defined social objects in mind. For example, in Twitter one can view and interact with microblogs of the users she follows and can also share information that can be seen by everyone interested in the content.

In PUSHPIN, the social objects are, *researchers* and *publications* and every supported social interaction is around these objects. For example, users can share publications, recommend publications to other users, and also similar to Twitter, follow other researchers.

Currently in PUSHPIN we have 248 active users, who have uploaded 8,911 publications that in total have 105,759 references and 301,474 authors. Also we have 20,108 institutions that our system recognizes. We also have 497 disciplines which can be assigned to user/publication by the user or the publication discipline can also be extracted from Mendeley. In total we have 175 manually assigned disciplines and 22,660 disciplines that have been extracted from Mendeley. Furthermore, 275 distinct tags have been given by the users to other users and/or publications, which has resulted in 389 user tags and 256 publication tags.

Having stated that almost every interaction in PUSHPIN is oriented around the two well-defined social objects—researcher and publication—the most powerful interactive feature that combines these two objects is the *recommendation*. Recommendations are often on the basis of either the data entered by the user, or on the actions performed by a user on the objects, or on the basis of some semantic operations performed on the object. Relying on just any one of the approach has a high probability of producing irrelevant results. So to make it more legitimate, PUSHPIN combines the user data/actions with the semantic operations. PUSHPIN also provides the user an option to choose which of the two should be given a higher priority.

Last but not the least, PUSHPIN also makes use of email as a powerful enabler of social interaction. This feature not only makes users aware of the updates they make themselves but also of the updates made by others. These updates might be in the form of new followers, new messages, upload of a publication that might be your's, your publication being rated by someone, a publication being recommended to you, weekly newsletters etc. These features keep PUSHPIN's users up-to-date with the latest news and happenings in PUSHPIN, while also making them aware of new and current research updates in their area of interest.

Outlook

Within the project's runtime, PUSHPIN has reached a certain level of maturity and has already attracted a number of researchers from all over the world. However, future developments in web technology will always provide room for improvement. The areas that can be enhanced in the future could be an improved recommendation, which takes into account the uncommon data to generate a more specific and quantified similarity score as against the data that is currently considered in PUSHPIN, viz. co-citations, bibliographic coupling etc., which are common between two entities such as publication-publication, user-user and user-publication.

An enhanced user-user recommendation would incorporate collaborative recommenders, e.g. taking the follower-relationship into account and thus recommending users that other users that follow similar people also follow. Another feature that could be added is the ability to reject a recommendation once and never see it again. A recommendation system where in the user could personalize the weights for recommendations would be a useful addition in one of the following versions of PUSHPIN.

Currently, for an uploaded publication, the extracted (and displayed) meta-data cannot be changed by the user. Since one cannot always rely on machines to be correct, an improvement here would be to allow the user to edit this meta-data. The 'Author Name Disambiguation' could be improved by including author affiliation, full-text similarity score, etc. In case of publication-publication matching a more definitive approach would be to consider full-text similarity, keywords, references etc., and in case of reference-publication (vice-versa) and reference-reference would be to use better similarity computing algorithms.

More data implies better and more specific comparative results. For PUSHPIN this fits perfectly. More users would result in more publications, which would result in better and more accurate recommendations.

Acknowledgements The research presented in this article was financially supported by a funding from the University Paderborn's Commission for Research and Young Scientists. We also thank the other members of the PUSHPIN project for their efforts.

References

1. Abbassi Z, Amer-Yahia S, Lakshmanan LV, Vassilvitskii S, Yu C (2009) Getting recommender systems to think outside the box. In: Proceedings of the third ACM conference on recommender systems, RecSys '09. ACM, New York, NY, USA, pp 285–288. DOI 10.1145/1639714.1639769. URL http://doi.acm.org/10.1145/1639714.1639769
2. Adomavicius G, Tuzhilin A (2005) Toward the next generation of recommender systems: a survey of the state-of-the-art and possible extensions. IEEE Trans Knowl Data Eng 17(6):734–749. URL http://ieeexplore.ieee.org/lpdocs/epic03/wrapper.htm?arnumber=1423975
3. Blair A (2010) Information overload, the early years. The Boston Globe. Available online http://www.boston.com/bostonglobe/ideas/articles/2010/11/28/information_overload_the_early_years/

4. Blair A (2011) Google Scholar's New Updates are "Recommended for You". Online College. org. Available online http://www.onlinecollege.org/2012/08/17/google-scholars-new-updates-recommended-you/
5. Blair A (2011) Information Overload's 2,300-Year-Old History. Harvard Business Review. Available online http://blogs.hbr.org/cs/2011/03/information_overloads_2300-yea.html
6. Borthakur D, Gray J, Sarma JS, Muthukkaruppan K, Spiegelberg N, Kuang H, Ranganathan K, Molkov D, Menon A, Rash S, Schmidt R, Aiyer A (2011) Apache hadoop goes realtime at facebook. In: Proceedings of the 2011 ACM SIGMOD international conference on management of data, SIGMOD '11. ACM, New York, NY, USA, pp 1071–1080. DOI 10.1145/1989323.1989438. URL http://doi.acm.org/10.1145/1989323.1989438
7. Bush V (1945) As We May Think. Atlantic Magazine, Available online http://www.theatlantic.com/magazine/archive/1945/07/as-we-may-think/303881/
8. Lee Giles C, Bollacker KD, Lawrence S (1998) CiteSeer: An automatic citation indexing system. In: Witten I, Akscyn R, Shipman F III (eds) Proceedings of the third ACM conference on Digital libraries, ACM Press, New York, pp 89–98
9. Connor J (2012) Scholar updates: making new connections. Google Scholar Blog. Available online http://googlescholar.blogspot.de/2012/08/scholar-updates-making-new-connections.html
10. Councill IG, Giles CL, yen Kan M (2008) Parscit: An open-source crf reference string parsing package. In: International language resources and evaluation. European Language Resources Association
11. Dimiduk N, Khurana A (2012) HBase in action. Manning Publications, ISBN: 9781617290527
12. Elmagarmid AK, Ipeirotis PG, Verykios VS (2007) Duplicate record detection: A survey. IEEE Trans Knowl Data Eng 19(1):1–16
13. Engeström J (2005) Why some social network services work and others don't — or: the case for object-centered sociality. Available online http://bit.ly/eJA7OQ (accessed 31 December 2010)
14. George L (2011) HBase: The definitive guide. O'Reilly Media, ISBN: 9781449396107
15. Gipp B, Beel J, Hentschel C (2009) Scienstein: a research paper recommender system. In: Proceedings of the international conference on emerging trends in computing (ICETiC'09), pp 309–315
16. Gruson-Daniel C (2012) Science et curation: nouvelle pratique du web 2.0. URL http://blog.mysciencework.com/2012/02/03/science-et-curation-nouvelle-pratique-du-web-2-0.html
17. Jack K (2011) Mendeley: recommendation systems for academic literature. Available online http://www.slideshare.net/KrisJack/mendeley-recommendation-systems-for-academic-literature
18. Jack K, Hristakeva M, de Zuniga RG, Granitzer M (2012) Mendeley's open data for science and learning: a reply to the datatel challenge. Int J Tech Enhanced Learn 4(1/2):31–46
19. Koren Y, Bell R (2011) Advances in collaborative filtering. In: Ricci F, Rokach L, Shapira B, Kantor PB (eds) Recommender systems handbook. Springer, New York, pp 145–186
20. Kraker P, Leony D, Reinhardt W, Beham G (2011) The case for an open science in technology enhanced learning. Int J Tech Enhanced Learn 3(6):643–654. URL http://know-center.tugraz.at/download_extern/papers/open_science.pdf
21. Li H, Councill IG, Bolelli L, Zhou D, Song Y, Lee WC, Sivasubramaniam A, Giles CL (2006) Citeseerx: a scalable autonomous scientific digital library. In: Proceedings of the 1st international conference on scalable information systems, InfoScale '06. ACM, New York, NY, USA
22. Lopez P (2009) Grobid: combining automatic bibliographic data recognition and term extraction for scholarship publications. In: Proceedings of the 13th European conference on research and advanced technology for digital libraries, ECDL'09. Springer, Berlin, Heidelberg, pp 473–474. URL http://dl.acm.org/citation.cfm?id=1812799.1812875
23. Lops P, Gemmis M, Semeraro G (2011) Content-based recommender systems: State of the art and trends. In: Ricci F, Rokach L, Shapira B, Kantor PB (eds) Recommender systems handbook. Springer, New York, pp 73–105
24. MacLeod H (2007) Social objects for beginners. Gapingvoid. Available online http://gapingvoid.com/2007/12/31/social-objects-for-beginners/

25. Manouselis N, Drachsler H, Verbert K, Duval E (2012) Ecommender systems for learning. Springer, Berlin/Heidelberg
26. Manouselis N, Drachsler H, Vuorikari R, Hummel HGK, Koper R (2011) Recommender systems in technology enhanced learning. In: Kantor PB, Ricci F, Rokach L, Shapira B (eds) Recommender systems handbook. Springer, Berlin, pp 387–415
27. McNee SM, Riedl J, Konstan JA (2006) Being accurate is not enough: how accuracy metrics have hurt recommender systems. In: CHI '06 extended abstracts on human factors in computing systems, CHI EA '06. ACM, New York, NY, USA, pp 1097–1101. DOI 10.1145/1125451.1125659. URL http://doi.acm.org/10.1145/1125451.1125659
28. Otlet P (1903) The science of bibliography and documentation. In: Rayward WB (ed) The international organization and dissemination of knowledge: selected essays of Paul Otlet (translated and edited, 1990). Elsevier, Amsterdam
29. Owen S, Anil R, Dunning T, Friedman E (2011) Mahout in action. Manning Publications, ISBN 9781935182689
30. Priem J, Hemminger B (2010) Scientometrics 2.0: New metrics of scholarly impact on the social web. First Monday [Online] 15(7)
31. Priem J, Taraborelli D, Groth P, Neylon C (2010) Alt-metrics: A manifesto (v.1.0). Available online http://altmetrics.org/manifesto accessed 18 August 2011
32. Rayward WB (1994) Visions of Xanadu: Paul Otlet (1868–1944) and hypertext. J Am Soc Inform Sci 45(4):235–250
33. Reinhardt W (2012) Awareness support for knowledge workers in research networks. Available online at http://bit.ly/PhD-Reinhardt. Ph.D. thesis, Open University of the Netherlands
34. Reinhardt W, Kadam P, Varlemann T, Surve J, Ahmad MI, Magenheim J (2012) Supporting Scholarly Awareness and Researchers' Social Interactions using PUSHPIN. In: Moore A, Pammer V, Pannese L, Prilla M, Rajagopal K, Reinhardt W, Ullmann TD, Voigt C (eds) Proceedings of the 2nd workshop on awareness and reflection in technology-enhanced learning, CEUR Workshop Proceedings, vol 931. URL http://ceur-ws.org/Vol-931/
35. Reinhardt W, Mletzko C (2012) Understanding the meaning of awareness in research networks. In: Moore A, Pammer V, Pannese L, Prilla M, Rajagopal K, Reinhardt W, Ullmann TD, Voigt C (eds) Proceedings of the 2nd workshop on awareness and reflection in technology-enhanced learning, CEUR Workshop Proceedings, vol 931. URL http://ceur-ws.org/Vol-931/
36. Reinhardt W, Mletzko C, Drachsler H, Sloep PB (2012) Design and evaluation of a widget-based dashboard for awareness support in research networks. Interact Learn Environ, DOI: 10.1080/10494820.2012.707126
37. Ricci F, Rokach L, Shapira B, Kantor PB (eds) (2011) Recommender systems handbook. Springer, New York
38. Schein AI, Popescul A, Ungar LH, Pennock DM (2002) Methods and metrics for cold-start recommendations. In: Proceedings of the 25th annual international ACM SIGIR conference on research and development in information retrieval, SIGIR '02. ACM, New York, NY, USA, pp 253–260. DOI 10.1145/564376.564421. URL http://doi.acm.org/10.1145/564376.564421
39. Shirky C (2008) It's not information overload. It's filter failure. Talk delivered at the Web 2.0 Expo NY 2008. Available at http://bit.ly/shirky-filter-failure accessed 16 December 2011
40. Shneiderman B (2008) Science 2.0. Science 319(5868):1349–1350
41. Waldrop M (2008) Science 2.0. Sci Am 298(5):68–73
42. White T, Romano R (2012) Hadoop: the definitive guide. O'Reilly Media, ISBN: 9781449311520

Printed in the United States
By Bookmasters